Transformational Embodiment in Asian Religions

This volume examines several theoretical concerns of embodiment in the context of Asian religious practice. Looking at both subtle and spatial bodies, it explores how both types of embodiment are engaged as sites for transformation, transaction, and transgression.

Collectively bridging ancient and modern conceptualizations of embodiment in religious practice, the book offers a complex mapping of how body is defined. It revisits more traditional, mystical religious systems, including Hindu Tantra and Yoga, Tibetan Buddhism, Bon, Chinese Daoism, and Persian Sufism, and distinctively juxtaposes these inquiries alongside analyses of racial, gendered, and colonized bodies. Such a multifaceted subject requires a diverse approach, and so perspectives from phenomenology and neuroscience as well as critical race theory and feminist theology are utilized to create more precise analytical tools for the scholarly engagement of embodied religious epistemologies.

This a nuanced and interdisciplinary exploration of the myriad issues around bodies within religion. As such, it will be a key resource for any scholar of Religious Studies, Asian Studies, Anthropology, Sociology, Philosophy, and Gender Studies.

George Pati is Associate Professor of Theology and International Studies and the Surjit S. Patheja Chair in World Religions and Ethics at Valparaiso University, USA. His research interests include religious literature in the Malayalam language, South Asian devotional traditions, the mediation of Hindu devotion through texts, rituals, and performances of Kerala, South India, and the body and religion. He is the author of *Religious Devotion and the Poetics of Reform: Love and Liberation in Malayalam Poetry* (Routledge 2019).

Katherine C. Zubko is Associate Professor of Religious Studies and NEH Distinguished Professor of the Humanities at University of North Carolina Asheville. Her research interests include aesthetics, ritual, performance, dance anthropology, and embodied religion in South Asia. She is the author of *Dancing Bodies of Devotion: Fluid Gestures in Bharata Natyam* (Lexington 2014).

Routledge Studies in Religion

The Role of Religion in Gender-Based Violence, Immigration, and Human Rights
Edited by Mary Nyangweso and Jacob K. Olupona

Italian American Pentecostalism and the Struggle for Religious Identity
Paul J. Palma

The Cultural Fusion of Sufi Islam
Alternative Paths to Mystical Faith
Sarwar Alam

Hindi Christian Literature in Contemporary India
Rakesh Peter-Dass

Religion, Modernity, Globalisation
Nation-State to Market
François Gauthier

Gender and Orthodox Christianity
Edited by Helena Kupari and Elena Vuola

Music, Branding, and Consumer Culture in Church
Hillsong in Focus
Tom Wagner

Transformational Embodiment in Asian Religions
Subtle Bodies, Spatial Bodies
Edited by George Pati and Katherine C. Zubko

For more information about this series, please visit: https://www.routledge.com/religion/series/SE0669

Transformational Embodiment in Asian Religions

Subtle Bodies, Spatial Bodies

Edited by
George Pati and
Katherine C. Zubko

Routledge
Taylor & Francis Group
LONDON AND NEW YORK

First published 2020
by Routledge
2 Park Square, Milton Park, Abingdon, Oxon OX14 4RN

and by Routledge
52 Vanderbilt Avenue, New York, NY 10017

Routledge is an imprint of the Taylor & Francis Group, an informa business

British Library Cataloguing-in-Publication Data
A catalogue record for this book is available from the British Library

Library of Congress Cataloging-in-Publication Data
A catalog record has been requested for this book

ISBN: 978-0-367-37555-3 (hbk)
ISBN: 978-0-429-35605-6 (ebk)

Typeset in Sabon
by codeMantra

Dedicated to Rebecca S. Norris and Richard M. Carp

Contents

List of figures ix
Notes on transliteration xi
Notes on contributors xiii
Acknowledgments xvii

Introduction 1
KATHERINE C. ZUBKO AND GEORGE PATI

1 The subtle body of vital presence in contemplative practices of Abhinavagupta's Trika Śaivism and Longchenpa's Great Perfection 15
KERRY MARTIN SKORA

2 Daoist body-maps and meditative praxis 36
LOUIS KOMJATHY 康思奇

3 Yuasa Yasuo's contextualization of the subtle body: phenomenology and practice 65
EDWARD J. GODFREY

4 Dismembering demons: spatial and bodily representations in the fifteenth-century *Ekaliṅgamāhātmya* 86
ADAM NEWMAN

5 Subtle body: rethinking the body's subjectivity through Abhinavagupta body 108
LORILIAI BIERNACKI

6 Embodied experience in the *Mahārthamañjarī* of Maheśvarānanda 128
STHANESHWAR TIMALSINA

Figures

2.1	Representative sampling of Daoist body-maps Source: Various; author's collection	45
2.2	Early extant illustrations Source: *Huangting yuanshen jing* 黄庭元神經 (DZ 1032, 14.4b-11a; left) and *Yutang neijing yushu* 玉堂內景玉書 (DZ 221, 2.13a-17b; right)	45
2.3	Inner landscape map Source: Nanjing zuantu jujie 難經纂圖句解, DZ 1024, 4ab	47
2.4	Mystical cranial locations Source: *Zazhu jiejing* 雜著捷徑, DZ 263, 18.2a	49
2.5	Contemporary neuroscientific brain-regions Permission granted courtesy of Jiang Sheng (Sichuan University) ed. *Zhongguo daojiao kexue jishu shi* (History of Taoism and Science). Beijing: Kexue chubanshe, 2002	50
2.6	Body as mountain Source: Duren shangpin miaojing neiyi 度人上品妙經內義, DZ 90, 8ab; also Jindan daoyao tu 金丹大要圖, DZ 1068	51
2.7	Painting (left) and stele rubbing (right) of *diagram of internal pathways* Source: Author's collection	53
2.8	The Yang-spirit Source: Shangqing dadong zhenjing 上清大洞真經, DZ 6, 5.1b	54

Notes on transliteration

This book includes various languages (Sanskrit, Chinese, Japanese, Arabic), and the authors have employed accepted forms of transliteration in the respective languages.

Notes on contributors

Loriliai Biernacki (Ph.D., University of Pennsylvania) is Associate Professor and Director of Graduate Studies in the Department of Religious Studies at the University of Colorado at Boulder. Her research interests include Hinduism, gender, and the interface between religion and science. Her first book, *Renowned Goddess of Desire: Women, Sex and Speech in Tantra* (Oxford, 2007), won the Kayden Award in 2008. She is co-editor of *God's Body: Panentheism across the World's Religious Traditions* (Oxford 2013). She is currently working on a study on the eleventh-century Indian philosopher Abhinavagupta within the framework of wonder, the New Materialisms, and conceptions of the body-mind interface.

Patrick J. D'Silva (Ph.D., University of North Carolina) is a lecturer in the Department of Philosophy at the University of Colorado Colorado Springs. His dissertation, "The Science of the Breath in Persianate India," analyzes how a series of divination practices centered on the breath is translated from Sanskrit into Persian in pre- and early-modern India, and how these practices were received by medieval (and modern) Iranian scholars as well as British orientalists. More information is available at patrickjdsilva.com.

Edward J. Godfrey (Ph.D., Temple University) focuses on phenomenological approaches to discussing the lived body, both through the lens of contemporary scientific materialism and the imagery of Tantra and Yoga. With this dichotomy in mind, his current research investigates the exclusivity of prevailing material narratives of the body and how alternative modalities of self-understanding/reflection are inhibited by its presupposition. He has also published within the field of Religion and Film and has co-translated a book on the philosophy and physical measurement of the subtle body.

Matthew R. Hotham (Ph.D., University of North Carolina, Chapel Hill) is Assistant Professor of Religious Studies at Ball State University. His dissertation investigated depictions of the Prophet Muhammad's body in the poetry of Nizami Ganjavi. His publishing and teaching interests include religion and animals, the role of affect and emotion in American Islamophobia, Islamic mysticism, and medieval Persian poetry.

Jay Johnston (Ph.D., University of Sydney) is an interdisciplinary researcher in the Department of Studies in Religion, University of Sydney. Central to her research is the concept of "subtle subjectivity" and its interrelation with beliefs about the body, senses, desire, aesthetic experience (cultivation of perception), and ethics. She has researched subtle body concepts and practices for over 20 years. Her publications include *Angels of Desire: Esoteric Bodies, Aesthetics and Ethics* (2008) and she is co-editor (with Geoffrey Samuel) of *Religion and the Subtle Body in Asia and the West: Between Mind and Body* (2011). A new monograph *Stag and Stone: Religion, Archaeology and Esoteric Aesthetics* (Equinox) is forthcoming.

Louis Komjathy 康思奇 (Ph.D., Religious Studies; Boston University) is Associate Professor of Chinese Religions and Comparative Religious Studies at the University of San Diego (home.sandiego.edu/~komjathy). A leading teacher-scholar of Daoism (Taoism) and Contemplative Studies, he has particular interests in contemplative practice, embodiment, and mystical experience. He is also founding co-chair (2004–2010) of the Daoist Studies Unit of the American Academy of Religion, founding co-chair (2010–2016) of the Contemplative Studies Unit of the American Academy of Religion, and manager of the Contemplative Studies Website (www.sandiego.edu/cas/contemplativestudies). His work in Contemplative Studies was recently recognized through appointment as a Mind & Life Institute Fellow. He has published widely on Daoism, both in premodern China and as a contemporary global religion. Some of his recent book-length publications on Daoism include *The Way of Complete Perfection: A Quanzhen Daoist Anthology* (State University of New York Press, 2013), *The Daoist Tradition: An Introduction* (Bloomsbury Academic, 2013), *Daoism: A Guide for the Perplexed* (Bloomsbury Academic, 2014), and *Taming the Wild Horse: An Annotated Translation and Study of the Daoist Horse Taming Pictures* (Columbia University Press, 2017). With Harold Roth of Brown University, he is currently working on a new contextual, contemplative, and annotated translation of the *Daode jing*.

Adam Newman (Ph.D., University of Virginia) concentrates on the religious traditions of India, with a particular emphasis on Hinduism in medieval Rajasthan. His research focuses on the religious and political history of South Asia, representations of sacred landscapes in Hindu Sanskrit narratives, and the construction of political and religious identity in the Mewar region of Rajasthan. Broadly, he is interested in sacred spaces and landscapes, religious conceptions of the body and embodiment, and the relationship between political power and religious authority in early South Asian history.

Keun-Joo Christine Pae (Ph.D., Union Theological Seminary, New York) is Associate Professor of Religion and Ethics and chair of the Religion Department at Denison University, Granville, Ohio. She is also affiliated with the college's Women's and Gender Studies Program and Queer Studies Program. Taking social ethics as a discipline, she teaches and researches the intersectionality of militarism and religion through the lens of race, gender, class, and sexuality, transnational feminist ethics, spiritual activism, and Asian/Asian American feminist theology and ethics. As a co-chair, Pae currently serves on the steering committee of the Women and Religion Unit at American Academy of Religion. She is also an ordained priest in the Episcopal Church.

George Pati (Ph.D., Religious Studies and South Asian Languages and Cultures, Boston University) is Surjit S. Patheja Chair in World Religions and Ethics and Associate Professor of Theology and International Studies at Valparaiso University, Indiana. His research interests include Hinduism, particularly the mediation of Hindu devotion, *bhakti*, through texts, rituals, and performances in the Malayalam language, and body and religion. He is the author of *Religious Devotion and the Poetics of Reform: Love and Liberation in Malayalam Poetry* (Routledge, 2019), as well as several chapters and articles, including "Movements, Miracles, and Mysticism: Apotheosis of Sree Narayana Guru of Early Twentieth Century Kerala," in Diana Dimitrova and Tatiana Oranskaia, eds., *Divinization in South Asian Traditions* (London: Routledge, 2018), pp. 115–130. His second monograph, *Hindu Bodies as Threshold: Rituals and Performances of Kerala, South India* (Routledge) is forthcoming. He is on the editorial board of the journal, *Body and Religion* and currently serves on steering committees for two groups at the American Academy of Religion: Arts, Literature, and Religion, and Body and Religion.

Matthew I. Robertson (Ph.D., University of California Santa Barbara) teaches and researches in the field of South Asian Religious Studies. His work draws upon the diverse methods of philology, philosophy, history, and digital humanities to illuminate the social and ideological complexities of ancient and pre-classical India. Recent publications can be found in the *Journal of Hindu Studies*, the *Journal of Indian Philosophy*, and the *Journal of Religion and Violence*. His first monograph, currently under review, investigates the literary history and historical development of concepts of personhood in the religious, political, and medical traditions of ancient India.

Kerry Martin Skora (Ph.D. in Religious Studies, University of Virgina; B.A. in Mathematics, University of Chicago) is an independent scholar. He is the author of several articles on Abhinavagupta, the renowned exponent of the non-dual Trika Śaivism of Kashmir, in which he analyzes the category of the lived body from a phenomenological perspective. As recent Fulbright Scholar in Bhutan, his thinking has taken a turn toward ecological phenomenology and semiotics, applied to both Abhinavagupta and the Tibetan Buddhist polymath Longchenpa, with special focus on ideas of spaciousness and consciousness. Now a Woodrow Wilson Teaching Fellow at Duquesne University, he will be teaching mathematics in Pittsburgh Public Schools beginning this year and plans to write about the relationships between mathematical thinking and thinking about Being.

Sthaneshwar Timalsina (Ph.D., Martin Luther University, Halle, Germany) is Professor of Religious Studies at San Diego State University. He works in the areas of Hindu and Buddhist religions and philosophies. The primary areas of his research include consciousness studies and Tantric studies. Besides four books, *Seeing and Appearance* (Shaker Verlag, 2006), Consciousness *in Indian Philosophy* (Routledge, 2009), *Tantric Visual Culture: A Cognitive Approach* (Routledge, 2015), and *Language of Images: Visualization and Meaning in Tantras* (Peter Lang, 2015), he has published over five dozen essays in his areas of research.

Katherine C. Zubko (Ph.D., West and South Asian Religions, Emory University) is Associate Professor of Religious Studies and NEH Distinguished Professor of the Humanities at University of North Carolina Asheville. Her areas of expertise include aesthetics, ritual, performance, dance anthropology, and embodied religion in South Asia. Zubko is the author of *Dancing Bodies of Devotion: Fluid Gestures in Bharata Natyam* (Lexington 2014), as well as several articles, including "Dancing the *Bhagavadgita*: Embodiment as Commentary" in the *Journal of Hindu Studies*. Zubko is the book review editor for the *Journal of Hindu Christian Studies* and currently serves on steering committees for two groups at the American Academy of Religion: Teaching Religion, and Body and Religion.

Acknowledgments

The essays in this volume were presented during different sessions of the American Academy of Religion, and we want to thank the various constituencies for peer reviewing and accepting these papers. The Body and Religion Unit was the hub for most of the presentations, and we dedicate this volume to the founding members of this unit, Rebecca Norris and Richard Carp, for their vision in creating this scholarly space for developing productive conversations on the intersection between practice and discourse around bodies and embodiment. The institutions that we work for have supported us in numerous ways, and we want to thank the University of North Carolina Asheville and Valparaiso University. The time and resources to complete this volume were provided in part by the Surjit S. Patheja Chair in World Religions and Ethics at Valparaiso University, Indiana, and the NEH Distinguished Professor in the Humanities at University of North Carolina Asheville.

The editorial team at Routledge has been very encouraging of this project from the very outset, and we are thankful to Joshua Wells, Editor for Religion at Routledge, for enthusiastically endorsing this project, and his team for bringing the manuscript through the many stages of the publication process. We are also extremely grateful to the two anonymous reviewers, who offered constructive and positive suggestions, especially an insightful restructuring idea.

In particular, we thank Natalia Zubko for her assistance in reformatting the images in Chapter 2.

Both of us would like to thank our families, friends, and colleagues who have shown unwavering encouragement and support during the writing of this volume.

Introduction

Katherine C. Zubko and George Pati

"What is body?" This collection of essays arose out of a continued quest for engaging this question through bringing two allied categories in body studies together for the first time: subtle bodies and spatial bodies. Subtle bodies, by definition, exist as a more porous and dynamic mental, affective and/or energetic interconnective materiality formulated beyond any isolated notion of an individual self. Analogously, spatial bodies delineate the ways bodies are interactively configured through various exchanges and actions that occur across physical and social transcultural spaces. The pairing of subtle bodies with spatial bodies reveals important dimensions of how both types of bodies function as sites for transformation, transaction, and transgression. These boundary-crossing, multilayered embodiments consider not just the overlap of mental, affective, and physical aspects experienced within an individual subject or system, but demonstrate how embodiment is mutually informed by intentions, contexts, agency, relationality, intersubjectivity, and purpose.

This volume revisits more traditional, mystical religious systems, including Hindu Tantric and Yogic, Tibetan Buddhist, Bon, Chinese Daoist and Persian and South Asian Sufi texts and praxis, but distinctively juxtaposes these inquiries alongside analyses of gendered and colonized bodies to reveal overlapping constructions of multiple coexisting, permeable, dynamic dimensions of embodiment. The theoretical and methodological landscape matches this diverse examination, drawing from phenomenology and neuroscience to feminist theology. This volume collectively bridges ancient and modern conceptualizations of bodied understandings and practices to constitute a complex mapping of how bodies are defined. What this expanded understanding of bodies is capable of creating illuminates new dimensions within each demarcated context, but also offers more precise analytical tools for the scholarly engagement of embodied religious epistemologies.

A main impetus for this project came from the call for further interdisciplinary and comparative work noted in the foundational volume that gathered cross-cultural strands on subtle body topics together for the first time: Geoffrey Samuel and Jay Johnston's (2013) *Religion and the Subtle Body in Asia and the West: Between mind and body.*[1] This book includes clear overviews of subtle bodies as grounded in each of their particular contextualized systems, from Tantra and Daoism to Sufism and Plato, but then in its fourth section, it begins to open a window into analyzing these subtle body concepts in comparison to Western and Eastern philosophical notions of intersubjectivity, feminist forms of relationality, alternative medicine practices, and ethical considerations of self and other. This volume builds further off of Samuel and Johnston's work on subtle bodies by providing a set of case studies that make visible what these embodied conceptualizations create as they move across different contexts and are engaged through new translocative and comparative lenses that deepen these lines of inquiry.[2] In particular, our volume uniquely creates a conversational intersection between subtle bodies and spatial bodies due to commonalities in how both processual conceptualizations of materiality envision bodies in their relational interactions with cosmic, social, and environmental spaces.

The remainder of this introduction provides brief overviews of scholarship engaging with both types of bodies, subtle and spatial, in part to elucidate why bringing these two categories into juxtaposition creates opportunities for new insights to emerge. Some allied theories and scholarly areas, including material religion and affect,[3] are not part of these overviews as the contributors chose not to highlight these analytical lenses in particular, but could become the thematic basis for future projects. A final section identifies comparative threads across the chapters, maps out the chapters of the book, and gives examples of the type of cross-comparative conversations that this volume makes possible through the pairing of subtle and spatial lenses.

Subtle bodies

The origin of scholarly work on subtle bodies is strongly rooted in mostly South and East Asian conceptualizations of the body as dynamic, porous, processual, and interactive with its surroundings through exchange, energies, and flows. In this section, we identify the main broader contexts of influence on constructions of subtle body concepts and practices, although each contains multiple distinct variations of embodied personhood under each system. Definitions pertinent to each context are noted.

1 *South Asian Yogic and Tantric Contexts.* The most well-known area of work on subtle bodies is originally connected to the *sūkṣma śarīra*, a term often translated as "subtle body" in wide use in Vedanta as interpreted through the work of Śaṇkara (eight c.). *Sūkṣma śarīra* denotes one of three bodies, the others being physical (*sthūla śarīra*) and causal (*kāraṇa śarīra*). It also is used in reference to a larger system of multiple coexisting, layered aspects of embodiment envisioned as multiple sheaths (*kośas*) surrounding the *ātman* or self, consisting of physical/food, *prāṇa* (vital force/breath), *manas* (heart-mind), intellect,

and *ānanda* (bliss). Subtle bodies and their components reflect various degrees of materiality and consciousness that are not conceived as separate from, but rather coextensive with, denser forms of physicality. The aforementioned schemas are only two of many varying iterations.[4]

As part of yogic and tantric developments (eighth–eleventh c.),[5] bodies include the recognition of an energetic circulatory system, flowing through channels (*nāḍīs*) in the body and meeting in centers (*cakras*) along the primary trunk channel (*suṣumṇā*) that runs from the base of the spine to the crown of the head. Yogic and tantric bodies engage with this energy through practices of breath, physical postures, visualization, and/or sexual intercourse among other possible ritually intentional actions. Engaging with this energy that corresponds with cosmic and/or divine energies produces multiple possible effects, from healing to liberatory experiences of *mokṣa* or *nirvana*. In David White's *Tantra in Practice*, nearly 20 forms of Tantra are noted in Hindu contexts alone, in addition to influential Daoist and Tibetan, Chinese, Korean, and Japanese Buddhist schools.[6] While many of the subtle body concepts in South Asia draw from ancient and medieval traditions, in the modern period, further ideas arose with gurus such as Aurobindo. A variety of teachers and key public practitioners imported Aurobindo's delineation of integral yoga, along with other guru-based systems into Western contexts.[7] The South Asian strand continues to revisit and expand on analysis of subtle body systems through transformed lenses related to divinity, devotion, performance, and gender, as explored in several of the essays in Barbara Holdrege and Karen Pechilis' *Refiguring the Body: Embodiment in South Asian Religions*.[8] Biernacki, Timalsina, Skora, and Robertson in this volume present work by interpreters and practitioners from areas within this evolving South Asian branch.

2 *East Asian Daoist Contexts*. Subtle body anatomies develop prominently within Daoism in relation to alchemy practices across various schools. Daoist bodies include a circulatory system of energy (*chi/qi/ki*) that can be cultivated through breath, diet, exercises, sexual energy exchange or control, and so forth to enhance health, longevity, and the conditions for immortality. Primordial *qi* is cosmic *qi*, and if a person transforms their body to be in complete alignment with this energy, they may bypass the transition of death that results from a lifetime of gradual depletion of *qi*. Livia Kohn's *Daoist Body Cultivation* details various techniques for engaging with *qi* and the desired outcomes for practitioners.[9] Within East Asian contexts, select Chinese and Japanese forms of Chan/Zen and Tantric Buddhisms also develop subtle body anatomies.[10] The chapters by Komjathy and Godfrey are based within East Asian contexts.

3 *Shamanistic Contexts*. While not a central focus of this volume, it is worth noting that among various indigenous groups throughout the

world, many shamans practice forms of ecstatic flight and vision quest through dream, trance, or other altered states of consciousness to access knowledge and facilitate healing work to benefit individuals and communities. These practices assume types of subtle bodies capable of conscious astral travel, bodies and objects that can transverse physical barriers or transform shapes, interrelational subjectivities with environments, plants and animals, and other expanded notions of embodiment specific to each localized tradition.[11] Many of these indigenous knowledge systems have been culturally appropriated by Europeans and Americans during the nineteenth and twentieth centuries as part of hybridized New Age spiritualities.[12]

4 *Spiritualist and New Age Contexts.* Great interest arose in Asian and indigenous understandings of body beginning in the late nineteenth century. Helena Blavatsky and Henry Olcott's Theosophical Society, and Rudolph Steiner's later iteration of anthroposophy were both at the forefront of adapting especially South Asian conceptions of subtle bodies for a wider global audience.[13] What marks many of these types of subtle body understandings is a mélange of sources, often unattributed, and with an emphasis on empowering transformation on individual and collective levels removed from religious, cultural, and national identities. Kurt Leland's *Rainbow Body* and Jeffrey Kripal's *Esalen*,[14] a history of one of the headquarters for New Age spiritual transformation, provide thorough overviews of the adoption of subtle body motifs and related practices in constructions of embodiment amongst New Age adherents.[15]

5 *Monotheistic and Western Philosophical Contexts.* Another area of scholarship centers on examining subtle body concepts in the Abrahamic traditions and Western philosophical traditions, from ancient to contemporary. While interpretations and critiques of heterodox theologies' embrace of body-soul and body-mind dichotomies loom large within scholarship, the exploration of mystical branches and subtle body constructs as part of these monotheistic and philosophical traditions illuminates an unexamined diversity of body constructs within these systems. The Samuel and Johnston volume on subtle bodies includes discussions on ancient Mediterranean, Neoplatonic and Sufi contexts. Jay Johnston's *Angels of Desire* bridges Eastern and Western esoteric philosophical and feminist implications, from intersubjectivity in Luce Irigaray to Buddhist *śūnyatā* (emptiness).[16] In this collection, D'Silva and Hotham offer chapters related to Sufi traditions of subtle bodies.

Attention to subtle bodies across these and other contexts has turned it into a more ubiquitous concept for analyzing the ways bodies disrupt assumptions of static, fixed, isolated, or dichotomous/dualistic characteristics or qualities. As discussed in the next section, the engagement with spatial bodies furthers dynamic constructions of subtle exchanges with elements and environments that illuminate porous rather than rigid boundaries of embodied personhood.

Spatial bodies

Scholars from various trajectories (primarily cultural geographers) have engaged in space and spatial analysis. Geographer Lily Kong, in her article, "Mapping 'new' geographies of religion: politics and poetics in modernity," emphasizes geographic significance of examining religion and the interconnectedness between social and spatial, private and public, and politics and poetics.[17] Kong proposes that future research must consider sites of religious practice beyond the official sacred, sensuous sacred geographies, religions in different historical and place-specific contexts, various geographical scales of analysis, and different constitutions of population, dialectics, and moralities.[18] Another cultural geographer, Doreen Massey, in her work, *For Space*, suggests that space is a product of interrelations in which plurality exists and is always under construction.[19]

The recent turn to spatial analysis is rooted in the works of the French theorists, Henri Lefebvre, Michel Foucault, and Michel de Certeau, and postcolonial theorist, Homi K. Bhabha. In *The Production of Space*, Lefebvre critiques notions of space as a static and passive entity and details the ways in which bodies are porously interacting with the spaces within which they exist.[20] Lefebvre specifically utilized the term "spatial bodies," emphasizing it to be dynamic, processual, and agentive. Foucault, in his work, *Of Other Spaces*, discusses the production of space and power and claims space to be a "heterotopia."[21] Foucault employs heterotopia to emphasize other place to have multiple meanings and relations, and that which is counter to utopia.[22] In *The Practice of Everyday Life*, de Certeau examines everyday practices and argues that space is practiced and embodied and is a nexus.[23] Bhabha, in his work, *The Location of Culture*, considers the production of third space as a site of identity negotiation and resistance toward hegemony.[24] Influenced by Lefebvre's work, Edward Soja in *Thirdspace* investigates space and spatiality, challenging dualistic approaches, and in *Seeking Social Justice*, he suggests the existence of a "mutually influential and formative relation between the social and the spatial dimensions of human life, each shaping the other in a similar way."[25] These studies on space and spatiality articulate the production of space, the fluid and porous characteristic of space, as well as problematizes delimiting space.

Though historians of religion Mircea Eliade, in his volume, *The Sacred and the Profane: The Nature of Religion*, closely examines sacred space and its connection to time in the study of religion,[26] and Jonathan Z. Smith, in his books *Map is Not a Territory* and *To Take Place*, argues that space is dynamic and socially defined as sacred and profane, and that space is a product of sacralization,[27] focus on spatial body analysis in Religious

Studies is a more recent derivation of this earlier trajectory within the field that shifted scholarly attention from a focus on belief to a focus on practice, and its related spheres of space, ritual, body, identity, and lived religion. Drawing insights from various studies on space and place, religion scholar Kim Knott in *The Location of Religion* articulates a spatial methodology, suggesting ways to analyze the location of religion: the body as the sources of space, dimension of space, properties of space, aspects of space, and dynamics of space.[28] Following Henri Lefebrve's lead, Thomas Tweed in *Crossing and Dwelling: A Theory of Religion* brings spatial embodied metaphors of homemaking and itinerancy in the religious life of transnational migrants without using the term "spatial bodies."[29] Drawing upon spatial and aquatic tropes, Tweed states, "Religions are confluences of organic-cultural flows that intensify joy and confront suffering by drawing on human and suprahuman forces to make homes and cross boundaries."[30] Tweed's use of spatial metaphors of dwelling and crossing signals religion to be a space of movement as he concludes his analysis of the itinerant spatial body by stating, "religions are flows, translocative and transtemporal crossings."[31] Spatial bodies, then, are dynamic spaces, as Veikko Anttonen states, "inside and outside of the human body are in transition."[32]

For example, such spatial concept of crossing in the Hindu religion is seen in Diana Eck's work, *India: A Sacred Geography*, as she bases her discussion of sacred geography in India based on pilgrimage places, *tīrtha*, literally meaning fords or crossings, derived from the Sanskrit root verb *tṛ* meaning, "to cross over."[33] The crossing over does not only refer to a pilgrim place or a ford or river, but also to the soul transitioning and transforming as per the *Upaniṣads*. Exploring space and embodiment, Kapila Vatsyayan maintains,

> all ancient civilizations (and many contemporary societies of some parts of the world) organized space, established a physical center, made enclosures, and gave it a mythical and cosmic significance. This was a method of re-integration, of re-affirmation of the relationship of the micro-macro, terrestrial and celestial.[34]

George Pati in examining body in *kaḷaricikitsā*, an alternative medicine practiced in *kaḷari*, martial arts complex, in Kerala, South India, furthers the notion of spatial bodies reinforcing the devotional-processual body as a nexus of the terrestrial, corporeal, and celestial.[35] These examples reinforce the spatiality of the body. Ritual theorist Catherine Bell in *Ritual Theory, Ritual Practice* contends the body to be "always conditioned by and responsive to a specific context," and that space and time are redefined by the "circularity to the body's interaction with the environment."[36] These studies shed light on the usefulness of analyzing spatiality and provides insight into analyzing spatial bodies discussed in this volume. For example,

Komjathy, Newman, Hotham, and Robertson's chapters emphasize the spatial processual dimension of bodies.

Attention to embodiment in Religious Studies includes methodological trajectories worth noting. Historians Carolyn Walker Bynum in *Holy Feast and Holy Fast* and Peter Brown in *The Body and Society* launched analyses of ancient and medieval documents through new embodied lenses detailing Christian renunciation practices.[37] An anthropological turn in Religious Studies since the 1990s supported in-depth case studies of how bodies and embodied practices were not only contextualized within specific spaces, but often challenged the very nature of assumed boundaries and interactive flows between bodies and the spaces which they inhabit, for example, Sarah Lamb's *White Saris and Sweet Mangoes: Aging, Gender and Body in North India* and Deidre Sklar's *Dancing with the Virgin: Body and Faith in the Fiesta of Tortugas, New Mexico.*[38]

Alongside the anthropological and historical explorations into embodiment, intersectional questions about race, gender, sexuality, nationality, and ongoing forms of oppression and effects of coloniality are increasingly incorporated into studies on religion and the body, persuading us to ask questions about the commodification and subjugation of the body.[39] In *Discipline and the Other Body: Correction, Corporeality, Colonialism*, Anupama Rao and Steven Pierce, eds., present colonialism as a management of difference and violation of the bodies of colonial subjects.[40] Along these lines, Achille Mbembé in "Necropolitics" explains, "Sovereignty meant occupation, and occupation meant relegating the colonized into a third zone between subjecthood and objecthood."[41] More importantly, Mbembé argues,

> the notion of necropolitics and necropower to account for the various ways in which, in our contemporary world, weapons are deployed in the interest of maximum destruction of persons and the creation of death-worlds, new and unique forms of social existence in which vast populations are subjected to conditions of life conferring upon them the status of living dead.[42]

The chapter by Pae furthers this understanding.

While most of these works advance understandings of embodiment and religion within particular contextualized spaces and time, a few propose more interactive dynamic exchanges between spaces and bodies without utilizing the explicit concept of "spatial bodies." These studies point at the production of space including various aspects of religion: sacred space, ritual space, embodied phenomenon, and intersectional spaces, corroborating Pierre Bourdieu's claim in *The Outline of Theory of Practice* that explores the mediation of the body via a dialectics of embodied social and physical habitus of practitioners and argues that the body is *the locus* for coordination of all levels of bodily, social, and cosmological experience.[43]

Chapter mapping and comparative threads

In bringing these two categories of analysis together, several thematic commonalities emerge that extend upon and help reframe epistemologies of religious embodiment, namely, (1) multiplicity and non-dualities, (2) practice as body, (3) embodied mappings (cosmic, natural, and built), (4) political (in)visibilities, and (5) knowing/sensing the processual body. The following section presents the focus of each individual chapter while highlighting the thematic connections across the chapters as they are in conversation with each other, emphasizing the fluidness of bodies and boundaries and the interconnectedness between subtle and spatial bodies.

1 *multiplicity and non-dualities*: Kerry Skora, in Chapter 1, "The Subtle Body of Vital Presence in Contemplative Practices of Abhinavagupta's Trika Śaivism and Longchenpa's Great Perfection," compares the works of Abhinavagupta and Longchenpa and points to a spontaneous process taking place in contemplative practices. Skora suggests that the subtle body is where Reality enfolds at once both Consciousness and matter, and is connected and yet irreducible to the physical body and Being or Consciousness. Analogously, Louis Komjathy, in Chapter 2, "Daoist Body-Maps and Meditative Praxis," sheds light on Daoist body maps, visual representations of indwelling gods co-dwelling within a practitioner's body, and argues spatial representation of Daoist body maps as a site of transformation and movement as it involves contemplative, transpersonal, and mystical form of (non)identity in which one overcomes habituation and activates a subtle body. These chapters illustrate the multiplicity and non-dualities of the body.
2 *Practice as body*: Edward Godfrey, in Chapter 3, "Yuasa Yasuo's Contextualization of the Subtle Body: Phenomenology and Praxis," expands upon the work of Yuasa Yasao, a Japanese philosopher, in light of Maurice Merleau Ponty's work on the "habit-body" and argues that Yuasa's unconscious quasi-material body strips the "subtle body" of its epistemological and ontological mystery and accounts for its diversity. Similarly, Adam Newman, in Chapter 4, "Dismembering Demons: Spatial and Bodily Representations in the Fifteenth-Century *Ekaliṅgamāhātmya*," illustrates how the body serves as the blueprint for cosmic and political order and that body and place are mutually articulative in shaping each other. Spatial practices engage bodies directly in the constant struggle against the dangers of primordial chaos and political instability.
3 *Embodied mappings (cosmic, natural, and built)*: The subsequent three chapters re-center practice as not what preexistent bodies do, but rather as a part of the construction of processual embodiment itself. Loriliai Biernacki, in Chapter 5, "The Subtle Body," assesses multiple divine agencies in Abhinavagupta's (eleventh c.) works and how these schemata

might be potentially mapped. Biernacki's appraisal of the human body in a medieval Indian Tantric vision of the subtle body acknowledges the multiplicity of agencies that make up human volition. Sthaneshwar Timalsina, in Chapter 6, "Embodied Experience in the *Mahārthamañjarī* of Maheśvarānanda," explores body-centric visualization practices in a Tantric tradition and argues that the spiritual awakening in the philosophy of Maheśvarānanda is orgasmic and the language he uses to describe it is visceral, suggesting the body to be "the placeholder of subjectivity, the bodily subject." Matthew Hotham, in Chapter 7, "Sensing the Ascent: Embodied Elements of Muhammad's Heavenly Journey in Nizami Ganjavi's Treasury of Mysteries," examines Muhammad's embodied ascension, revealing the importance of the physical body to Sufi understandings of mysticism.

4 *Political (in)visibilities*: Patrick D'Silva, in Chapter 8, "Bodies in Translation: Esoteric Conceptions of the Muslim Body in Early-modern South Asia," draws on examples from the *svarodaya* and *`ilm-i dam* corpus in the South Asian context, exploring how the breath operates within the body as imagined by the texts and demonstrating the subtle aspects of the body. Along these lines, Keun-Joo Christine Pae, in Chapter 9, "The Colonized Body of Military Prostitution: U.S. Military Prostitution in South Korea as a Site of Spiritual Activism," offers insight into the political (in)visibility and spatiality of the body and illustrates the agency of body among subjugated and marginalized South Korea prostitutes from a Christian perspective. In both these examples, the subtle and the spatial bodies emphasize political (in)visibility.

5 *Knowing/sensing the processual body*: Jay Johnston, in Chapter 10, "Frisky Methods: Subtle Bodies, Epistemological Pluralism and Creative Scholarship," discusses the implications on shifting the focus to hard-to-define bodies, arguing that "Frisky Methods" are required due to the subjectivity necessitating multiple modes of knowing the body asserting epistemological plurality and difference. This chapter delineates why the way that we study and write about body matters, noting the complexity, plurality, and the translocative aspect of bodies as part of our very scholarly praxis. Likewise, within the context of mystical practices, Matthew Robertson, in Chapter 11, "Bliss and Bodily Disorientation: The Autophagous Mysticism of Georges Bataille and the Taittirīya Upaniṣad," suggests the significant role the *enfleshed* body plays in mystical experience, problematizing the uncritical acceptance of fixed bodies as a locus of orientation for our thinking about spatial bodies. These chapters highlight the processual and dynamic nature of the body.

The essays in this volume, *Transformational Embodiment in Asian Religions: Subtle Bodies, Spatial Bodies*, do not provide an instant definition of subtle or spatial bodies but allows for definitions to evolve and expand through a critical examination of bodies in various social and religious contexts. Subtle bodies and spatial bodies are, in many ways, interrelated, and while these two lenses offer new insights into understanding the body in religion, they also persuade us to ask new questions of the nature of "body" itself.

Notes

1 Geoffrey Samuel and Jay Johnston, eds., *Religion and the Subtle Body in Asia and the West: Between Mind and Body* (New York: Routledge, 2013), 7.
2 Kimberly Patton and Benjamin Ray, eds. *In Comparison a Magic Dwells* (Berkeley: University of California Press, 2000).
3 For excellent overviews of these fields, see the introductions to the following volumes: S. Brent Plate, *Key Terms in Material Religion* (New York: Bloomsbury, 2015) and Melissa Gregg and Gregory J. Seigworth, eds. *The Affect Theory Reader* (Durham, NC and London: Duke University Press, 2010).
4 See John Bowker, "Subtle body," in *The Oxford Dictionary of World Religions*, ed. J. Bowker (Oxford: Oxford University Press, 1997), 924.
5 Gavin Flood, *The Tantric Body: The Secret Tradition of Hindu Religion* (New York: I.B. Tauris & Co., 2006), 157–162; Geoffrey Samuel, *The Origins of Yoga and Tantra: Indic Religions to the Thirteenth Century* (Cambridge: Cambridge University Press, 2008), 271–290. Samuel places the development of subtle anatomies a bit earlier than Flood, and so I have included the range of dates.
6 David Gordon White, ed. "Introduction," in *Tantra in Practice* (Princeton, NJ: Princeton University Press, 2000), 7.
7 Aurobindo, *Integral Yoga: Sri Aurobindo's Teaching and Method of Practice* (Twin Lakes, WI: Lotus Press, 2015); Stephanie Syman, *The Subtle Body: The Story of Yoga in America* (New York: Farrar, Straus and Giroux, 2010).
8 Barbara Holdrege and Karen Pechilis, eds. *Refiguring the Body: Embodiment in South Asian Religions* (New York: State University of New York Press, 2016).
9 See Kristofer Schipper, *The Daoist Body* (Berkeley: University of California Press, 1988) and Livia Kohn, ed., *Daoist Body Cultivation* (Twin Lakes, WI: Three Pines Press, 2006).
10 Charles Orzech, Henrik Sorenson and Richard Payne, eds., *Esoteric Buddhism and the Tantras in East Asia* (Leiden: Brill, 2011); Taiko Yamasaki, *Shingon: Japanese Esoteric Buddhism* (Boulder, CO: Shambala, 1988); and Thomas Kasulis, Roger Ames and Wimal Dissanayake, eds., *Self as Body in Asian Theory and Practice* (New York: SUNY Press, 1992), the latter including both South and East Asian contexts.
11 See Graham Harvey, *Shamanism: A Reader* (New York: Routledge, 2003).
12 See Andrei Znamenski, *Beauty of the Primitive: Shamanism and the Western Imagination* (Oxford: Oxford 2007) and Philip Jenkins, *Dream Catchers: How Mainstream America Discovered Native Spirituality* (Oxford: Oxford 2005).
13 See Gordon Djurdjevic, *India and the Occult: The Influence of South Asian Spirituality on Modern Western Occultism* (New York: Palgrave, 2014) and the first chapter in Jay Johnston, *Angels of Desire: Esoteric Bodies, Aesthetics and Ethics* (New York: Routledge 2008), for overviews of the forms of body developed in these two systems.
14 Kurt Leland, *Rainbow Body: A History of the Western Chakra System from Blavatsky to Brennan* (Lake Worth, FL: Ibis Press, 2016); Jeffrey Kripal, *Esalen: America and the Religion of No Religion* (Chicago, IL: University of Chicago Press, 2007). See also Jeffrey Kripal, *Secret Body: Erotic and Esoteric*

Currents in the History of Religions (Chicago, IL: University of Chicago, 2017) for an examination of how traditions related to paranormal experience and scholars studying traditions with subtle body practices have influenced the way religion has been studied historically.

15 Kripal, *Secret Body* (Chicago, IL: University of Chicago, 2017) examines how traditions related to paranormal experience and scholars studying traditions with subtle body practices have influenced the way religion has been studied historically.

16 Glenn Peers, *Subtle Bodies: Representing Angels in Byzantium* (Berkeley: University of California Press, 2001); Jay Johnston, *Angels of Desire: Esoteric Bodies, Aesthetics and Ethics* (New York: Routledge, 2008).

17 Lily Kong, "Mapping 'new' geographies of religion: politics and poetics in modernity," *Progress in Human Geography* 25, no. 2 (2001): 211–233.

18 Ibid., 228; See also, Kim Knott, "Religion, Space, and Place: The Spatial Turn in Research on Religion," *Religion and Society: Advances in Research* 1 (2010): 29–43.

19 Doreen Massey, *For Space* (London: Sage Publications, 2005).

20 Henri Lefebvre, *The Production of Space* (Oxford and Cambridge, MA: Blackwell, [1974] 1991).

21 Michel Foucault, "Of Other Spaces." Translated by Jay Miskowiec. *Diacritics* 16, no. 1 (Spring 1986): 22–27.

22 Ibid.

23 Michel de Certeau, *The Practice of Everyday Life* (Berkeley: University of California Press, 1984).

24 Homi K. Bhabha, *The Location of Culture* (London and New York: Routledge, 1994).

25 Edward W. Soja, *Thirdspace: Journeys to Los Angeles and Other Real-and-Imagined Places* (Oxford and Cambridge, MA: Blackwell, 1996); Edward W. Soja, *Seeking Spatial Justice* (Minneapolis: University of Minnesota Press, 2010).

26 Mircea Eliade, *The Sacred and the Profane: The Nature of Religion* (Hamburg and Berlin, Germany: Rowohlt Taschenbuch Verlag GMBH, 1957).

27 Jonathan Z. Smith, *Map Is Not a Territory: Studies in the History of Religions* (Chicago, IL: University of Chicago Press, 1978); Jonathan Z. Smith, *To Take Place: Toward Theory in Ritual* (Chicago, IL: University of Chicago Press, 1987).

28 Kim Knott, *The Location of Religion: A Spatial Analysis* (London and Oakville, CT: Equinox, 2005).

29 Thomas Tweed, A. *Crossing and Dwelling: A Theory of Religion* (Cambridge, MA: Harvard University Press, 2006).

30 Tweed, *Crossing and Dwelling*, 54.

31 Tweed, *Crossing and Dwelling*, 158.

32 Veikko Anttonen, "Space, Body, and the Notion of Boundary: A Category-Theoretical Approach to Religion." *Temenos: Nordic Journal of Comparative Religion* 41, no. 2 (2005): 187–202, 191.

33 Diana L. Eck, *India: A Sacred Geography* (New York: Three River Press, 2012), 7. See also, Diana L. Eck, *Banaras: City of Light* (New York: Columbia University Press, 1991).

34 Kapila Vatsyayan. "Performance: The Process, Manifestation and Experience," in *Concepts of Space Ancient and Modern*, ed. Kapila Vatsyayan (New Delhi: Indira Gandhi National Center for the Arts, 1991), 381–394, 381.

35 George Pati, "Body as Sacred Space in Kaḷaricikitsā of Kerala, South India." *Religions of South Asia* 3, no. 2 (2009): 235–250.

36 Catherine Bell, *Ritual Theory, Ritual Practice* (New York: Oxford University Press, 1992), 99.

37 Carolyn Walker Bynum, *Holy Feast and Holy Fast* (Berkeley: University of California Press, 1987); Peter Brown, *The Body and Society* (New York: Columbia University Press, 1988).
38 Sarah Lamb, *White Saris and Sweet Mangoes: Aging, Gender and Body in North India* (Berkeley: University of California Press, 2000); Deidre Sklar, *Dancing with the Virgin: Body and Faith in the Fiesta of Tortugas, New Mexico* (Berkeley: University of California Press, 2001).
39 See these works: Jinhua Jia, Xiaofei Kang and Ping Yao, *Gendering Chinese Religion: Subject, Identity and Body* (Albany: State University of New York Press, 2014); Helen Kim and Noah Leavitt, *JewAsian: Race, Religion and Identity for America's Newest Jews* (Lincoln: University of Nebraska Press, 2016); Paul Reeve, *Religion of a Different Color: Race and The Mormon Struggle for Whiteness* (New York: Oxford University Press, 2015); Heather Kopelson, *Faithful Bodies: Performing Religion and Race in the Puritan Atlantic* (New York: Oxford University Press, 2014); and Santa Arias and Raul Marrero-Fente, eds., *Coloniality, Religion and the Law in the Early Iberian World* (Nashville: Vanderbilt University Press, 2014).
40 Anupama Rao and Steven Pierce, eds., *Discipline and the Other Body: Correction, Corporeality, Colonialism* (Durham, NC: Duke University Press, 2006).
41 J. A. Mbembé, Translated by Libby Meintjes, Necropolitics. *Public Culture* 15, no. 1 (Winter 2003), 26.
42 Ibid., 40.
43 P. Bourdieu, *Outline of a Theory of Practice.* Translated by Richard Nice (Cambridge: Cambridge University Press, 1977).

Bibliography

Anttonen, Veikko. "Space, Body, and the Notion of Boundary: A Category-Theoretical Approach to Religion." *Temenos: Nordic Journal of Comparative Religion* 41, no. 2 (2005): 187–202.

Arias, Santa and Raul Marrero-Fente, eds. *Coloniality, religion and the law in the early Iberian world.* Nashville: Vanderbilt University Press, 2014.

Aurobindo. *Integral Yoga: Sri Aurobindo's Teaching and Method of Practice.* Twin Lakes, WI: Lotus Press, 2015.

Bell, Catherine. *Ritual Theory, Ritual Practice.* New York: Oxford University Press, 1992.

Bhabha, Homi K. *The Location of Culture.* London and New York: Routledge, 1994.

Bourdieu, Pierre. *Outline of a Theory of Practice.* Translated by Richard Nice. Cambridge: Cambridge University Press, 1977.

Brown, Peter. *The Body and Society.* New York: Columbia University Press, 1988.

Bynum, Carolyn Walker. *Holy Feast and Holy Fast.* Berkeley: University of California Press, 1987.

de Certeau, Michel. *The Practice of Everyday Life.* Berkeley: University of California Press, 1984.

Djurdjevic, Gordon. *India and the Occult: The Influence of South Asian Spirituality on Modern Western Occultism.* New York: Palgrave, 2014.

Eck, Diana L. *India: A Sacred Geography.* New York: Three River Press, 2012.

Eliade, Mircea. *The Sacred and the Profane: The Nature of Religion.* Hamburg and Berlin, Germany: Rowohlt Taschenbuch Verlag GMBH, 1957.

Flood, Gavin. *The Tantric Body: The Secret Tradition of Hindu Religion.* New York: I.B. Tauris & Co., 2006.

Foucault, Michel. "Of Other Spaces." Translated by Jay Miskowiec. *Diacritics* 16, no. 1 (Spring, 1986): 22–27.Gregg, Melissa and Gregory J. Seigworth, eds. *The Affect Theory Reader.* Durham, NC and London: Duke University Press, 2010.
Harvey, Graham. *Shamanism: A Reader.* New York: Routledge, 2003.
Holdrege, Barbara and Karen Pechilis, eds. *Refiguring the Body: Embodiment in South Asian Religions.* New York: State University of New York Press, 2016.
Jenkins, Philip. *Dream Catchers: How Mainstream America Discovered Native Spirituality.* Oxford: Oxford University Press, 2005.
Jia, Jinhua, Xiaofei Kang and Ping Yao. *Gendering Chinese Religion: Subject, Identity and Body.* Albany: State University of New York Press, 2014.
Johnston, Jay. *Angels of Desire: Esoteric Bodies, Aesthetics and Ethics.* New York: Routledge 2008.
Kasulis, Thomas, Roger Ames and Wimal Dissanayake, eds. *Self as Body in Asian Theory and Practice.* New York: SUNY Press, 1992.
Kim, Helen Kiyong and Noah Leavitt. *JewAsian: Race, Religion and Identity for America's Newest Jews.* Lincoln: University of Nebraska Press, 2016.
Knott, Kim. *The Location of Religion: A Spatial Analysis.* London and Oakville, CT: Equinox, 2005.
———. "Religion, Space, and Place: The Spatial Turn in Research on Religion." *Religion and Society: Advances in Research* 1 (2010): 29–43.
Kohn, Livia, ed. *Daoist Body Cultivation: Traditional Models and Contemporary Practices.* Magdalena, NM: Three Pines Press 2006.
Kong, Lily. "Mapping 'New' Geographies of Religion: Politics and Poetics in Modernity." *Progress in Human Geography* 25, no. 2 (2001): 211–233.
Kopelson, Heather. *Faithful Bodies: Performing Religion and Race in the Puritan Atlantic.* New York: New York University Press, 2014.
Kripal, Jeffrey. *Esalen: America and the Religion of No Religion.* Chicago, IL: University of Chicago Press, 2007.
———. *Secret Body: Erotic and Esoteric Currents in the History of Religions.* Chicago, IL: University of Chicago, 2017.
Lamb, Sarah. *White Saris and Sweet Mangoes: Aging, Gender and Body in North India.* Berkeley: University of California Press, 2000.
Lefebvre, Henri. *The Production of Space.* Oxford and Cambridge, MA: Blackwell, 1991 [1974].
Leland, Kurt. *Rainbow Body: A History of the Western Chakra System from Blavatsky to Brennan.* Lake Worth, FL: Ibis Press, 2016.
Massey, Doreen. *For Space.* London: Sage Publications, 2005.
Mbembé, J. A. trans. by Libby Meintjes, Necropolitics. *Public Culture* 15, no. 1 (Winter 2003): 11–40.
Orzech, Charles, Henrik Sorenson and Richard Payne, eds. *Esoteric Buddhism and the Tantras in East Asia.* Leiden: Brill, 2011.
Pati, George. "Body as Sacred Space in Kaḷaricikitsā of Kerala, South India." *Religions of South Asia* 3, no. 2 (2009): 235–250.
Peers, Glenn. *Subtle Bodies: Representing Angels in Byzantium.* Berkeley: University of California Press, 2001.
Plate, S. Brent, *Key Terms in Material Religion.* New York: Bloomsbury, 2015.
Rao, Anupama and Steven Pierce, eds. *Discipline and the Other Body: Correction, Corporeality, Colonialism.* Durham, NC: Duke University Press, 2006.
Reeve, Paul. *Religion of a Different Color: Race and the Mormon Struggle for Whiteness.* New York: Oxford University Press, 2015.

Samuel, Geoffrey. *The Origins of Yoga and Tantra: Indic Religions to the Thirteenth Century*. Cambridge: Cambridge University Press, 2008.

Samuel, Geoffrey and Jay Johnston, eds. *Religion and the Subtle Body in Asia and the West: Between Mind and Body*. New York: Routledge, 2013.

Schipper, Kristofer. *The Taoist Body*. Translated by Karen Duval. Berkeley: University of California Press, 1988.

Sklar, Deidre. *Dancing with the Virgin: Body and Faith in the Fiesta of Tortugas, New Mexico*. Berkeley: University of California Press, 2001.

Smith, Jonathan Z. *Map Is Not a Territory: Studies in the History of Religions*. Chicago, IL: University of Chicago Press, 1978.

———. *To Take Place: Toward Theory in Ritual*. Chicago, IL: University of Chicago Press, 1987.

Soja, Edward W. *Seeking Spatial Justice*. Minneapolis: University of Minnesota Press, 2010.

———. *Thirdspace: Journeys to Los Angeles and Other Real-and-Imagined Places*. Oxford and Cambridge, MA: Blackwell, 1996.

Syman, Stephanie. *The Subtle Body: The Story of Yoga in America*. New York: Farrar, Straus and Giroux, 2010.

Tweed, Thomas A. *Crossing and Dwelling: A Theory of Religion*. Cambridge, MA: Harvard University Press, 2006.

Vatsyayan, Kapila. "Performance: The Process, Manifestation and Experience." In *Concepts of Space Ancient and Modern*, edited by Kapila Vatsyayan, 381–394. New Delhi: Indira Gandhi National Center for the Arts, 1991.

Yamasaki, Taiko. *Shingon: Japanese Esoteric Buddhism*. Boulder, CO: Shambala, 1988.

White, David Gordon, ed. *Tantra in Practice*. Princeton, NJ: Princeton University Press, 2000.

Znamenski, Andrei. *Beauty of the Primitive: Shamanism and the Western Imagination*. Oxford: Oxford University Press, 2007.

1 The subtle body of vital presence in contemplative practices of Abhinavagupta's Trika Śaivism and Longchenpa's Great Perfection

Kerry Martin Skora

Introduction

This essay is a cross-cultural comparison of subtle body theory and practice, as expressed in the Trika Śaiva tradition of Abhinavagupta (c. 975–1025 C.E.) and the Tibetan Buddhist Great Perfection (*rdzogs pa chen po*) tradition of Longchenpa (*Klong chen pa*; 1308–1364 C.E.). I am interested in the body that is activated by means of visualization and full-bodied contemplative practices.[1] Abhinavagupta and Longchenpa are perfect candidates for such a comparative study. Both provide us with grand syntheses of their lifeworlds while articulating the subtle body in relation to Being (*gzhi*; *anuttara*) and its penetrating and pervading grounding of human development. Abhinavagupta focuses on contemplative practices of the subtle body in the fifth chapter of the *Light on the Tantra* (*Tantrāloka*), on the topic of "the embodied way [to liberation]" (*āṇava-upāya*); Longchenpa focuses on contemplative practices of the subtle body in the eighth chapter of the *Precious Treasury of Words and Meanings* (*Tshig don rin po che'i mdzod*), on the topic of "the pathways of primordial gnosis (*ye shes*) (in the human body)."[2]

The pioneering scholarship of Lilian Silburn on Abhinavagupta[3] and David Germano on Longchenpa[4] aid me in this task. Both take the subtle body seriously, interpreting it as connected—yet irreducible—to the physical body and as resonant with Being or Consciousness. At the same time, because of the complexity and profundity of the subject, further interpretation is necessary. Standing on their shoulders, however, I go beyond their initial translations and interpretations to practice "comparative religious studies." My primary model here is Jeffrey Kripal.[5] Kripal's work is significant in creating a robust model for comparison and in assessing and critiquing the discipline of Religious Studies. Taking a panoramic view of our field, he suggests that one of its purposes is to learn more about Consciousness, defining "Humanities" as the study of Consciousness coded in Culture.[6] I take this to mean, echoing Paul Ricoeur,[7] that the primary purpose should be to learn more about ourselves, our realities.

When we study Abhinavagupta and Longchenpa, of course, we should study the cultural matrices in which they find themselves—always giving rise to complex differences. Ironically, such differences also reveal similar patterns underlying Consciousness. Thus, we need to also ask, "How do such cultural expressions evoke something beyond culture?" In this chapter, instead of focusing on culture, I turn my vision in order to focus on Consciousness or Being itself. Thus, I compare Abhinavagupta and Longchenpa in order to find that which eludes contextualist studies, a common pattern in how Consciousness manifests in, through, and as our own bodies. I begin with Abhinavagupta, tapping into the scholarship of Silburn and others and integrating my own translations and interpretations, as entry into comparative religious studies. I will then turn to Longchenpa, drawing on both the translations and interpretations of David Germano to set up my examples for comparison.

In particular, I am focusing on the "subtle body of vital presence." This is the body that attains a peak state of flow, energy, and vitality by recovering its connection to Consciousness. I am signaling that such a body is remarkably similar to what has been called "Soul" in other places and times, if we focus on its corresponding connection to Being and the wonderful implications of such connecting for this very life, bracketing any notions of transmigration or life after death. A.H. Almaas notes that, even in our own "Western" lineages, for most of history we have allowed for the existence of Soul,[8] and have understood that Soul is able to know both Being and Universe; that these three are interrelated aspects of one Reality.[9] The same problems that we have understanding Soul are transferable to the understanding of subtle body. Theories—as well as our language, hermeneutics, and understanding—about souls and subtle bodies need to be correspondingly subtle. Following Abhinavagupta's and Longchenpa's leads, I suggest that the subtle body is where Reality enfolds at once both Consciousness and matter.[10] Notably, Germano makes similar connections, also calling for a comparative study focused on the subtle body. He notes the cross-cultural significance of "spiritual breath" and "inner winds" (*rlung*; *prāṇa*) of subtle body practice and the cross-cultural identification of this notion with notions of life and soul. Inspired by various other thinkers, including the psychologist Harry T. Hunt,[11] I will show how these various notions are gathered together in the notion of "vital presence."

Abhinavagupta's dazzling bright and spinning wheel of fire

I now describe three examples of contemplative practices related to the subtle body. My first example is from Abhinavagupta's fifth chapter of the *Tantrāloka*, in which he focuses on using the breath, mind, and body as objective supports for the contemplation, and thus as the means by which the practitioner is able to access Ultimate Reality, or Consciousness. Abhinavagupta first introduces the subtle body practices:

> Ultimate Reality lights up, in our intellect-vital breath-body complex. These are not separate from the Light, which is only Consciousness. Because of Consciousness's freedom, It has two qualities: the body of Consciousness, and insentience.[12]

For Abhinavagupta, Reality is made of both Consciousness and matter, yet not in any simple dualistic way. These, in fact, intertwine—most precisely in the human being, who may use their breath, mind, and body to access Consciousness. Reality enfolds both Consciousness and matter. This enfolding takes its most complex shape in the human individual, in the Self or Soul.

The first of five practices described by Abhinavagupta is contemplative visualization (*dhyāna*). Abhinavagupta, master of both religion and aesthetics, is certainly aware of the rich history of *dhyāna* in India, beginning with the *ṛṣi*s and continuing with all creative artists and visionaries, up to Abhinavagupta himself.[13] Abhinavagupta's actual presentation, as always, is dense, and was meant to be used with the guidance of a lineage teacher. I will rely on the brilliant guide Christopher Wallis provides. Wallis has translated parts of the corresponding chapter of Abhinavagupta's summary text, *Essence of the Tantra* (*Tantrasāra*), supplemented with his own extra-textual guide to the contemplative practices.[14] Here is my paraphrased summary of the essential parts of Walllis' meditative guide that will allow us to make more sense of Abhinavagupta's descriptions in the *Tantrāloka*:

> First, center one's awareness in the Heart. Second, visualize the subtle body, i.e., visualize one's body as containing three channels. One breathes in through the top of the head to the Heart through the left channel, which is imagined as glowing as the breath-energy flows through. One retains the breath, being centered in the Heart. Then one breathes out starting at the Heart through the right channel and out through the top of the head. One continues, slowly extending length of pause, until a bodily-felt energy, the Fire of Mahābhairava, suddenly flashes forth in the Heart. Third, one visualizes the energy as a fire wheel with twelve spokes, pulsing and spinning in the Heart, exiting through one of the sense openings (eye, ear, or another opening). The wheel leaves the body and rests on a sense object, corresponding to the sense opening (a visual object; for example, if the wheel exited through the eyes, and so on). Fourth, as the pulsating, spinning wheel rests on the object, the practitioner imagines that the object is an emission of their own consciousness and is being filled with divine energy. Then, dissolve the object in the fire wheel as it reenters the body through

> same sense opening as before and then rises through central channel to dissolve in Void at the top of the head as one exhales. Fifth, after the wheel has rested into the silence of the space at the top of the head, one rests there in complete stillness of the Void. Sixth, repeat process, now using the memory of the object instead of a real object.

Returning to Abhinavagupta's description of contemplative visualization, the practice traditionally involves gathering one's awareness in the Heart, and then making contact with Being. Abhinavagupta begins his description by stating that to know Reality is to know what is inside one's Heart. This is not the physical Heart, but nonetheless accessible to the practitioner through their own body. Abhinavagupta continues:

> Moon-Sun-Fire, one should contemplate on their fusion, thinking nothing else. From the rubbing together of the firesticks of this contemplation, the oblation-eating fire of Mahābhairava, in the great sacrificial pit of the Heart, intensely setting aflame, one should make it flourish. One should meditate on the abodes of knower, known, and the knowing, indivisible with the radiant presence of Bhairava and his expansive power.[15]

This practice involves breathing both in and out for successively longer periods of time and then the fusing together of these two different breaths; finding the perfect still-point or balance.[16] The reference to moon and sun and fire tells us that Abhinavagupta is referring to subtle body visualization.[17] The terms "sun," "moon," and "fire" refer to the three channels, the three phases of knowing, the three breaths (inward, outward, and their fusion), and the three goddesses of Abhinavagupta's Trika tradition (Parā, Parā-Aparā, and Aparā).

The practitioner is visualizing the Self as a hollow container of channels, while also feeling movement. Three channels, well known in subtle body discourses, are most important: the light of the moon channel, on the left; the light of the sun channel, on the right; and the light of the fire channel, the central channel. Significantly, the practitioner transcends their former body image and self-identity, now seeing and feeling themselves as a body of light.[18] The practitioner evokes the cycle of Consciousness, the processes of knowing and perception, and the various types of breaths or wind energies. Finally, Lilian Silburn notes that the practitioner "reunite[s] all the energies of body, thought, and speech in order to blend them into a single current of intense vibrations," gathering them together into one center.[19] The bodily energies of the practitioner—the subtlest levels of how they breathe and, therefore, how they perceive, know, and are conscious—tend to be chaotically distributed throughout the body; the process involves moving from a chaotic fragmented state to a unitary state.

Abhinavagupta continues:

> This No-Thing-Higher Cakra, from the Heart, flows out through the spaces of the eyes [and the other senses],[20] into the various fields of

> sense-objectivity. Thus, onto the sensory field of sound and so forth, through the pathway of the space of the sensory organ of hearing and so forth, through this Cakra falling, [the practitioner] recognizes [the field and the Cakra] as identical [to Bhairava]. Like a powerful lord, the universal emperor, this [Dazzling Bright Spinning Wheel, the Cakra which has become the Fiery Bhairava, the Great Tremendum], the nature of all, wherever it falls through this process [is followed by its senses, just as the emperor is followed by his subjects].[21]

We see here a practice of energy leaving through or entering one of the sense openings, creating a flow of energy between inside and outside, outside and inside. This flow is an important focal point for analysis.[22] Additionally, the intense contemplation leads to the fused energy becoming the presence of Bhairava in the Heart, a great blaze suddenly flashing forth, into which the whole sensory field, the whole universe now dissolves.[23] Notably, the divine pervades both the human and the universe. Again, we find the three important aspects of Reality: Being, Soul, and Cosmos. The process also integrates both light and spontaneity. Finally, with the metaphor of the universal emperor, Abhinavagupta suggests that a non-egoic, autonomous, spontaneous process takes place. This is the activation of the subtle body. All the sensory modalities are enlivened. This is an activating, enlivening, and revitalizing process, with all the sensory modalities being drawn together and gathered harmoniously around this autonomous entity, the true Self, or true Consciousness.[24]

Abhinavagupta's articulating sounds that rise in the body

My second example is Abhinavagupta's *uccāra* practice. This term can be translated in a variety of ways: "utterance," "recitation," "enunciation," "rising," or "elevation." As used by Abhinavagupta, the term simultaneously refers to vocalization as well as upward movement in the body,[25] initially indicating that the practice integrates sensory modalities of hearing, tactility, and kinesthetics. As with contemplative visualization, the purpose is to activate the subtle body process. Abhinavagupta states at the beginning of his description that the practitioner engages the vital breath (*prāṇa*) in order to allow Being, the None Higher (*anuttara*), to expand or unfold.[26]

This practice, like the contemplative visualization practice, is also summarized in Abhinavagupta's own *Essence of the Tantra*, for which we have the insightful synthesis provided by Christopher Wallis. Here again is my paraphrased summary of the essential parts of Wallis's synthesis:[27]

> First, gather one's awareness in the Heart. Second, as one breathes out, one feels energy flowing out through one's sense channels, and imagines their awareness leaving the body and resting on an object, feeling energy flowing through sense channels and manifesting as the object. Third, while imagining one's Self as underlying all things, one breathes

> in, feeling revitalized, and seeing the object as part of the Self. Overcoming separation, one becomes free of desire. Fourth, the equalizing breath suddenly, without effort, arises in the Heart, fusing and uniting the in-breath and out-breath; one now rests in this unity. Fifth, the fire of the up-breath rises and the practitioner absorbs within the three aspects of the "dynamic flow of consciousness," the three aspects of knower, known, and the knowing process. This is practiced through visualization or may happen spontaneously and even forcefully. The three aspects become united and absorbed in the Ground of Being, the Supreme Knower. This corresponds to the energy (*śakti*) of the vital breath—connected to *kuṇḍalinī* in some contexts—suddenly rising up the central channel, to the highest center. Sixth, the fire of absorption, having reached the Sky of Consciousness at the crown center, burns out, with only spacious stillness remaining. The Pervasive Vital Energy emerges and overflows from the center, flowing into and filling both body and environment with liquid bliss. Liberation is attained, as the True Self is recognized as one's identity and underlying the whole universe.

Additionally, Wallis describes variations of this basic practice, such as those including the use of *mantra*s or seed-syllables—the latter also being visualized as sparks of light as the sound travels up through the central channel. These may be coordinated with *mudrā*s, or hand gestures.[28]

Especially significant is the blissful rising of *kuṇḍalinī* coordinated with the rising of *mantra* in the body. The pulsating, radiating, bodily experience of rising *kuṇḍalinī*—felt by the practitioner as upward movement of energy through the subtle central channel or even as full-bodied ascension—is simultaneously the bodily-felt sense of the *mantra* rising in the form of subtle sound or subtle vibration. Here we are reminded of Margaret Laski's uncovering of "quasi-physical sensations" underlying mystical bliss or ecstasy. These sensations range from bodily experience expressed with metaphoric images—feeling uplifted—to more extreme experiences—actually feeling one is flying.[29] In a tradition that recovers the early cremation grounds experience of becoming Bhairava flying-in-the-sky, the more extreme experience would be an ever-present possibility. "Flying" (*plavana*) is one of ten yogic experiences enumerated by Jayaratha, in glossing Abhinavagupta's later section on the reactions of the practitioner who touches the fullness of Reality (*pūrṇatāsparśa*).[30] In any case, the rising of *kuṇḍalinī* along with the rising of *mantra* is again a clear crossing of sensory modalities.

Thus, as in the contemplative practice of *dhyāna*, various sensory modalities are also fused together in a pre-discursive, preconceptual unitive experience. This more complex practice involves visualization, but also hearing, tactility, inner and outer kinesthetics, and even imagination being integrated, or "entrained," spontaneously flowing into one integrative experience.[31] Even though the two sets of practices appear different, this essential pattern underlies both—and this may not be so surprising. Here, we note that for Merleau-Ponty, all pre-discursive, preconceptual experience is unitive and synaesthetic. Separation of the different sensory modalities is an abstraction that occurs only after stepping out of experience and reflecting on it from the outside.[32]

Additionally, this parallels the practice of phonematic emanation that Abhinavagupta describes in the third chapter of the *Tantrāloka*. Because Consciousness manifests as the body of the universe through the emission of sound, beginning with subtle sounds leading into grosser levels, the practitioner who embodies the Cosmos may reverse this process, dissolving the gross universe of sound, moving through subtler levels of the universe equated with sound, and, finally, reaching Pure Consciousness. More particularly, the emanation of the universe by Śiva is understood as the articulation of the fifty Sanskrit phonemes that collectively embody the True Self. Recollection of the phonemes is salvific in that the practitioner reverses the process of manifestation, gathering together all the aspects of Śiva dispersed into the world, and uniting them within the Self. Gathering together the phonemes by the practitioner is precisely an embodied process of being. With Jean-Louis Chrétien, we may say the Divine touches the practitioner, "collected whole and gathered up by the Other."[33] Recollection of the phonemes is also understood as recovering within the body the precognitive impulse or power (*icchā-śakti*) that gives rise to manifestation. Notably, this is a precognitive and pre-discursive bodily experience. For Abhinavagupta, sounds arise out of and dissolve back into Consciousness embodied in the Self. Sounds are accessible and felt in the body as divine energy. The *uccāra* practice is an example of this general principle.

Finally, we perhaps see here how the subtle body functions as a kind of "Soul" and, therefore, why some theorists connect the subtle body to the "Soul." We have seen how for Abhinavagupta, Consciousness and matter enfold one another, meeting in the subtle body. We also see Abhinavagupta playing with the notion of the finite being able to touch the infinite, pushing the boundaries of the body-self to reach the divine.[34] In the context of this practice, for example, Abhinavagupta refers to hearing that which cannot be heard. More than that, the whole point is to reach the unreachable—the None-Higher (*anuttara*), ontologically different from this body and this universe. Again, the practice allows the practitioner to overcome the ordinary body image, associated with the egocentric cognition that constructs a world of dualism, materialism, reductionism, and rationalism. In such transcendence—or dissolution even—the body is no longer separate from Being. The finite body is pushed to its limits, hearing that which cannot be heard, the whole body becoming an "organ of Being," a channel for the Other. Divine sound is bodily felt. And it is precisely our soulful and primordial touch that lies at the limits, with Self reaching out to be caressed by the Other.

Longchenpa's eating of wind-energies

In this section, I turn to the scholarship of David Germano who, through brilliant translations and interpretations gives us closer access to the subtle body contemplative practices Longchenpa describes. I will focus on one contemplative practice, the yoga of food. As I turn to a different system, I want to emphasize that I am purposely "decontextualizing."[35] An example from a different system—different tradition, time, place, and context—provides our project more complexity and more power of knowledge. Again, the goal is to uncover patterns that underlie subtle body practices that might otherwise remain hidden. Such a methodology is also inspired and influenced in part by Herbert Guenther, the renaissance scholar who initiated Longchenpa Studies in 1975.[36] Guenther reveals the relevance of Longchenpa's discourses and practices to all others, in whatever time and place.[37] Guenther continues Longchenpa's humanistic dialogue by translating, interpreting, and conveying the tradition to Western listeners by essentially creating new language and models for understanding connected to phenomenology, the experience of the Self and the world. Because of the incredible complexity and difficulty of his work, Guenther has been ignored by most scholars, with the exception of a few daring to follow his trailblazing path, including David Germano. Guenther's powerful methodology is transferable to our other fields, including Abhinavagupta Studies and Subtle Body Studies.

In a triune set of scholarly works, David Germano, in addition to translating and interpreting Longchenpa's masterly synthesis of Great Perfection discourse and practice, provides us with detailed translations and interpretations of seven sets of contemplative practices that form, according to Longchenpa, the Great Perfection preliminary practices.[38] Although each is relevant to the subtle body practices being interpreted here, it will suffice to narrow our field down to one example within those seven sets. One set includes three main yogas of food,[39] and, within that, Germano focuses on one specific yoga of food, the "eating of winds."[40] These "winds" are similar to the breaths portrayed by Abhinavagupta. Germano explicitly describes the winds as energy currents, flows, or streamings. Similar to Abhinavagupta's understanding is the deep connection between the wind energies and awareness or Consciousness itself. Focusing on the wind energies is equivalent to becoming aware of awareness, being able to watch how Consciousness operates in one's very own body. Significantly, William James defines Consciousness using these very same terms, "streamings," "flows," and "currents."[41] James's work is one of the primary influences in the thought of Harry T. Hunt, which I will use later to help us think more deeply about the subtle body discourses and practices that I am synthesizing here.

Amongst many similar descriptions, the following presentation by Longchenpa of the yoga of food, translated by Germano, immediately highlights the synaesthetic nature of the practice, the deconstructing of normative body image, and the arising of vital presence:

> You join the upper and lower winds [of the body], pull them into the flavor channel (with inhalation via the nostrils), and imagine the throat wheel is thus filled with the flavor of ambrosia. By means of concealing the earth and water winds [i.e., yellow and blue in color], all appearances become food for you and dissolve within the throat and flavor channel. Through meditating on them as pervaded by the bliss of meditative states, you accomplish the yoga of food.[42]

As interpreted by Germano, the general idea is that the practitioner "ingests wind-energies." Again, this signals the breaking down of the normative relationship between body-self and environment. While breathing in, one is also visualizing that one is ingesting the energies' underlying appearances. Thus, the practitioner overcomes both separation from environment as well as the consequent afflictive desire. Significantly, the wind-energies enter the body of the practitioner through the nostrils and then go to the right channel, known as the "flavor channel" associated with eating food. In a similar set of exercises, the practitioner meditates on the sky and eats the blue winds experienced as the essential energies underlying all appearances. This sky-blue energy then pervades the body, filling it with pure joy. We are immediately reminded of the blissful nectar pervading the body in Abhinavagupta's practices. In addition to involving the rhythms of breathing with visualization, this practice would seem to involve taste, as the notions of "eating" and "flavor" indicate, and perhaps even the sense of smell. The practitioner continues to ingest winds until the throat wheel overflows and the energies become redistributed throughout the mind-body complex, nourishing and revitalizing both mind and body.

Longchenpa's breathing exercise bears significant similarities to Abhinavagupta's exercise. As Germano points out, "the body's lower currents of energy" are pulled up, and "upper currents of energy" are pressed down, and then "concealed," or concentrated or fused together in what is known as the "vase," a central part of the body near the navel.[43] Similarly, the practitioner moves from a chaotic state, in which the breath-energies are fragmented and uncoordinated, to a harmonious state of synchrony. According to Germano, concentrating energies implies using energy efficiently and smoothly, rather than wasting and dissipating energy, a natural consequence of feeling separate from one's environment, and, hence, in an imbalanced state of desire, eating mindlessly in a futile effort to fulfill endless desire. The practitioner, with a body-image based on such separation, suffers because of unwholesome dependence on desirable food. The exercise breaks this separation, again establishing a flowing relationship between inside and outside, connecting the body-self to an environment of expansive and re-vitalizing energy.

Longchenpa elucidates a related technique, further translated and interpreted by Germano, that has clear connections to the cremation grounds culture. Now, the practitioner visualizes a yoginī slicing the upper part of their own heart with a sickle, so that blood can then flow out of the yoginī's vagina and into the practitioner's heart.[44] The blood flows as white and red drops, the seminal nuclei of enlightenment, so that the heart fills and then overflows, saturating the whole body with the bliss of liberation. Again, a flowing relationship is established between inside and outside. Simultaneously, the visualization deconstructs the practitioner's normative view of body-self and its relation to its surroundings. A static view, where the body and environment are simply inert, separate and solid, with the body in afflictive, needy dependence on the environment and its coarse food, is replaced by a processual view, where the body is nourished and vitalized, as one contemplates flowing energy. The wind-energies are equivalent to the essences of the elements of the natural world, "elemental essences," pervading the environment. To gather them together again is to intensify this energy or vitality, allowing it to overflow in the body. As Germano notes, the practitioner moves from coarse food to contemplative food, becoming liberated from limited and obsessive body images, also corresponding to limited and obsessive images of materiality. Again, synaesthesia is involved, the flowing and the colors indicating a crossing of tactile and visual sensory modalities. In sum, all of these contemplations are concerned with transformations of Consciousness. In ordinary awareness, because of the separation of body-self and external Reality, afflictive attachment or repulsion arises. With the activation of subtle body, one's former image of body-self is deconstructed, replaced by a flow of energy between "here" and "there," involving bodily-felt sense, as the practitioner becomes aware of being located in a surrounding array.[45]

Concluding remarks: vital presence, flowing energies, and bodies of light

In his masterpiece *On the Nature of Consciousness*, published in 1995, and various journal articles,[46] Harry T. Hunt presents nothing less than a grand synthesis of Consciousness Studies. It goes back to Ancient Greece and India and continues to the present day, in dialogue with both Asian and Western traditions and thinkers, and accesses different disciplines, including analytical and continental philosophy, phenomenology of body and ecology, and cognitive and transpersonal psychology.[47] Like both Abhinavagupta and Longchenpa, Hunt honors the reality of Consciousness. And while understanding that these very bodies of ours are often limited by dimmed-down awareness, imprinted and constrained by their social environments, Hunt refuses to reduce Consciousness to culture or cognition. Like Abhinavagupta and Longchenpa, Hunt explores the artificial constraints that the body can transcend in order to reach more spacious and expansive forms of awareness. Hunt's conversation parallels the attempts by both Abhinavagupta and Longchenpa to present a dynamic whole wherein spirit and matter, Consciousness and body, inside and outside, and Being and Universe intertwine. Hunt recognizes the Self to be a process that serves as the field where all of this intertwining may take place. Thus, while being keenly attuned to important differences between different subtle body traditions,[48] most significantly, Hunt intentionally goes beyond contextualism, constructivism, and other forms of reductionism to unveil the significant common patterns shared between different subtle body traditions. For these reasons, his work is essential to any contemporary theory regarding subtle body discourse and practice.

Hunt is not a contextualist. He does not use differences of era, place, or culture to argue that each subtle body system is a mere construction that works or makes sense solely in its own specific context. At the same time, Hunt is clearly aware of the clever ways in[49] which any society constrains the beleaguered body-self by continually imposing its oppressive norms, laws, customs, routines, and historical conventions. I would characterize Hunt as a "post-constructivist, post-contextualist," much like Abhinavagupta and Longchenpa. Abhinavagupta, for example, proclaims a processual antidote to the brutal Brahmanical hegemony of his day. He defines this external, socio-historical system of values determining the world and identity of a false self in eight particular ways. For Abhinavagupta, the false self is literally possessed—as we ourselves today might find ourselves living restrained, inauthentic, wasted lives—by eight demons, called "Seizer-Demons" (*graha*). These are the demons of socio-religious hierarchies of power; mere scholastic learning of texts; local values and status taken to be universal; following rules construed as universally correct; attachment to the body-ego as one's true Self; narrow-minded patriotism, regionalism, and parochialism; anyone-and everyone's consensually validated reality; and lust for power, money, and more possessions.[50] Hunt already recognizes the dangers of reducing Reality to a local context. His goal is different now—namely, to seek essential patterns underlying human beings, the very patterns that allow us to break out of context. Hunt suggests then that the *sine qua non* of subtle body experience is the sense of "vital presence." Comparing "vital presence" to Abraham Maslow's "peak experience" and Mihaly Csikszentmihalyi's "flow experience,"[51]Hunt, like Abhinavagupta and Longchenpa, takes seriously the notion of what we would term transpersonal experience, the experience of transcending the ordinary body-ego.

A.H. Almaas's understanding of the transpersonal experience of "essence," with two primary poles, "openness" and "presence," inspires Hunt's understanding of religious experience. Openness is the impersonal encounter with transcendence "based on the experience of openness and space."[52] An example of openness is the "light-of-the-void" experience, recognized in various traditions, including Western introspection and Tibetan

Buddhist traditions.[53] Relevant to our topic is the other pole of "presence" that Hunt describes as the more personal side of religious experience. This is the full-bodied experience of "I am." One is fully existing—and simultaneously aware that one is fully existing. Hunt and others have compared this, and I think rightly so, to "lucid dreaming." In lucid dreaming, one is fully engaged in the activity of dreaming while simultaneously aware that one is dreaming. Imagine now that one is fully engaged in the activity of existing while knowing one is existing—fully aware of the body-self and all its experiences, fully aware of the environment in which one is placed, all the while watching oneself being engaged in life. Spontaneously, one finds themselves in the rare situation of suddenly, completely realizing that one is alive, bringing all awareness and accompanying energies to one's "immediate here-and-now experience for its own sake."[54] Being aware that one is present in a particular environment, one would become fully and maximally present and alive, accompanied by the "increased [bodily-felt] sense of clarity, immediacy, and freedom also described by Maslow as part of peak experience."[55]

Hunt's explication of Consciousness is relevant to both Abhinavagupta and Longchenpa. Hunt has applied his understanding to the experience of vital presence in different contexts, including schizophrenia, classical introspection, bioenergetics, and, most importantly for us, meditation.[56] Even more significantly, with his understanding, Hunt illuminates a particular set of Tibetan Buddhist practices focused on subtle body activation. He primarily relies on accounts by Garma C.C. Chang and Geshe Kelsang Gyatso. Although Hunt refers at times to Longchenpa, his references to Longchenpa do not include the yoga of food or, for that matter, any of the yogas described by Longchenpa in the same chapter that is devoted to contemplative subtle body traditions. Hunt does not refer at all to Abhinavagupta. Therefore, I now want to draw on Hunt's theories to show how three main themes are applicable to the subtle body practices of Abhinavagupta and Longchenpa.

First, each of the subtle body contemplations involve flow states that activate complex synaesthetic patterns. The flow state, spontaneous and revitalizing, involves feeling energy flowing within one's body-self and between the body-self and the environment. As we try to recognize something that goes beyond culture, it is important to take seriously both Abhinavagupta and Longchenpa. Such states are not simply imaginary fantasies; these luminaries are not making this up. If we superimpose our own alien body-self-image onto this other lifeworld, of course it is difficult to imagine. Hunt, a psychologist, synthesizes and extrapolates from vast amounts of other research, including but not limited to that of Andras Angyal on schizophrenia, both William Reich and A.H. Almaas's on bioenergetics and contemplative practices including some related to the subtle body, Paul Schilder on classical introspection, and Heidegger scholar and phenomenologist, Eugene Gendlin, on focusing. Building upon all of this, Hunt explains: our body-self is normally in a state of contracted or stepped-down consciousness, far from any state of vital presence, having accepted the body as viewed from the outside as our real Self, and thus experiencing an extremely lifeless, unintelligent, static, and solid body separate from its environment, with all the resulting contractions and oppressions and limitations literally stored within, in the form of uptightness and rigidity. Consciousness and its accompanying energies are literally trapped with nowhere to go.[57] In contemplative experience, similar to experiences through introspection and bioenergetic practices and even to the spontaneous experiences of schizophrenics, it is possible to let go of this old body image—as well as all the accompanying limitation and suffering—by accessing and activating a subtler Self, a truer Self, and paying attention only to what we experience, what we actually feel.

The implications here are enormous. Imagine a map of Reality based on multi-dimensional deep experience, rather than two-dimensional, artificially constructed ideas. The difference is directly related to the gap between constructivist models of Reality and those of post-constructivists. Martin Heidegger, inspired by Rudolph Otto and attuned to the vast multi-dimensional lifeworld of experience, alerts us to this gap.[58] The encounter with the Numinous, with Awesome Being, is complex and bodily felt, completely separate from religious conceptual maps or schema. Schema are mere representations that freeze then reduce the original bodily-felt, expansive experience of immediacy, openness, spaciousness, and clarity.

We are in a better position now to understand that for Abhinavagupta and Longchenpa, the flow state does, actually, spontaneously take over. We can discern two different phases of the practices. At the beginning of each practice, the practitioner appears to have to force themselves to breathe in a certain manner, purposely crossing sensory modalities. They are guided by the tradition and seem to "fake" it. That this is a necessary part of the practice would make some scholars conclude that the body is always constrained by tradition[59] or that one is only imagining some fantasy self in some fantasy world.[60] Here, we encounter a central paradox in the study of religion that Jeffrey Kripal highlights: both rationalist scholars and reflexive scholars are necessary. Any one scholar works out of their own integrity to make sense of religion. However, in Kripal's terms, the Human is Two—an ego who has not been traumatized—or "cooked enough"—as it were, and a new Self, creatively arising into Being—"cooked" through trauma, crisis, or spiritual emergency. Thus, any one scholar may focus exclusively on one of the two human dimensions.[61]

After following the initial guidelines of the text and tradition, something amazing happens: preconceptual and pre-discursive flow takes over, activating synaesthetic patterns. Abhinavagupta, for example, refers to all the sensory modalities working harmoniously, comparing the blazing wheel of

Bhairava that arises as being like a universal emperor, while the senses, being like the subjects, naturally fall in line and follow their lord. Longchenpa's references to overflowing, revitalizing, and reenergizing also point to a spontaneous process taking over. He is explicit about this at times, concluding one description of a contemplative practice: "A blissful, clear and non-conceptual state of contemplation spontaneously arises, and the meditator becomes divested of attachment to food and clothes."[62] Additionally, these examples involve kinesthetic experiences of flowing energies—one truly feels movement in the body—blending with visual modalities and, in more advanced practices, sometimes with sound, such as listening and chanting. Finally, in Longchenpa's description of "eating ambrosia," and the simultaneous energization of the "flavor" channel, we even see visualization crossing with taste and, possibly, smell.

Additionally, in subtle body activation, the practitioner overcomes their ordinary body image, going beyond ordinary states that consist of limited and distorted images of body as merely objective. The body is no longer seen as a stable object separate from a stable environment. The body-self becomes a body of light, an energy body in a flowing relationship with its environment.[63] In Abhinavagupta's contemplative visualization practice; for example, the spinning wheel of fire falls on the object with the practitioner contemplating that the object has arisen from Consciousness, is maintained by Consciousness, and dissolves back into Consciousness. In this way, appearances are seen as illusory in that they are not separate from Consciousness. The practitioner recognizes the intertwining of internal sensing and outward sensing. One first becomes centered in the heart, recovering awareness, and then one is made to see the connection between inner awareness and the sensory field—between consciousness of the inside and consciousness of the outside. The body becomes more permeable, open, and expansive.

Finally, because body image is bounded to image of external surroundings, the practitioner lets go of the ego separating them from their environment, recovering a sense of vital presence, tantamount to the bodily-felt sense, "I am here," a pre-discursive bodily-felt sense of their ground of being, of the sense that "I am here." With such vital presence also comes grace and wonder, clarity and freedom. The practitioner not only experiences Self as divine, but their whole surrounding environment as being filled with divine grace. The practitioner begins seeing themselves as a body of light, not separate from the environment, and establishing a flowing circuit of energy between inside and outside. We are reminded of eco-philosopher, Andreas Weber's "enlivenment"[64] meant to replace the rationalist term "enlightenment," and referring to the highest capacity of the human being to overcome their separation from nature and, thus, to become fully alive, attaining "self-ablazedness," as they experience "pure grace in whose presence the splendor of creation unfolds with ever greater complexity in ever more delicate forms."[65]

Notes

1 See, on this distinction, André Padoux, *The Hindu Tantric World: An Overview* (Chicago: The University of Chicago Press, 2017), 75. I differ from Padoux in his assessment that such a body is completely imaginary. I argue that the subtle body certainly is real; we simply need to expand our understanding of reality.
2 David Germano, "Poetic Thought, the Intelligent Universe, and the Mystery of Self: The Tantric Synthesis of rDzogs Chen in Fourteenth Century Tibet" (PhD diss., University of Wisconsin, 1992).
3 See Lilian Silburn, *Kuṇḍalinī: Energy of the Depths*, trans. Jacques Gontier (Albany: State University of New York Press, 1988), especially 25–79, which includes translations and interpretations of the fifth chapter of the *Tantrāloka*; and Lilian Silburn and André Padoux, ed. and trans., *Abhinavagupta, La Lumière sur les Tantras, Chapitres 1 à 5 du Tantrāloka* (Paris: Collège de France, 1998).
4 See Germano, "Poetic Thought, the Intelligent Universe, and the Mystery of Self: The Tantric Synthesis of rDzogs Chen in Fourteenth Century Tibet" (most important for us is Germano's translation of the eight chapter, along with his interpretations in his annotations); "Food, Clothes, Dreams, and Karmic Propensities," in *Religions of Tibet in Practice*, ed. Donald S. Lopez, Jr. (Princeton, NJ: Princeton University Press, 1997): 293–312; and "The Elements, Insanity, and Lettered Subjectivity" in *Religions of Tibet in Practice*, ed. Lopez, Jr., 313–334.
5 See Jeffrey J. Kripal, *Authors of the Impossible: The Paranormal and the Sacred* (Chicago: The University of Chicago Press, 2010); Jeffrey J. Kripal, et al., *Comparing Religions: Coming to Terms* (Malden, MA: Wiley-Blackwell, 2014); and Jeffrey J. Kripal, *Secret Body: Erotic and Esoteric Currents in the History of Religions* (Chicago: The University of Chicago Press, 2017).
6 See Kripal, *Comparing Religions*, 86–87; and also Kripal, *Secret Body: Erotic and Esoteric Currents in the History of Religions*, 206 ff.
7 See Paul Ricoeur, "The History of Religions and the Phenomenology of Time Consciousness," in *The History of Religions: Retrospect and Prospect*, ed. Joseph M. Kitagawa (New York: Macmillan Publishing Company, 1985), 28–29.
8 See A. H. Almaas, *The Inner Journey Home: Soul's Realization of the Unity of Reality* (Boston, MA: Shambhala, 2004), 3–14.
9 See Almaas, *The Inner Journey Home*, 6–8. Perhaps the most rigorous modern accounts of Reality as threefold are found in Raimundo Panikkar's life corpus, reaching a peak in his most recent *Rhythm of Being: The Gifford Lectures* (Maryknoll: Orbis Books, 2010).
10 Here I am also inspired by Laura U. Marks. See her *Enfoldment and Infinity: An Islamic Genealogy of New Media Art* (Cambridge, MA: MIT Press, 2010), 271.
11 Most important will be Harry T. Hunt, *On the Nature of Consciousness: Cognitive, Phenomenological, and Transpersonal Perspectives* (New Haven, CT: Yale University Press, 1995).
12 *Tantrāloka* 5.7a-8b. All translations of the *Tantrāloka* are my own. I am most grateful for all the previous pioneering work on the *Tantrāloka* that inspired and aided my own, especially the elucidating translations and interpretations of Raniero Gnoli in Italian, and Lilian Silburn and André Padoux in French. See Raniero Gnoli, ed. and trans., *Abhinavagupta, Luce dei Tantra, Tantrāloka* (Milano: Adelphi Edizioni, 1999); and Silburn and Padoux, ed. and trans., *Abhinavagupta, La Lumière sur les Tantras, Chapitres 1 à 5 du Tantrāloka.* Also most helpful and relevant is Lilian Silburn, *Kuṇḍalinī*, 25–79; and the

remarkable translating and interpreting of essential parts of *Tantrāloka* 5 by Mark S. G. Dyczkowski. See Dyckzkowski, trans., *The Stanzas on Vibration* (Albany: State University of New York Press, 1992), 271–273. Finally, my understanding has also benefitted from the illuminating work of Christopher D. Wallis, in his *Tantra Illuminated: The Philosophy, History and Practice of a Timeless Tradition* (Second Edition; Petaluma, CA: Mattamayūra, 2013), especially 385–402, on Abhinavagupta's presentation of *dhyāna* and *uccāra* in the *Tantrasāra*.

13 See Jan Gonda, *Vision of the Vedic Poets* (The Hague: Mouton, 1963); and Kerry Martin Skora, "Bodily Gestures and Embodied Awareness: *Mudrā* as the Bodily Seal of Being in the Trika Śaivism of Kashmir," in *Refiguring the Body: Embodiment in South Asian Religions*, ed. Barbara A. Holdrege and Karen Pechilis (Albany: State University of New York Press, 2016), 96.

14 Wallis, *Tantra Illuminated*, 385–394.

15 *Tantrāloka* 5.22a–25a.

16 This practice, sometimes called "vase breathing," is found across traditions, in both India and Tibet, including Longchenpa's tradition. See Silburn, *Kuṇḍalinī*, 41–43; Dyczkowski, *Stanzas on Vibration*, 271–272; and Wallis, *Tantra Illuminated*, 392.

17 See Wallis, *Tantra Illuminated*, 388–392; and Dyczkowski, *Stanzas on Vibration*, 391–392, note 16.

18 Abhinavagupta begins his description of *dhyāna* stating that Consciousness-Light dwells within the Heart of the practitioner: *Tantrāloka* 5.20a. Thus, Wallis, for example, says that subtle body visualization means meditating on being a body of light: Wallis, *Tantra Illuminated*, 386. Germano interprets Longchenpa similarly, as a body containing and revitalized by enlightenend energy: Germano, "Food, Clothes, Dreams, and Karmic Propensities," 296–297. The important point is that the body is reimagined and experienced anew as in fact a container for channels of light or energy, recovering its primordial relationship to Consciousness. See also Hunt, *On the Nature of Consciousness*, 204–205.

19 See Silburn, *Kuṇḍalinī*, 32.

20 Karl Ove Knausgaard is awestruck by David Eagleman's *The Brain: The Story of You*. I summarize his insightful and helpful response with three key points: First, seeing something actually means that more information is truly outward toward the object, rather than the other way. I would add that this means that neuroscientists now recognize that awareness is flowing outward toward the object. Second, seeing involves the whole body and all the other senses. The state of flow is real and has a neurological basis. And, third, human beings really do have the capacity to overcome the sense of ordinary body-self. This is simultaneous with becoming totally immersed in the world. See Knausgaard, "By the Book: Karl Ove Knausgaard," *Book Review*, *New York Times*, August 17, 2017, (accessed January 30, 2019). https://www.nytimes.com/2017/08/17/books/review/karl-ove-knausgaard-by-the-book.html.

21 *Tantrāloka* 5.27b-31a.

22 This is one of the essential characteristics of subtle body practices. We will see that this is part of Longchenpa's practices, also.

23 See also Padoux, *The Hindu Tantric World*, 128–129.

24 See Wallis, *Tantra Illuminated*, 385; and Silburn, *Kuṇḍalinī*, 75.

25 There are many permutations of this practice. For example, Abhinavagupta's disciple, Kṣemarāja, presents the *uccāra* practice of the mystical syllable *OṂ* in his commentaries on the *Netratantra* and *Svacchandatantra*: see André Padoux, *Vāc: The Concept of the Word in Selected Hindu Tantras*, trans. Jacques Gontier (Albany: State University of New York Press, 1990), 403–410.

26 *Tantrāloka* 5.43a-43b.
27 See Wallis, *Tantra Illuminated*, 395–396.
28 Ibid.
29 See Harry T. Hunt, *On the Nature of Consciousness*, 202–203.
30 See Silburn, *Kuṇḍalinī*, 72.
31 See Wallis, *Tantra Illuminated*, 395–396.
32 See Kerry Martin Skora, "The Pulsating Heart and Its Divine Sense Energies: Body and Touch in Abhinavagupta's Trika Śaivism," *Numen: International Review for the History of Religions* 54, no. 4 (2007): 438–442. We are also reminded that sound and touch might actually share the same neurobiological roots; and that all sensory modalities might ultimately go back to touch, to feeling.
33 Jean-Louis Chrétien, *The Call and the Response*, trans. Anne A. Davenport (New York: Fordham University Press, 2004), 131. See also Kerry Martin Skora, "Bodily Gestures and Embodied Awareness: *Mudrā* as the Bodily Seal of Being in the Trika Śaivism of Kashmir," 92–93.
34 See Kerry Martin Skora, "The Bodily Efflorescence of Words: The Crossing of Divine-Voice and the Body-Self in Abhinavagupta's Cosmology," *Southeast Review of Asian Studies* 35, no. 1 (2013): 70–89.
35 Decontextualization is a natural process underlying various fields of knowledge, starting with what Michel Foucault understood as, rightly so I think, our tightest system of knowledge, mathematics. Mathematical insight is gained when patterns are revealed by comparing two apparently different objects and recognizing that they share patterns at a higher level of abstraction. This process works in other disciplines. Thus, philosopher Ben-Ami Scharfstein has provided a rigorous argument against contextualization, and for decontextualization. His remarkable vision is still relevant today, perhaps even more so, because of the tendency found in our own field of religious studies for exclusive contextualization. Again, this is not to deny that contextualization is essential. The underdog here is decontexutalization, and my argument, and Scharfstein's, is only a response to exclusive contextualization. See Ben-Ami Scharfstein, "The Contextual Fallacy," in *Interpreting Across Boundaries: New Essays in Comparative Philosophy*, ed. Gerald James Larson and Eliot Deutsch (Princeton, NJ: Princeton University Press, 1988): 84–97.
36 I am marking the beginning of Longchenpa Studies with Guenther's first full study and translation of Longchenpa, as far as I am aware, complete with his unique phenomenological method, in the *Kindly Bent to Ease Us* trilogy: Herbert V. Guenther, *Kindly Bent to Ease Us*, 3 volumes (Emeryville, CA: Dharma Publishing, 1975–1976).
37 See Herbert V. Guenther, *Matrix of Mystery: Scientific and Humanistic Aspects of rDzogs-chen Thought* (Boulder, CO: Shambhala, 1984): 1, where Guenther makes clear his methodology: "Here, 'essential' is to be understood as that which is relevant to the actuality of man's existential predicament. As such it has nothing to do with cultural artifacts, museum pieces, and other playthings of those in the humanities who have failed to distinguish between that which can still make a claim on contemporary man in all his situational complexities and those fossilized cultural patterns which survive merely by virtue of gathering dust. It is this failure that accounts, to a very large part, for the growing suspicion and hence fear—completely justified—that the humanities are in fact no longer relevant." My goal in this article is to continue Guenther's project of making Religious Studies and the Humanities relevant.
38 See my bibliographic note on David Germano above.
39 Germano, "Food, Clothes, Dreams, and Karmic Propensities," 295–296.
40 Germano, "Food, Clothes, Dreams, and Karmic Propensities," 296: "'eating' one's own energized breath."

41 See Harry T. Hunt, *On the Nature of Consciousness*, 11–12, 123–124, and 210.
42 Germano, "Food, Clothes, Dreams, and Karmic Propensities," 296.
43 Germano, "Food, Clothes, Dreams, and Karmic Propensities," 296–297.
44 Here and below, I am following Germano, "Food, Clothes, Dreams, and Karmic Propensities," 297.
45 Here I am using the language of Harry T. Hunt, to whom I turn in my next and concluding section. Hunt himself is inspired by James J. Gibson. See Hunt's synthesis of Gibson's phenomenology of perception and his key concept of the ecological array: Harry T. Hunt, *On the Nature of Consciousness*, 63–72.
46 Harry T. Hunt, *On the Nature of Consciousness: Cognitive, Phenomenological, and Transpersonal Perspectives*; "'Dark Nights of the Soul': Phenomenology and Neurocognition of Spiritual Suffering in Mysticism and Psychosis," *Review of General Psychology* 11, no. 3 (2007): 209–234; "'The Heart Has Its Reasons': Transpersonal Experience as Higher Development of Social-Personal Intelligence, and Its Response to the Inner Solitude of Consciousness," *The Journal of Transpersonal Psychology* 48, no. 1 (2016): 1–25. See also Harry T. Hunt, *Lives in Spirit: Precursors and Dilemmas of a Secular Western Mysticism* (Albany: State University of New York Press, 2003).
47 See also the exchange on the nature of Consciousness between, on one hand, Hunt and colleagues, Oliver Sacks, Antonio Damasio, and others, and, on the other hand, world-renowned neuroscientist Christoph Koch, in "Exclusive: Oliver Sacks, Antonio Damasio, and Others Debate Christoph Koch on the Nature of Consciousness," *Mind Guest Blog, Scientific American*, accessed February2,2019,https://blogs.scientificamerican.com/mind-guest-blog/exclusive-oliver-sacks-antonio-damasio-and-others-debate-christof-koch-on-the-nature-of-consciousness/.
48 See Hunt, *On the Nature of Consciousness*, 307–308, note 1.
49 Also relevant and significant is the integrated essay by Geoffrey Samuel: "Subtle-body processes: Towards a non-reductionist understanding," in *Religion and the Subtle Body in Asian and the West*, ed. Geoffrey Samuel and Jay Johnston (London: Routledge, 2013), 249–266. Samuel directs us to the important scholarship of Edward Kelly and others, which points to Consciousness as primordial and separate from matter, to argue against naive physicalism. However, in his essay, perhaps due to scope only, he takes a less radical position focusing on Consciousness as emergent yet autonomous, bracketing the idea of whether or not Consciousness precedes matter. This is clearly different, and Samuel recognizes this, from some of the assumptions of the various traditions studied in his edited volume. Of course, they are different from the views of Abhinavagupta and Longchenpa, who understand Consciousness as not only autonmous, but as primary. In this essay, I am tending toward the more radical position: any theory or model applied to Abhinavagupta and Longchenpa should accordingly recognize Consciousness as primary.
50 My translations are meant to emphasize these concepts' existential weight and relevance. For the Sanskrit and more literal translations, see Alexis Sanderson, "Purity and Power Among the Brahmans of Kashmir," in *The Category of the Person: Anthropological and Philosophical Perspectives*, ed. Michael Carrithers, Steven Collins, and Steven Lukes (Cambridge: Cambridge University Press, 1985), 211–212, note 69. Silburn provides related insight on Abhinavagupta's views of scholastic learning, and on how systems of purity and impurity oppress and contract the body-self: see Silburn, *Kuṇḍalinī*, 92, and 163–165.
51 See Hunt, *On the Nature of Consciousness*, 199–200.
52 See Hunt, *On the Nature of Consciousness*, 209.
53 See Hunt, *On the Nature of Consciousness*, 158–160.
54 Hunt, *On the Nature of Consciousness*, 200.

55 Hunt, *On the Nature of Consciousness*, 226. See also James H. Austin, *Zen and the Brain: Toward an Understanding of Meditation and Consciousness* (Cambridge, MA: MIT Press, 1988), 324–325; and Kerry Martin Skora, "A Day in the Life of an Aesthetic Tāntrika: From Synaesthetic Garden to Lucid Dreaming and Spaciousness," *Religions* 9, no. 3 (2018): 14–16.
56 See Hunt, *On the Nature of Consciousness*, 200–209.
57 See Hunt, *On the Nature of Consciousness*, 200–204.
58 See Hunt, *Lives in Spirit*, 15–16.
59 See, for example, Gavin Flood, *The Tantric Body: The Secret Tradition of Hindu Religion* (London: I. B. Tauris, 2006), 157–162.
60 I have addressed this, responding to André Padoux and Alexis Sanderson, in my "The Pulsating Heart and Its Divine Sense Energies." See especially 446–453.
61 Kripal, *Authors of the Impossible*, 266–269; and *Comparing Religions*, 284–286.
62 Germano, "Food, Clothes, Dreams, and Karmic Propensities," 297–298.
63 Neuroanatomist Jill Bolte Taylor provides insight into Consciousness, describing her energy-body experience following a stroke. See Jill Bolte Taylor, "My Stroke of Insight," *TED2008*, February 2008, accessed February 4, 2019, https://www.ted.com/talks/jill_bolte_taylor_s_powerful_stroke_of_insight. See also Jeffrey Kripal's brilliant interpretation of the experience and its implications for the study of Consciousness, in *Authors of the Impossible*, 259–261 and 265–269.
64 See Andreas Weber, *The Biology of Wonder: Aliveness, Feeling, and the Metamorphosis of Science* (Gabriola, BC: New Society Publishers, 2016), 1–5.
65 See Andreas Weber, *Matter and Desire: An Erotic Ecology* (White River Junction, VT: Chelsea Green Publishing, 2017), 54.

Bibliography

Abhinavagupta. *The Tantrāloka of Abhinavagupta with the Commentary [Tantrālokaviveka] of Jayaratha*, ed. R. C. Dwivedi and Navajivan Rastogi. 8 vols. Delhi: Motilal Banarsidass, 1987 [1918–1938].

Almaas, A. H. *The Inner Journey Home: Soul's Realization of the Unity of Reality*. Boston, MA: Shambhala, 2004.

Austin, James H. *Zen and the Brain: Toward an Understanding of Meditation and Consciousness*. Cambridge, MA: MIT Press, 1988.

Chrétien, Jean-Louis. *The Call and the Response*. Translated by Anne A. Davenport. New York: Fordham University Press, 2004.

Dyczkowski, Mark S. G., trans., *The Stanzas on Vibration*. Albany: State University of New York Press, 1992.

Flood, Gavin. *The Tantric Body: The Secret Tradition of Hindu Religion*. New York: I. B. Tauris, 2006.

Germano, David. "The Elements, Insanity, and Lettered Subjectivity." In *Religions of Tibet in Practice*, edited by Donald S. Lopez, Jr., 313–334. Princeton, NJ: Princeton University Press, 1997.

Germano, David. "Food, Clothes, Dreams, and Karmic Propensities." In *Religions of Tibet in Practice*, edited by Donald S. Lopez, Jr., 293–312. Princeton, NJ: Princeton University Press, 1997.

Germano, David. "Poetic Thought, the Intelligent Universe, and the Mystery of Self: The Tantric Synthesis of rDzogs Chen in Fourteenth Century Tibet." PhD diss., University of Wisconsin, 1992.

Guenther, Herbert V. *Kindly Bent to Ease Us*. 3 vols. Emeryville, CA: Dharma Publishing, 1975–1976.

Guenther, Herbert V. *Matrix of Mystery: Scientific and Humanistic Aspects of rDzogs-chen Thought*. Boulder, CO: Shambhala, 1984.

Gnoli, Raniero, ed. and trans. *Abhinavagupta, Luce dei Tantra, Tantrāloka*. Milano: Adelphi Edizioni, 1999.

Gonda, Jan. *Vision of the Vedic Poets*. The Hague: Mouton, 1963.

Hunt, Harry T. "'Dark Nights of the Soul': Phenomenology and Neurocognition of Spiritual Suffering in Mysticism and Psychosis." *Review of General Psychology* 11, no. 3 (2007): 209–234.

Hunt, Harry T. "'The Heart Has Its Reasons': Transpersonal Experience as Higher Development of Social-Personal Intelligence, and Its Response to the Inner Solitude of Consciousness." *The Journal of Transpersonal Psychology* 48, no. 1 (2016): 1–25.

Hunt, Harry T. *Lives in Spirit: Precursors and Dilemmas of a Secular Western Mysticism*. Albany: State University of New York Press, 2003.

Hunt, Harry T. *On the Nature of Consciousness: Cognitive, Phenomenological, and Transpersonal Perspectives*. New Haven, CT: Yale University Press, 1995.

Hunt, Harry T., Oliver Sacks, Antonio Damasio, et. al. "Exclusive: Oliver Sacks, Antonio Damasio, and Others Debate Christoph Koch on the Nature of Consciousness." *Mind Guest Blog, Scientific American*. Accessed February 2, 2019. https://blogs.scientificamerican.com/mind-guest-blog/exclusive-oliver-sacks-antonio-damasio-and-others-debate-christof-koch-on-the-nature-of-consciousness/.

Klong chen rab 'byams pa. *Tshig don mdzod*. Gangtok, Sikkim: Sherab Gyaltsen and Khyentse Labrang, 1983.

Knausgaard, Karl Ove. "By the Book: Karl Ove Knausgaard." *Book Review, New York Times*, August 17, 2017. Accessed January 30, 2019. https://www.nytimes.com/2017/08/17/books/review/karl-ove-knausgaard-by-the-book.html.

Kripal, Jeffrey J. *Authors of the Impossible: The Paranormal and the Sacred*. Chicago: The University of Chicago Press, 2010.

Kripal, Jeffrey J. "Edgewalker: An Interview with Jeffrey J. Kripal." Interview by Erik Davis. *Reality Sandwich*, 2013. Accessed February 3, 2019. http://realitysandwich.com/148059/edgewalker_interview_jeffrey_j_kripal/.

Kripal, Jeffrey J. *Secret Body: Erotic and Esoteric Currents in the History of Religions*. Chicago: The University of Chicago Press, 2017.

Kripal, Jeffrey J., et al. *Comparing Religions: Coming to Terms*. Malden, MA: Wiley-Blackwell, 2014.

Marks, Laura U. *Enfoldment and Infinity: An Islamic Genealogy of New Media Art*. Cambridge, MA: MIT Press, 2010.

Padoux, André. *The Hindu Tantric World: An Overview*. Chicago: The University of Chicago Press, 2017.

Padoux, André, *Vāc: The Concept of the Word in Selected Hindu Tantras*. Translated by Jacques Gontier. Albany: State University of New York Press, 1990.

Panikkar, Raimundo. *Rhythm of Being: The Gifford Lectures*. Maryknoll, NY: Orbis Books, 2010.

Ricoeur, Paul. "The History of Religions and the Phenomenology of Time Consciousness." In *The History of Religions: Retrospect and Prospect*, edited by Joseph M. Kitagawa, 13–30. New York: Macmillan Publishing Company, 1985.

Samuel, Geoffrey. "Subtle-body processes: Towards a non-reductionist understanding." In *Religion and the Subtle Body in Asian and the West*, edited by Geoffrey Samuel and Jay Johnston, 249–266. London: Routledge, 2013.

Sanderson, Alexis. "Purity and Power Among the Brahmans of Kashmir." In *The Category of the Person: Anthropological and Philosophical Perspectives*, edited by Michael Carrithers, Steven Collins, and Steven Lukes, 190–216. Cambridge: Cambridge University Press, 1985.

Scharfstein, Ben-Ami. "The Contextual Fallacy." In *Interpreting Across Boundaries: New Essays in Comparative Philosophy*, edited by Gerald James Larson and Eliot Deutsch, 84–97. Princeton, NJ: Princeton University Press, 1988.

Silburn, Lilian. *Kuṇḍalinī: Energy of the Depths*. Translated by Jacques Gontier. Albany: State University of New York Press, 1988.

Silburn, Lilian and André Padoux, ed. and trans. *Abhinavagupta, La Lumière sur les Tantras, Chapitres 1 à 5 du Tantrāloka*. Paris: Collège de France, 1998.

Skora, Kerry Martin. "The Bodily Efflorescence of Words: The Crossing of Divine-Voice and the Body-Self in Abhinavagupta's Cosmology." *Southeast Review of Asian Studies* 35, no. 1 (2013): 70–89.

Skora, Kerry Martin. "Bodily Gestures and Embodied Awareness: *Mudrā* as the Bodily Seal of Being in the Trika Śaivism of Kashmir," in *Refiguring the Body: Embodiment in South Asian Religions*, edited by Barbara A. Holdrege and Karen Pechilis, 89–107. Albany: State University of New York Press, 2016.

Skora, Kerry Martin. "A Day in the Life of an Aesthetic Tāntrika: From Synaesthetic Garden to Lucid Dreaming and Spaciousness." *Religions* 9, no. 3 (2018): 1–18. https://doi.org/10.3390/rel9030081.

Skora, Kerry Martin. "The Pulsating Heart and Its Divine Sense Energies: Body and Touch in Abhinavagupta's Trika Śaivism." *Numen: International Review for the History of Religions* 54, no. 4 (2007): 420–458.

Taylor, Jill Bolte. "My Stroke of Insight." *TED2008*, February 2008. Accessed February 4, 2019. https://www.ted.com/talks/jill_bolte_taylor_s_powerful_stroke_of_insight.

Wallis, Christopher D. *Tantra Illuminated: The Philosophy, History and Practice Timeless Tradition*. 2nd ed. Petaluma, CA: Mattamayūra, 2013.

Weber, Andreas. *The Biology of Wonder: Aliveness, Feeling, and the Metamorphosis of Science*. Gabriola, BC: New Society Publishers, 2016.

Weber, Andreas. *Matter and Desire: An Erotic Ecology*. White River Junction, VT: Chelsea Green Publishing, 2017.

2 Daoist body-maps and meditative praxis[1]

Louis Komjathy 康思奇

Considered as a whole, the Daoist (Taoist) tradition, as expressed by its various communities, movements, and associated textual corpuses, contains sophisticated mappings of the "Daoist body."[2] This is the body discovered and/or actualized through Daoist practice. In other publications, I have emphasized the ways in which such corporeal cartographies and the corresponding somatic topographies (geographies) relate to what I refer to as the "Daoist alchemical body" and "Daoist mystical body."[3] That is, depending on the relevant theoretical and comparative issues, this body may be viewed as a site for refinement and transmutation, even rarefication and divinization, and for experiencing the sacrality of the Dao in/as/through the body.[4]

Many of the Daoist body-maps that I will explore in this chapter could be the focus of an independent discussion. However, I am increasingly less interested in hyper-specialized and hyper-historical studies, although I recognize the importance of such research. I am more interested in the deeper dimensions of contemplative practice and contemplative experience as well as in larger interpretive questions derived from and applicable to the comparative and cross-cultural study of religion.

Thus, in this discussion, I focus on representative Daoist body-maps, with particular attention to their relationship to specific types of Daoist meditation. I begin with a brief overview of the types of Daoist meditation, including their association with different historical periods and Daoist movements. This is followed by an attempt to trace the "history of the Daoist body," that is, the emergence and development of specific Daoist views related to and practices for exploring human personhood and embodiment. These views became the basis for what I refer to as "Daoist body-maps" in the late medieval period. These are usually illustrated diagrams of the Daoist alchemical or mystical body; that is, the body discovered and/or actualized through the associated Daoist training regimens. In the third section, I examine some representative examples of these "corporeal cartographies" and "somatic topographies." In the final section, I offer a "contemplative autobiographical account" in which I draw upon my 25+ years of Daoist contemplative practice in order to advance an experiential understanding of the historical materials, and perhaps, in the process, chart a new contemplative methodology and interpretive approach. This is one that makes space of scholar-practitioners and "critical adherent discourse."

Types of Daoist meditation

There is an intricate relationship between Daoist meditative praxis and Daoist body-maps. Each informs and is expressed in the other. By way of background, there are at least five major types of Daoist meditation.[5]

1 Apophatic or quietistic meditation. Designated by various Chinese Daoist technical terms such as "fasting the heart-mind" (*xinzhai* 心齋), "guarding the One" (*shouyi* 守一), "sitting-in-forgetfulness" (*zuowang* 坐忘), and later "quiet sitting" (*jingzuo* 靜坐)
2 Ingestion (*fuqi* 服氣)
3 Visualization (*cunxiang* 存想)
4 Inner observation (*neiguan* 內觀)
5 Internal alchemy (*neidan* 內丹). Also "female alchemy" (*nüdan* 女丹)

Briefly stated, apophatic meditation emphasizes emptying and stilling the heart-mind, the seat of emotional and intellectual activity from a traditional Chinese perspective, until one becomes empty and still. It is primarily contentless, nonconceptual, and non-dualistic.[6] Ingestion (literally, "eating qi") involves taking the energies of the cosmos into one's body and incorporating them into one's being. Typical examples include ingesting solar, lunar, and astral effulgences and cosmic ethers or vapors. Visualization (literally, "maintaining thought") involves visualizing (possibly "imagining" or "actualizing") specific deities, constellations, colors, and so forth. There is some overlap between visualization and ingestion.[7] If one were more radical, one might categorize ingestion as a form of Daoist dietetics as well as of meditation. It is also a major Daoist health and longevity (*yangsheng* 養生) technique. Adapted from Buddhist *vipassana* (Skt.: *vipaśyana*) practice, Daoist inner observation generally involves maintaining non-discriminating awareness of all phenomena and/or exploring the body as an internal landscape.[8] Finally, internal alchemy utilizes complex, stage-based practices aimed at psychosomatic, including physiological and energetic, transformation. It often incorporates and systematizes the four other types. Later, methods specifically for women, called "female alchemy," developed.[9]

These types of Daoist meditation in turn emerged during specific periods and are associated with specific Daoist movements or sub-traditions.

1 Classical Daoism: Warring States (480-222 BCE) to Early Han (206 BCE-9 CE). Texts: *Laozi* 老子, *Zhuangzi* 莊子, and sections of the *Guanzi* 管子, *Huainanzi* 淮南子, *Lüshi chunqiu* 呂氏春秋, etc. Associated movement: Classical inner cultivation lineages

2 Early and early medieval Daoism: Later Han (25–220 CE) to Period of Disunion (220–581). Texts: *Laozi zhongjing* 老子中經, *Huangting jing* 黃庭經, *Dadong zhenjing* 大洞真經, etc. Associated movements: Taiping太平, Taiqing太清, and Shangqing 上清
3 Early and early medieval Daoism: Later Han (25–220 CE) to Period of Disunion (220–581), although many of the influential texts date from the next period of Daoist history. Texts: *Taiqing fuqi koujue* 太清服氣口訣, *Fuqi jingyi lun* 服氣精義論, etc.
4 Late medieval Daoism: Tang (618–907). Texts: *Neiguan jing* 內觀經, *Dingguan jing* 定觀經, and sections of other Tang-dynasty meditation manuals. Associated movement: Late medieval Daoism (monastic system), specifically later Shangqing
5 Late medieval and late imperial Daoism: Tang to Qing (1644–1911). Texts: *Chuandao ji* 傳道集, *Wuzhen pian* 悟真篇, *Dadan zhizhi* 大丹直指, etc. Associated movements: Zhong-Lü 鐘呂, Nanzong 南宗, Quanzhen 全真, etc.[10]

Apophatic or quietistic meditation is the earliest form; it is associated with the inner cultivation lineages of classical Daoism. Ingestion and visualization are particularly connected to the early Shangqing (Highest Clarity) movement of early medieval Daoism, although there are earlier precedents. Inner observation emerged in the context of the fully integrated Tang-dynasty monastic system. Finally, internal alchemy, as a developmental stage-based approach, was first articulated in the late Tang and early Song dynasty, with the Quanzhen (Complete Perfection) and so-called Nanzong (Southern School) movements being especially influential.[11] Each of the five types exist in the modern world, but apophatic meditation and internal alchemy are the most widely practiced.

Fragments for a history of the Daoist body

Following the monumental three-volume *Fragments for a History of the Human Body* by Michel Feher and his colleagues,[12] we can trace the history of specific sociohistorical constructions of embodiment and the history of specific bodies. Of course, like references to "the brain," it is somewhat problematic and inaccurate to speak of "the body" as distinct from a larger understanding of personhood and being, including subjectivity, embodied experience, and individual lives.[13] Nonetheless, this approach brings attention to the body not only as an anatomical structure, physical given, and locomotive agent, but also as a psychosocial phenomenon, historical site, and cultural artifact. This relates to the body as a cultural, symbolic, and technological subject, with the latter suggesting the use of various *tékhnē* ("arts/methods/skills") to develop distinct forms of being, embodiment, movement, and presence.[14] As I have suggested in other publications,[15] one might, in turn, focus on posture (i.e., specific body configurations) as expressions of associated techniques, training regimens, and worldviews. In any case, the "history of the Daoist body" highlights the fact that there is a *history* of Daoist ways of viewing, interacting with, and developing human embodiment, including uniquely Daoist analogies, conceptions, mythologies, and symbolism.

It is obviously beyond the present contribution to provide a complete history, but I would like to highlight some key moments in the ongoing formation of the "Daoist body." To begin, we find germinal ideas in the texts of classical Daoism, especially in the *Laozi* 老子 (Book of Venerable Masters),[16] which is more commonly known by its honorific title of *Daode jing* 道德經 (Scripture on the Dao and Inner Power).[17]

> Empty the heart-mind and fill the belly;
> Weaken the will and strengthen the bones. (chapter3)
> Cherishing the people and governing the country, can you abide in non-knowing? (chapter10)
> One who takes self as the world can be entrusted with the world.
> One who cares for self as the world can be relied on by the world. (chapter13)

While the contextual meaning of these and related passages is open, and while the *Daode jing* is often framed as a philosophical tract or manual of statecraft, in the larger Daoist tradition such statements are frequently read in terms of self-cultivation; there are analogical and symbolic associations. In the third set of lines, the Chinese character here translated as "self" is *shen* 身, which depicts the human torso viewed from the side. It may also refer to "body" and "personhood."[18] The phrase designating "world," *tianxia* 天下, more literally means "under-sky/heavens." The admonition to view the body/self-as-world established an important precedent for later Daoist macrocosmic/microcosmic views, with the head identified as the "heavens" in the human body. In addition, in the first passage we find germinal ideas for the eventual Daoist idea (discovery and actuality) of the "belly" (*fu* 腹) or navel region as the storehouse of qi, or vital breath (see below). Finally, the body also became viewed as the "country" (*guo* 國), and references to "governing the country" (*zhiguo* 治國) became read as "regulating the body" (*zhishen* 治身). For example, the second-century CE *Laozi zhangju* 老子章句 (Chapter-and-Verse Commentary on the *Laozi*; DZ 682; ZH 556),[19] which is attributed to the obscure recluse and Yangsheng 養生 (Nourishing Life) practitioner Heshang gong 河上公 (Master Dwelling-by-the-River; ca. 160 CE?) and which is one of the most influential Daoist commentaries, contains relevant exegesis. As expressed in the commentary on chapter 59, which is titled "Guarding the Dao,"

> *When one possesses the mother of the country, one can become long lasting.*

> The country is the body. The mother is the Dao. When we protect the Dao within the body, qi remains unlabored and the five spirits [of the yin-organs] are free from vexation. Then one attains longevity. (DZ 682, 3.19b-20a)

In addition, there is a whole series of classical Daoist technical terms that eventually became utilized to designate esoteric corporeal locations and vital substances, including Celestial Gates (*tianmen* 天門; LZ 10), a.k.a. Gates of Heaven, as the senses, third-eye, and/or crown-point; Mysterious Female (*xuanpin* 玄牝; LZ 4) as physical respiration, original qi, and/or original spirit; and Tailbone Gate (*weilü* 尾閭; ZZ 17) as the coccyx.

Moving into the beginnings and early phases of organized Daoism, there are a number of texts that articulated and supplied additional technical terminology related to Daoist embodiment. Both the late second-century CE *Laozi ming* 老子銘 (Inscription on Laozi) and the possibly early fourth-century *Huangting waijing jing* 黃庭外景經 (Scripture on the Outer View of the Yellow Court; DZ 332) reference subtle body locations, complete with esoteric names. The *Scripture on the Yellow Court* is particularly noteworthy. Although the original provenance remains unclear, with the text possibly associated with a currently unidentified southern Daoist movement, the *Scripture on the Yellow Court* became central in the Shangqing 上清 (Highest Clarity) movement, which was one of the most influential subtraditions of early medieval Daoism. In fact, it appears that Highest Clarity adherents composed the associated fourth-century *Huangting neijing jing* 黃庭內景經 (Scripture on the Inner View of the Yellow Court; DZ 331). For present purposes, *jing* 景 in the title is noteworthy. Under one reading, the character may refer to "effulgences," inner numinous energies or corporeal spirits. Under another reading, it refers to "landscape" and/or "view"; from this interpretive perspective, the texts represent inner/esoteric and outer/exoteric teachings, respectively. As we will see, the phrase *neijing* became especially significant in later Daoist body-maps. In any case, these two scriptures discuss the Daoist body using various esoteric terms to designate associated corporeal locations. While the actual locations are often open to interpretation and have different associations in different systems, common identifications are as follows: "elixir field" (*dantian* 丹田)/navel, "yellow court" (*huangting* 黃庭)/spleen, "gate of life" (*mingmen* 命門)/area between the kidneys, "mysterious pass" (*xuanguan* 玄關)/kidneys, "jade pond" (*yuchi* 玉池)/mouth, and so forth. The *Scripture on the Yellow Court*, along with other key Highest Clarity texts like the fourth-century *Dadong zhenjing* 大洞真經 (Perfect Scripture of Great Profundity; DZ 6), documented and became the basis of the movement's ingestion and visualization practices. That is, the latter were informed and actualized by Daoist corporeal cartographies.

Although some dimensions of Highest Clarity Daoism could be labelled proto-*neidan* (that is, the fifth major type of Daoist meditation) it was not until the late medieval period, specifically during the late Tang (618–907) and early Song (960–1279) dynasties, that internal alchemy became formalized and systematized. This type of Daoist meditation not only incorporated the other four earlier forms, but also helped to articulate and explore a more "standardized Daoist body," which is explored in the next section. Internal alchemy integrated diverse sources, including classical Daoist texts, correlative cosmology, *Yijing* 易經 (Book of Changes) symbology,[20] meditational and physical disciplines of Yangsheng, cosmological dimensions and technical terminology of *waidan* 外丹 (external alchemy), Chinese medical theory, and even Buddhist soteriology and Confucian moral philosophy. In terms of the "history of the Daoist body," internal alchemy was particularly important for the development of what I refer to as the "alchemical body." This is the body explored and actualized through *neidan* training; that is, through stage-based praxis that centers on subtle centers and an energy system and that aims at complete transmutation, or "immortality" in Daoist terms. This is the Daoist body as consisting of various "elixir fields" and energy channels, with the latter forming a complex, interconnected network. Late medieval *neidan* eventually resulted in additional material expressions, namely, the creation of illustrated diagrams of the Daoist body. That is, although there may have been now-lost, earlier visual depictions, it was from the eleventh to the fourteenth centuries that Daoists composed the earliest extant examples of what I refer to as "Daoist body-maps" (*shentu* 身圖). These types of Daoist material religion continued to be executed and commissioned through the next periods of Daoist history, with some of the most influential emerging in the late imperial period.[21]

Daoist body-maps

Moving into the Daoist body-maps, and more generally, meditative praxis, are corporeal cartographies, including illustrations related to the alchemical or mystical body. This is the body discovered and/or actualized through the associated training regimens. There are cross-cultural and comparative examples, such as Indian Tantric and Yogic expressions utilizing the *chakra-nādī-prāna* system. Such somatic mappings are often related to specific training regimens and stages on the contemplative path. Here I would again emphasize a technical understanding of "praxis" as including specific views, practices, experiences, and goals.[22] Body-maps are, in turn, informed by and expressions of contemplative practice, and they point towards associated contemplative experiences. They also articulate distinct contemplative psychologies, a concept first developed by the Dutch transpersonal psychologist Han de Wit.[23] Contemplative psychologies, or what I have referred to as "psychologies of realization" that develop Richard King's notion of "epistemologies of enlightenment," are views of consciousness and being that inform, are informed by, and utilized within contemplative practice.[24]

Shifting attention to our Daoist materials, Daoist body-maps are Daoist corporeal cartographies and somatic topographies. They are usually illustrated diagrams of the Daoist alchemical or mystical body. This is the body discovered and/or actualized through the associated Daoist training regimens. There are many examples, especially as extant in wood-block illustrations in the *Daozang* 道藏 (Daoist Canon; 1,487 texts; dat. 1445/1607), the primary Daoist textual collection.[25] There are also some paintings and steles. These Daoist body-maps are informed by and expressions of the five major types of Daoist meditation discussed previously, especially ingestion, visualization, inner observation, and internal alchemy. They have often been and often are utilized as meditation aids. In a comparative frame, one might consider the "Taima Mandala" as employed within the context of early medieval Chinese Pure Land Buddhist visualization.[26] In any case, these Daoist body-maps envision a transformed ontological condition in which the human body is comicized, divinized, and rarified. In some sense, the practitioner becomes a new being, infused with pure and refined energy and pervaded by the Dao's sacred presence. In my way of thinking, these Daoist body-maps thus relate to the three-fold aspect of Daoist practice: cultivation, embodiment, and transmission.

Viewed as a whole, Daoist body-maps illustrate the constituents of what became the "standardized Daoist body."

1 Sun (left eye) and moon (right eye)
2 Descending Bridge (tongue) (*jiangqiao* 降橋), Crimson Dragon (tongue) (*chilong* 赤龍) , Twelve Storied Tower (trachea) *shier zhong lou* 十二種樓), Sweet Dew (saliva) (*ganlu* 甘露), etc.
3 Five yin-organs (*wuzang* 五臟)
   liver (east/green/dragon), heart (south/red/bird), spleen (center/ yellow/—),
   lungs (west/white/tiger), kidneys (north/black [purple]/snake-turtle)
4 Three elixir fields (*dantian* 丹田)
   Ocean of Qi (lower; navel), Scarlet Palace (middle; heart), Niwan (upper; head)[27]
5 Three Treasures (*sanbao* 三寶)
   Vital essence (*jing* 精), subtle breath (*qi* 氣), spirit (*shen* 神)
6 Meridians (*jing* 經/*luo* 絡/*mai* 脈)
   12/8: Governing, Conception, Belt, Thrusting
7 Three Passes (*sanguan* 三關)
   Tailbone Gate (lower; coccyx), Paired Passes (middle; mid-spine), Jade Pillow (upper; occiput)

Most of these are straightforward, but the more esoteric ones require some explanation. As attentive readers will note, Daoist numerology tends to privilege triads. From a Daoist perspective, three is a pure yang number, and multiples of threes, particularly nine (3x3), are prevalent. The latter is often referred to as "redoubled yang" (*chongyang* 重陽) and represents complete alchemical transformation. In the previous list, we find the "three elixir fields" and "three treasures." As we saw in the previous section, "elixir field" is a Daoist name for subtle body locations. Interestingly, recalling the various influences on internal alchemy, *dan* 丹, more literally "pill," derives from an ingredient utilized in external alchemy formulas. Specifically, *dan* refers to "cinnabar," or mercuric sulfide (HgS).[28] As the name indicates, internal alchemy sought to create an "inner elixir" through the transmutation of various substances *within the body*. In any case, the standardized Daoist body consists of three elixir fields associated with the internal three treasures. The former may refer to the perineum/navel/head or navel/heart/head. The associations in the former are clearer: perineum/vital essence, navel/qi, and head/spirit. Also associated with bodily fluids (e.g., saliva, sweat), vital essence is considered the most substantial and corresponds to foundational vitality. The character contains the *mi* 米 ("rice") radical, thus suggesting a more substantial substance. Vital essence is housed in the kidneys and relates to one's constitution, partially indebted to ancestry ("genes"). It is associated with semen in men and menstrual blood in women. While also designating physical respiration, qi is a more subtle breath or "energy" stored in and circulating through the body. The standard character consists of *qi* 气 ("steam") over *mi* 米 ("rice"), thus suggesting a more subtle presence. Qi also circulates through the world, universe, and all things, and there are many types.[29] For Daoists, the most important is the "qi of the Dao" (*daoqi* 道炁), which designates a sacred, numinous presence and sometimes corresponds to "original qi" (*yuanqi* 元氣). Finally, "spirit" is the most subtle or rarified; it is housed in the heart and corresponds to consciousness and divine capacities more generally. The character consists of *shi* 示 ("omen") and *shen* 申 ("extend"). While the latter is usually taken as a phonetic, under one reading spirit suggests the ability to connect to invisible or barely noticeable presences.

Simplified and standardized internal alchemy systems tend to frame alchemical transformation in terms of a three-stage process: (1) Transforming vital essence to qi; (2) Transforming qi to spirit; and (3) Transforming spirit to return to the Void. That is, a process of rarefaction, transmutation, and even divinization is at work, which culminates in "immortality" in Daoist terms. The three elixir fields and internal Three Treasures relate to other triads, including the Three Purities, Three Heavens, and external Three Treasures.[30] The meridians, also referred to as "channels" or "vessels," are the energy conduits and networks in the body. They are utilized in both Chinese medicine and Daoism, which partially explains the conflation of these traditions in the popular imagination. The standard system consists of the twelve primary organ-meridians and the "eight extraordinary vessels." The latter tend to be more central in Daoist training regimens. These meridians are as follows: (1) Governing Channel, which moves up the middle of the spine; (2) Conception Channel, which moves up the center of the front torso; (3) Thrusting Channel, which moves through the center of the torso; and (4) Belt Channel, which moves around the waist and is the only horizontal meridian. In Daoist practice, the other four tend to be understood as two moving down the outside and up the inside of the arms, and two following a similar path through the legs.[31] Finally, the Three Passes are the three places along the spine through which it is difficult for qi to circulate. Interestingly and as explored later, they are often imagined as mountain passes and relate to a practice known as the Microcosmic Orbit.

Daoist body-maps are, in turn, visual representations of the Daoist body. As previously discussed, they incorporate earlier (non-illustrated) Daoist views of human personhood. They are part of Daoist material culture or "material religion," often expressing refined artistic and aesthetic qualities. They are frequently utilized as meditation and visualization aids. They may be thought of as corporeal cartographies and somatic topographies, including the Daoist inner landscape and somatic geography. Here, we again encounter Daoists as expert mapmakers.[32] Daoist body-maps have wide-ranging content, but especially fascinating examples depict the human body as a whole. The earliest extant examples date from late medieval period, around the tenth century. Some of the most famous examples were executed during the imperial period, specifically the nineteenth century. This dimension of the Daoist tradition has been extensively studied by Catherine Despeux, Susan Shih-shan Huang, Livia Kohn, Joseph Needham et al., Kristofer Schipper, and myself.[33]

There are a variety of Daoist somatic views related to Daoist anthropology (conceptions of personhood) and psychology (conceptions of *psyche*) expressed in these body-maps. They include body-as-county, as-cosmos, as-crucible, as-landscape, and as-mountain, with the latter being particularly interesting and distinctive. Let us begin our exploration with a representative sampling (see Figure 2.1).

In terms of types, these include abstract, symbolic, and largely indecipherable (to the uninitiated) depictions through illustrations of specific anatomical regions and structural details (e.g., organs and head) to diagrams of the entire torso and even the full body. As briefly mentioned, and as will be explored momentarily, there are also esoteric somatic terms, including diverse names for the same location. For example, the final image at the bottom-right identifies the navel region as the "lower elixir field," "Central Yellow," "Gate of Life," "Ocean of Qi," "True Earth," and so forth.

Two early extant illustrations depict the animal-emblems and the seven stars of the Big Dipper as related to specific organs (see Figure 2.2).

These diagrams come from the eleventh and twelfth centuries, but they illustrate early medieval methods. They have some connection to the Highest Clarity movement and relate to ingestion and visualization techniques (see previous section). The left image depicts the spirits of the five yin-organs, which correspond to the Five Phases (*wuxing* 五行), namely, Wood/east/green, Fire/south/red, Earth/center/yellow, Metal/west/white, and Water/north/black (purple). This system, which is part of traditional Chinese

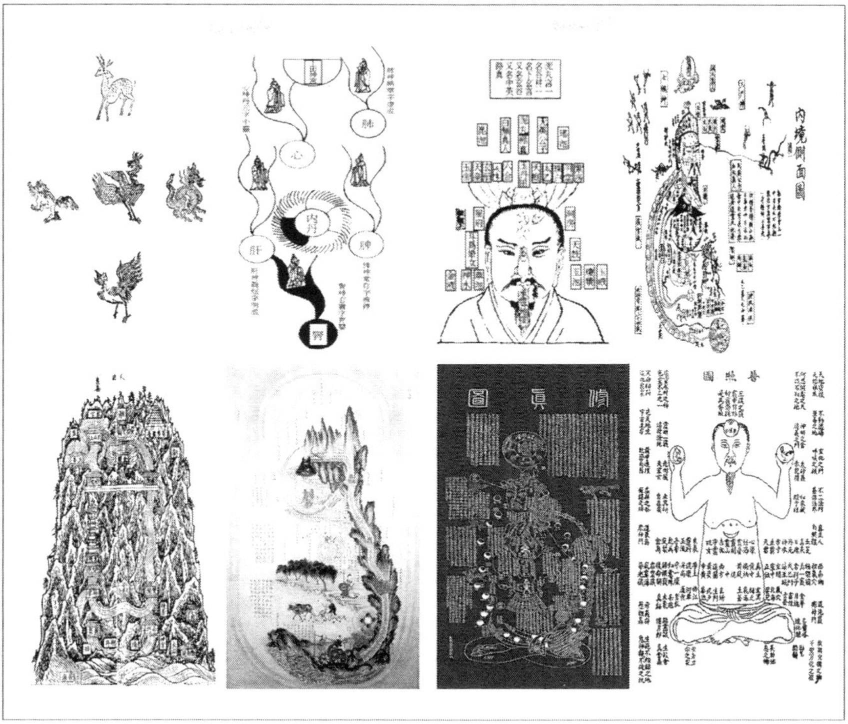

Figure 2.1 Representative sampling of Daoist body-maps.
Source: Various; author's collection.

Figure 2.2 Early extant illustrations.
Source: Huangting yuanshen jing 黃庭元神經 (DZ 1032, 14.4b-11a; left) and *Yutang neijing yushu* 玉堂內景玉書 (DZ 221, 2.13a-17b; right).

cosmology and of a traditional Chinese worldview more generally, is also referred to as correlative cosmology and the system of correspondences. According to this diagram, the associated animal emblems are as follows: two-headed black deer/kidneys (top); vermilion bird/heart (bottom); white tiger/lungs (left); azure dragon/liver (right); and golden phoenix/spleen (center). In later representations, the Mysterious Warrior (snake-turtle) replaces the deer, while the center tends not to have an emblematic or totemic animal.[34] The right image depicts stars of the Northern Dipper (Big Dipper; Ursa Major) and the associated organs.

Starting from the top right/dipper bowl and going to the lower left/handle, the esoteric stellar names are: (1) Yangming 陽明 (Yang Brightness)/heart; (2) Yinjing 陰精 (Yin Essence)/lungs; (3) Zhenren真人 (Perfect One)/liver; (4) Xuanming 玄冥 (Mysterious Darkness)/spleen; (5) Danyuan 丹元 (Cinnabar Prime)/stomach; (6) Beiji 北極 (North Culmen)/kidneys; and (7) Tianguan 天關 (Celestial Pass)/eyes. These diagrams thus express Daoist macrocosmic/microcosmic views: The energies of the directions/seasons and of the Dipper stars come to infuse the practitioner's body. In some sense, the body is the universe, and the universe is the body.

We also have an early illustration of the "Daoist inner landscape" (see Figure 2.3), which dates from the thirteenth century and purports to elucidate the *Nanjing* 難經 (Classic of Difficulties), a classical Chinese medical text.

Interestingly, although this diagram contains the *jing* 境-landscape character, it recalls the previously mentioned *neijing* 內景 ("inner view") version of the *Scripture on the Yellow Court* and anticipates the more famous *neijing* 內經 ("inner pathways") diagram examined later. As will become clear momentarily, the *Inner Landscape Map* became seminal in later periods. The diagram depicts the human torso viewed from the right side. The base of the spine, spinal column, and head are particularly prominent. This includes esoteric names for mystical cranial locations, which will be discussed shortly. The diagram also references the so-called Three Death-bringers (*sanshi* 三尸) and Seven Po (*qipo* 七魄; Corporeal Souls), which are present on either side of the head. Alternatively rendered as "Three Corpses" and sometimes appearing as "Three Worms" (*sanchong* 三蟲), the Three Death-bringers are conventionally understood as three bio-spiritual parasites residing in the human body. They reside in the previously-mentioned three elixir fields, namely, Palace of Nirvana (center of head), Vermilion Palace (heart region), and Ocean of Qi (lower abdomen). The ninth-century *Chu sanshi jiuchong jing* 除三尸九蟲經 (Scripture on Expelling the Three Death-bringers and Nine Worms; DZ 871, 7a-8a) contains illustrations of the Three Death-bringers,[35] wherein they are identified as follows: Peng Ju 彭踞 (upper), Peng Zhi 彭躓 (middle), and Peng Jiao 彭蹻 (lower) (see also DZ 817). Thus, they are sometimes referred to as the "Three Pengs" (*sanpeng* 三彭). Other texts, such as the *Sanshi zhongjing* 三尸中經 (Central Scripture on the Three Death-bringers; *Yunji qiqian*, DZ 1032, 81.15b-17a), provide alternative names: Qinggu 青古

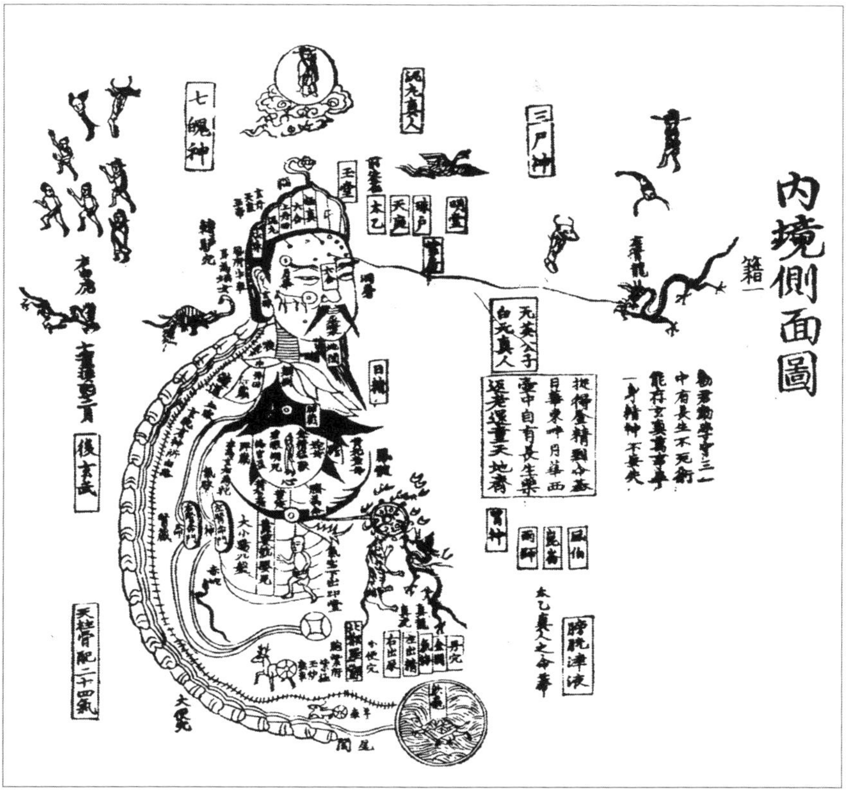

Figure 2.3 Inner landscape map.
Source: Nanjing zuantu jujie 難經纂圖句解, DZ 1024, 4ab.

(Blue Decrepitude; upper), Baigu 白姑 (White Hag; middle), and Xueshi 血尸 (Bloody Corpse; lower) (also DZ 303, 4a). Various malevolent and harmful influences are attributed to them, including inciting people to become greedy, angry, forgetful, deluded, sexually deviant, and so forth.

From an early medieval Daoist perspective, the Seven Po are also bio-spiritual entities which exert negative influences on the individual and which lead to dissipation, and often to premature death. In the eleventh century encyclopedia *Yunji qiqian* 雲笈七籤 (Seven Tablets from a Cloudy Satchel; DZ 1032), they are identified as follows: (1) Shigou 尸狗 (Corpse Dog), (2) Fushi 伏矢 (Concealed Arrow), (3) Queyin 雀陰 (Sparrow Yin), (4) Tunzei 吞賊 (Seizing Thief), (5) Feidu 飛毒 (Flying Poison); (6) Chuhui 除穢(Oppressive Impurity), and (7) Choufei 臭肺 (Putrid Lungs) (54.7ab). Visual representations appear in the *Scripture on Expelling the Three Death-bringers and Nine Worms* (DZ 871, 3a). According to that text,

> The Seven Po consist of yin and deviant qi. They are ghosts. They can make people into walking corpses, causing them to be stingy and greedy, jealous and full of envy. They give people bad dreams and make them clench their teeth. They command the mouth to say 'yes' when the heart-mind thinks 'no'. In addition, they cause people to lose their vital essence in sexual passion and become dissipated by hankering after luxury and ease. Through them, people completely lose their purity and simplicity
>
> (2a)

Taken collectively, the Three Death-bringers and Seven Po are bio-spiritual parasites, malevolent somatic entities, and negative psycho-spiritual states that would result in a weakening of physical vitality and premature death. There are, in turn, various practices aimed at expelling or eradicating them, including alchemical formulas and ascetic regimens such as elimination diets using specific herbs and minerals as well as intermittent fasting.

In addition to the inner landscape that depicts the organs or torso, there also are maps of particular areas of the human body, such as mystical cranial locations (see Figure 2.4).

This diagram is titled *Yanluozi shoubu tu* 煙蘿子首部圖 (Diagram of Master Yanluo's [Smoky Turnip] Head) and preserved in the *Xiuzhen shishu* 修真十書 (Ten Works on Cultivating Perfection; DZ 263), which is a thirteenth century anthology on internal alchemy, especially the systems associated with the so-called Southern School. It reveals a hidden or secret energetic body within the ordinary body. Specifically, it alludes to the so-called Nine Palaces (*jiugong* 九宮) of the head region.

1 Mingtang 明堂 (Hall of Light). One inch in from Yintang 印堂 (Seal Hall; third-eye)
2 Dongfang 洞房 (Grotto Chamber). Two inches in from Yintang
3 Dantian 丹田 (Elixir Field). Three inches in from Yintang
4 Liuzhu 流珠 (Flowing Pearl). Four inches in from Yintang
5 Yudi 玉帝 (Jade Thearch). Five inches in from Yintang
6 Tianting 天庭 (Celestial Court). One inch above Mingtang
7 Jizhen 機真 (Secret Perfection). One inch above Dongfang
8 Xuandan 玄丹 (Mysterious Elixir). One inch above Dantian
9 Taihuang 太皇 (Great Sovereign). One inch above Liuzhu

(*Yuandan shangjing* 元丹上經, DZ 1345, 2b-8a; also *Suling jing* 素靈經, DZ 1314, 12b-22a)

In my way of thinking, in addition to being esoteric, these somatic spaces are "mystical" because they are non- or only semi-spatial, are primarily become opened through practice, and lead to expansions of consciousness. One method involves bringing the gaze and the intention in through the third-eye and into the center of the head. As one concentrates on that area, each palace

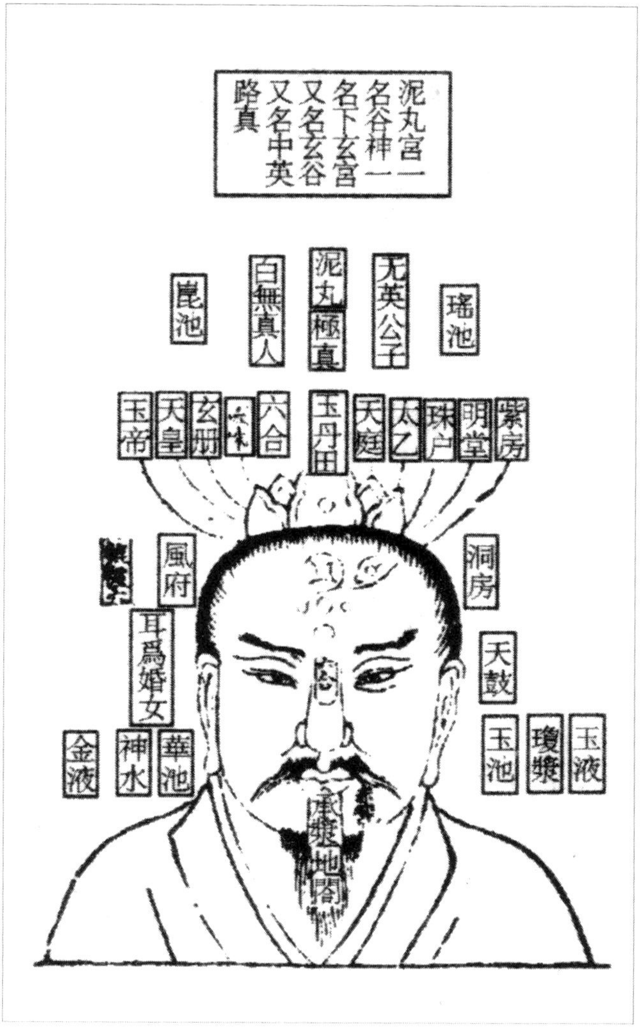

Figure 2.4 Mystical cranial locations.
Source: Zazhu jiejing 雜著捷徑, DZ 263, 18.2a.

opens in sequence. The practitioner, in turn, finds portals and even infinite space within the head. Here it is interesting to imagine a potential connection with contemporary neuroscientific brain-regions (see Figure 2.5).

That is, one wonders about potential neuroanatomical/physiological changes and expansions of consciousness as documented by modern neuroimagining technologies.

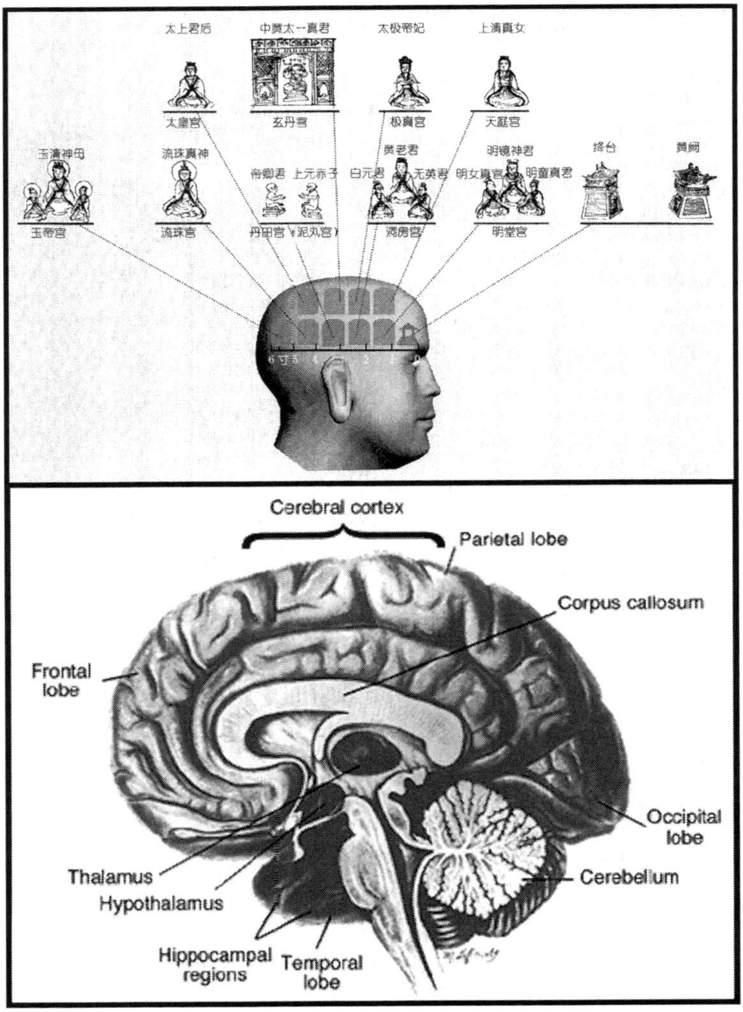

Figure 2.5 Contemporary neuroscientific brain-regions.
Permission granted courtesy of Jiang Sheng (Sichuan University) ed. *Zhongguo daojiao kexue jishu shi* (History of Taoism and Science). Beijing: Kexue chubanshe, 2002.

We also encounter Daoist views and maps of the body as a mountain (see Figure 2.6).

Titled *Tixiang yinyang shengjiang tu* 體象陰陽升降圖 (Diagram of Ascent and Descent of Yin-Yang in the Body), this is an early thirteenth century illustration of unclear provenance. It depicts the Daoist body from the left-side. It highlights the spine and the Twelve-Storied Pagoda (trachea; center-left). It also emphasizes the importance of connecting the two

Figure 2.6 Body as mountain.
Source: Duren shangpin miaojing neiyi 度人上品妙經內義, DZ 90, 8ab; also Jindan daoyao tu 金丹大要圖, DZ 1068.

primary Extraordinary Vessels. These are the Governing Channel (moving up the spine; center-right) and the Conception Channel (moving down the front center-line of the torso; center-left). As mentioned, from a classical Chinese medical and Daoist perspective, the body consists of a series of twenty meridians, or energy channels. In the diagram, qi, subtle breath or vital energy, is depicted as flowing water, so there is a specific fluid physiology at work.[36]

The illustration, in turn, draws our attention to the central importance of mountains in Daoism. For example, in a highly influential passage from the *Baopuzi neipian* 抱朴子內篇 (Inner Chapters of Master Embracing Simplicity; DZ 1185) by Ge Hong 葛洪 (Baopu 抱樸 [Embracing Simplicity]; 283–343), we are told,

> All of those seeking the Dao and preparing medicines, as well as those fleeing political disorder and living as hermits, go to the mountains. Many, however, meet with harm or even death because they do not know the method for entering mountains. Hence the saying, "At the foot of the great Mount Hua, bleached bones lie scattered." Everyone knows that someone may have special knowledge about one thing, but one cannot know everything about all things. Some people set on the search for life drive themselves to their own deaths. (17.1a)

Generally speaking, "mountains" may refer to actual mountains, stillness, meditative absorption, seclusion, refuge, altars, and, more generally, the self. So, when Daoists speak of "entering the mountains" (*rushan* 入山), they may mean mountain seclusion, ritual activity, meditation practice, or any combination.[37] Moreover, to go deeper into the mountains involves going deeper into the self, and vice versa.

One of the most famous Daoist body-maps, of which I have published an in-depth study, is the *Neijing tu* 內經圖 (Diagram of Internal Pathways) (see Figure 2.7), which again recalls the "inner view" of the *Scripture on the Yellow Court* and the *Inner Landscape Map*.

A nineteenth-century depiction of the Daoist alchemical body, this illustration exists in what appears to be the original painting, preserved in a Beijing medical museum, and a stone stele, preserved at Baiyun guan 白雲觀 (White Cloud Temple), also in Beijing. It is most well-known in the modern world through rubbings derived from the stele. As even a rudimentary engagement with this Daoist body-map reveals, there are too many details to cover in this article. (I have previously written a detailed analysis, including a complete annotated translation; interested individuals may consult that study.[38]) Here I simply want to draw attention to a few features. Like the previous *Inner Landscape Map*, it represents the human torso viewed from the side, but in this case the left-side is depicted in a manner parallel to the *Diagram of Ascent and Descent*, with the spine especially prominent. Here the spine consists of a series of mountain passes (Three Passes), which lead into the mountains of the head (lower-right to upper-right). The diagram is frequently engaged as a visual aid related to the Microcosmic Orbit (*zhoutian* 周天; a.k.a. Celestial Cycle) practice, which is also known as the Waterwheel (*heche* 河車). This involves circulating qi, or energy, up the spine and down the front centerline of the torso. The diagram draws attention to this fact by depicting the Governing and Conception Channels as containing five bands each, specifically associated with the energy of the five (six) yang-organs

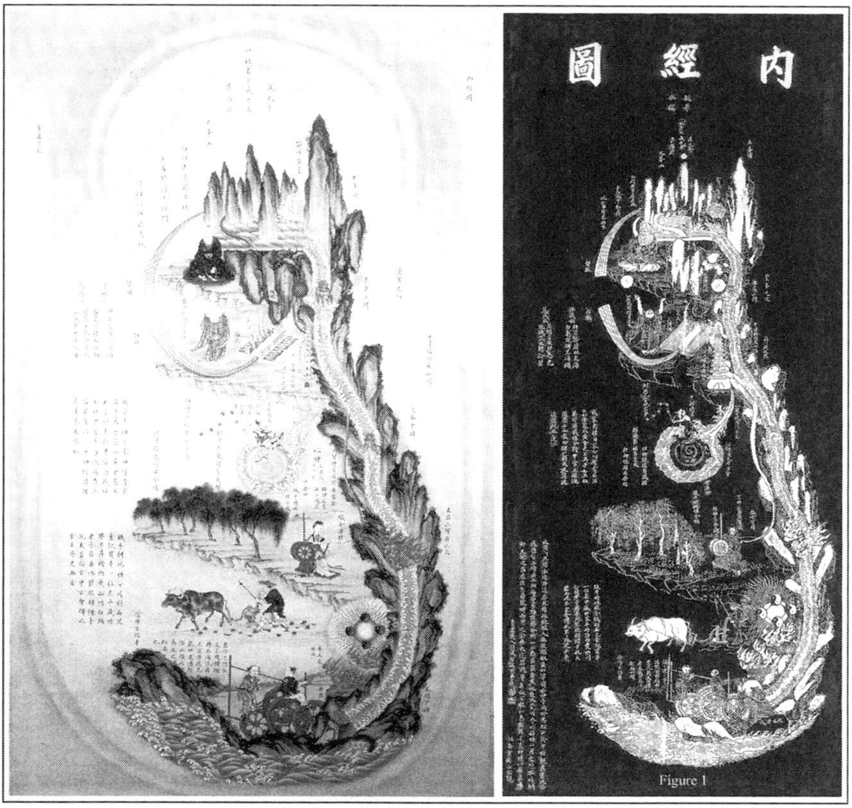

Figure 2.7 Painting (left) and stele rubbing (right) of *diagram of internal pathways*.
Source: Author's collection.

and five yin-organs (upper-left), respectively. This is partially accomplished by touching the tip of the tongue (the Descending Bridge; upper-center) to the upper palate. Thus, the Microcosmic Orbit practice leads not only to a unified energetic being, but also to overall health of the entire organ-meridian system. We also note the left-eye as the sun and right-eye as the moon (upper-center). That is, the landscape and the cosmos are contained in our own bodies. In this Daoist vision, one looks outside to discover the corporeal landscape, and one looks inside to discover the cosmos.

The diagram also contains a golden or white sphere, possibly a pearl, above the crown-point, the mountain-summit (upper-center). This generally refers to the "yang-spirit" (*yangshen* 陽神), also known as the "body-beyond-the-body" (*shenwai shen* 身外身) and the "immortal embryo" (*xiantai* 仙胎) (see Figure 2.8).[39] The yang-spirit is the transcendent spirit *created* through alchemical praxis and accompanying transformation. It

Figure 2.8 The Yang-spirit.
Source: Shangqing dadong zhenjing 上清大洞真經, DZ 6, 5.1b.

is the ultimate goal of Daoist internal alchemy. It ensures personal postmortem survival and entry into the Daoist sacred realms.

According to the standard account, at the moment of death, the practitioner sends out the yang-spirit through the crown-point, which thereupon enters the Daoist sacred realms or celestial locales.

To summarize, Daoist body-maps are visual depictions of the Daoist body, the human body understood from a Daoist perspective and encountered/

actualized through Daoist praxis. We encounter the human body as country, cosmos, crucible, landscape, and mountain. Such illustrations are rooted in classical and foundational Daoist cosmogony, cosmology, and theology as well as classical, early, and early medieval Daoist anthropology. They reveal the Daoist "alchemical body" and "mystical body," which consists of elixir fields, energy channels and networks, mystical cranial locations, and so forth. These diagrams also demonstrate the complex nature of Daoist praxis, in which specific views, practices, experiences, and goals are interrelated and mutually informing. Such Daoist body-maps are also utilized as meditation aids and maps of transformation. They point towards Daoist forms of embodiment and ways of being.

Towards a contemplative autobiographical account

A conventional discussion would have ended here. However, as I wish to help advance a critical first-person approach to the academic study of contemplative practice, mystical experience, and Religious Studies more generally,[40] let me push the bounds of decorum and academic discourse, especially as framed by the secular materialist and social constructivist hegemonic study of religion. Specifically, the emerging interdisciplinary field of Contemplative Studies recognizes the potential contribution of critical subjectivity, including what I have referred to as "critical adherent discourse," and scholar-practitioners. It makes space for theory informed by practice, and practice informed by theory. From my perspective, it opens up the possibility of disciplined investigation of my own and your own and our own contemplative experiences. This is what I refer to as "theorizing from the inside out."[41]

I have been engaging in dedicated and sustained Daoist training for over twenty-five years.[42] This includes familiarity with the previously mentioned five major types of Daoist meditation, although I am most conversant with quietistic and alchemical techniques. In these twenty-five years, I have experienced many of the transformative effects documented in the Daoist body-maps explored herein. Significantly, I found the illustrations subsequent to many of the experiences. That is, it was not social conditioning via Daoist material culture that led to these experiences. Some of these experiences include the following: common/standard ones, such as awareness of subtle presence in the *dantian* 丹田 (elixir fields) and meridians; communal attunement (flow); Twelve Storied Pagoda; energetic unraveling; embryonic respiration; Nine Palaces as well as crown-point and fontanelle opening; absorption/disappearance in the heart; disappearance of bones; dream-teachings and immortal transmissions, especially related to lineage; simultaneity of time; and "seeing through." It would obviously take an entire article to recount my "subtle" or "energetic history," that is, the history of *my own Daoist body*. Here I will be content to provide a few pivotal examples, with attention to the Daoist body-maps previously explored.

On the most basic level, I had a variety of more general energetic experiences. When I first started preliminary and foundational training in 1991 in New Hampshire, I began learning Yang 楊-style Taiji quan 太極拳 (Yin-Yang Boxing). My teacher emphasized the cultivation of qi and moving in unison, especially with a sense of ease, fluidity, and harmony. One day during practice I felt the entire group, approximately twenty people, as a single energetic field and kinesthetic symphony. This was my first discernable energetic experience, although I had a number of unitive mystical experiences while a teenager. Along these lines, after more formal, intensive Daoist training in Seattle from 1993–1998, I began to have a more all-encompassing "energetic perception" and "energetic experiencing," in which I experienced every person, place, and situation as energetic in nature. That is, rather than being simply physical or emotional, there was an underlying qi signature and pattern. Somewhat akin to movement patterns and effects, this became evident in each and every encounter and interaction, especially with respect to organic and sentient beings like humans. I consider the other "advanced" or "higher" experiences, particularly those related to the Daoist subtle and alchemical body, to be deeper, supplemental forms of unfolding and/or activation.

In terms of the previously explored Daoist body-maps, during various intensive, solitary meditation sessions, I had a variety of alchemical experiences. Here I will briefly describe five of them. First, as we saw, some Daoist body-maps depict the unification of the Governing and Conception Channels, specifically through the practice of the Microcosmic Orbit. While I practiced the latter method, I have clearly felt qi moving up the center of the spine and down the front centerline of the torso. After some time of "cycling" and "circulating," these united into a single band or sphere, which felt like the deeper "structure" of my physical body.

The second experience relates to the trachea as the Twelve Storied Tower. When I first heard this description, I viewed it to be poetic and symbolic. However, one day while meditating in a large meditation hall, my neck began to relax and lengthen spontaneously. Then I felt my trachea begin to extend section by section, as what appeared to be twelve rungs in total. My spine had extended in a manner like the *Diagram of Internal Pathways*, and it felt as though my head was touching the ceiling. That is, my body seemed to have become about twenty feet tall and filled the entire room.

Third, with respect to the Nine Palaces, I have had a number of experiences in which spaces in head spontaneously opened. At times, this seemed as though "doors" were opening consecutively or as though there were deeper, successive layers in the head region. Eventually, the head became expansive to the point where it felt like infinite space.

On a more esoteric and less visual level, Daoist alchemical texts often allude to "embryonic respiration" (*taixi* 胎息) and the "disappearance of bones" (*sangu* 散骨; *xiaogu* 消骨). While the latter may invoke the idea of decomposition after physical death, from a Daoist alchemical perspective it refers to the transmutation of the bones, the apparently most physical and substantial aspect of body/self. In any case, with respect to "embryonic respiration," here referring to the apparent cessation of physical respiration along the lines of "breathing" in a mother's womb, my breathing has decreased to the point that it seemed as though my lungs were no longer active. While on a phenomenological level, I would see this as more of a lengthening, deepening, and slowing of respiration, it did seem that respiration had been suspended. As something like a state of meditative and/or mystical absorption, I do not know how long this lasted, but when I returned to a more differentiated state of awareness (i.e., aware of myself as "not breathing"), my lungs reactivated spontaneously. Similarly, I have experienced the "disappearance of bones," in the sense that my bones felt like they became more insubstantial, almost hollow, and porous. I then felt energy and something like luminous light infusing them.

Finally, what I refer to as "seeing through" designates a transformed state of consciousness and perceiving in which one discerns a hidden or underlying energetic dimension and condition. Specifically, one "sees through" appearances and recognizes real intentions, motivations, and psychosomatic conditions. This recalls key insights of classical Daoism, including as expressed in the fourth-century BCE "Neiye" 内業 (Inward Training; chapter 49) chapter of the *Guanzi* 管子 (Book of Master Guan),[43]

A complete heart-mind at the center
Cannot be concealed or hidden.
It will be known through your appearance;
It will be seen in the color of your skin.
If you encounter others with exceptional qi,
They will be kinder to you than your brothers.
If you encounter others with harmful qi,
They will injure you with their weapons.
The reverberation of the wordless
Is more rapid than the drumming of thunder.
The shape of qi and the heart-mind
Is more luminous than the sun and moon.
It is more manifest than the concern of parents.
Rewards are insufficient to encourage goodness;
Punishments are insufficient to discourage transgression.
And yet, once this exceptional qi is attained,
All under the heavens will come to be contained.
Once this complete heart-mind is stabilized,
All under the heavens will come to listen.

(chapter 18; see also chapters 16 and 26)

Combining this with early medieval Daoist views, there is a talismanic dimension of practice, one in which one is simultaneously protected and others are revealed. From a committed Daoist perspective, one remains connected to the sacred and remembers what is real. Everything is clear.

In short, from my perspective and in my experience, Daoist practice does, in fact, result in an ontological transformation, in the formation of a new being, a Daoist body. This involves a movement from more habituated conditions to more realized ones. It is a contemplative, transpersonal, and mystical form of (non)identity in which one overcomes habituation and activates a subtle body. This subtle body includes a heightened energetic sensitivity, one that is attentive to the deeper and more encompassing reality of human existence. In Daoist terms, it is the Dao encountered in/as/through one's very own body. So, turning this critical autobiographical account back on our historical materials, we may reapproach the Daoist contemplative corporeal cartographies. This includes developing a viable experiential methodology.

If contemplative practice is about *practice*, then is it not worthwhile, even necessary, to develop an appropriate and disciplined, first-person approach? This might include participant-observation, scholar-practitioners, and critical adherent discourse (CAD). While I recognize that this challenges certain conventional academic views, and even mandated requirements for participation, there are other ways of knowing, being, and experiencing. A contemplative approach to corporeal cartographies and somatic topographies, especially one rooted in and expressing specific practices and experiences, requires at least some researchers to have direct, first-hand experience with the associated practices. This might be referred to as "the view from within." From a lived, experiential perspective, these body-maps make larger claims. They reveal distinctive contemplative psychologies, ones that express the possibility of being and psychologies of realization. The body depicted in Daoist body-maps is my body, and my body reveals the potential of the human body in general. Each practice leads to a specific way of being and experiencing the world, of participating in a carnal, somatic, and relational network. Thus, embodiment is not simply about "having a body"; it is about what types of bodies we cultivate and actualize. It is about what we contain and manifest as physically and energetically existing beings. This includes the possibility of contemplative and mystical embodied being-in-the-world. For this, Daoist body-maps chart and reveal the body as landscape and the landscape of the body.

Notes

1 The present chapter uses Pinyin Romanization for Mandarin pronunciations of Chinese characters. Dao, Daoism, and Daoist derive from this system, while Tao, Taoism, and Taoist, which are still pronounced with a "d" sound, derive from the older Wade-Giles system.

2 For overviews of the Daoist tradition see Louis Komjathy, *The Daoist Tradition: An Introduction* (London and New York: Bloomsbury Academy, 2013); idem., *Daoism: A Guide for the Perplexed* (London and New York: Bloomsbury Academy, 2014). As outlined in these publications, "classical Daoism" and "organized Daoism" replaces the inaccurate and outdated constructs of so-called "philosophical Daoism" and so-called "religious Daoism." These publications also include my argument for understanding Daoism as a religious community and tradition from the beginning.

3 See Louis Komjathy, *Cultivating Perfection: Mysticism and Self-Transformation in Early Quanzhen Daoism* (Leiden: Brill, 2007); idem., "Mapping the Daoist Body: Part I: The *Neijing tu* in History," *Journal of Daoist Studies* 1 (2008): 67–92; idem., "Mapping the Daoist Body: Part II: The Text of the *Neijing tu*," *Journal of Daoist Studies* 2 ((2009): 64–108; idem., "The Daoist Mystical Body," in *Perceiving the Divine through the Human Body: Mystical Sensuality*, eds. Thomas Cottai and June McDaniel (New York: Palgrave MacMillan, 2011), 67–103.

4 The Dao 道 is sacred or ultimate concern of Daoists. It has four primary defining characteristics: (1) Source of everything (*yuan* 元); (2) Unnamable mystery (*xuan* 玄); (3) All-pervading sacred presence (*ling* 靈); and (4) Universe as transformative process (*hua* 化). See Komjathy, *The Daoist Tradition*; idem., *Daoism: A Guide.*

5 For a general overviews of Daoist meditation see Komjathy, *The Daoist Tradition*; idem., *Daoism: A Guide*; idem., "Daoist Meditation: From 100 CE to the Present," in *The Oxford Handbook of Meditation*, eds. Miguel Farias, David Brazier, and Mansur Lalljee, (Oxford and New York: Oxford University Press, 2019).

6 On classical Daoist apophatic meditation see Harold Roth, *Original Tao: Inward Training (Nei-yeh) and the Foundations of Taoist Mysticism* (New York: Columbia University Press, 1999).

7 On ingestion and visualization see Livia Kohn, ed., *Taoist Meditation and Longevity Techniques* (Ann Arbor: Center for Chinese Studies, University of Michigan, 1989); Isabelle Robinet, *Taoist Meditation: The Mao-shan Tradition of Great Clarity* (Albany: State University of New York Press, 1993).

8 On inner observation see Livia Kohn, *Seven Steps to the Tao: Sima Chengzhen's Zuowanglun* (St. Augustin/Nettetal: Monumenta Serica, 1987); idem., *Taoist Meditation.*

9 On internal alchemy see Kohn, *Taoist Meditation*; Lowell Skar and Fabrizio Pregadio, "Inner Alchemy," in *Daoism Handbook*, ed. Livia Kohn (Leiden: Brill, 2000): 464–497; Komjathy, *Cultivating Perfection*; idem., *The Way of Complete Perfection: A Quanzhen Daoist Anthology* (Albany: State University of New York Press, 2013); idem., *Contemplative Literature: A Comparative Sourcebook on Meditation and Contemplative Prayer* (Albany: State University of New York Press, 2015); Unfortunately, we have yet to see a book-length study of female alchemy. A brief overview appears in Komjathy, *The Daoist Tradition.* See also idem., "Sun Buer 孫不二: Early Quanzhen Matriarch and the Beginnings of Female Alchemy," *Nan Nü: Men, Women and Gender in China* 16, no. 2 (2014): 171–238.

10 For information on these various texts and those referenced below see Judith Boltz, *A Survey of Taoist Literature: Tenth to Seventeenth Centuries* (Berkeley: University of California, Institute of East Asian Studies, 1987); Kristofer Schipper and Franciscus Verellen, eds., *The Taoist Canon: A Historical Guide* (Chicago: University of Chicago Press, 2004).

11 An overview of these various movements with guidance for further reading appears in Komjathy, *The Daoist Tradition.* See also Livia Kohn, ed., *Daoism*

Handbook (Leiden: Brill, 2000); Fabrizio Pregadio, ed., *The Encyclopedia of Taoism* (London and New York: Routledge, 2008).

12 Michel Feher, with Ramona Naddaff and Nadia Tazi, eds., *Fragments for a History of the Human Body* (New York: Zone Books, 1989).

13 Depending on the conceptualization, it is also problematic to speak of "embodiment." This is especially the case if one assumes mind/body dualism, as though the former is some *thing* being embodied in the latter. See, e.g., Thomas Csordas, ed., *Embodiment and Experience: The Existential Ground of Culture and Self* (Cambridge: Cambridge University Press, 1994); José Luis Bermúdez, Anthony Marcel, and Naomi Eilan, eds., *The Body and the Self* (Cambridge, MA: MIT Press, 1998); Komjathy, *Cultivating Perfection*.

14 For some insights on "praxis," including "spiritual disciplines" and "techniques of self," see Pierre Bourdieu, *Outline of a Theory of Practice* (Cambridge and New York: Cambridge University Press, 1977); Luther Martin, Huck Gutman, and Patrick Hutton, eds., *Techniques of the Self: A Seminar with Michel Foucault* (Amherst: University of Massachusetts Press, 1988); Marcel Mauss, *Techniques, Technology and Civilization* (New York and Oxford: Berghahn Books/ Durkheim Press, 2006); Komjathy, *Cultivating Perfection*; idem., *Contemplative Literature*; idem., *Introducing Contemplative Studies* (West Sussex, England and Hoboken, NJ: Wiley-Blackwell, 2018); idem., "Praxis," in Timothy Knepper and Gerreon Kopf, eds., *Global-Critical Philosophy of Religion* (New York: Springer Publishing Company, forthcoming).

15 Komjathy, *Cultivating Perfection*; idem., *Contemplative Literature*; idem., *Introducing Contemplative Studies*; idem., "Praxis." In the latter, I have also drawn attention to the ways in which specific traditions become embodied and expressed as specific movement patterns.

16 Hereafter, the *Laozi* will be abbreviated as "LZ." Similarly, the *Zhuangzi* 莊子 (Book of Master Zhuang), which is another central and influential classical Daoist text, will be abbreviated "ZZ."

17 Unless otherwise indicated, all translations are my own. Harold Roth (Brown University) and I are in the process of completing a new contextual, contemplative, and annotated translation of the *Daode jing*. My translations are indebted to our collaborative work.

18 On classical Chinese technical terms related to "body" see Livia Kohn, "Taoist Visions of the Body," *Journal of Chinese Philosophy* 18 (1991): 227–252; Roger Ames, "The Meaning of Body in Classical Chinese Philosophy," in *Self as Body in Asian Theory and Practice*, ed. Thomas Kasulis (Albany: State University of New York Press, 1993), 157–177; Komjathy, *Cultivating Perfection*.

19 Catalogue numbers for Daoist textual collections follow Louis Komjathy, *Title Index to Daoist Collections* (Cambridge, MA: Three Pines Press, 2002); idem., "Title Index to the *Zhonghua daozang* 中華道藏 (Chinese Daoist Canon)," *Monumenta Serica* 62 (2014): 213–260. DZ refers to *Daozang* 道藏 (Daoist Canon), which is the primary and standard Daoist textual collection.

20 The *Yijing* is an ancient Chinese text, neither Ruist ("Confucian") nor Daoist, and consists of 64 hexagrams (six-line diagrams), which are also analyzed according to the eight trigrams (three-line diagrams). Take collectively, these are said to describe all of the changes in the universe. Each trigram and hexagram consists of solid or broken lines, which are read from bottom to top and correspond to yang and yin, respectively. In the context of Daoist internal alchemy, these become utilized to designate specific corporeal locations, vital substances, and/or psychosomatic transformations. For example, the Gen-mountain ☶ trigram consists of one yang-line above two yin-lines. Under one reading, this represents the stillness of mountains, and meditation by extension. That is, the stability of earth (yin) creates the foundation for the clarity of heaven (yang).

21 For some resources on Daoist material culture see Stephen Little, *Taoism and the Arts of China* (Berkeley: University of California Press, 2000); Susan Shih-shan Huang, *Picturing the True Form: Daoist Visual Culture in Traditional China* (Cambridge, MA: Harvard University Press, 2012).
22 Komjathy, *Cultivating Perfection*; idem., *Contemplative Literature*; idem., *Introducing Contemplative Studies*; idem., "Praxis."
23 See Han de Wit, *Contemplative Psychology* (Pittsburgh: Duquesne University Press, 1991); also Komjathy, *Contemplative Literature*; idem., *Introducing Contemplative Studies*.
24 Richard King, *Orientalism and Religion: Postcolonial Theory, India, and 'The Mystic East'* (London and New York: Routledge, 1999); Komjathy, *Cultivating Perfection*; idem., *Contemplative Literature*; idem., *Introducing Contemplative Studies*.
25 See Komjathy, *Title Index*; Schipper and Verellen, *Taoist Canon*; Komjathy, *The Daoist Tradition*.
26 See Kenneth Tanaka's contribution in Komjathy, *Contemplative Literature*.
27 Niwan 尼丸 literally means "mud-ball." It is generally understood as a transliteration of *nirvana*, but may also derive from an alchemical substance utilized in external alchemy. On a more symbolic level, it recalls the view of realized consciousness as a lotus flower.
28 On the use of Western alchemy to translate indigenous Chinese terms, such as *neidan* (lit., "inner cinnabar/pill") as "internal alchemy," see Komjathy, *Contemplative Literature*.
29 See, e.g., Komjathy, *The Daoist Tradition*.
30 These associations are discussed in Komjathy, *The Daoist Tradition*; idem., *Daoism: A Guide*.
31 Under one view of classical Chinese embryogenesis, the Governing and Conception Channels are the first meridians to form. That is, in the womb and in early stages of fetal development, human beings are a single, unified energy form.
32 See Komjathy, "Mapping the Daoist Body."
33 Kristofer Schipper, "The Taoist Body," *History of Religions* 17, no. 3/4 (1978): 355–386; idem., *The Taoist Body* (Berkeley: University of California Press, 1993 [1982]); Joseph Needham et al., *Science and Civilisation in China*, vol. V.: *Chemistry and Chemical Technology*, part 5: *Spagyrical Discovery and Invention: Physiological Alchemy* (Cambridge: Cambridge University Press, 1983); Kohn, "Taoist Visions of the Body"; Catherine Despeux, *Taoïsme et corps humain. Le Xiuzhen tu* (Paris: Guy Trédaniel, 1994); Komjathy, "Mapping the Daoist Body"; idem., "The Daoist Mystical Body"; Huang, *Picturing the True Form*.
34 There are additional correspondences that are utilized in Daoist ingestion and visualization practice, including the Five Marchmounts (sacred mountains) and Five Planets. For an overview see Komjathy, *The Daoist Tradition*.
35 See Komjathy, *The Daoist Tradition*.
36 For an attempt to explore "inner elixir formation" based on classical Chinese fluid physiology see Komjathy, *Cultivating Perfection*.
37 The seminal discussion of these views is Schipper, *The Taoist Body*.
38 Komjathy, *Mapping the Daoist Body*.
39 See Komjathy, *Cultivating Perfection*; idem., *The Way of Complete Perfection*; idem., *Contemplative Literature*.
40 This approach was first explicitly advanced in de Wit, *Contemplative Psychology*. It was subsequently developed in Harold Roth, "Contemplative Studies: Prospects for a New Field," *Teachers College Record* 108, no. 9 (2006): 1787–1815. For a more integrated discussion, including as "critical

subjectivity," see Komjathy, *Contemplative Literature*; idem., *Introducing Contemplative Studies*.

41 This has parallels with the so-called "insider/outsider problem" and scholarship-practitioners. For some of my thoughts on these and related issues, in which I also engage the relevant literature, see Louis Komjathy, "Field Notes from a Daoist Professor," in *Meditation and the Classroom*, eds. Judith Simmer-Brown and Fran Grace (New York: State University of New York Press, 2011), 95–103; idem., "Möbius Religion: The Insider/Outsider Question," in *Religion: A Next-Generation Handbook for Its Robust Study*, ed. Jeffrey Kripal (New York: Palgrave MacMillan, 2016), 305–323; idem., *Introducing Contemplative Studies*.

42 I began my Daoist training in 1991 under Deneal Amos (1928–2001), a Buddho-Daoist teacher and then-director of the New Canaan Academy (Lyme, New Hampshire); engaged in intensive Daoist training from 1993–1998 under Harrison Moretz (b. 1952), director of the Taoist Studies Institute (Seattle, Washington); and then trained under Chen Yuming 陳宇明 (b. 1962), then vice-abbot of Yuquan yuan 玉泉院 (Temple of the Jade Spring), the base-monastery of Huashan 華山 (Mount Hua; Huayin, Shaanxi). The latter included living as a recluse and visiting monastic, and eventually resulted in formal ordination as a Daoist priest (*daoshi* 道士) in the Huashan lineage of Quanzhen (Complete Perfection) Daoism. My primary ordination name, which locates me in the 26th-generation, is Wanrui 萬瑞 (Myriad Blessings). See Komjathy, "Notes from a Daoist Professor"; David Palmer and Elijah Siegler, *Dream Trippers: Global Daoism and the Predicament of Modern Spirituality* (Chicago: University of Chicago Press, 2017).

43 For an annotated translation and study see Roth, *Original Tao*.

Bibliography

Ames, Roger. "The Meaning of Body in Classical Chinese Philosophy." In *Self as Body in Asian Theory and Practice*, edited by Thomas Kasulis, 157–177. Albany: State University of New York Press, 1993.

Bermúdez, José Luis, Anthony Marcel, and Naomi Eilan, eds. *The Body and the Self*. Cambridge, MA: MIT Press, 1998.

Boltz, Judith. *A Survey of Taoist Literature: Tenth to Seventeenth Centuries*. Berkeley: University of California, Institute of East Asian Studies, 1987.

Bourdieu, Pierre. *Outline of a Theory of Practice*. Cambridge and New York: Cambridge University Press, 1977.

Csordas, Thomas, ed. *Embodiment and Experience: The Existential Ground of Culture and Self*. Cambridge: Cambridge University Press, 1994.

Despeux, Catherine. *Taoïsme et corps humain. Le Xiuzhen tu*. Paris: Guy Trédaniel, 1994.

de Wit, Han. *Contemplative Psychology*. Pittsburgh, PA: Duquesne University Press, 1991.

Feher, Michel, with Ramona Naddaff and Nadia Tazi, eds. *Fragments for a History of the Human Body*. New York: Zone Books, 1989.

Huang, Susan Shih-shan. *Picturing the True Form: Daoist Visual Culture in Traditional China*. Cambridge, MA: Harvard University Press, 2012.

King, Richard. *Orientalism and Religion: Postcolonial Theory, India, and 'The Mystic East.'* London and New York: Routledge, 1999.

Kohn, Livia, ed. *Daoism Handbook*. Leiden: Brill, 2000.

———. *Seven Steps to the Tao: Sima Chengzhen's Zuowanglun*. St. Augustin/Nettetal: Monumenta Serica, 1987.
———, ed. *Taoist Meditation and Longevity Techniques*. Ann Arbor: Center for Chinese Studies, University of Michigan, 1989.
———. "Taoist Visions of the Body." *Journal of Chinese Philosophy* 18 (1991): 227–252.
Komjathy, Louis, ed. *Contemplative Literature: A Comparative Sourcebook on Meditation and Contemplative Prayer*. Albany: State University of New York Press, 2015.
———. *Cultivating Perfection: Mysticism and Self-transformation in Early Quanzhen Daoism*. Leiden: Brill, 2007.
———. *Daoism: A Guide for the Perplexed*. London and New York: Bloomsbury Academy, 2014.
———. "Daoist Meditation: From 100 CE to the Present." In *The Oxford Handbook of Meditation*, edited by Miguel Farias, David Brazier, and Mansur Lalljee. Oxford and New York: Oxford University Press, forthcoming.
———. "The Daoist Mystical Body." In *Perceiving the Divine through the Human Body: Mystical Sensuality*, edited by Thomas Cottai and June McDaniel, 67–103. New York: Palgrave MacMillan, 2011.
———. *The Daoist Tradition: An Introduction*. London and New York: Bloomsbury Academy, 2013.
———. "Field Notes from a Daoist Professor." In *Meditation and the Classroom*, edited by Judith Simmer-Brown and Fran Grace, 95–103. New York: State University of New York Press, 2011.
———. *Introducing Contemplative Studies*. West Sussex, England and Hoboken, NJ: Wiley-Blackwell, 2018.
———. "Mapping the Daoist Body: Part I: The *Neijing tu* in History." *Journal of Daoist Studies* 1 (2008): 67–92.
———. "Mapping the Daoist Body: Part II: The Text of the *Neijing tu*." *Journal of Daoist Studies* 2 (2009): 64–108.
———. "Möbius Religion: The Insider/Outsider Question." In *Religion: A Next-Generation Handbook for Its Robust Study*, edited by Jeffrey Kripal, 305–323. New York: Palgrave MacMillan, 2016.
———. "Praxis." In *Global-Critical Philosophy of Religion*, edited by Timothy Knepper and Gerreon Kopf. New York: Springer Publishing Company, forthcoming.
———. "Sun Buer 孫不二: Early Quanzhen Matriarch and the Beginnings of Female Alchemy." *Nan Nü: Men, Women and Gender in China* 16, no. 2 (2014): 171–238.
———. *Title Index to Daoist Collections*. Cambridge, MA: Three Pines Press, 2002.
———. "Title Index to the *Zhonghua daozang* 中華道藏 (Chinese Daoist Canon)." *Monumenta Serica* 62 (2014): 213–260.
———. *The Way of Complete Perfection: A Quanzhen Daoist Anthology*. Albany: State University of New York Press, 2013.
Little, Stephen. *Taoism and the Arts of China*. Berkeley: University of California Press, 2000.
Martin, Luther, Huck Gutman, and Patrick Hutton, eds. *Techniques of the Self: A Seminar with Michel Foucault*. Amherst: University of Massachusetts Press, 1988.

Mauss, Marcel. *Techniques, Technology and Civilization*. New York and Oxford: Berghahn Books/Durkheim Press, 2006.

Needham, Joseph, et al. *Science and Civilisation in China*, vol. V.: *Chemistry and Chemical Technology*, part 5: *Spagyrical Discovery and Invention: Physiological Alchemy*. Cambridge: Cambridge University Press, 1983.

Palmer, David, and Elijah Siegler. *Dream Trippers: Global Daoism and the Predicament of Modern Spirituality*. Chicago: University of Chicago Press, 2017.

Pregadio, Fabrizio, ed. *The Encyclopedia of Taoism*. 2 vols. London and New York: Routledge, 2008.

Robinet, Isabelle. *Taoist Meditation: The Mao-shan Tradition of Great Clarity*. Translated by Julian Pas and Norman Girardot. Albany: State University of New York Press, 1993.

Roth, Harold. "Contemplative Studies: Prospects for a New Field." *Teachers College Record* 108, no. 9 (2006): 1787–1815.

———. *Original Tao: Inward Training (Nei-yeh) and the Foundations of Taoist Mysticism*. New York: Columbia University Press, 1999.

Schipper, Kristofer. "The Taoist Body." *History of Religions* 17, no. 3/4 (1978): 355–386.

———. *The Taoist Body*. Translated by Karen Duval. Berkeley: University of California Press, 1993 [1982].

Schipper, Kristofer, and Franciscus Verellen, eds. *The Taoist Canon: A Historical Guide*. 3 vols. Chicago: University of Chicago Press, 2004.

Skar, Lowell, and Fabrizio Pregadio. "Inner Alchemy." In *Daoism Handbook*, edited by Livia Kohn, 464–497. Leiden: Brill, 2000.

3 Yuasa Yasuo's contextualization of the subtle-body

Phenomenology and praxis

Edward J. Godfrey

Introduction

Japanese philosopher YUASA Yasuo's (1925–2005) philosophy of the subtle-body offers a complementary understanding of embodiment that begins with the assessment of lived experience. He offers a structure to the mind-body that is heavily influenced by Zen Buddhism and the philosophy of NISHIDA Kitarō that approaches the subtle-body by means of eschewing objective assumptions and metaphysics, to start with the lived experience of one's own body. Yuasa thematically situates his investigation of the subtle-body by drawing from the work of French phenomenologist Maurice Merleau-Ponty. Beginning from the phenomenological standpoint of presuming that the body is none other than the condition of experience itself, he introduces four information circuits of the body that structure experience. These circuits begin with the familiar sensory-motor circuit, followed by the circuit of coenesthesis,[1] and then the emotional-instinct circuit. The fourth circuit he proposes is the unconscious quasi-body. The first three are more or less accounted for by Merleau-Ponty, but this novel fourth circuit reflects Yuasa's understanding of the subtle-body, a topic reasonably unaddressed by Merleau-Ponty. This "unconscious quasi-body," according to Yuasa, is both psychologically unconscious and physically invisible, and it enters conscious awareness only indirectly through the other three circuits. By expanding upon the familiar field of phenomenology, Yuasa situates an ordinarily elusive topic (i.e., the subtle-body) in an established domain of discourse.

In addition to this philosophical contextualization, this paper recasts the fundamental question that structures the investigation of the subtle-body. Rather than ask, "what is the subtle-body?," Yuasa asks "how can I know the subtle-body?," changing the domain of inquiry from ontology to practical embodied expression. That is, he stresses that this is not an appropriate topic for abstract intellectual analysis alone, but a living project to be cultivated by an individual. To clarify the importance of the distinction between these two orientations, we may draw upon the philosophy of T.P. Kasulis. His categories of "intimacy" and "integrity," and their respective epistemological paradigms, affirm the importance of recasting the "what" of traditional ontology, to the "how" affirmed by Yuasa. Kasulis introduces what he calls an "elitist epistemology" that arises only after years of practice. The benefits of Yuasa's practical phenomenological orientation are twofold. It first places the term in a realm of discourse that demystifies an otherwise elusive topic, and second, with help from Kasulis, identifies the realms of discourse that distort and otherwise obscure the subtle-body.

Body as condition of experience

Yuasa begins his philosophy with the phenomenology of Merleau-Ponty as this orientation presupposes an epistemology wherein more traditional objective methods for approaching and understanding the workings of consciousness (e.g., mind-body dualism, medical materialism) are set aside in favor of turning to the phenomena themselves.[2] This is done in order to favor a description of the experience of one's own lived body. He defines this position in contradistinction to Kant, offering the critique that Kant's philosophy was ultimately based too heavily upon "analytic reflection."[3] Merleau-Ponty proposes that reducing the world to abstract ideas distances the individual from their own experience, and thus their bodies. As he warns,

> The whole life of consciousness is characterized by the tendency to posit objects, since it is consciousness ...only in so far as it takes hold of itself and draws itself together in an identifiable object. And yet the absolute positing of a single object is the death of consciousness, since it congeals the whole of existence, as a crystal placed in a solution suddenly crystallizes it.[4]

Merleau-Ponty explains that it is when one "absolutely posits" an object, whether an external object or an abstract internal object, consciousness, as he says, "dies." We may interpret this to mean that dividing mind and body by positing them into two categories and then elevating mind over body is the death of consciousness. By this he asserts that in his understanding, the natural domain of consciousness is not constricted by this "positing" of objects. In addition, he states that whatever the nature of consciousness is, it is broader and more elusive than the nature of "positing." These presuppositions of consciousness and the variety of questions that follow are what apparently drew Yuasa to Merleau-Ponty as they both saw the "crystallization" of matter and mind as obstructive.[5] Merleau-Ponty wanted to employ a form of meaningful intentionality divorced from both realism and idealism that was more extensive than a mere cogito bearing within itself a cogitatum.[6] He sought a phenomenological orientation that was more inclusive; something expressive, something living. Merleau-Ponty proposed a paradigmatic shift starting with the lived experience of the body.[7]

Further defining this shift, Merleau-Ponty explains that the body is not merely a thing that acts within the world, but, as he writes, "The body is our general medium for having a world."[8] This presents a radically different understanding of space, moving away from the Cartesian "container model" of space and the "natural body," toward space defined by the inseparability of things in relation to the expression of the human body.[9] This expression is at the very heart of Merleau-Ponty's phenomenology, expressed pithily as, "Consciousness is... not a matter of 'I think that' but of 'I can'."[10] That is to say, our being is expressed by doing. Crucial to action is Merleau-Ponty's concept of "depth," which expresses an inherent existential immersion in the world. Contrary to a purely objective understanding of one's being with respect to the environment, which may perhaps be referred to as a "container model of being" that presupposes the three-dimensional volume of space into which discreet objects are placed, from Merleau-Ponty's perspective, according to Steinbock, "Depth is the dimension where things envelop one another, overlap, antagonize, encroach; ...[it] immediately discloses ...the fact that perceiver and perceived are intertwined and yet never coincide completely."[11] Steinbock presents an example proposed by Merleau-Ponty, which is the case of walking into a familiar room and opening the curtains, and how the overall presence of the room changes – the hidden and reclusive things spring to life and readiness. That which was uninviting and gloomy, upon the opening of the curtains, reveals a word of familiar possibilities.[12] It is in the context of this immersive understanding that action finds its place.[13]

Merleau-Ponty identifies a modality of being wherein the expressiveness of actions constitutes one's very world. As he explains, "...in the normal person the subject's intentions are immediately reflected in the perceptual field, polarizing it, or placing their seal upon it, or setting up in it, effortlessly, a wave of significance."[14] This is what was suggested by Steinbock's example: when we approach familiar objects, they are illuminated by an immediately felt significance defined by that object's usefulness in relation to the degree that it allows the body to express its will. This is what Merleau-Ponty called the "habit-body" which becomes accustomed to reacting to familiar stimuli, such as a hand responding to a door knob. Although this may be understood objectively incorporating the object-body's physical function and practical outcome, Merleau-Ponty would warn that this is a secondhand abstraction of what is immediately expressed through the subject-body.

Merleau-Ponty uses the example of a typewriter, and the habituated ease with which accustomed fingers express the body's will immediately and without deliberation. He writes,

> [Habit] is knowledge in the hands, which is forthcoming only when bodily effort is made, and cannot be formulated in detachment from that effort. The subject knows where the letters are on the typewriter

> as we know where one of our limbs is, through a knowledge bred of familiarity which does not give us a position in objective space.[15]

"Forthcoming only when bodily effort is made," demonstrates the body's learning that does not at all transfer immediately to bright and clear conscious awareness. With the example of the typewriter, or to modernize, a computer's keyboard, we may reasonably suspect that most people would not be able to readily draw a keyboard from memory without painstakingly physically reenacting typing familiar words and extrapolating the movement of the fingers. The same could be said of playing a song on an instrument, the progression of which may only be recalled after physically playing out the fingering of the song. In explanation, Merleau-Ponty states that it is "a knowledge bred of familiarity which does not give us a position in objective space." That is, the fingers, after they have learned how to type, cease to register in one's conscious conception of space.

Once such an action becomes set as habit, Merleau-Ponty claims that one's perception of one's self-expression changes with respect to space. He writes,

> In so far as I have a body through which I act in the world, space and time are not, for me, a collection of adjacent points nor are they a limitless number of relations synthesized by my consciousness, and into which it draws my body. I am not in space and time, nor do I conceive space and time; I belong to them, my body combines with them and includes them.[16]

Here, Merleau-Ponty is very clearly criticizing the Newtonian worldview wherein space and time are understood to be strictly *a priori* categories. Instead, he recognizes that his body is a spatial and temporal expression itself which cannot be pulled from this nexus of rationality, save through abstract and artificial means (e.g., the construction of the object-body). This expression is surely what he has in mind when he writes, "…to look at an object is to inhabit it, and from this habitation to grasp all things in terms of the aspect which they present to it."[17] For the object-body to "inhabit" another object is a patent logical absurdity, but when the immediacy of one's phenomenological experience is taken with respect to the object's habituated usefulness to the individual and the individual's particular understanding, the object joins with the individual's intentional expression.

Merleau-Ponty saw the individual primarily in terms of the expressiveness of the body and its utility toward the world.[18] To verbalize this expressiveness, he required an epistemological assumption that broke away from the presumption of objectivity and material reductionism. The importance of Merleau-Ponty's phenomenology will be evident in the following section, as this philosophy heavily influenced Yuasa's understanding of how the subtle-body can be known.

Yuasa

This section introduces the philosophy of Yuasa Yasuo, specifically his fourfold body schema which expands upon the insights of Merleau-Ponty, adding an additional, deeper level. Yuasa also adds to this discussion, suggesting the use of the gestalt foreground/background paradigm and a criticism of mind–body dualism, taking consciousness to be something that converges between the two fields of psychology and physiology, not accepting a compromise or stopping at correlativity, but instead employing a third-term between the two. As the term may carry a number of contemporary interpretations, by "mind-body correlativity," I mean only to suggest a general awareness of the inseparability of mind and body which stands in contradistinction to "mind-body dualism." Also expanding beyond the scope and methodological assumptions of Merleau-Ponty, Yuasa centralizes self-cultivation (*shugyō*) as the means for deliberately training the unconscious functions of the subtle-body. In doing so, Yuasa makes a case for what he terms the "unconscious quasi-body."

In this section, Yuasa's understanding of the body will be established as an expansion of Merleau-Ponty's body schema. Yuasa's building upon Merleau-Ponty's schema takes into account more explicit neurological and physiological aspects of human physiology, while introducing elements of Eastern philosophy, also unaccounted for in Merleau-Ponty, most notably *ki (ch'i)*-energy, which is one expression of the subtle-body.

Yuasa's four circuits of the body

Yuasa's account of the body begins where Bergson and Merleau-Ponty began – with the sensory-motor circuit. This circuit is an expression of the common everyday function of one's experience defined by the relationship that exists between sensory information perceived from the environment and motor responses whose actions are expressive of the body's utility toward the world. This stimulus and response loop is habituated through action and repetition.[19] Merleau-Ponty's insight into this matter comes in identifying an additional, deeper layer to the body—the habit body—beneath the sensory-motor circuit that was foundational for the human being and was fundamentally expressive in nature. Yuasa, expanding upon these insights, introduces further layers of the mechanisms that give rise to phenomenological experience which more exactly articulates the mechanism at work in the unconscious regions of experience. Yuasa expands Merleau-Ponty's depiction of the body, separating the elements that comprised the habit-body into a more gradual spectrum of components, more carefully systemizing four levels of the body. These circuits are (1) the sensory-motor circuit, (2) the circuit of coenesthesis, (3) the emotional-instinct circuit, and (4) the unconscious quasi-body.

To begin Yuasa's depiction of his body schema, the first layer is the sensory-motor circuit as defined by Merleau-Ponty. He adds that underneath the sensory-motor circuit, there is a second layer which he calls the "internal information apparatus." The internal information apparatus is the domain of one's internal awareness wherein one receives information about the state of one's body beyond the scope of ordinary "sensing" from the first layer. Yuasa breaks down this second layer into two parts, the first of which he calls the "circuit of kinesthesis." He designates this term as the system of nerves which provides feedback as to the body's movement, functioning as the support for the sensory-motor circuit by providing a stream of feedback to one's bodily actions. The second portion of Yuasa's internal information apparatus is the splanchnic nerves, which comprise the circuit of somesthesis, which transfers information about the condition of the organs to include feelings from the skin, muscles, tendons, and internal organs, and the sensation of balance.[20]

Yuasa notes that there is a fundamental difference between one's awareness of each of these first two circuits. The former is bright and clear such that one's movements and physical sensations are easily localized within the awareness of one's body. For example, in picking up a small and delicate object, one is explicitly aware that it is being held, for example, gently with the finger tips. The clarity is necessary as the feedback in this circuit is required for subtle acts of dexterity and balance, like applying just enough pressure to, perhaps, hold a paper cup upright and with just enough pressure to keep it secure without crushing it. Splanchnic sensation, however, does not usually possess this lucidity, as one does not have an immediately clear understanding of the position or state of the internal organs (or any of their messages they may have for conscious awareness) unless there is something wrong with one of them. Yuasa explains that this is because there is a larger area in the cerebral cortex designated to the former. As a result, as Yuasa writes, "We take the motor sensation to be at the periphery of ego-consciousness, the splanchnic sensation is further behind it, formed at the base of a vague, dark consciousness."[21] Yuasa terms these two circuits of the internal information apparatus when taken together as the circuit of coenesthesis, which he likens to a feedback apparatus.

Following the sensory-motor circuit and the circuit of coenesthesis is the third layer of the experience of the body, which Yuasa terms the "emotional-instinct circuit," which consists of the autonomic nervous system (sympathetic and parasympathetic) which regulates and maintains the function of the internal organs. Yuasa notes that special attention must be paid to this circuit's unique character as it is more on the periphery of ordinary consciousness than the previous two. That is, in the same sense as mentioned earlier concerning how the circuit of somesthesis is less connected to the cerebral cortex than the circuit of kinesthesis, the autonomic nervous system does not connect to the cerebral cortex at all. Centripetally, this circuit regulates such functions as digestion and heart rate, which are regulated entirely unconsciously, ordinarily by the parasympathetic nervous system. Centrifugally, this circuit communicates only through stress and emotion which are diffused throughout the body. This is to say that the information given out from the emotional-instinct circuit is entirely unlocalized.

This circuit is central for the maintenance of life, as well as the source of sexual and other instinctual energy. To return to Merleau-Ponty for a moment, it is this level of unconscious energy that drives the intentional arc, deriving its driving energy from basic energetic impulses of the body.[22] Merleau-Ponty's famous case of a man named Schneider, who, due to a traumatic brain injury, was unable to apply this energy to his world; as such, his world became barren of meaning, and he became pathologically emotionally neutral to his world. One's emotional coloring of the world, according to Merleau-Ponty, whether sexual desire or desire to express one's thoughts on a typewriter, derives from something he believed to be sexual at its basis. But as this energy functions at the level of the emotional-instinct circuit, its energy is diffused throughout one's experience.

This third circuit, as well as the somesthesis of the second circuit, Yuasa notes, is insufficiently paid attention to by Western science; however, the exception is depth psychology, which is keen to recognize the potential for an unconscious source to some psycho-physical maladies.[23] To explain in more detail, Yuasa defines the habit body as the second circuit, to which those who have trained their body diligently have more access. That is, the first circuit more easily "hands off control," as it were, to inculcated sub-routines habituated through practice. According to Yuasa, the ease with which someone performs such an action can be disrupted by emotion, such as anxieties that arise during public speaking, or frustrations that arise during participation in sports. In a more mundane sense, this may apply to any number of emotional agitations that arise at any time, even in the case of something such as interacting with a cashier at the grocery store, or simply being out in public. This third circuit, Yuasa claims, is primarily neglected, as training the body is ordinarily limited to the first two circuits, as they are focused on athletic actions such as speed and strength, whereas the training of this third circuit trains the emotional responses and inhibitions of the whole person.

To acquire an understanding of how such stray emotions upset the individual, Yuasa states that one must begin cultivating the third emotional-instinct circuit through meditation, which focuses the mind such that it is no longer disturbed by the arising of agitating emotion and by the intrusions of the "over-thinking" mind. This is to say that both unconscious emotional agitation and the conscious overcorrections of ratiocination perturb the expression of the body. As Yuasa writes,

> ...if a person can maintain calmness without being swayed by emotion, the movements of the mind and body will coincide with each other smoothly and freely. In short, controlling emotion in self-cultivation

> enhances the degree of correlativity between the movement of the mind and body, and develops a more intimate relation of union between mind and body.[24]

One may cultivate such awareness and control in a specific art, such as swordsmanship or meditation, but the benefits of learning to more harmoniously maintain one's emotional-instinct circuit applies to the entire personality.[25] The mindfulness and awareness of one's lived-body cultivated in order to excel, for example, in archery, entirely transfer to such mundane aspects of negotiating life, such as not losing one's temper in traffic and dealing with emotional agitation in the case of the everyday people with which one happens to come in contact – both their agitation and one's own.

These secondary effects of cultivating the emotional-instinct circuit are not merely coincidental or accidental, but are at the very heart of self-cultivation. On the point of the big picture of such training, Yuasa writes,

> Training solely for technique without concern for the perfection and enhancement of the personality has usually been regarded as heretical in Eastern cultivation theories. No matter how one may excel in bodily skills or scholarship, one cannot win respect as long as there is a flaw in one's human sentiments. The preoccupation with technique alone is taken to be dangerous.[26]

Although potentially construed as foreign or mysterious, this sentiment is not entirely out of place in popular Western modes of physical cultivation. Although the "perfection and enhancement of the personality" is not ordinarily discussed forthright, the discipline formed by practicing a sport ultimately influences other aspects of one's character. This is especially true with respect to youth athletics, where young people learn, alongside the basic fundamentals of a sport, values such as teamwork, discipline, and practice, which clearly translate off the field.

One may perhaps take a more cynical view with respect to professional athletics. It is a matter of conjecture that the measure of success, for example, in professional tackle football, has relatively little to do with the cultivation of one's personality as the standards are strictly physical.

This emphasis on physicality may safely be reduced to an environment that emphasizes the cultivation of the first and second information circuits as defined by Yuasa, in many respects ignoring the third.

The unconscious quasi-body

The first three circuits of the body's information system, as presented by Yuasa, are in accord with conventional physiological and psychological understanding of the human body, and there appears to be nothing overtly contentious that accompanies their introduction. His fourth circuit, however, requires the expansion of the ordinary understanding of the mind-body in introducing Yuasa's particular formulation of the subtle-body: the unconscious quasi-body.

Yuasa introduces his fourth circuit of the body's information system under a handful of terms: the "circuit of *ki* (気; Chinese, *qì/ch'i*)," "visceral-meridian system," and "unconscious quasi-body."[27] The latter term will be primarily used in this section as it is more general than tradition-specific terminology (i.e., "*ki*" and "meridian system"). This will be done for the sake of simplicity and focus. Although it will not be addressed in this chapter, it should be noted that Yuasa draws heavily from these respective fields in order to contextualize his point. Drawing from traditional Chinese medicine, qigong, and the meditative teachings of the likes of Kūkai and Dōgen, Yuasa makes it clear that he is not inventing anything by this term, but merely re-presenting something quite old in a contemporary fashion.

To begin to unpack this term, we return once again to Merleau-Ponty's body schema. Yuasa presents Merleau-Ponty's body schema as a Western example, as his philosophy brings much insight to the issue. He writes,

> The mode of a 'bodily scheme,' throwing a net of potential actions toward the external world—linking it to the physiological bodily system, while incorporating within it a placement in the external world—can be grasped neither by an analysis of psychological functions experienced immediately in consciousness nor by an analysis of positivistic physiological functions.[28]

These psychological and physiological components of Merleau-Ponty's body schema are accessible neither to the individual who experiences them, nor to the psychologist or physician who studies them secondhand in a clinical setting. What Yuasa suggests is that, as he explains, there "remains a 'third term' mediating between the psychological and the physiological-physical... inferred based on manifest functions in consciousness and the physical dimension...."[29] A consequence of this inference is that the analysis of psychological functions experienced immediately in consciousness and the analysis of positivistic physiological functions are, in fact, grasped in part by both, as they each recognize that something very clear is indeed occurring, yet neither represent an exclusive standpoint from which to authoritatively define the observation. The nature of this inference demonstrates that whatever this third term may be, it is neither strictly psychological nor strictly physiological. It is this formulation of "neither psychological, nor physiological" that requires attention.

Merleau-Ponty seemed to have been aware of this very phenomenon, using the same expression of a "third term" between the psychological and the physiological.[30] He suggests this fundamental unity all the more explicitly, stating, "The union of soul and body is not an amalgamation between two mutually external terms, subject and object, brought about by arbitrary decree. It is enacted at every instant in the movement of existence."[31] Here we see Merleau-Ponty patently rejecting the mind-body dualism of Descartes, while at the same time emphasizing one's fundamental being as expressed through the body.

The point to be emphasized here is that the "substance" of the subtle-body, if that term may be used at all, "lies in the region of the psychologically unconscious and the physiologically invisible."[32] As such, knowledge of this fourth circuit of the unconscious quasi-body is derived only indirectly; that is, it must be inferred. Such examples of this inference can be found in such systems such as depth psychology, which makes inferences about the nature of the psyche based on analysis, and acupuncture which bases its inferences on its observed curative effects. However, such knowledge may not be accessible to most people, especially those ensconced in a paradigm that views the very problem explicitly one-sidedly, for example, materialism.

Yuasa explains that through various means, one may come to develop an awareness of this third term. Yuasa uses the example of "hearing a voice without seeing the person producing it."[33] I am, however, partial to the analogy of a submarine traveling well beneath the surface of the water, detectable only by the subtle wake it leaves behind. In this analogy, the submarine represents the movements of the unconscious quasi-body, which is not immediately detectible as it is "underwater," that is, psychologically unconscious and physically invisible. However, this movement leaves a trace that may be detected in other layers of the body's information system, for example, in felt sensations in the viscera or the skin, or image experiences that emerge from the unconscious. In this way, the psychologically unconscious and physically invisible unconscious quasi-body makes itself known.

With this in mind, it naturally follows that the unconscious quasi-body occupies a foundational space that is neither reducible to idealism nor realism, that it is neither purely psychological nor physiological while possessing characteristics of both. With respect to the idea of a standpoint, it appears that neither position – the psychological or the physiological – can fully account for this phenomenon. This lack of clearly defined standpoint makes discussion of the subtle-body problematic. In order to approach the unconscious quasi-body, a form of bracketing must be performed, wherein one's inclinations toward the reductionism of idealism or realism (or any other position, for that matter) must be suspended, and a new more deliberately ambiguous position must be taken into consideration.

In order to discuss the subtle-body and its various expressions, such as Yuasa's unconscious quasi-body, a new logical paradigm is needed, as the either/or paradigm loses its potency when confronted by such a topic. In the case of the unconscious quasi-body, we find that the expression "neither psychological nor physiological" simply does not make sense, as such a definition seems to excuse the unconscious quasi-body from conversation. It is all the more so a grave error to dismiss as nonsense the unconscious quasi-body for no better reason than that it does not easily nestle into established reductionist categories and modalities of inquiry. It is the contention of this project that perhaps the greatest inhibitor to the understanding of the subtle-body is the either/or paradigm. If this is the case, then a more fundamental and inclusive paradigm is required.

Intimacy and integrity: legitimizing new domains

In this section, a pair of philosophical paradigms will be introduced that will assist this investigation, which is the position presented by T.P. Kasulis in his *Intimacy or Integrity: Philosophy and Cultural Difference* (2002). In a piece that predated this publication, Kasulis describes this as a "contextual grid" that is superimposed over an object of consideration by an individual or even by a larger group at a cultural level.[34] The problem he identifies is that this grid often obfuscates certain aspects of the object of consideration, creating blind spots relative to the chosen standpoint. As he explains, "the more intently we look for the answer in terms of the grid, the more impossible the task becomes." He suggests that the only way to address these problems is to adjust the grid.

In his *Intimacy or Integrity*, Kasulis presents two "contextual grids" or what he explains to be two philosophical paradigms, intimacy and integrity, making the argument that cultural differences can be better understood by looking at them in terms of whether an individual or a culture tends to prioritize, or hold in the foreground, one standpoint or the other.[35] Cultural difference aside, these categories will help discuss the issue at hand, primarily with respect to Kasulis' assertion of the gestalt paradigm in the sense that he proposes entirely different paradigms of perceiving the world and oneself that are merely hidden in the background of our own orientations, hidden in plain sight. With this current project in mind, as will be shown later, in light of Kasulis, the assumptions of the Scientific Revolution and its ensuing problems can be more meaningfully cast in terms of intimacy and integrity.

Kasulis notes that these terms are not at all absolute, as he proposes them simply for their heuristic value. I offer them in the same light in the sense that I do not want to establish psychological truths, essences, or a typology, but instead offer a means of addressing the "intimate" aspects of being that were overlooked during the enlightenment. Kasulis warns against one-sided and reductionist perspectives when engaging in dialogue, which is central to this current project. To a certain degree, such initial assertions of difference may be useful as they set the stage for conversation. As a kindred example, writing on discussing difference in the context of Jung, Clarke writes,

> In hermeneutical terms it does of course make sense to create some kind of initial distance between interlocutors, but phrases such as these carry a huge weight of prejuduce [sic] which can only serve to frustrate

> the whole attempt at dialogue... [Leaving any categorical distinctions] unanalysed and unqualified [is] grossly inadequate and misleading.[36]

C.G. Jung, for example, drew perhaps extreme overgeneralizations between cultures in terms of "extroversion" and "introversion" that were simply untrue and generally disruptive, while carrying only a modicum of usefulness. Kasulis explicitly warns against this sort of one-sidedness.

In contrast to this one-sidedness, Kasulis emphasizes correlativity, suggesting that the matter of standpoint or orientation is never an either/or matter, and that intimacy and integrity vary from person to person in spite of what one may say about generalizations about cultures. Yet it is the assumption of this paper, that integrity has been predominantly influential in Greece and Europe, which is now global in scope. This predominance has in turn generated a perspectival bias. As Clarke writes, "...in the passage of ideas from East to West, where the languages and cultures of the latter have assumed the status of world domination, may we not be witnessing something less like an innocent conversation and more like an imperial annexation?"[37] This is very strongly worded, but perhaps appropriately so. The point made by both Clarke and Kasulis is that the hegemony of the Western worldview has historically run rough-shod over alternative standpoints, and, as such, a more favorable means of discussing difference is in order. Counter-reductionism and correlativity will be the methods emphasized here so that the marginalized position of intimacy may be given room to make a point.

Integrity

Integrity will be introduced first as this position represents the standpoint that accounts for the methods and assumptions of "*theōria*" and the scientific method which predominates. To explain the term, Kasulis lists five characteristics of integrity that define it in contradistinction to intimacy.[38] To begin, (1) integrity is a position that represents that which is objective and publicly verifiable. This is to say, it presumes that nothing is concealed, and its arguments are "bright and clear," open, and accessible to all. This also incorporates the criteria of verifiability and peer review of the scientific community. (2) In the standpoint of integrity, relationships are external. To explain this, Kasulis uses the example of losing one's wallet.[39] The money in one's wallet belongs to him or her; it is a matter of property rights, ownership, and the legal entitlement to what is earned. This Kasulis refers to as "belonging-to." In contrast, Kasulis notes how different the loss of money is from the loss of a cherished picture of a loved one carried in the same lost wallet. This Kasulis refers to as "belonging-with," which is a principle of intimacy to be further addressed later in the chapter. External relationships are clearly defined and independent of whoever is inspecting them. (3) In integrity, knowledge is empty of affect. That is, emotional tones and other personal elements that accompany one's knowledge are understood to be essentially irrelevant, if not disruptive and undesirable; a fact is a fact independent of how one feels about it. (4) Knowledge is strictly intellectual and symbolic – purely conceptual. This establishes that symbols are the only acceptable language of integrity. (5) Knowledge within the standpoint of integrity is bright and open, or "self-conscious of its own grounds." In tandem with (1), if information is objective, it must be obvious and clearly so. Nothing can remain hidden or obscured.

Intimacy

Integrity should strike the reader as familiar, as Kasulis suggests this is the prevailing standpoint that guides scientific and rational discourse. Although markedly different in nature, so too should the standpoint of intimacy. Intimacy, as defined by Kasulis, is the standpoint defined by interdependence, synthesis, and holism, and as such the assumptions of integrity do not apply. For example, even the expression "standpoint" is compromised. "Standpoint" suggests the position from which a domain is constructed and viewed, and in the Greek context, this suggests "*theōria*." However, Kasulis defines the standpoint of intimacy quite differently – as the position "*in medias res*," or "in the midst of things."[40] As an example, WATSUJI recognizes this difference in what he has in mind by the expression "resignation to life," which is the standpoint, he claims, arises when one is perpetually smothered by nature and life in a monsoon-fed jungle.[41] From this position, the role of the individual is not minimized, but, instead, one assumes an exhaustively immersive position of highly personal immediacy and interconnectedness.

To further clarify, Kasulis introduces five characteristics of intimacy that each stands in contradistinction to the aforementioned five characteristics of integrity. To begin, (1) intimacy is still objective, but personal rather than public, for example, learning about a sport versus playing a sport. There is an immediate, embodied, and personal understanding that is still objective, but is not something that can be explained outside of actually doing. For example, two athletes may be able to discuss the nuances of playing their sport that a non-athlete may objectively understand, but their knowledge will simply be unlike in kind. (2) Relationships are intimate and personal. This is the aforementioned "belonging-with." In the case of the lost wallet, one has a very different relationship with the lost photos as they represented something invaluable that was established through experience over time. This is also suggested in Watsuji's discussion of the meaning of the Japanese term chosen for "human being," which is *ningen* (人間). Watsuji argues against discreet and isolated (integrity) definitions of the human being based on some combination of mind and body, and instead emphasizes the fundamental relationships between human beings that truly establish our humanity, what he calls "betweenness."[42] Such relationships are inseparable from the individual.[43] We may also return to Merleau-Ponty's phenomenological relationship to a typewriter. The immediate expressiveness of one's fingers when they interact with the typewriter fits best in the paradigm of intimacy. (3) Knowledge has an affective dimension. That is, our knowledge is simply that; our knowledge. For example, knowledge about the immediate inner workings of one's self is, by definition, intimate. A pithy example of this was once shared by Albert Einstein. When asked if he believed that everything could be explained in a scientific way, he responded, "Yes, it is possible, but it would not make sense. It would be an inadequate representation, as if one described a Beethoven symphony in terms of air pressure waves."[44] In this inadequacy, something is distinctly missing. (4) Knowledge is somatic as well as psychological. Knowledge is embodied and assimilated through experience; it is not merely a learning of the mind, but a learning of the body, and it is a learning that is a result of doing. This suggests that such learning takes a great deal of mental and/or physical effort. Learning to golf would be one such example as there is simply no substitute for regularly repeating the requisite patterns of motion and spending time learning how to intuitively read the greens. (5) The ground of intimacy is dark and esoteric.[45] Dark knowledge is that which arises over time, and it cannot be immediately or easily shared. In order to gain this knowledge, one must set oneself on a path and practice it for a long time. For example, take driving a manual transmission vehicle. There are surely purely mechanical means of explaining the underlying principles, but practice is simply the only way to know how to drive a manual transmission. "You just have to develop a feel for it," is an expression of intimacy.[46]

Concerning the body, integrity looks at it with principles, to include objective sciences like biology, physics, and psychiatry, which rely on mathematical methods and the postulation of universals to define a particular. Intimacy, on the other hand, looks at the body as *your* lived body, which is indifferent to mathematical systemization and defined by personal growth and creative expressiveness. We see here two very different strains of thought at work; one analyzing the human being, breaking it up into its component parts from afar in order to identify the principles that guide it, and the other dynamically integrating the human being further into its environment, its relationships, and even its own body through action.

Benefits of the gestalt paradigm

Central to Kasulis's categories is the relationship between the two, which is defined by the gestalt paradigm of foreground and background. The advantage of this situational arrangement is that moving between each standpoint does not require movement, *per se*. It is a matter of adjusting one's focus or one's "contextual grid" in order to bring what was in the background to the foreground and vice versa. That is, as in the case of this paper, it is a matter of moving between the standpoint of detached objectivity, to *in medias res*.

Briefly, an example provided by Kasulis can be introduced as a means of defining how this relationship *does not* function. It is a familiar story with Indian roots, although interpreted creatively by Kasulis, of five blind sages touching an elephant.[47] Here, each sage feels the elephant (some matter to be investigated) and exclaims, "it feels like a thick snake," "a palm leaf," and so forth, each roughly describing the portion of the elephant from their respective standpoints. Bad phenomenology aside,[48] such a view of perspective suggests the relative situation of each, and perhaps that one merely needs to adopt the position of the other (literally or figuratively, in this case) and their perspective of the matter will change. But this, Kasulis states, is not at all how one goes about changing perspective. This understanding is based on the assumptions of either/or reductionist thinking, which is a property of integrity.

Instead, Kasulis proposes that such differences are better captured by the gestalt paradigm, using the classic example of Rubin's vase. This is the picture of two faces looking at each other, and the space between them indicates a vase – and/or a vase that has a silhouette that looks like two close-together faces. This is an exceedingly fitting example for Kasulis, as, from the standpoint of integrity, it is faces *or* a vase, but from the standpoint of intimacy, it is faces *and* a vase.[49] To identify which is prioritized, the relationship of the two images is a matter of which is held in the *foreground* and which recedes into the *background*, which suggests that when one image is present (i.e., in the foreground), the other recedes and may even be obscured. Note here how these epistemological assumptions contrast with the previous metaphor of the five blind sages and the elephant. In the first, that which is hidden is literally beyond the range of experience (either present or absent), while in the second, the observer has access to both positions, yet only notices one—at least at first. If one is to move between the standpoint of *theōria* and *in medias res*, "movement" is defined quite differently. In order to grasp the other standpoint, the only new thing introduced is how one sees.

It is worthwhile to note that the gestalt paradigm contains elements of both positions and can be explained from either—that it is both a seamless whole (intimacy) and consisting of two different parts (integrity). When such a diagram is encountered, one may see only two faces for a while, but then suddenly, the vase may appear. Although one perspective may be favored, this sudden inversion demonstrates an innate capability of seeing both perspectives. This is arguably Kasulis' greatest point; that there are complementary perspectives, utterly invisible to our own, that we intrinsically have access to. Not just negations of our affirmations, but utterly incomprehensible differences that will remain hidden in plain view until such a perspectival shift is undergone.[50]

By centralizing the gestalt paradigm, Kasulis is asserting (1) that people already have immediate access to all the information needed and that although the standpoint of intimacy may appear incomprehensible and unfamiliar, it is far more accessible and familiar than one may at first believe. The gestalt paradigm also asserts (2) that understanding another perspective necessarily entails that one must also temporarily leave one's current standpoint or contextual grid with which one is more familiar. This second point seems lost on those who hold that their position is absolute, for that which is absolute cannot be set aside. This is all the more compounded when cast in the either/or paradigm where the intimate intertwined relationship is discarded in favor of strong-arm labels such as "true" and "false."

Kasulis asserts that if we wish to become more mindful of this situation, sensitizing ourselves to what usually rests in the background, we must learn to become "bi-orientational" which has as its goal the understanding of one's own perspectival bias along with recognizing the merits of other seemingly incompatible perspectives.[51] Learning to see (or to live) both is what Kasulis has in mind.

Intimacy and verification of the subtle-body

With intimacy in mind and the value of training the emotions established, let us next return to Yuasa's epistemology. Although Yuasa acknowledges that some people are born naturally sensitive to the movements of the unconscious quasi-body and *ki*-energy,[52] for most, an experience with these obscure aspects of being require training. As such, Yuasa explains the difference between how the knowledge claims based on such a theory of the body are verified.

Yuasa defines the "Western pattern of thinking" as being "democratic" in nature, where truth claims must be bright and clear, and available to public scrutiny. In contrast, he writes that,

> [T]he traditional Eastern pattern of thinking is an 'elitist' theory with a goal which only a few can reach through their efforts. [And as such,] ...the Eastern elitist view of human being does not take the essence of human nature simply as a given, but takes it as an unknown which needs to be practically investigated. Self-cultivation is an endeavor to discover the true self through this practical investigation and to actualize it.[53]

"Elitist," while a potentially polarizing term, in the context of *shugyō*, suggests "exclusivity" in the sense that few people thoroughly undergo this training, and it is the few who are then uniquely qualified after many years of training to comment on the nature of what their studies have revealed.

To elaborate on the exclusivity of such knowledge claims, an unlikely ally in this discussion is none other than Sam Harris, who claims to have made his own modest attempts at contemplative practice. Earlier in his career, Harris offered the analogy of "building one's own telescope." He explains,

> ...the problem with a contemplative claim ...is that you can't borrow someone else's contemplative tools to test it. Imagine where astronomy would be if everyone had to build [their] own telescope before [they] could even begin to see if astronomy was a legitimate enterprise. ...To judge the empirical claims of contemplatives, you have to build your own telescope. ...to judge whether certain experiences are possible ... we have to be able to break our identification with discursive thought... [which] ...is not work that our culture knows much about.[54]

This apt metaphor of the telescope, full of the tension between intimacy and integrity, reiterates the need for practice in experiencing the subtle-body, and the exclusivity of those qualified to comment on it.

By way of this metaphor, in "building one's own telescope," one engages in a self-cultivation practice that enables access to experience of the unconscious quasi-body. The body thus cultivated reveals something which is the psychologically unconscious, physiological, invisible, internal structure of the mind-body that can be accessed through practice.

Subtle-body as project

It is this idea of "practice" that we turn to next, which is essential to Yuasa's body schema. He is not merely proposing an ontology of the subtle-body, but instead proposes that self-cultivation practices are the means by which one may come to know the unconscious quasi-body, albeit indirectly. In contradistinction to *theōria* or integrity, his project is practical in nature, emphasizing the *praxis* of intimacy. Rather than ask what the mind-body is, Yuasa asks, how can we improve it? In his words, "[Western] mind-body theories have a strongly held attitude of asking theoretically what is the relationship between the mind and body, but [Eastern] mind-body theory takes the attitude of asking how the mind-body relationship becomes or changes through training and practice."[55] This sentiment is shared by Geoffrey Samuel who notes that Eastern theories of the body were not proposed in order to merely describe the body itself, "but because they wanted people to *do* something in relation to them" [emphasis added].[56] For example, Sarukkai notes that in yogic practice, "The phenomenological consequence of the [*āsanas*] lies in their ability to allow us a grasp on the internal 'structure' of the body and place it in the 'same level of visibility' as the external hand."[57] Such practice was meant to "bring to light" the underlying structures of human being which are ordinarily obscured in darkness.

However *praxis* may be construed, through *shugyō*, a new definition of "health" arises. In contrast, Merleau-Ponty was also astutely aware of health, but the patients he studied were predominantly cases of young men returning from war with shrapnel in their skulls. "Health," as defined in this context, was to look at a damaged young man's brain, and deduce what *was not* happening, adopting a definition of "health" as the absence of damage. In this model, one is either healthy or unhealthy, normal or abnormal. In Yuasa's "elitist" view, this model is expanded. One who cultivates the body attains a "super-normal" understanding of the body, along with super-normal health, introducing a radically different paradigm of health.[58] As such, this more clearly demonstrates how Yuasa expands upon Merleau-Ponty's understanding of the body, incorporating the practices of intimacy and this notion of super-health. A point to be emphasized is that although Merleau-Ponty identified the expressiveness of the body vis-à-vis his body schema, he never advocated training or cultivating it in the way suggested by Yuasa.

Conclusion

In this chapter I have presented philosophical stepping stones that, with the help of T.P. Kasulis, meaningfully contextualize Yuasa's understanding of the subtle-body. In using his four-circuit body schema and his articulation of the "psychologically unconscious and physiologically invisible" unconscious quasi-body, we may generate a working space in which the subtle-body, in its myriad manifestations, may be inspected. Foremost, Yuasa's unconscious quasi-body strips the "subtle body" of its epistemological and ontological mystery and accounts for its wild diversity. Framing the problem as he does, the unconscious quasi-body is known indirectly through the mind and body, and its ontological structure is beyond the domain of immediate rational inquiry.

With these distractions set aside, a more sterile environment arises in which the subtle-body may be inspected, especially through the lens of culture, anthropology, and depth psychology. Barbara Duden reminds us that "if we start from the assumption that the imaginations and perceptions of a given period have the power to generate reality, we can approach phenomena that are usually rendered invisible because of some a priori axiom of what is natural."[59] In Yuasa's four-circuit body schema, the "subtle-body" may be understood as a culturally, physically, and psychologically informed expression of the unconscious quasi-body, and his philosophy generates a space in which to inspect this unconscious, invisible foundation of being that lies underneath.

Notes

1 That is, general awareness of one's own body.
2 It is, of course, a problematic assertion that phenomena are immediately accessible to the mind, as the presuppositions of the mind – social or otherwise – shape how phenomena appear. "Immediate" experience is most certainly mediated.
3 Johnston addresses this divergence in *Angels of Desire*, emphasizing mind and Kant's impoverished view of desire and aesthetics.
4 Maurice Merleau-Ponty, *Phenomenology of Perception*, ed. Colin Smith (New York: Routledge, 2005), 82.

5 Samuel identifies each of these positions as naïve materialism and naïve idealism, or blind reductionist attitudes that presume subtle-body phenomenon to be either wholly material or idealist. Geoffrey Samuel and Jay Johnston, eds. *Religion and the Subtle Body in Asia and the West* (New York: Routledge, 2013), 252–253.
6 Edmund Husserl, *Cartesian Meditations: An Introduction to Phenomenology*, trans. Dorian Cairns (Dordrecht: Kluwer Academic Publishers, 1999), 33.
7 He makes this change in standpoint clear when he writes, "...I observe external objects with my body... but my body itself is a thing which I do not observe: in order to be able to do so, I should need the use of a second body which itself would be unobservable." He suggests here a position that is immediately present to conscious experience, while rejecting any position that is mediated through idealized abstraction. Merleau-Ponty, *Phenomenology*, 104.
8 Merleau-Ponty, *Phenomenology*, 169. For the sake of comparison, this expression, "The body is our general medium for having a world," appears right at home in *Sāṃkhya*, seemingly suggesting the *tanmātras* or the conditions of the subtle-body that allow for one's experience of the elements (*mahābhūtas*).
9 "[T]here is nothing 'natural' about bodies, that bodies are not neutral masses of inert material, but rather are actively lived, defined, conceptualized and affected by cultural discourses." Jay Johnston, "Cyborgs and Chakras: Intersubjectivity in Spiritual and Scientific Somatechnics," in *Religion and Retributive Logic: Essays in Honour of Professor Garry W. Trompf*, eds. C. Cusack and C. Hartney (Leiden: Brill, 2010), 314.
10 Merleau-Ponty, *Phenomenology*, 159.
11 Anthony J. Steinbock, "Merleau-Ponty's Concept of Depth," *Philosophy Today* 34, no. 4 (1987): 337.
12 Steinbock, "Merleau-Ponty," 338.
13 This understanding is not in accord with Sundar Sarukkai's position, wherein he defines "depth" to be purely a matter of that which is "outside" the individual, whereas Steinbock does not draw this distinction. However, this distinction does not weigh on this general synopsis. Sundar Sarukkai, "Inside/Outside: Merleau-Ponty/Yoga," *Philosophy East and West*, 52, no. 4 (2002): 465.
14 Merleau-Ponty, *Phenomenology*, 151.
15 Ibid., 166.
16 Ibid., 162.
17 Ibid., 9.
18 "The body is essentially an *expressive space*." Ibid., 169.
19 Yuasa Yasuo, *The Body: Toward an Eastern Mind-Body Theory*, trans. Shigenori Nagatomo and T.P. Kasulis (Albany: SUNY Press, 1987), 169.
20 Yuasa Yasuo, *The Body, Self-Cultivation and Ki-Energy*, trans. Shigenori Nagatomo and Monte S. Hull (Albany: SUNY Press, 1993), 46.
21 Ibid., 46.
22 Merleau-Ponty, *Phenomenology*, 182.
23 For example, the effects of trauma and stress on health.
24 Yuasa, *The Body, Self-Cultivation and Ki-Energy*, 55.
25 One may also reflect on how the effects of alcohol function in a disastrously similar fashion as they are both means of "dealing" with disruptive emotions and overthinking, the former meaningfully resolving emotion and the latter chemically suppressing it.
26 Yuasa, *The Body: Toward an Eastern Mind-Body Theory*, 209.
27 Yuasa, *The Body, Self-Cultivation and Ki-Energy*, 111.
28 Yuasa, *The Body: Toward an Eastern Mind-Body Theory*, 172.
29 Yuasa, *The Body, Self-Cultivation and Ki-Energy*, 141.
30 Ibid., 122.

31 Merleau-Ponty, *Phenomenology,* 102.
32 Yuasa, *The Body, Self-Cultivation and Ki-Energy*, 117.
33 Ibid., 116.
34 Yuasa, *The Body: Toward an Eastern Mind-Body Theory*, 1.
35 Yuasa, as well as Kasulis, emphasize the "westernness" of medical materialism and the "easternness" of self-cultivation practices, but this distinction offers little to the discussion, other than affix a general place to an idea. Ultimately, as a citizen of planet earth, both as separate manifestations of the heritage of the collective species must be taken, recognizing the insights of both without essentializing the value of "westernness" or "easternness." That is to say, from a planetary perspective, these distinctions are not very useful. However, as I contend, the distinction between intimacy and integrity, regardless of where they find their roots, is quite useful.
36 J.J. Clarke, *Jung and Eastern Thought: A Dialog with the Orient* (New York: Routledge, 2001), 162.
37 Ibid., 166.
38 T.P. Kasulis, *Intimacy or Integrity: Philosophy and Cultural Difference* (Honolulu: University of Hawai'i Press, 2002), 25.
39 Ibid., 37–38.
40 Ibid., 95.
41 Watsuji Tetsurō, *Watsuji Tetsurō's* Rinrigaku, trans. Yamamoto Seisaku and Robert E. Carter (Albany: SUNY Press, 1996), 21.
42 Ibid., 13–14.
43 The consequence of childhood development in the absence of such relationships is catastrophic. For example, the case of Oxana Malaya who was raised by dogs. This suggests that relationships, or betweenness, are essential, which compromises ontological claims of one's essence being reduced to the mind and/or body. Elizabeth Grice, "Cry of an Enfant Sauvage," *The Telegraph*, July 17, 2006, accessed 4 February, 2015.
44 "*Ja, das ist denkbar, aber es hätte doch keinen Sinn. Es wäre eine Abbildung mit inadäquaten Mitteln, so als ob man eine Beethoven-Symphonie als Luftdruckkurve darstellte.*" Max Born, *Physik im Wandel meiner Zeit* (Braunschweig: Vieweg Verlag, 1957), 292.
45 "Esoteric" often carries the connotation of that which is passed on to an initiate by a guru, but this is not suggested by Kasulis' use of the term as such passage is strictly objective in nature and thus falls under the purview of integrity.
46 One may note that the tension between Romanticism and the European Enlightenment can be construed as an interplay between intimacy and integrity.
47 Kasulis, *Intimacy or Integrity*, 156.
48 Don Ihde, *Experimental Phenomenology: An Introduction* (Albany: SUNY Press, 1986), 29–30.
49 In this light, Kasulis' use of "or" in the title of his book becomes conspicuous. He addresses this, stating that due to the nature of academic writing, he is forced into the perspective of integrity, although he could rewrite the book someday from the perspective of intimacy. Kasulis, *Intimacy or Integrity,* 161.
50 Although a text that seems to intentionally avoid its own philosophical analysis, Kuriyama's *The Expressiveness of the Body and the Divergence of Greek and Chinese Medicine* is a sterling example of how the human body has historically been assessed through intimacy and integrity in the East and the West.
51 Kasulis, *Intimacy or Integrity,* 156.
52 Yuasa, *The Body, Self-Cultivation and Ki-Energy*, 112.
53 Ibid., 63.
54 Sam Harris, "The Problem with Atheism." Sam Harris. https://samharris.org/the-problem-with-atheism/.

55 Yuasa, *The Body, Self-Cultivation and Ki-Energy*, 64.
56 Samuel and Johnston, *Religion and the Subtle Body*, 250.
57 Sundar Sarukkai, "Inside/Outside: Merleau-Ponty/Yoga" *Philosophy East and West*, 52, no. 4 (2002): 471.
58 Yuasa, *The Body: Toward an Eastern Mind-Body Theory*, 62–64.
59 Samuel and Johnston, *Religion and the Subtle Body*, 91.

Bibliography

Born, Max. *Physik im Wandel meiner Zeit*. Braunschweig: Vieweg Verlag, 1957.

Clarke, J.J. *Jung and Eastern Thought: A Dialog with the Orient*. New York: Routledge, 2001.

Gerke, Barbara. "On the 'Subtle Body' and 'Circulation' in Tibetan Medicine." In *Religion and the Subtle Body in Asia and the West*, edited by Geoffrey Samuel and Jay Johnston, 83–99. New York: Routledge, 2013.

Grice, Elizabeth. "Cry of an Enfant Sauvage." *The Telegraph*, July 17, 2006. Accessed February 4, 2015. https://www.telegraph.co.uk/culture/tvandradio/3653890/Cry-of-an-enfant-sauvage.html.

Harris, Sam. "The Problem with Atheism." Sam Harris. Accessed January 27, 2014. https://samharris.org/the-problem-with-atheism/.

Husserl, Edmund. *Cartesian Meditations: An Introduction to Phenomenology*. Translated by Dorian Cairns. Dordrecht: Kluwer Academic Publishers, 1999.

Ihde, Don. *Experimental Phenomenology: An Introduction*. Albany: SUNY Press, 1986.

Johnston, Jay. *Angles of Desire: Esoteric Bodies, Aesthetics and Ethics*. Oakville: Equinox Publishing Ltd, 2008.

———. "Cyborgs and Chakras: Intersubjectivity in Spiritual and Scientific Somatechnics." In *Religion and Retributive Logic: Essays in Honour of Professor Garry W. Trompf*, edited by C. Cusack and C. Hartney, 306–315. Leiden: Brill, 2010.

Kasulis, T.P. *Intimacy or Integrity: Philosophy and Cultural Difference*. Honolulu: University of Hawai'i Press, 2002.

KURIYAMA Shigehisa. *The Expressiveness of the Body and the Divergence of Greek and Chinese Medicine*. New York: Zone Books, 2002.

Merleau-Ponty, Maurice. *Phenomenology of Perception*. Edited by Colin Smith. New York: Routledge, 2005.

Samuel, Geoffrey and Jay Johnston, eds. *Religion and the Subtle Body in Asia and the West*. New York: Routledge, 2013.

Sarukkai, Sundar. "Inside/Outside: Merleau-Ponty/Yoga." *Philosophy East and West* 52, no.4 (2002): 459–478.

Steinbock, Anthony J. "Merleau-Ponty's Concept of Depth." *Philosophy Today* 34, no.4 (1987): 336–351.

WATSUJI Tetsurō. *Watsuji Tetsurō's* Rinrigaku. Translated by Yamamoto Seisaku and Robert E. Carter. Albany: SUNY Press, 1996.

YUASA Yasuo. *The Body, Self-Cultivation and Ki-Energy*. Translated by Shigenori Nagatomo and Monte S. Hull. Albany: SUNY Press, 1993.

———. *The Body: Toward an Eastern Mind-Body Theory*. Translated by Shigenori Nagatomo and T.P. Kasulis. Albany: SUNY Press, 1987.

4 Dismembering demons

Spatial and bodily representations in the fifteenth-century *Ekaliṅgamāhātmya*

Adam Newman

Introduction

This chapter examines representations of divine and human bodies and spatial practices in the fifteenth-century Sanskrit Hindu narrative entitled *Ekaliṅgamāhātmya* (*The Glorification of Ekaliṅga*). I argue that to understand the importance of Ekaliṅga temple and its function as the royal center of political power and religious authority in the Mewar region of early medieval Rajasthan, we have to examine the textual representations of divine and human bodies as they relate to the built environment and the geographical landscape. Bodies, human and divine, serve as blueprints for the geographical landscape and for the Hindu temple, and as such they mediate between structured order on the one hand, and chaos—represented mythologically as cosmogonic time before the creation of geographical place, and politically by geographical spaces outside of political control—on the other. In the *Ekaliṅgamāhātmya* (*ELM*), the body serves as the blueprint for cosmic and political order that is in constant struggle against the dangers of primordial chaos and political instability.

The *Ekaliṅgamāhātmya* in historical context

The *ELM* is a fifteenth-century mythico-historical account of the establishment of a temple in honor of the Hindu deity Śiva, known locally as Ekaliṅga. Situated within a walled-off complex with roughly 108 other smaller temples, Ekaliṅga temple is located in the southern region of modern Rajasthan, in the small village of Kailashpuri. Based upon an inscription attributed to the Lakulīśa Pāśupata sect of Śaivism, the earliest date for the establishment of Ekaliṅga temple is 971 CE.[1] Ekaliṅga temple served as the royal temple of the rulers of this region of Rajasthan, known as Mewar, from at least the thirteenth century. From this early date, it is clear that Ekaliṅga temple was closely connected to the royal court of the kingdom of Mewar through its affiliation with an early ruler named Bappaka.[2] From 971 CE until the early fourteenth century, the kingdom of Mewar grew in political strength and expanded its boundaries through military conquest and the absorption of smaller and weaker ruling lineages in the region. However, in the early fourteenth century, the rulers of Mewar lost control of their most strategic fort in the region, Chittorgarh, to Alā-al Dīn Khaljī, the ruling sultan of Delhi. From the early fourteenth to the early fifteenth century, the inscriptional record coming out of Mewar is silent, indicating that the kingdom had lost much, or most, of its political control in the region. Ekaliṅga temple is once again mentioned during the reign of Rāṇā Mokala (1420–1429) in an inscription dated 1425.[3] This inscription, written partly in the vernacular language of Mewari, is an important indication of the new sociopolitical environment existing in early fifteenth-century Mewar. We know that from the late thirteenth century until approximately 1420, the record had gone silent in reference to Ekaliṅga temple, and it's not entirely clear what the status of the temple was during that period, and to what degree the temple had fallen into disrepair. As evidenced in the Mokal inscription of 1428, there is a renewed interested in the Ekaliṅga site, and a reference to the construction of a rampart around the temple complex indicates the previous destruction of part of the temple and the continued threat from invaders into the region, both Muslim and tribal.[4]

It is during the reign of Mahārāṇā Kumbhā (1433–1468) that we see a forceful reassertion of political, and indeed cultural, control over the region. It is also during Mahārāṇā Kumbhā's reign that the *ELM* was written. Composed sometime in the mid to late fourteenth century, the *ELM* is, I argue, a political and cultural "rebranding" of the kingdom after its partial destruction and the near extinction of the royal lineage during the Islamic incursions in the early fourteenth century. This "rebranding" took the form of the reestablishment of the territorial boundaries of the kingdom through the creation, in both narrative and geographic space, of temples, bathing tanks, and other built structures. In cosmological and political terms, what lay beyond the boundaries of the kingdom represented a threat to the political and religious order of Mewar. More concretely, beyond the boundaries of Mewar lived tribal groups and other "outsiders" who presented a constant threat to the political stability of the kingdom, as I will demonstrate later in the chapter. In real political and spatial terms, these tribal groups presented a constant threat of military invasion and remained a constant concern for the royal court of Mewar. For the authors of the *ELM*, who were tasked with re-envisioning Mewar's place in a new Hindu cosmology, what lay beyond the boundaries of Mewar was unstructured, chaotic, and dangerous space populated by demons and other impure and threatening beings. Because of this, what became of foremost importance to the author(s) of the *ELM*, and by extension to the royal court of Mewar, was the maintenance and protection of the boundaries of the kingdom. Later, I will investigate the ways in which the kingdom of Mewar, through the *ELM*, represented and negotiated these dangerous beings that lay beyond its boundaries. Toward this end, I will first begin with a discussion of space and place in Western academic theory, and then move on to the *ELM* specifically.

Space and place in the *Ekaliṅgamāhātmya*

This chapter will be concerned with the relationship between bodies—both human and divine—and territorial and political boundaries. In the *ELM*, boundaries between bodies and between political and territorial spaces, including "sacred" spaces, become locations of contestation and negotiation in both mythological and political terms. In this chapter, I will argue that representations of the human body in the *ELM* are coextensive with political and geographical territory, and interactions between the two take place at the very limits of each, that is, at boundary locations in the geographical landscape and boundaries between human and divine bodies. Representations of the human body and representations of territorially and politically bounded spaces are mapped on to each other, and it is through the interaction between these two symbolic realms that the *ELM* was able to construct a cognitive and cosmic map of the kingdom of Mewar. In this formulation, I am following several scholars of religion, including Veikko Anttonen who writes,

> Just as the body is an entity with boundaries, the bodily openings are border zones through which life flows in or out in a similar manner as people transgress international borders in entrance and exit sites. The human body and territory are always in symbolic interaction.[5]

The interaction between bodily and territorial boundaries in the *ELM* – and the dangers that crossing these boundaries represented—had real implications for how the rulers of Mewar attempted to control the dangerous and chaotic forces that lay just beyond the actual political limits of their kingdom.

The argument of this chapter relies on a particular understanding of "sacred space," a scholarly term, the definition of which is debated. I understand sacred spaces to be physical places that are set apart from other "profane" geographical locations through ritual practices that transform ordinary space into sacred space. Sacred spaces, furthermore, are inherently relational and contested, and are the locations of economic, political, social, and symbolic power. In my analysis of space, place, and embodiment in the *ELM*, I will draw from several theoretical models, most importantly Henri Lefebvre, Viekko Anttonen, and Thomas Tweed. The writings of these scholars emphasize the situational and fluid notion of space and the body, such that territorially bounded regions and physically bounded human bodies obtain their very sacredness through a constant process of boundary negotiation as well as through the dynamics of various expressions of symbolic power. Ritual is central to the understanding of sacred space, because it is ritual that consecrates everyday space and sets it apart as extraordinary and imbued with the divine. Ritual, of course, is performed by embodied beings, and so the body is a fundamental element of sacred space, serving in many ways as a metaphor for the natural, geographical landscape as well as for the built environment. Even if only temporary, sacred spaces can serve as political centers in contrast to the ordinary, profane, and, at times, dangerous peripheral spaces that exist beyond their boundaries.

I want to emphasize the important role of center and periphery, boundary and limit, and other metaphorical and literal understandings of orientation in the idea of the sacred. The sacred is relational, but sacred spaces often become centers of religious, political, and social power. In order to understand the role of sacred space in the lives of religious practitioners, we have to attend not only to these spaces as centers of geographical, social, and cosmic orientation, but we must also attend to the boundaries, borders, and peripheries that surround such sacred centers. Sacred space provides orientation—local, national, cosmic—but the actual power of these spaces is precisely at their boundaries and limits, because the sacred itself is defined in opposition to what lies beyond those very boundaries: the profane, the impure, and the dangerous. The boundaries of the sacred, and what lies beyond them, can be as small as the walls of a temple or, as I argue here, as large as the boundaries of a kingdom. Peripheries and boundaries are central in the construction of religious, political, and social identities because of the ideological work they do in defining who, or what, is inside and outside of those boundaries. On this issue, Thomas Tweed remarks,

> Religions position women and men in natural terrain and social space. Appealing to supranatural forces for legitimation, they prescribe social locations: you are this and you belong here...Religions, in other words, involve homemaking. They construct a home—and a homeland. They delineate domestic and public space and construct collective identity. Religions distinguish us and them—and prescribe where and how both should live.[6]

Taking Tweed's understanding of the ways in which religions orient people in their natural and social landscapes, I argue for the orienting and identity-shaping power of sacred space, particularly when those spaces serve doubly as the very markers of political territory.

I also follow Tweed who argues for a fluid definition of religion, which emphasizes not only place-making through the building of homes, temples, and other social centers but also movement through social space and across boundaries. Tweed pushes against a static understanding of religion, arguing instead for a dynamic definition that not only stresses homemaking and dwelling but also movement, contestation, negotiation, and reorientation. Religion, therefore, is a process of orientation – to the home, to the immediate landscape, and to the cosmos—and *as a process*, religion constantly struggles against the ever-present threat of disorientation and chaos. If we understand religions as fluid and dynamic cartographies of orientation, then "we can understand religions as always-contested and ever-changing maps that orient devotees as they move spatially and temporally. Religions are partial, tentative, and continually redrawn sketches of where we are, where we've been, and where we're going."[7] What Tweed stresses, and what I would like to demonstrate in this chapter, is that religion as a map of geographic, social, and cosmic orientation does not stay fixed, and that center and periphery are relative terms in constant tension.

What does this mean for the representations of the sacred space in the *ELM*? The political boundaries of the kingdom of Mewar are of foremost concern to the authors of the text, and, as such, the text begins with the formation of the earth, which in the narrative is coextensive with the boundaries of the kingdom of Mewar (Medinī or Medapāṭa in Sanskrit) itself. As I will describe later in this chapter, the earth was formed from the fat and other body parts of two demons killed by Viṣṇu, after which their bodies served as the territorial limits of the kingdom. What is beyond the boundaries of the kingdom's territory, and what is beyond the boundaries of the (divine) body, are described as dangerous, chaotic, and impure. One of the implicit goals of the author(s) of the text, then, is to protect the boundaries of the kingdom through the establishment and maintenance of temples, bathing tanks, and other sacred spaces that function at the same time as the limits of the divine body. In the following section, I will make clear the relationship between embodiment, the built environment, and the geographical landscape.

Body, temple, landscape

In Hinduism, as in other religious traditions, there is an intimate relationship between the body and social space. In fact, following Lefebvre, social space implies the body and follows from it:

> The whole of (social) space proceeds from the body, even though it so metamorphoses the body that it may forget it altogether—even though it may separate itself so radically from the body as to kill it. The genesis of a far-away order can be accounted for only on the basis of the order that is nearest to us—namely the order of the body.[8]

Body and territory are coterminous, the one implying the other. What I want to stress is the very intimate relationship between geographical landscape and the human body, as very frequently Hindu traditions make this very same argument. I will follow Veikko Anttonen here who argues that the relationship between body and territory is related to the relationship between center and periphery and the visible and invisible. Anttonen, in "Rethinking the Sacred: The Notions of 'Human Body' and 'Territory' in Conceptualizing Religion," makes the argument for the coterminous nature of body and territory through the notion of the visible and the invisible, where the visible is continuous with the external body and the inside of the territory, and the invisible is continuous with the internal body and the outside of the territory. Anttonen writes:

> I argue that any cultural system can exist only when there is symbolic interaction between the inside and the outside and between the visible and the invisible. The outside of the human body is continuous with the inside of the territory; they are both perceivable aspects of social life. The inside of the human body is continuous with the outside of the territory; they are both invisible.[9]

In the premodern Indian context, the natural landscape, the built environment, and representations of bodies all interrelate to establish the political order of the kingdom—its inner and outer boundaries—and they serve to symbolically represent the dangers that lay beyond those limits.

Of course, the role of the body—human, animal, divine—has a long history in the religious narratives of Hindus in India. Hindu religious narratives imagine a topography that is absolutely imbued with the divine; mountains, rivers, lakes, forests, and other natural landforms are often connected to sacred narratives that relate the stories of their physical emplacement within the larger topography of the Indian subcontinent. The physical presence of natural topographic features within the larger Indian landscape often takes place with reference to divine bodies—their eruption from the earth, or their dismemberment—and the ways in which those bodies make up the geographical space of India. The body of the divine, distributed across the physical landscape is, I argue, the primary metaphor for the creation of sacred space within the Indian Hindu tradition. This metaphor of the distributed divine body upon the physical landscape is important for an understanding of how human actors negotiate sacred places, and it is also important for an understanding of how regional and transregional identities were imagined and reimagined in early medieval Mewar.

From very early on in the Hindu religious world, we have divine bodies being used as the foundation of the geographical landscape. In fact, one of the earliest hymns in the Vedic tradition speaks of the dismemberment of a cosmic giant and the subsequent transformation of his body parts into a newly formed world. In one of the most well-known hymns in the *Ṛg Veda*, the *Puruṣa Sūkta* ("The Hymn of Man"), the entire earth, and even what lay beyond the earth, are pervaded by a cosmic giant who has, "a thousand heads, a thousand eyes, a thousand feet."[10] From this cosmic giant all beings were born, including animals, humans, and even the Gods Agni and Indra. Naturally, as all beings were born from this cosmic Man, so did the division of the universe emerge from the parts of his body: "From his navel the middle realm of space arose; from his head the sky evolved. From his two feet came the earth, and the quarters of the sky from his ear. Thus they set the worlds in order."[11] This hymn is telling us something very specific about the order of the world, namely, that space and place do not exist apart from the body. Edward Casey, reflecting on the relationship between place and body in a similar dismemberment myth in the Babylonian *Enuma Elish*, writes, "If the Babylonian legend is telling us anything, it is that body and place belong together from the very beginning. Their fate is linked—not only at the start but at subsequent stages as well."[12] Bodies are the very foundation of reality itself; the body, cosmic or otherwise, is the locus of world creation and the source for the very establishment of one's orientation in the physical world. The myth found in the *Puruṣa Sūkta* is making the claim that bodies come first, not only mythologically and cosmologically, but also experientially. It is the human body that first brings meaning to a place, and regional or trans-regional identities emerge from the contact between body and landscape. As Jonathan Z. Smith has noted, "It is the relationship to the human body, and our experience of it, that orients us in space, that confers meaning to a place. Human beings are not placed, they bring place into being."[13] This is plainly evident in the *Puruṣa Sūkta* myth: the body of "man" was the source of the very foundation of place itself, and it was from this body that India as a meaningful landscape emerged.

The body is not only the foundation of the earth in Hindu mythological narratives, but it is also central in understanding local, regional, and trans-regional sites of sacrality; the Hindu geographical landscape is covered with mountains, rivers, forests, and fields that are connected, in one way or another, to the body of the divine. One of these mythological motifs is the story of the *śākta pīṭha*s, places variously numbered across India where the dismembered body of the goddess fell to earth.[14] A prominent version of the story begins with Śiva's destruction of Dakṣa's sacrifice and his subsequent mourning of his deceased wife Satī, Dakṣa's daughter. Śiva, distraught over the death of his wife, is said to have danced across the earth, with the body of Satī over his shoulder. The gods, needing to put an end to this dance, either entered the body of Satī through yoga, making the body fall apart piece by piece, or, according to another version, Viṣṇu is said to have cut Satī's body to pieces with his discus. Both narratives say that the places where the dismembered parts of Satī's body fell became *śākta pīṭhas*—seats of feminine divine power—and embodied in physical temples. These temples became pilgrimage sites distributed all across the Indian subcontinent, and they continue to be important locations for the worship of the divine feminine. This myth tells us that not only is there a correspondence between body and sacred landscape, but also there is a clear relationship being made between temple, body, and sacred landscape. Like the myth of the dismemberment of *Puruṣa*, the cosmic giant, the geographical landscape becomes imbued with sacred meaning through the association of the physical topography of India with a mythic body; physical landscape and mythic landscape converge to establish sacred places such as the goddess temples, which then become locations for ritual and the concomitant expression of regional and trans-regional religious identities.

Just as the landscape is inseparable from the body, so the Hindu temple is also modeled on the form of the human body. Indeed, one of the most important correlations made in Indian architecture is between the Hindu temple and the human form. This correlation goes back to ancient Vedic sacrifice where the orientation and the construction of the sacrificial altar were based on the measurements of the human body, and a square shape was used in the construction of these altars in which a human body was imagined.[15] The connection between the body of the sacrificer and the sacrificial altar is one of homology where the altar becomes the body of the one performing the ritual; the microcosmic body and the macrocosmic universe are both renewed in the performance of the Vedic sacrificial ritual. Stella Kramrisch notes that, "In building up the sacrificial body, the altar, the sacrificer in so doing becomes the very altar itself; he builds for himself a sacrificial body and by doing so he is beyond time and death."[16] The homologue between the human body and the sacrificial altar in the Vedic period was passed on into the period of Hindu temple-building. The diagram used in the building of Hindu temples, the *vāstupuruṣamaṇḍala*, is a schematic map of the temple structure that uses proportions of the human body in order to visualize and measure the temple space. Regarding the continuation of the Vedic fire altar and the temple, together with its proportions based upon human anatomy, Kramrisch writes:

> The image of the Vāstupuruṣa coterminous and one with the *maṇḍala* is drawn in the likeness of man. His head lies in the East, in the *maṇḍala* of 64 squares, the legs opposite; body and limbs fill the square. Now bricks are laid down which had been identified with the several parts of his body. The bricks were square; now squares are drawn, lines separate and connect those parts and limbs and are their joints and vital parts. These must not be hurt. The lines too (*nāḍī*), belong to the anatomy of the subtle body of Vāstupuruṣa, they are channels of energy as the nerves are and the arteries in the gross body. Their prototypes are Prāṇa and Vāyu. The spine (*vaṃśa*) of this Puruṣa of 64 squares, is the middle line of the plan of the temple, as it is of the altar.[17]

As this demonstrates, the role of the body in Hinduism (and in South Asian religion more generally) is central in the creation of sacred landscapes and in the construction of sacred architecture such as temples. Bodies, divine or human, are used as the physical material out of which the earth itself is made and by which sacred temples are measured out and constructed. The centrality of the physical body in place-making and world construction is evident in all of this.

Cosmogenesis as topogenesis[18]

In the *ELM*, there is a similar story of divine dismemberment and place-making, very similar to what is described in the *Puruṣa Sūkta*. In the early chapters of the *ELM*, the story of Madhu and Kaitabha is given as the source of the physical landscape of the earth. The story of the killing of Madhu and Kaitabha is found in other Puranic narratives, but its inclusion in the *ELM* is important for understanding place and sacred landscape in the geographical imagination of the author(s) of that text. For the author(s) of the *ELM*, physical place had to emerge first in the larger telling of the history of Ekaliṅga temple. The *ELM* is not only the story of the establishment of Ekaliṅga temple, but of the entire world. According to the *ELM*, two demons (*daitya*) named Madhu and Kaitabha emerge from the earwax of Viṣṇu, who were bent on killing the God Brahmā. The goddess, in the form of yogic sleep, awakens Viṣṇu, and after a 5,000-year battle, the two demons are defeated, and their bodies dismembered. The blood, fat, and bones of the two demons are then laid out as the foundation of the earth by the mythic king Pṛthu.[19] The *ELM* reads:

> O Hari, the two evil demons Madhu and Kaiṭabha, who even the gods had difficulty defeating, were confused by Mahāmāyā [great delusion] and said [to Viṣṇu], "You, praiseworthy beloved one, are the death of us two. [However] You will not conquer the two of us where the earth is overflowing with water." "So be it," said the Lord who bears the conch, disc, and mace. Having placed them on his hip he cut their two heads off with his discuss. After that this earth, which was bathed with their fat, was filled with it. The earth is called Medinī for that reason… In the past there was a beloved king named Pṛthu, who was righteous, who performed sacrifice, and was pure. He saw the earth filled with the bones, fat, and blood derived from the bodies of Madhu and Kaṭabha. Pṛthu then made the earth level [by spreading out the dismembered bodies of Madhu and Kaiṭabha].[20]

For the author(s) of the *ELM*, world creation and place-making begins in the same fashion as other Hindu mythological accounts, that is, with the dismemberment of divine (or demonic) bodies and the construction of the physical landscape from those body parts. The text is constructing a mythological narrative to account for the Sanskrit name of Mewar—Medinī or Medapāṭa, the land extended (*pāṭa*) by fat (*medas*).[21] From the very beginning, then, the author(s) of the *ELM* make clear the relationship that those who dwell in Mewar have with bodies and embodied being. The cosmological macrocosm, envisioned as the dismembered bodies of the two demons, is localized as the microcosmic regional landscape. Presenting the mythic past in such a way, through the incorporation of the local landscape of Mewar into the larger frame of universal world place-making, the *ELM* collapses the macro and transcendent into local, regional, and immediately present.

Because of the dismemberment of Madhu and Kaitabha, the entire region of Mewar—which is continuous with the territorial limits of the kingdom of Mewar—is the body of those two demonic beings. Within that landscape, as its religious and political center, is the temple of Ekaliṅga, modeled on the blueprint of the human form. According to the *ELM*, the temple of Ekaliṅga was constructed over the *liṅga* (phallus) of Śiva that emerged from the earth.[22] That there is a connection between divine bodies, Hindu temples, and the geographical landscape is clear from these relationships.

Built structures such as Ekaliṅga temple function as "centers" not only in a cosmological sense as described earlier, but also in the social and political sense. Due to this, the geographical landscape and the built environment are directly connected not only to the bodies of celestial beings, but to the bodies of those beings, human or non-human, who visit sacred spaces through pilgrimage and travel. Linking the temple to the divine body, and to the larger physical and sacred landscape, says something very powerful about the way that human bodies conceive of and move through space. It is common in South Asia for large temples to be embedded in a network of smaller temples and pilgrimage places such as lakes, rivers, and bathing tanks. Ekaliṅga temple, as represented in the *ELM*, is embedded in such a network of pilgrimage locations that serve as a mythic and actual map of Mewar and the surrounding kingdom in the fifteenth century. Therefore, performing pilgrimage to Ekaliṅga and its surrounding affiliated architectural and geographical sites constituted a deep religious and social engagement with the imagined landscape of Mewar, and with the body of the divine. The depiction of pilgrimage in the *ELM*, even if only in an imagined and ideal sense, is a depiction of the possibility of bodily movement through the divine landscape.

Furthermore, movement through the divine landscape—the body of the deity - is as important socially and politically as it is religiously. Bodily movement through such a space is central to the construction of regional identity and political control. Anne Feldhaus, in her study of region, pilgrimage, and geographical imagination in Maharashtra, writes about the relationship between body and landscape:

> Passing through an area with one's body, or imagining oneself—or someone else—doing so, gives one a sense of the area as a region. In most pilgrimages in South Asia, the pilgrims enact their conviction that they *can* move through a region by in fact doing so. At the same time, they reinforce the same conviction for those who, though they remain at home, are aware of the pilgrim's journeys. Movement through an area with one's own body, or a clear realization of the possibility of such movement, is a condition for being able to image the area as a region in *any* coherent sense.[23]

Physical place and body, then, codetermine a pilgrim's experience of the sacred landscape and create a larger conception of regional identity through the actual, or even imagined, movement through that landscape. As I describe later, in the presentation of the various pilgrimage sites surrounding

Ekaliṅga, the *ELM* is describing, and circumscribing, the central religious and political region of Mewar. The very landscape in which Ekaliṅga temple is embedded was made religiously and politically central through the imagined movement of bodies across the sacred landscape. This movement was narrativized in the *ELM* in the form of pilgrimage routes. In the *ELM*, we are presented with two very different literary descriptions of pilgrimage: the first, a Brahman goes on a pilgrimage through the center of the kingdom around the temple of Ekaliṅga; the second, a wish-granting cow goes on a pilgrimage to the borders of Mewar. Both of these pilgrimages serve to define the center and periphery of the kingdom of Mewar, and by doing so defines the very limits of political and cosmic order in the kingdom.

Ekaliṅga temple and the *Aṣṭatīrthas*

The *ELM* describes many important pilgrimage places (*tīrtha*s) spread throughout the actual physical landscape near Ekaliṅga temple, and in fifteenth-century Mewar, the physical landscape constituted a web of interconnecting religious centers based around the royal temple. Undoubtedly, certain pilgrimage places existed in the region before the writing of the *ELM*, but this text presents a new map—a newly constituted sacred landscape—for the purpose of administrative and social unification during a time of political change and military expansion. The ability of pilgrimage places to create a new sacred landscape that is at the same time a place of political legitimation and religious power is, again, because of the real or imagined movement of bodies through that landscape.

The *ELM* describes eight pilgrimage places (*aṣṭatīrtha*) that surround the main temple of Ekaliṅga. These eight *tīrtha*s are local bathing tanks located near Ekaliṅga temple or within the temple complex.[24] Perhaps the most interesting feature of these *tīrtha*s is that they are listed as eight in number. The number eight is important in Indian religious traditions, often being used as a reference for the totality of physical space, that is, the four cardinal and four intermediate directions. It is possible, then, to understand these eight pilgrimage places as markers of the spatial core of the Ekaliṅga cult in the fifteenth century. The *ELM* is in strong support of this argument, as it provides the cardinal directions for four of these *tīrtha*s. Specifically, the *ELM* states that Kuṭila bathing tank is in the west, Takṣakeśa is in the south, Vindhyavāsinī is in the north, and Amṛta is in the east.[25]

Having described the placement of the bathing tanks in the various directions, the *ELM* goes on to say that at these bathing tanks dwell "pure-minded ascetics" who are engaged in different types of spiritual practice.[26] This reference to ascetics—Brahmans—dwelling at these *tīrtha*s and engaging in religious practice is important for an understanding of just how these eight pilgrimage places were understood by the author(s) of the *ELM*, and how they may have been used. By narratively (and perhaps physically) placing Brahmans at these eight pilgrimage places, the *ELM* is in effect claiming Brahmanical control over these important spiritual sites, the center of which is Ekaliṅga temple, the body of the divine itself, and this control was as much political as it was religious. Relatively large kingdoms in Rajasthan, such as the kingdom of Mewar in the fifteenth century, expanded the boundaries of their states through a process of military aggression as well as through a process of ideological conquest and control. This generally occurred through the pacification and "Sanskritization" of local gods and goddesses and, in the case of Mewar, the "Rajputization" of tribal populations.[27] This ideological (and social) process of expansion and control over the local population involved not only the adoption of local deities, but also the building of temples and pilgrimage networks supported by the royal center and administered by Brahman priests who were often given land grants and other monetary gifts to maintain those temples. Hermann Kulke, in his study of the growth of state power in Orissa, notes three main ways in which central powers controlled peripheral powers through ideological means. Specifically, he mentions: (1) royal patronage of pilgrimage places, (2) settlement of Brahmans, and (3) construction of new imperial temples.[28] Royal temples, and their surrounding networks of related sacred ponds, bathing tanks, and shrines, were the physical embodiment in the landscape of royal authority and priestly control in these expanding regional kingdoms.

The *ELM* concludes its description of the eight pilgrimage places by stating that the entirety of the town of Nāgahrada, where the temple of Ekaliṅga and these eight pilgrimage places are located, has the distance of "five *krośa*s," (*pañcakrośa*), a measure that varies according to different sources.[29] Diana Eck discusses the term "*krośa*" in her description of the geographical limits of Kāśī, also known as Banaras or Vārāṇasi. According to Eck, the modern city of Banaras is divided into smaller and smaller circles that demarcate its sacred geographical boundaries, and as one approaches the inner center of the city, sacred power is thought to increase. The area referred to as Kāśī constitutes the largest of the five circles, everything else being included in that geographical limit. Eck equates the five *krośa*s with the five *kośa*s, or sheaths, that constitute the human body:

> Its largest circle—Kāśī—encloses a sacred area which extends far into the countryside to the west of the city. As one approaches the center, each sacred zone becomes increasingly charged with power. In a mystical sense, one might say that just as there are five *koshas* (literally "sheaths," a word interchanged in this context with *krosha*, a unit of measurement) in the human person, layered like the leaf sheaths on a stalk of grass, so there are five *koshas* in Kāshī: Kāshī, Vārānasī, Avimukta, Antargriha, and, finally, the innermost *linga* of Vishvanātha.[30]

The *ELM* seems to be modeling itself on the geographical landscape of Banaras, and so it is perhaps appropriate to imagine that the same process of increasing 'zones' of sacred power was at play in Nāgahrada and Mewar as it was in Banaras. The town of Nāgahrada, with Ekaliṅga temple at its center, constituted the sacred center of the region, with power being condensed most powerfully at the very heart of the kingdom, Ekaliṅga temple itself. As one made their way to the territorial limits of the kingdom, and to the limits of the bodies of Madhu and Kaiṭabha whose fat was spread out to construct those limits, the sacred power of those spaces diminished, and danger and impurity increased.

After describing the Brahmans dwelling at the eight *tīrtha*s surrounding Ekaliṅga temple, the *ELM* states that at these very *tīrtha*s various Bhil tribal groups were made to abandon violence and become devotees of Śiva.[31] The pacification of Bhil tribal people through their conversion to Hinduism was a particularly important concern during the reign of Mahārāṇā Kumbhā, and we see this process take place through the process of control over the pilgrimage sites surrounding Ekaliṅga. The Bhil tribe served in a way as the symbol of the danger and impurity that existed just beyond the boundaries of the kingdom. As the territorial limits of Mewar is coterminous with the dismembered bodies of Madhu and Kaiṭabha, so the tribal groups beyond the limits of the kingdom were mythologized as dangerous, violent, and in need of pacification. Chapter 28 describes in great detail the eight pilgrimage sites and the various sages and devout religious practitioners at those sacred places. The author(s) of the text make it clear that it is here among these Hindu sages and sacred spaces that the dangerous Bhils are pacified and converted to Hinduism through devotion to Śiva. At the center of the kingdom—indeed, at the very center of the divine and cosmically ordered body—the chaotic and politically dangerous forces represented by tribal groups are pacified and made politically submissive.

By being at the center of the kingdom and at the center of the divine and properly structured body of landscape and temple, these religiously impure and politically destabilizing beings are, in turn, made pure through their conversion to Brahmanical orthodoxy. As one moves away from the center of the kingdom and the order that the body brings, however, political and cosmic order becomes threatened. This is mythologized through the travels of the wish-granting cow through the political and religious map of Mewar, particularly as she approaches the boundaries of the kingdom.

Beyond the boundaries: chaos and danger

Just as the *ELM* described specific pilgrimage locations (*tīrtha*) surrounding the political and religious center of the kingdom, so the narrative also describes what lay beyond those boundaries. At the beginning of this chapter I stressed the relational and contingent nature of the sacred, and I placed emphasis on the relationship between center and periphery in how I define sacred spaces. In this section I want to look further at how the *ELM* mythologized that which existed beyond its boundaries—those dangerous and chaotic spaces outside of political and cosmological limits.

I argue that we can understand boundaries as liminal spaces with respect to the territorial limits of a kingdom or other culturally bounded region. It is because of this liminality that these spaces are regarded as dangerous, chaotic, and, often, impure in the view of the imperial court of Mewar. Victor Turner argues that liminal spaces are often characterized by ambiguity and danger, owing to their non-incorporation into accepted classificatory boundaries.[32] In the *ELM*, this danger takes the form of non-Hindu groups that threaten the political stability of the kingdom because of their perceived impurity and military aggression. The Bhils were the tribal group most dominant in the Mewar region of Rajasthan in the fifteenth century. The Bhils are outside of the Hindu *varṇa* classificatory system, and as such are considered impure in the eyes of the orthodox Hindu tradition. The worldview put forward in the *ELM* is a clear assertion of political and cultural boundaries that stress the (imagined) community that lay within the limits of the kingdom, and those on the outside, existing as they do in the chaotic and liminal spaces beyond political control and cosmic order, and are constant threats to the stability of the kingdom.

The author(s) of the *ELM*, and those in the royal court that supported the worldview of that narrative, imagined what lay within the boundaries of the kingdom as a type of "homeland," a space inhabited by an imagined community with a more or less homogeneous identity. Homelands emerge through a process of homemaking, a constant negotiation and renegotiation of territorial boundaries. On this matter, Tweed writes,

> Homemaking does not end at the front door. It extends to the boundaries of the territory that group members allocentrically imagine as *their* space, but since the homeland is an imagined territory inhabited by an imagined community, a space and group continually figured and refigured in contact with others, its borders shift over time and across cultures.[33]

The *ELM*, focused as it is on the creation and enforcement of political and cultural boundaries, is making a clear argument about the dangers of those living outside of the homeland and beyond the boundaries of the kingdom. The narrative does this through the story of a wish-granting cow and her creation of temples, bathing tanks, and other built structures that mark the limits of the territory of Mewar. By paying attention to the representations of place and people on the inside and outside of sacred spaces, we can more fully attend to the ways in which religious and political actors exercise a "politics of exclusion."[34] The limits of Mewar, the very boundaries of the kingdom, become central to the narrative of the *ELM* because of this notion of exclusion. Who, or what, is included within the boundaries of the kingdom, and excluded from them, becomes part of the larger narrative of sacred space in the text.

Chapters 13–18 of the *ELM* describe the sacred geography of Mewar. These same six chapters describe the journey of the wish-granting cow across the geographical and political landscape of Mewar. In these chapters, the wish-granting cow is often described establishing *liṅga*s at the borders of the kingdom as she traverses the landscape, the meaning of which is that she is building temples to Śiva at the territorial limits of Mewar. In my analysis, this is a clear process of using the Hindu temple—as a representation of the human and divine body in the built environment—as a marker of political and religious inclusion/exclusion. By creating these boundaries marked with Hindu temples, the author(s) of the *ELM* are making a claim to the inner space of the kingdom as a unique region protected from the dangers that exist beyond its borders. Body and landscape, therefore, work together to establish a space with a specific regional identity. As Casey writes:

> Body and landscape present themselves as coeval epicenters around which particular places pivot and radiate. They are, at the very least, the bounds of places. In my embodied being I am *just at* a place as its inner boundary; a surrounding landscape, on the other hand, is *just beyond* that place as its outer boundary. Between the two boundaries—and very much as a function of their differential interplay—implacement occurs. Place is what takes place between body and landscape.[35]

It is quite clear that the author(s) of the *ELM* use the narrative of the wish-granting cow to define the political territory of Mewar through her establishment of temples to Śiva in the literary landscape. Let me now turn to the specific narratives of the wish-granting cow to place this point clear.

In the mythological narrative of the creation of Ekaliṅga temple, a wish-granting cow (*kāmadhenu*) pours her milk down upon the ground that covers a hidden *liṅga*. That *liṅga* is Ekaliṅga himself who had been forced to dwell in the underworld (*pātāla*) due to a curse placed upon it by the goddess Pārvatī. The wish-granting cow spills her milk upon the earth, and Ekaliṅga, arising from the underworld into Mewar, states that from that moment forward the wish-granting cow will wander the entire earth establishing *liṅga*s, which will serve as equivalent but separate forms of Ekaliṇga.[36] Importantly, Ekaliṅga also says that the wish-granting cow will take the form of Brahmans, or Hindu priests, and will become impassible at the border of the kingdom. *ELM* 8.53 reads:

> Having taken on the form of [multiple] Brahmans, you [the wish-granting cow] will be impassible in your control over the border [of the kingdom]. Those [people] who have passed over you at the borders of fields, villages, and temples will become [as if] the killers of Brahmans.[37]

This verse is telling us something quite important about how power—political, religious, and symbolic—is being exercised in fifteenth-century

Mewar. This verse is an *active* claim to the territorial limits of the kingdom, such that any foe trespassing beyond the boundaries of Mewar—presumably in order to commit violence – should be understood as a killer of Brahmans (*brahmaghna*), perhaps one of the most vile and polluting types of people in the world according to Hindu thought. We again see that Brahmans are used as symbolic tools that enforce the political and religious boundaries of the kingdom, in contrast to the polluting and chaotic forces that may attempt to traverse those boundaries.

The narrative of the wish-granting cow comes early in the *ELM* – chapter eight of 32 chapters—and it takes place immediately after Ekaliṅga emerges from the underworld into the kingdom of Mewar. This mythic moment is the most important expression of the territorial limits of Mewar since the opening myth of the dismemberment of Madhu and Kaitabha described earlier. After the region of Mewar was constructed from the fat of the two demons, the next expression of spatial boundaries is in the movements of the wish-granting cow across, and up to the very limits of, Mewar. As we saw, the macrocosmic space created from the bodies of the two dismembered demons was coextensive with the limits of the kingdom of Mewar, and those beings that live beyond the boundaries of the kingdom, whether they are tribal groups, demons, or ghosts, present a very real cosmic and political threat to the stability of the kingdom. Hence the establishment of Hindu temples, populated with Brahmans, created by the wish-granting cow in her movement across the social, political, and religious landscape. What is being expressed in the narrative of the wish-granting cow is an active engagement on the part of the author(s) of the *ELM* toward the "inside" and the "outside" of Mewar as a cultural and political territory, a territory whose rulers were constantly negotiating relationships of power at the centers and peripheries of that region. As a political space, the rulers of Mewar had to make the most forceful claims to the control of territory at the peripheries, for the obvious reason that it is on the boundaries and peripheries where the kingdom's stability was most at risk.

In chapter 16, the *ELM* presents an interesting episode, again involving the dangers that exist just beyond the limits of Mewar. When the gods come to Bṛhaspati and ask how they remove the sins acquired after killing the demon Vṛtra, Bṛhaspati tells the gods to go to the limits of Mewar (*medapāṭāntikaṃ*) and bathe in the Kurumā River.[38] The Kurumā River—today known as the Karmoī River—flows through the Chittorgarh district in Rajasthan, east of the temple of Ekaliṅga and near the modern border of Rajasthan and Madhya Pradesh. The *ELM* also states that there is a bathing tank, known as Karttarī Kuṇḍ—situated at the bank of the river—that removes all sin.[39] The role of the wish-granting cow with regard to the travels of the gods to the Kurumā River is unclear, but the *ELM* states that after the gods bathed in this river at the limits of Mewar, they left for their individual abodes, while the wish-granting cow continued on (possibly beyond) the limits of Mewar, and as she was admiring the beauty of the scenery, she saw a great army of the Kirāta people. The term "Kirāta" is something of a generic term in Sanskrit literature referring to tribal groups living in the mountains and other "wild" places. According to the editor of the *ELM*, the Mewari language commentary in the *ELM* states that the term "Kirāta" is referring to the Bhil tribe.[40] After seeing this army of the Bhils, who are described as carrying all manner of weapons, the wish-granting cow became angry at the sight of them. The *ELM* states that the wish-granting cow knew that those in the tribal army were of a wicked nature (*duṣṭabhāvaṃ*), and she attacked them with her horns, hooves, snout, and tail. After attacking the tribal army and driving them away in the four directions, the wish-granting cow placed a curse on them. She proclaims that in the future, this tribe will be subservient to preeminent kings and will always have a fear of waterborne illnesses (*jalādrogabhayaṃ*). Similarly, but in opposition to this curse given to the tribal people, the wish-granting cow states that any king living in the Mewar region will not have any fear of waterborne illnesses, nor will they have any fear of the tribal people either. After uttering this curse, the wish-granting cow continued with her journey.[41]

This incident is important for several reasons. First, we again are given another characterization of the Bhil tribal people as violent, prone to war, and outside of the Brahmanical fold. As the wish-granting cow is at the very margins of the kingdom of Mewar, I think it is reasonable to assume that the tribal army in this episode is either at the borders of the kingdom or just beyond. By routing the tribal army, the wish-granting cow—or more to the point, the authors of the *ELM*—are making claims to the territorial boundaries of the kingdom. By characterizing the tribal army as wicked and warlike, the author(s) of the *ELM* are stating that what exists beyond the boundaries of the kingdom, and beyond the boundaries of the dismembered body of the two demons Madhu and Kaitabha, is dangerous and a threat to the kingdom's political stability. This is a claim to territory, both political and religious, on the part of the rulers of Mewar, and it is an expression of symbolic power over center and periphery in a politics of property.

This claim to territory is expressed through the curse given to the tribal group by the wish-granting cow. As described earlier, the wish-granting cow stated that, besides being subservient to preeminent kings, the tribal people living in the region would always have a fear of waterborne sickness. What this curse means exactly is not altogether clear, but I will venture an analysis based on my understanding of sacred space and political territory described thus far. I understand this curse to mean that the tribal groups living either within or outside of the territory of the kingdom will have a fear of water in bathing tanks and other sacred bathing areas, such as rivers. Bathing tanks are an important element of the built environment in Hinduism because they serve as locations of purity where a devotee can, essentially, wash the sins off of their physical and spiritual body. By cursing the Bhil people to be afraid of water is to exclude those people from participation in this orthodox Hindu ritual. What I believe is happening here is the appropriation of the geographical and built environment through a politics of exclusion, and this is done by defining who or what is fit—sacred—enough to bath in these tanks and rivers. As the non-Hindu body is considered biologically and inherently impure, the Bhil tribal people are excluded from all such sacred places and pushed deeper past the boundaries of the kingdom. The symbolic and political appropriation of space and property is fundamental in the exercise of political power in Mewar, as in other places and times in human culture. As Chidester writes, "The sacred character of a place can be asserted and maintained through claims and counter-claims on its ownership. The sacrality of place, therefore, can be directly related to a politics of property."[42] What this "curse" does, in part, is to define both political and religious boundaries between those dangerous groups who live beyond the borders of the kingdom and those who live within.

Conclusion

At the beginning of his well-known essay "Map is Not Territory," Jonathan Z. Smith relates a story of his experience as a young man on a dairy farm in upstate New York. In this anecdote, Smith describes the locative map that the farmer, his employer, constructed of his world—a world which was a microcosmic map of the larger cosmos in which that farmer dwelled. Smith describes the space that the farmer constructed wherein everything had its assigned place and role in the social and natural environment. By operating in conformity to the natural word such as the planting season and the breeding season, and by conforming to the social world delineated by the boundaries of fences, walls, and other borders, the farmer ordered his world in conformity to the social world of personal and private property:

> What he [the farmer] established within the walls of his house and within the fences that surround his farm was the carving out of a space which was separate from other spaces and yet in harmony with his perception of the larger social and natural environments. By limiting the space over which he had dominion, he strove to maximize all of the possibilities of that space. He sought to create, in both his home and farm, a microcosm in which everything had its place and was fulfilled by keeping its place...He conferred value upon that place by his cosmology of home and farm and by the dramatization of his respect for the integrity of their borders...I would term this cosmology a locative map of the world and the organizer of such a world, an imperial figure.[43]

What I have proposed in this chapter is something very similar to what Smith describes for his farmer. Through the establishment of built structures at the center of the kingdom of Mewar, and through building smaller temples, bathing tanks, and other structures on the borders of the kingdom, the imperial figures who composed the *ELM* and disseminated the text throughout the territory created a locative, microcosmic map that was meant to be organized in harmony with the larger map of the Hindu cosmos. Body and place are mutually articulative, each influencing the other.

What lay beyond the boundaries of the kingdom of Mewar was mythologized as chaotic, dangerous, and impure in relation to the inside of the kingdom, particularly as one comes closer to the center of the region and its most important site of political and religious power, Ekaliṅga temple. What I have demonstrated is the manner in which this temple and other built structures on the periphery of the kingdom are mediated between cosmic chaos and political instability beyond the borders of the kingdom on the one hand, and proper political rule and cosmically harmonious geographical place on the other.

Notes

1 D.R. Bhandarkar, "An Eklingji stone inscription and the origin and history of the Lakuliśa Sect," *Journal of the Bombay Branch of the Royal Asiatic Society* XXII, 154–155. The earliest literary references to the Pāśupatas are probably found in the *Mahābhārata*. In the *Śāntiparvan* of the *Mahābhārata*, four religious doctrines are mentioned—Sāmkhya, Yoga, Pāñcarātrā, and Pāśupata. In the commentary written on the Pāśupatasūtra, entitled Pañcārthabhāsya, Kaundinya writes that Śiva assumed the body of a Brahman and manifested on earth at Kāyāvatarana or Kāyāvarohana, after which he went to Ujjayinī where he transmitted his teachings to his disciple Kuśika. This story is found in many later records, including the Ekaliṅga inscription of 971 discussed in this chapter. The most developed literary accounts of the birth of Lakulīśa are found in the *Vāyupurāṇa* and *Liṅgapurāṇa*, and these accounts no doubt directly influenced the birth narrative of Lakulīśa found in the Ekaliṅga record of 971 CE.

2 Bappaka, also known as Bappā Rāwal, is considered to be the founder of the lineage of the ruling house in Mewar. However, before the thirteenth century, Bappaka was an important figure, but not recorded as the progenitor of the royal lineage. The first inscription to mention Bappaka is the Ekliṅgji inscription of 971 CE. In this record, he is described as an important member of the Guhila royal lineage and as a king ruling in Nāgahṛda, the ancient capital of Mewar and a center of Pāśupata activity. In a slightly later inscription from 977 CE, Guhadatta is listed as the founder of the lineage for the first time, according to the available records. This record does not list Bappā at all, an absence that is striking given his importance in the Ekliṅgji inscription if he were indeed considered to be the founder of the Guhila lineage. It is only in 1274, and later 1285, that we have the first references to Bappā or Bappāka as the founder of the Guhila lineage. Importantly, Guhila is said to be the son of Bappā in the 1285 record. See *Indian Antiquary*, vol. XXXIX, 186–191; Mount Abu Stone Inscription of Samarasiṃha, 1285 CE, *Indian Antiquary*, vol. XVI, 345–353; Chittaurgarh Stone Inscription of Samarasimha, 1274 CE, *URI*, 176.

3 G.N. Sharma, "A Note on Rāṇā Mokal's Plate V.S. 1482 (1425 A.D.)," *Indian Historical Quarterly*, XXX, 178–182.

4 Śṛngi-ṛṣi Inscription of Prince Mokala (1428), *Epigraphia Indica XXIII*, 230–241.

5 Veikko Anttonen, "Rethinking the Sacred: The Notions of 'Human Body' and 'Territory' in Conceptualizing Religion," in *The Sacred and Its Scholars: Comparative Methodologies for the Study of Primary Religious Data*, eds. Thomas A. Idinopulos and Edward A. Yonan (Leiden: E.J. Brill, 1996), 52.
6 Thomas Tweed, *Crossing and Dwelling: A Theory of Religion* (Cambridge: Harvard University Press, 2006), 75.
7 Tweed, *Crossing and Dwelling*, 74.
8 Henri Lefebvre, *The Production of Space*, trans. Donald Nicolson-Smith (Cambridge, Blackwell, 1991), 405.
9 Antonnen, "Rethinking the Sacred," 42.
10 Wendy Doniger, sel., trans., and annot. *The Rig Veda: An Anthology* (New York: Penguin Books, 1981), 30.
11 Doniger, *The Rig Veda*, 31.
12 Edward Casey, *Getting Back into Place: Toward a Renewed Understanding of the Place-World* (Bloomington: Indiana University Press, 1993), 45.
13 J.Z. Smith, *To Take Place: Toward Theory in Ritual* (Chicago: The University of Chicago Press, 1987), 28.
14 For a fuller investigation of this myth, see Sircar, D.C. *The Śākta Pīṭhas*. Delhi: Motilal Banarsidass, 1973.
15 Stella Kramrisch, *The Hindu Temple vol. I* (Delhi: Motilal Benarsidass, 1976), 22 et passim.
16 Kramrisch, *The Hindu Temple*, 69.
17 Kramrisch, *The Hindu Temple*, 71.
18 I take this phrasing from Casey, *Getting Back into Place*, 19.
19 *Ekaliṅgamāhātmyam* (*ELM*) 2.16-17ab.
20 *ELM* 2.12-17.
21 The name "Mewar" is a vernacularization of the Sanskrit name "Medapāṭa." The early history of the name Medapāṭa and its meaning is unclear. In an inscription during the time of the Guhila ruler Samarasiṃha, it is briefly noted that the name Medapāṭa is such because the land was bathed in the fat (Sanskrit: *medas*) and blood of the enemies of Bappaka, the early ruler of Mewar. See Shyamaldas, Kaviraj. ed., "Achaleśvara Inscription of Samarasiṃha, AD 1285", *Vir Vinod*, vol. I, Delhi, 1986, 397–401.
22 *ELM* 7.11-13; 8.10. These types of *liṅga*s, known as "self-manifest" (*svayambhū*) *liṅga*s because they arise in the landscape naturally, are numerous in Rajasthan and elsewhere in India. Ekaliṅga temple, though very well known locally, does not have a claim to such pan-Indian status as the much more well-known *jyotirliṅga*s, of which there are 12 throughout India.
23 Anne Feldhaus, *Connected Places: Region, Pilgrimage, and Geographical Imagination in India* (New York: Palgrave Macmillan, 2003), 28.
24 Of these eight *kuṇḍa*s, I am aware of the actual presence of four: Bhairava Kuṇḍ, Takṣakeśa Kuṇḍ, Tulsi Kuṇḍ, and Kuraj Kuṇḍ. The two current bathing tanks within the Ekaliṅgajī temple complex itself—Tulsi Kuṇḍ and Kuraj Kuṇḍ—could, in fact, be two tanks on the *ELM* list, particularly Kuraj Kuṇḍ, which is also called Pārvatī Kund. My guess is that Tulsi Kund is Cakrapuṣkariṇīṃ Kuṇḍ—both names are clear references to Viṣṇu, and Tulsi Kund is directly behind a large temple dedicated to Viṣṇu within the Ekaliṅga temple complex.
25 *ELM* 28.2-41.
26 *ELM* 28.42-45ab.
27 Nandini Sinha Kapur. *State Formation in Rajasthan: Mewar During the Seventh-Fifteenth Centuries* (New Delhi: Manohar Publishers, 2002), 132–133.
28 Herman Kulke, "Royal Temple Policy and the Structure of Medieval Hindu Kingdoms" in *The Cult of Jagannath and the Regional Tradition of Orissa*, eds. Anncharlott Eschmann, et al. (New Delhi: Manohar, 1978,) 132.

29 *ELM* 28.55. According to Monier-Williams, a *krośa* is "the range of the voice in calling or hallooing', a measure of distance (an Indian league, commonly called a Kos= 1000 Daṇḍas = 4000 Hastas = 1/4 Yojana; according to others = 2000 Daṇḍas = 8000 Hastas = 1/2 Gavyūti)." Sir Monier-Williams, *A Sanskrit-English Dictionary Etymologically and Philologically Arranged with Special Reference to Cognate Indo-European Languages* (London: Oxford University Press, 1899), 322.
30 Diana Eck, *Banaras: City of Light* (New York: Knopf, 1982), 350.
31 *ELM* 28.45cd-28.46ab
32 Victor Turner, *The Ritual Process: Structure and Anti-structure* (Ithaka: Cornell University Press, 1969), 94 et passim.
33 Tweed, *Crossing and Dwelling*, 110.
34 I take the phrase "politics of exclusion" from Chidester and Linenthal who use it in reference to Gerardus van der Leeuw. See David Chidester and Edward T. Linenthal, "Introduction" in *American Sacred Space* (Bloomington: Indiana University Press, 1995), 8.
35 Casey, *Getting Back Into Place*, 29.
36 *ELM*: 8.48-49.
37 *ELM* 8.53.
38 Despite having performed something of a "good deed" for killing the demon Vṛtra, the demon was nonetheless a Brahman, and as such those responsible for his death accrue the "sin" of Brahmanicide that needs to be ritually removed.
39 *ELM* 16.15-17.
40 *ELM*, 198.
41 *ELM* 16.31-41
42 Chidester and Linenthal, *American Sacred Space*, 8.
43 Jonathan Z. Smith, "Map Is Not Territory," in *Map Is Not Territory* (Chicago, University of Chicago Press, 1993 [1978]), 292.

Bibliography

Anttonen, Veikko. "Rethinking the Sacred: The Notions of 'Human Body' and 'Territory' in Conceptualizing Religion." In *The Sacred and Its Scholars: Comparative Methodologies for the Study of Primary Religious Data*, edited by Thomas A. Idinopulos and Edward A. Yonan, 37–65. Leiden: E.J. Brill, 1996.

Casey, Edward. *Getting Back into Place: Toward a Renewed Understanding of the Place-World*. Bloomington: Indiana University Press, 1993.

Eck, Diana. *Banaras: City of Light*. New York: Knopf, 1982.

Ekaliṅgamāhātmyam. Edited and translated into Hindi by Dr. Shri Krishnan "Jugnu." Delhi: Aryavarta Sanskrity Sansthan, 2011.

Epigraphia Indica. New Delhi: Archeological Survey of India, 1888–Present.

Feldhaus, Anne. *Connected Places: Region, Pilgrimage, and Geographical Imagination in India*. New York: Palgrave Macmillan, 2003.

Indian Antiquary. Vols. 1–62. Bombay: Education Society's Press, 1872–1933.

The Indian Historical Quarterly. Calcutta: Calcutta Oriental Press, 1925–1963.

Journal of the Bombay Branch of the Royal Asiatic Society. Bombay: Asiatic Society of Bombay, [1955]–2002.

Kapur, Nandini Sinha. *State Formation in Rajasthan: Mewar During the Seventh-Fifteenth Centuries*. New Delhi: Manohar Publishers, 2002.

Kramrisch, Stella. *The Hindu Temple vol. I*. Delhi: Motilal Benarsidass, 1976.
Kulke, Herman. "Royal Temple Policy and the Structure of Medieval Hindu Kingdoms." In *The Cult of Jagannath and the Regional Tradition of Orissa*, edited by Anncharlott Eschmann, et al., New Delhi: Manohar, 1978.
Lefebvre, Henri. *The Production of Space*. Translated by Donald Nicolson-Smith. Cambridge, Blackwell, 1991.
Monier-Williams, Monier. *A Sanskrit-English Dictionary Etymologically and Philologically Arranged with Special Reference to Cognate Indo-European Languages*. London: Oxford University Press, 1899.
The Rig Veda: An Anthology. Translated by Wendy Doniger. New York: Penguin Books, 1981.
Smith, Jonathan Z. "Map Is Not Territory," in *Map Is Not Territory*. Chicago: University of Chicago Press, 1993 [1978].
———. *To Take Place: Toward Theory in Ritual*. Chicago: The University of Chicago Press, 1987.
Turner, Victor. *The Ritual Process: Structure and Anti-structure*. Ithaca: Cornell University Press, 1969.
Tweed, Thomas. *Crossing and Dwelling: A Theory of Religion*. Cambridge: Harvard University Press, 2006.

5 Subtle body

Rethinking the body's subjectivity through Abhinavagupta body

Loriliai Biernacki

Whose body?

> It is like this. As a caterpillar, having gone to the tip of a blade of grass, then draws itself together to approach another one, in this way, the self (*ātman*), having dropped this body, rendering it unconscious, that self draws itself together to approach another body.
>
> Bṛhadaraṇyaka Upaniṣad 4.4.3[1]

Darwin's famous rejection of God finds utterance in a pessimistic, if pithy, arraignment of nature's cruelty. He wrote, "I cannot persuade myself that a beneficent and omnipotent God would have designedly created the Ichneumonidae with the express intention of their feeding within the living bodies of Caterpillars."[2] This parasitic wasp injects its eggs into the caterpillar; as it matures, the wasp larva slowly eats away from the inside its live womb, the caterpillar's body. The idea of an enemy within, a wasp taking over the hapless caterpillar from the inside, violating the body's boundaries, infiltrating its organs against the will of the body's proper owner strikes Darwin as too sinister to countenance. It's the stuff of horror movies, evoking images from the movie "Alien," with the strange, ugly creature bursting out of Kane's chest.

We, and Darwin, tend to think of our bodies as our own inviolable property, a self marked off from others by the boundary of skin that makes us each an individual with our own separate desires. Perhaps more disturbing still are those other infiltrating organisms that do not just devour bodies, but control also the mind and desires of their victim, like the horsehair worm that secretes neurotransmitters into the brains of crickets enticing them to commit suicide in waters they would normally shun—these mind-controlling parasites elicit something more akin to an unconscious, visceral disgust in their sinister co-optation of something beyond the body, stealing away the mind and will of their victims. As if stealing the will and mind of a creature, even so humble a creature as a cricket, crosses a line. To bring it closer to home, we need only look so far as that best and ubiquitous of household pets, our feline companions. Joanne Webster, Jaroslav Flegr, and others have painstakingly tracked how even for humans, for those infected with a parasite we get from our cats, Toxoplasma gondii, our wills and minds are not quite our own, but rather managed by these tiny infectious manipulators of consciousness.[3]

As Webster and her colleagues document,[4] this tiny protozoa manages to alter dopamine production on a neuronal level – in the case of mice, it drives them to a reckless, fatal attraction for cat pheromones. For humans, the altered brain chemistry brings its own kinds of recklessness; infected persons are far more likely, statistically, almost three times more likely, to get into car accidents.[5] As Robert Sapolsky notes, the protozoa is also implicated in an increase in schizophrenia and suicide.[6] A tiny parasite in a human body becomes the author of human desires and actions. That such a tiny unintelligent creature could cause such deep volitional shifts in human behavior cannot help but give us pause. We think of our minds, our wills, as somehow our own, even more deeply our own than the bodies we possess. But what if the sense of self I habitually inhabit were somehow also an expression of more than just my familiar "I"? Here I am not suggesting that we consider the extensive and much-discussed influence we encounter through the self's construction in its interrelations with other human selves and society.[7] Rather, on a much more basic, bodily level, what if, indeed, my own desires are more than just me, are rather also the expressions of the various other beings that share my body space—the Toxoplasma gondii, the multiplicity of bacteria and viruses in the space of my body's microbiome? Or indeed even something altogether lacking even the basic sentiency of a protozoa—like the lead in drinking water which causes increased aggression, or the refined plant substance taken from a poppy to make a profoundly mind-controlling opioid? What if my will is simply the expression of one temporarily victorious puppeteer, among many of multiple agencies driving my desires?

For this chapter, I point to an oddly similar appraisal of the human body that we find in a medieval Indian Tantric vision of the subtle body—similar in its displacement of human agency in favor of a multiplicity of not visible, hard to discover, but potent agencies directing human actions. This medieval Indian portrait of the human body that we see in the writings of the eleventh-century Hindu thinker Abhinavagupta takes the subtle body as the locus of a multiplicity of agencies, as a panoply of deities, that drive human choices. There is, of course, a big difference between gods inhabiting, directing the desires of a human body, and mindless parasites doing so through manipulations of brain dopamine levels, yet what they both point to is a displacement of agency for human subjectivity. For this chapter, I address this key component of the subtle body within this medieval Indian context, namely, that it operates as a way of acknowledging the multiplicity of agencies that make up human volition. The subtle body in this respect affords a recognition that the human is not master in its own house, but rather that the house itself, the subtle body, instead points to an expansive ecology with multiple expressions of agency directing human choices.[8] What is so striking about this shift in perspective is that the very metaphor of "house," Freud's Western assumption of the body as some inert container, might not ever really work for something so complex and multiple as a human body.

In what follows, I first discuss Abhinavagupta's panentheist conception of the subtle body and its implications for understanding the idea of the body generally for our contemporary world. I argue for an understanding of the subtle body as a way of acknowledging the multiplicity of agencies that make up human volition. With this, the subtle body for Abhinavagupta affords a way of allowing differentiation within his non-dual philosophy, even as this capacity for difference is marked by human limitations. Following this, I examine a key problem the subtle body solves for an Indian context more generally, specifically, its function to carry the karma of person from one life to the next. After this, I address in greater detail Abhinavagupta's image of the subtle body as *puryaṣṭaka*, the "City of Eight." On the heels of this, we look at how Abhinavagupta's portrays the body as the abode of gods who direct its functions. Finally, by way of conclusion, we see that Abhinavagupta allows for a sense of unification of the self within the subtle body, simply through the use of the "I," the first-person perspective, as the "I" operates on multiple registers, embracing the multiple agencies that direct it as one's own.

Already it may be apparent that this conception of the subtle body is not particularly consonant with popular new-age versions of the subtle body, with their color-coded cakras pointing the way to spiritual enlightenment. And certainly, the subtle body also functions in other ways for medieval India; perhaps its most important function is as a means for explaining religious doctrinal points, such as reincarnation. It also operates as a mechanism for the kinds of magical powers, *siddhis*, that populate Indian religious traditions, and are entailed in this religiously shared Indian cosmology of proliferating ghosts and spirits.[9] This proliferation of spirits, indeed, is implicated in the enmeshed network of multiple agencies overdetermining human choices. In any case, what is remarkable about this displacement of human agency is how surprisingly it parallels a modern Western scientific displacement of human agency. Even apart from infectious protozoans, a thrust of much contemporary human biology is an understanding that human agency is preempted by biological imperatives, the mechanical functions of neurons, neurotransmitters, and hormones driving human behaviors, not at the behest of an individual's will, but rather more conspicuously serving the reproduction of genes. In this context, Sapolsky is not an outlier when he suggests that given the mechanisms of human biology, free will is a difficult concept to consider.[10] What these two very distant worldviews, separated by centuries and theology, share is just this abrogation of human agency.

With these similarities, the theology that Abhinavagupta's medieval model carries may seem to us today as excess baggage, an unnecessary addition to the nuts and bolts of biology. I suggest, however, that Abhinavagupta's theological inscription of deities driving human action offers something more: a way of thinking about selves and bodies that can be valuable in our own current moment of planetary neglect. The panentheism out of which Abhinavagupta fashions his conception of the subtle body enfolds within it an upgrade for the idea of bodies, of matter. Not ever entirely dead, but imbued with a lively intentionality as the body's own entangled deities. The theology Abhinavagupta presents offers a perspectival shift into recognizing the body's claims to intentionality also, an intentionality typically only accorded to spirit. With this, his model rejects a spirit-body duality where spirit is the true voice of the person possessing the body in favor instead of a continuum of an ever-expansive conception of what the idea of spirit, consciousness, might be in its highest expression as the "I," the pervasive sense of subjectivity animating all existence. The purest expression of spirit is simply the expansive embrace of a sense of "I" across bodies and deities.

Along these lines, I suspect that what is important about the understanding of the subtle body as made of deities is less its precise theological orientation of the body, an idea of this god or that god in this or that part of the body, and rather more the accompanying suggestion that various agencies drive human will, agencies with their own separate intentionalities. That Abhinavagupta offers different maps of which deities populate the various locations of the subtle body that do not agree in their details tends to suggest his own understanding of the subtle body concentrates less on which deity controls which part of human behavior and more as a nod to the body's inherent entanglements.[11] This panentheist theology is a way of underscoring a foundational liveliness to all that exists in our world. In this respect, Abhinavagupta's model of the subtle body with its multiplicity of agencies is surprisingly consonant with a new materialist reclamation of our world as not simply dead matter subject to human manipulations. Abhinavagupta's worldview shares with new materialisms an acknowledgment of an ecology of beings in which we humans are materially embedded. The implicit panpsychism of much of new materialism, its discovery of a vitality in things, a pervasive consciousness even in what appear to be mere objects, find a counterpart in this Indian model's basic panentheism, verging- n panpsychism, highlighting the liveliness of the world, in this portrait of a body variously enacting the entelechies of different deities.

It is important here to emphasize that Abhinavagupta's cosmology derived out of the traditions in medieval India called the Mantramārga[12] and its consequent map of the subtle body is not quite the same as other images of subtle bodies that we find elsewhere in India's religious landscape, medieval and beyond. Apart from the fact that conceptions of what the subtle body looks like can vary dramatically,[13] how the subtle body functions within a given cosmology also varies as well. Abhinavagupta's panentheism entails some different functionalities for the subtle body than other models, for instance, models of the subtle body predicated on dualist conceptions of cosmology. Similarly, Buddhist philosophical conceptions need the notion of the subtle body to explain reincarnation, a key component of the historical Buddha's discourse, yet given the philosophical imperative of the Buddhist *anātma* doctrine to not have some substance-based soul hanging around, going from life to life, a Buddhist conception of subtle body at times starts to look like an idea of the subtle body as information, mere data conserved from one point in time to the next, without an accompanying unifying intelligence.

What marks Abhinavagupta's conception of the subtle body against these other conceptions, dualist and self-free, is, in the end, precisely his panentheism which folds a conception of consciousness with its intelligence intimately within bodies, not separate from bodies. He tells us, for instance, that "'that,' consciousness alone, is the highest ultimate body (*vapuḥ*) of all entities."[14] Far from a dualist idea of a gulf between consciousness and matter, here, in contrast, consciousness itself is nothing other than a body. He does not entertain some idea akin to our familiar Cartesian split, which, even as we find this split in Sāṃkhya, Abhinavagupta rejects it. Rather, the model is one where consciousness itself molds itself into the multiplicity of beings with their bodies that make up the world. He writes, "on the back of the wall that is consciousness the picture of all beings becomes visible."[15] Consciousness itself is the stuff that makes up bodies, arranging itself in various ways. In this context, we hear him say that the ultimate expression of spirit and consciousness, the *Śiva tattva*, is also just a body: "The *Śiva* Archetype alone is the body of all things."[16] Very directly, he takes pains to clearly indicate his non-dualist cosmology to entail no difference between materiality and consciousness. Consciousness itself, in its highest, purest manifestation as the *Śiva tattva*, is, in fact, just the body; the material component of the world is itself spirit. The concomitant corollary of this is that there is also no place where there is matter that is dead, entirely free of at least a latent capacity to express sentiency.

As Abhinavagupta tells us, "Even the lifeless third person, if it sheds its lifeless form can take on the first and second person forms. As in, 'Listen, o stones' and 'Of mountains, I am Meru.'"[17] Here stones, which we and he typically understand as dead matter, are not ontologically bound to this lifeless state. By being addressed in the second person, he tells us, they lose their inert insentiency and take on the life that comes with being called "you," through the second-person address. Indeed, when we focus our attention on objects, the Buddha statue or the Catholic image of Mary on the altar, or even a favorite vase, the objects themselves appear to inhabit a kind of glow. Explaining the power of icons in a religious context usually invokes a notion that humans project human qualities onto objects. Abhinavagupta, in contrast, suggests that the stones or icons innately already possess a latent liveliness that merely comes to the surface by our address. The second example he gives, "Of mountains I am Meru," is spoken by the god Krishna to the warrior Arjuna in the *Bhagavad Gītā*; here Abhinava tells us, the mountain takes on the "I" feeling of the first grammatical person through this declaration, transforming it from object to subject. With this, no longer a dead configuration of stones and earth, it reclaims its deep essential nature as sentient subject.

So how does the subtle body play into this non-dual fusion of matter and consciousness? We often think of the subtle body as being about transcendence, a way for the spirit to leave the body behind in some abstracted, disembodied, and consequently more perfect, less entangled existence.[18] Abhinavagupta's model, in contrast, is very much about bringing things back to bodies, to materiality, no doubt, a materiality which is at base simply spirit in any case, yet one in which a lingering materiality as third-person object makes both interaction and multiplicity possible. What the subtle body does for Abhinavagupta is to allow this perspectival awareness to register the multiplicity that makes up the world. In relation to what the subtle body (*puryaṣṭaka*) does, he tells us,

> [I]n the state of that type of I-consciousness, which belongs to the Lord ignorance is entirely removed. So the notion, "this is blue," does not arise. Here that sort of lower I-consciousness needs to be developed which will not be so spotless and rarefied as to entirely remove the knowledge of object as other.[19]

In order to relate to others we need something different than the highest awareness of non-duality; rather, we need a lower sort of awareness. What the subtle body does is to afford us this lower awareness that makes it possible to differentiate others.[20] The subtle body is sufficiently enmeshed in the multiplicity of the world to register a difference between itself and another; it allows a person to notice some object nearby and to understand it as different from one's own self, to be able to interact with a blue something as outside of one's self, even if a truer gaze knows that its blue difference from me is merely provisional.

Abhinavagupta's conception of the subtle body

Abhinavagupta's conception of the subtle body is that it is simply consciousness, but consciousness which has become limited, contracted. He tells us:

> the inherent nature of this person is that of pure consciousness which has become contracted into the subtle body, the City of Eight in the state of Emptiness, and has acquired the habit of wandering from body to body, life after life.[21]

The term he uses here for the subtle body in accordance with his Tantric lineage is *puryaṣṭaka*, literally, the "City of Eight." We notice right away with the nomenclature that he uses, "City of Eight," that already the idea of the subtle body entails a plurality. Earlier we see "sūkṣma śarīra," literally, "subtle body," but here the very name of the subtle body references its inherent multiplicity. In any case, the subtle body, as the City of Eight, arises as a contraction of awareness, one that hinges upon deeper latent traces of a sense of limitation. Abhinavagupta describes this limitation in terms evocative of subconscious impulses that override what the conscious mind might say. He tells us:

> So, thinking, I am "equal to *Rudra*, etc.," and "I am that" [*Brahman*, Absolute] is fine, but to the extent that the latent residual impressions remain fully operative, it is reasonable that pride and anger, etc., will still arise. Consciousness, which here possesses latent traces, herself creates limitation. Consciousness is one alone, yet has a specific form where it consists of sound [form, taste] etc. which flow down and are absorbed, and from this the City of Eight is separated off from full consciousness.[22]

Even if we might tell ourselves we are the pure highest awareness of divinity, the "I am that" of the Upaniṣads,[23] nevertheless, so long as deeper impressions of limitation remain latent in ourselves, anger and pride will still pop up against our will. His description explains with a psychological lucidity how his monism can incorporate a conception of a subtle body that is limited. Not full consciousness, the subtle body instead offers a sense of self as limited and differentiated from other selves.

The subtle body also in his context is connected to the idea of Emptiness, the familiar Buddhist term of *śūnya*, which, for Abhinavagupta's context, is understood as a kind of grounding space out of which the materiality of the world arises. Delineating the relationship that the subtle body bears to Emptiness, *śūnya*, Abhinavagupta says,

> when "I-ness" is placed within Emptiness, it exists and is called the City of Eight. … To which they say: "The subtle body is also present in the state of meditative absorption in that particular deep meditation (*samādhi*) which is a merger into Emptiness." "I-ness" placed in Emptiness is the impeller, the one which agitates the five vital breaths and that "I-ness" takes the form of the function of the senses and it takes as its essence the City of Eight.[24]

Abhinavagupta understands a stance of subjectivity, "I-ness" (*ahantā*), as key to enlivening the breath to take on its form as the subtle body, which wanders from body to body, life after life. The subtle body remains present even in a deep meditative state. So rather than the erasure of a sense of a subtle body in a state of Emptiness, for Abhinavagupta, there is instead a close linkage between the subtle body and Emptiness.

The subtle body is also connected with the operations of bodily functions like smell, sight, and the breath, *prāṇa*. The flow of *prāṇa*, breath, includes both a physical element and simultaneously a non-physical energetic component. This doubly configured understanding of breath, *prāṇa*, as both material and subtle contributes to make up the subtle body. Abhinavagupta tells us that the subtle body, this

> City of Eight here includes the five vital breaths plus the two groups of sense organs [organs of knowledge (*buddhīndriya*) and organs of action (*karmendriya*)]. By accepting the inner organs as one essential capacity to ascertain things, we have the third.[25]

So the five vital breaths plus the two groups of sense organs make seven. The first group, the sense organs, includes the five senses: the capacity to hear, see, feel, taste, and smell. The second group, the five *karmendriya*, is connected to physical components of the body detailed in terms of function. They include the feet as the capacity to move, the hands as the capacity to grasp, the anus as the capacity to excrete, the genitals as the capacity to reproduce, and the mouth as the capacity for speech. The eighth component is the inner organ (*antaḥkaraṇa*), which includes lumped together the mind, intellect, and ego. This thus gives us a picture of the subtle body, first, as made of the breaths (*prāṇa*). Additionally, the subtle body has the capacity to see and hear, the capacity to grasp and speak, and also a capacity to think. This conception of the transmigrating subtle body with its powers to grasp and move looks like a bit more than a simple ghost, a transmigrating spirit that occasionally appears to the people left behind, and instead rather looks to have the powers of a poltergeist, grasping and speaking.

Explicating the subtle body in more detail, Abhinavagupta tells us that "this City of Eight is an extremely subtle body"[26] and at the same time, it is

> like the physical body, but does not have limitations in terms of its spatial dimensions. However, that [subtle body] is linked to time as a universal. … The City of Eight does in fact have the nature of a body, because the great elements [fire, earth etc.] inhere in it. Also, here, in order to remove delusion, he uses the word "body" precisely to preempt the objection that the word "body" [with its physical implications] should not be applied here.[27]

So the subtle body is like a physical body, but it does not have the same spatial limitations. It is connected to time as a universal, so it exists in time, but appears less constrained than the ordinary physical body.

Even so, Abhinavagupta tells us that its rarefied condition should not be construed to mean that this subtle body does not partake of the materiality associated with bodies. Rather, he emphasizes that the subtle body does indeed have the nature of a body. Still, as a body, it is not the same as the ordinary human physical body or other material objects.

Describing the subtle body in its confluence with Emptiness, Abhinavagupta says,

> these two, Emptiness and the City of Eight do have the nature of being an object. However, still there is a difference between these two and pots etc., because there is no association with the ability to produce pleasure and pain, since they lack contact with an external body. "Hence, in this way" he says, indicating that because of this difference, consequently they [physical bodies and pots] should not be considered [the same as] these two [Emptiness and the City of Eight].[28]

The subtle body is a body, yet not quite like the tangible familiar forms of matter, like clay pots, because the subtle body is subtle, not like familiar material objects we can touch, like pots and jars, or inert things we can manipulate. The picture we get of the subtle body is as a kind of quasi-materiality that includes a capacity for thought and even a capacity to move and grasp, along with sensory abilities, that is, a capacity to hear and see. Still, this body lacks the tactile physicality of a clay pot, and that affords it a different status than an ordinary human body.

There is also, however, some variance on what makes up the subtle body for Abhinavagupta's tradition. He notes that:

> some others say that the five subtle elements and the three inner organs are the City of Eight. Yet, because they include the five vital airs in the subtle element touch, the variety of viewpoints here turns out in reality to be no variety at all.[29]

That is, the idea of the five vital breaths is already included in a different version of what makes up the subtle body, so Abhinavagupta tells us that however the eight is configured, the five vital breaths are still included.[30]

The five breaths (*prāṇa*) carry links to various states of being. These are *prāṇa, apāna, samāna, udāna*, and *vyāna*. The *prāṇa* is the out-breath and is associated with the daytime and the waking state. The *apāna* is connected to nighttime, inwardness, and dreaming. Curiously, Abhinavagupta appears to reverse the understanding of *prāṇa* and *apāna* that one finds typically in contemporary discussions of the breath in yoga practices, where *prāṇa* indicates the in-breath. For Abhinavagupta, in contrast, *prāṇa* points to the out-breath, since it is the breath which causes the external world to appear, while the *apāna* points to the in-breath, because it signals the person going inward and resting in the self.[31] The equalizing breath, the *samāna,* is associated with deep sleep and also with states where one falls in a drunken stupor or a coma, or is chemically poisoned or is in a meditative awareness,[32] while the up-breath, *udāna,* is connected to an experience of transcendence.[33] Vyāna, the all-pervasive breath, is connected to an understanding of the self to be the totality.[34]

We can begin to see that the idea of the subtle body melds together elements of affect, various states of mind, with this, indirectly, emotions, cognitive deliberation, all then connected to bodily flows and autonomic processes involved in sleep and bodily processes. The subtle body maps these flows of breath and mind and senses. In this way, wrapped in and through the physical body is a subtle body delineated by the movements of energy flows and functions; this model of body supplies the cakras, the subtle body centers, vortexes, which have become popular in the New Age West.

These subtle body centers link places in the body to mental and emotional functions. Abhinavagupta tells us the heart is connected to the function of creation and linked to memory and dreams, since these are also creative acts, while the subtle body cakra in the throat is connected to keeping alive in awareness the forms around us, and is connected to the waking state and things that are perceived as common to a variety of viewers.[35] These functions are not simply mechanical operations of an insentient body, however, but are expressions of an ever-present dense network of deities residing in various centers in this body, with the god Brahmā in the heart and the god Viṣṇu in the throat, linking the human with a plethora of other beings, all sharing the space of the human body.

The gods in the body

As a number of scholars have noted, the subtle body historically for India is not patterned on the organs of the physical body. Dominik Wujastyk points out that "the Tantric body is yet another example of a non-anatomical body,"[36] and Gavin Flood offers an insightful analysis of the Tantric body as an overlay of a textual scriptural tradition.[37] This understanding of the human body as interlinked with a non-physical yet still somewhat material subtle body has a deep ancestry harkening back to Vedic antecedents invoking various deities in the body. The *Taittirīya Brāhmaṇa*, in its "easy invocation"[38] of various gods in the human body, describes it:

> Let Agni, the god of fire reside in my speech. Speech is in the heart. The heart is in me. I am in immortality. Immortality is in the sacred verbal formula. Let Vayu, the god of wind reside in my breath. The breath is in the heart. The heart is in me. I am in immortality. Immortality is in the sacred verbal formula. Let the Sun god reside in my eye. The eye is in the heart. The heart is in me. I am in immortality. Immortality is in the sacred verbal formula.[39]

The text continues to assign different gods to dwell in different parts of the body, yet in this early formulation, not all of the components assigned to the body seem to be gods. For instance, the text invokes strength for the arms (*bala*), herbs, and trees residing in one's hair (*oṣadhivanaspati*). These elements do not ever quite take on the deification that we see happening for Agni as the god of fire, Surya as the sun god, or Vayu as the god of wind. Nevertheless, this early instance of reflecting the macrocosm in the microcosm points toward a deification of the various things that a human body can do, such as speech, seeing, hearing, as well as having strength (*bala*) and a fiery personality (*manyu*), even as we also see what makes up the body, with earth (*pṛthivī*) as the element that makes for the material-body quality of a body (*śarīra*) and space residing in the ears. This pastiche of categorically dissimilar components linking the human body to the cosmos sets a template that echoes in later formulations of the subtle body as comprised of deities.[40]

With Abhinavagupta's Tantric articulation of the body in the eleventh century, we find the body parceled out into a framework of various deities governing its functions.[41] In Abhinavagupta's *Dehasthadevatācakrastotram (Hymn of the Gods Located in the Body)*, he praises a series of deities in the body, each associated with some aspect of human functioning. Beginning with Gaṇeśa, the elephant-headed god, always first to be praised, Abhinavagupta sings, "I praise Gaṇapati, who is the *prāṇa*, the breath in the body, worshipped first in a hundred different philosophies, who delights in giving what one desires, adored by multitudes of gods and demons."[42] From Gaṇeśa, he goes on to praise a variety of other gods, the god Vaṭuka as the *apāna*, the down-breath in the body,[43] the god Ānandabhairava, a blissful form of the god Śiva, in the center of the heart, and the goddess Ānandabhairavī as the form of awareness (*vimarśa*) that makes the body sentient. The intellect (*buddhi*) is instantiated by the goddess Brahmaṇī, ego (*ahaṁkāra*) by the goddess Śāṁbhavī, and the mind (*manas*) by the goddess Kaumarī. He proceeds to then assign goddesses to the five senses, from Vaiṣṇavī as the goddess who hears our sounds to, Lakṣmī who is the power in humans that smells. The components of the body that he outlines with this hymn loosely correspond to the elements that make up the subtle body.[44] Abhinavagupta notes how each of these functions of the human body, including the breath, the mental faculties of the mind, ego, and intellect, collectively known as the inner organ (*antaḥkaraṇa*), along with the five sensory capacities, works through the power of deities who embody these functions. With this he effectively delegates the capacities we humans have to smell, think, and breathe to a multiplicity of sentient others, beings who are gods making possible the variety of things a human body accomplishes. The body, which is the material instantiation of human living, is fundamentally a plurality of subjectivities. The plurality we find for the subtle body is not surprising, since, after all, as we saw earlier, the subtle body is all about making a space for difference, for a multiplicity of others. It is what makes it possible to experience objects like a blue something different from one's self.

What makes this idea of the body as a plurality of agencies different from a Western biological conception of the body driven by genetic predispositions, by the pull of the biome, by a biology barely or not at all conscious is that Abhinavagupta's multiple agencies retain their own conscious intentions. These gods in the body have their own subjectivities. On the one hand, like Sapolsky's model which sees biology driving human choices rather than a governing human person making choices, here also, the idea of an individual person's human will as the force directing the body is abandoned. On the other hand, instead of impersonal forces, like neuronal dopamine or even the manipulations of Toxoplasma gondii as the forces driving human behavior, here gods direct the body. Lakṣmī, the traditional goddess of wealth, does the smelling that the body performs; Indrāṇī is the force that sees; Śāṁbhavī directs the choice to drive fast or slow; and so on. Abhinavagupta's theological shift adds an element of subjectivity, conscious intentionality to the various agencies directing the body.

Abhinavagupta offers also a different map of gods directing the functions in the body than the one we find in the *Dehasthadevatācakrastotram*. In his philosophical opus, the *Īśvara Pratyabhijñā Vivṛti Vimarśinī*, he talks about the various gods in the body as a ladder leading up to the highest awareness. Referencing particular points in the body as energy centers, focally potent places in the body, Abhinavagupta tells us:

> In this way, the god *Brahmā* is in the heart; *Viṣṇu* is in the throat; *Rudra* is in the palate. *Īśvara*, the Lord, is in the space between the eyebrows. *Sadāśiva* is upward in the cranial opening at the soft spot on the top of the skull, and *Śakti*, the divine feminine Energy, has the nature of being in no particular abode. These are all the supreme reality in a six-fold body. The six forms serve as a cause making a ladder in the human body up to the level which is the supreme reality. [Utpaladeva] explains these forms designated by the scriptural texts as the inherent essential nature of each of these places, the heart and so on.[45]

The physical body is the abode of gods, and what happens on the subtle level, in this case on the level of particular deities, is replicated in this mundane lump of flesh as the material instantiation of particular energies. Thus, the creator god *Brahmā* is located in the heart, because the heart is understood as the place in the body where we create ideas, while Rudra is in the palate, because the palate represents the space where speech dissolves upward into silence. The essential nature of these places in the body, the heart, and so on is the functions ascribed to particular deities. These gods make a ladder, both physically and metaphysically in the body, lining up the energies, intentions, and affective impulses of various gods along the spine, in the familiar model of the cakra system, which Abhinavagupta references. This macrocosm-microcosm linkage between the human body and the greater world around us is not a new idea for Abhinavagupta; we saw it also in the Vedic "easy invocation" where the trees and herbs are understood as the hair of the human person, and where the god of fire, Agni, is invoked to reside in human speech.

In this way, Abhinavagupta offers deities as representations of particular affective and sensory bodily functions, here and as we saw earlier, in the *Dehasthadevatācakrastotram* where, for instance, our familiar experience of smell is the goddess of wealth offering fragrant flowers. With this he points to a radically different model of what it means to inhabit a human body than our routine, implicitly dualist, assumption that the body is a mere inert lump of flesh to manipulate, as simply the "house" for what is actually real, our consciousness, or soul.

Along these lines, as I noted earlier, I suspect that what is important about the understanding of the subtle body as made of deities is less its precise theological orientation of the body, an idea of this god or that god in this or that part of the body, and rather more the accompanying suggestion that various agencies, with their own separate intentionalities, direct human choices. The *Dehasthadevatācakrastotram* tells us that the god Ānandabhairava resides in the heart, while the *Īśvara Pratyabhijñā Vivṛti Vimarśinī* places the creator god Brahmā in the heart. That Abhinavagupta offers different maps for the gods in the body suggests his own understanding of the subtle body concentrates less on which deity controls which part of human behavior, and more on the map itself as a displacement of human control, a recognition of the human as embedded in a topology of multiple agencies.

The idea of deities within the body suggests that there is not a simple "soul" or "mind" of the person directing the body as inert object. Rather the notion of deity signals intentionality and awareness that supersedes the mind. The body's various parts, sensory capacities, and functions follow the directive of the residing deity. The god Brahmā in the heart, ruling over the creative life of dreams, causes dreams when we sleep that we do not control. Not fundamentally directed by the person or the person's mind or will, this conception of deity references intentionality within a schematic of sensory appreciation and desires. The idea of deity gets at the types of affective bodily processing that bypass the mind's chatter—the involuntary crinkling of the nose in the face of a nasty smell, or the body's hair rising at an unexpected scary turn in the movie. Abhinavagupta's use of the concept of deity allows for intentionality and the autonomy of the body's affective experiences in ways that can be expressed as different, sometimes contradictory, to the storyline that the mind repeats to itself about the self. Thus, in this Indian conception, the story the mind tells itself is the function of two components, the *manas*, mind chatter, and *ahaṁkāra*, the ego. What these Indian texts consider as the ego and the mind map nicely to what cognitive scientists like Merlin Donald,[46] George Lakoff, and Marc Johnson[47] point to as the cognitive executive function of the mind. Operating alongside these two, but with different trajectories, we find other, different intentional and autonomous affective processes of the body, the memory of smells, as Proust so eloquently demonstrated, the heightened mood of a meditative state. Their separate, rich life is highlighted by not reducing these functions to mechanical bodily processes, but affording them instead the sentiency of deity.

Brian Massumi also references this disjunct between what our minds say and the richness of our body's contradictory expressions in his seminal article, "The Autonomy of Affect."[48] He notes that our conscious expressions arise by dint of inhibition and he calls for a deeper examination of this multiple richness in the affects of the body. Massumi proposes that we understand this rich and contradictory expression of affect as a kind of virtual reality. Abhinavagupta instead reads the multiple registers of affect in the body as a theology. This theology of the body demonstrates affective states as a variety of deities. They inculcate a sense of multiple agencies, with intentionalities that are not always congruent with each other, or with the ego and mind.

In a sense, we might say that theology here registers a kind of respect for the affective processes of the body. Locating gods in the body is a way of acknowledging that not all in this human body is under the sway of that seeming uniquely human crowning glory of discursive mental thought that we call the mind. Sentiency, will, and desire pop up all over the body, not just as handmaidens of the mind. This theology of the body, moreover, proposes these multiple affective registers in a way that does not dwell, to either lament or rejoice, on the subsequent disappointment and loss of the sovereignty of the ego and its free will. So while Massumi strives to find a model to understand the complex, refractory affective flows of the body in a language of the virtual, Abhinavagupta instead reads this complexity of multiple affective flows through a lens of forces of deities with their own conscious trajectories. In this respect, this panentheist theology affords a foundational liveliness to the multiplicity of agencies that make up the body, here referenced in Abhinavagupta's map of the subtle body, which sees the body itself as an ecology of beings, materially embedded.

Conclusion

By way of conclusion, I will offer what I see as Abhinavagupta's response to a particular complication that follows from the idea of a multiplicity of deities directing human choices. How is it that these multiple agents, gods in the body, do not makes us into schizophrenic multiplicities, a self splintered into a profusion of voices and intentions? In terms of the biology from a Western perspective, we do already find something like a jungle of desires and intentions. Antonio Damasio tells us that we are made up of a multitude of cells, each undergoing its own encounters of birth, development, and death. Damasio says that individual cells also have things like desire and will, that is the desire to stay alive. Even as he notes that it is odd to think of cells having desire the way we have desire, nevertheless, he tells us, that this is still the case.[49] Similarly, Patrick McNamara suggests that a disunity of self goes all the way down to our genes, drawing from Haig's genetic research indicating that even for the fetus in the womb, maternal and paternal genes have opposing operations, with clashing drives, and they consequently compete for expression.[50] Tim Morton, looking to Lynn Margulis' work on endosymbiosis, points out that a host of life forms already live within us. Even a basic component of our cell structure, the mitochondria, is a relic symbiont, an other living entity with its own intentions, merging with our cell structure.[51]

Abhinavagupta, on the other hand, does not leave us with a fragmented multiplicity of vying agencies. Rather, the unity of the self arises in the midst of the multiplicity that is the subtle body with its accompanying deities, simply through reclaiming subjectivity, through embracing the first-person perspective. It is precisely the stance of subjectivity, "I-ness" (*ahantā*), which assimilates the multiplicity of the body with its various pulls. In laying out a possible argument against his conception of the subtle body, he says:

> One may object here—of course it is possible to declare the City of Eight as the manifestation of the Self since the City of Eight has this capacity to remain unseen in the normal way that we see a pot etc. But why is there the unnecessary addition of the "I" following from this imposed onto the City of Eight? [Utpaladeva] expresses this idea saying, "in the belief, the concept of 'I"'. To this objection [Utpaladeva] replies, "belonging to it, the 'I' alone." The word "alone" indicates that the "I" which appears to be an extraneous addition should be accepted as necessary to the City of Eight. In the absence of the perception of the "I," in fact, these attributes, [the subtle body etc.,] are accompanied by pure unadulterated ignorance. If the host of entities and things, blue etc., are not seen as belonging to the Self, then they would not have the capacity to manifest, but they do appear.[52]

The "I" (*aham*), the sense of subjectivity, is not an extraneous addition to the subtle body. The subtle body is instead the attribute of subjectivity. As we saw earlier, the subtle body arises through the contraction of pure consciousness. This consciousness is the sense of "I," the *ahantā*, "I-ness." This sense of "I-ness" enlivens the subtle body; with this it is what unifies the multiplicity of gods directing the body.

This host of gods in the body, that Abhinavagupta describes as a ladder, as we saw earlier, function to bring just this awareness to the person, that the self is not different from the highest God. Indeed, following on his description of the gods in the body that we saw above,

Abhinavagupta, quoting a line from the grammarian Bhartṛhari, tells us that this self, in the end, is itself the multiplicity of what exists, consisting of everything. All the gods in the body exist in this self; this self experiences everything:

> Dividing the Self by the Self, having created entities of different types, he places them separately; the lord of all, consisting of all, is the enjoyer, the experiencer in dreams, who sets things in motion.[53]

Notes

1 My translation draws from and modifies Olivelle's translation, Patrick Olivelle, trans., *Upaniṣads* (New York: Oxford University Press, 1996).

2 Richard Dawkins, *River Out of Eden: A Darwinian View of Life*, Reprint (New York: Basic Books, 1996).

3 Kathleen McAuliffe, *This Is Your Brain on Parasites* (Boston, MA: Mariner Books, Houghton Miflin Harcourt, 2016).

4 Emese Prandovsky, et al., "The Neurotropic Parasite Toxoplasma Gondii Increases Dopamine Metabolism," *PLoS One* 6, no. 9 (September 21, 2011): e23866, https://doi.org/10.1371/journal.pone.0023866.

5 McAuliffe, *Brain on Parasites*, 63. Sapolsky notes 3–4 times more likely in his interview with Edge TV, Robert Sapolsky, "Interview: Toxoplasmosis," *Edge TV*, accessed August 25, 2018, https://www.youtube.com/watch?v=m3x3TMdkGdQ.

6 McAuliffe, *Brain on Parasites*, 75.

7 What I will not do here is articulate for this context of the subtle body, the helpful and well-trod understanding of construction of a self through its engagement with an external social world. Much has been written about how identity, agency, and desires are enacted via the social world we inhabit, through advertising (I'm thinking of Pierre Bourdieu's work particularly, though much else is certainly available), through cultural expectations of gender (I think of Judith Butler here), and through our understandings of self in relation to others as a kind of inter-being with others (I think of Catherine Keller's brilliant work here). This understanding has also been followed in relation to ideas of the subtle body (I'm thinking of Gavin Flood, *The Tantric Body*: The Secret Tradition of Hindu Religion. New York: I.B. Tauris, 2006).

8 Here Freud's assumption of a Darwinian model which translates Darwin's deterministic drives into Freud's conception of id points to an underlying Western monothesim, *id* as singular source of human drives biological, psychological drives. In contrast, this conception of the subtle body replaces this monochromatic view with an expansive multiplicity.

9 See Fred Smith's excellent and expansive treatment of the various spirits that possess humans, for instance, p. 194, in Frederick Smith, *Self Possessed: Deity and Spirit Possession in South Asian Literature and Civilization* (New York: Columbia University Press, 2006).

10 Robert Sapolsky, *Stanford Biology Lectures #25*, 2010, https://www.youtube.com/watch?v=-PpDq1WUtAw&index=25&list=PL150326949691B199, beginning 3:09 minutes, especially 5:34 minutes, 25:38 minutes. Also, Robert Sapolsky, Sapolsky on Free Will, August 2018, https://www.youtube.com/watch?v=ihhVe8dKNSA, beginning 0:40 minutes.

11 We will look at the differences in these models below.

12 See Alexis Sanderson's seminal article on this nomenclature, Alexis Sanderson, "World's Religions," in *Śaivism and the Tantric Traditions*, ed. Stewart Sutherland, et al. (London: Routledge, 1988), 660–704.

13 See Geoffrey Samuel, "Subtle-Body Processes: Towards a Non-Redutionist Understanding," in *Religion and the Subtle Body in Asia and the West: Between Mind and Body*, eds. Geoffrey Samuel and Jay Johnston (Johnston. New York: Routledge, 2013), 249–266, Jay Johnston, "Subtle Subjects and Ethics: The Subtle Bodies of Post-Structuralist and Feminist Philosophy," in *Religion and the Subtle Body in Asia and the West: Between Mind and Body*, eds. Jay Johnston and Geoffrey Samuel (New York: Routledge, 2013), 239–248, also, Dory Heilijgers-Seelen, *The System of Five Cakras in Kubjikamatatantra 14-16: A Study and Annotated Translation* (Leiden: Brill, 1994).

14 Abhinavagupta, *Īśvara Pratyabhijñā Vivṛti Vimarśinī*, 3 vols. (Delhi: Akay Reprints, 1985), (hereafter Ipvv) vol. 3: 257: "*Tad eva ca sarvabhāvānām pāramārthikam vapuḥ.*" The "*tad*" here refers to the "*tat*" in the verse a few lines earlier on which Abhinavagupta comments, referencing "*matur,*" "belonging to the subject." That is, the subject who is conscious, since as Abhinavagupta notes immediately in his commentary, that the causality we find in the world cannot be attributed to insentient objects, but only to consciousness: "*jaḍe pratiṣṭhitaḥ kārya kāraṇa bhāvo na upapadyate, api tu cidrūpa eva.*"

15 Ipvv vol. 3: 257: *Tad bhitta pṛṣṭhe ca sarva bhāva citra nirbhāsa iti.*

16 Ipvv vol. 3: 257: *śivatattvaṃ hi sarva padārthānām vapuḥ.*

17 Abhinavagupta, "*Parātriṃśikāvivaraṇa*" (Goettingen Register of Electronic Texts in Indian Languages), 212: "*narātmāno jaḍā api tyaktatatpūrvarūpāḥ śāktaśaivarūpabhājo bhavanti, śṛṇuta grāvāṇaḥ* [\cf *Mahābhāṣya* 3.1.1; \cf *Vākyapadīya* 3 *Puruṣasamuddeśa* 2], *meruḥ śikhariṇām ahaṃ bhavāmi* [*Bhagavadgītā* 10.23]," accessed November 8, 2016, http://gretil.sub.uni-goettingen.de/gretil/1_sanskr/6_sastra/3_phil/saiva/partrvau.htm.

18 We see this idea in the Bṛhadaraṇyaka Upaniṣad, Śaṅkara and Bṛhadaraṇyaka, *Bṛhadaraṇyaka Upaniṣad with Śaṅkara's commentary*, Kanva recension with the commentary ascribed to Śaṅkara, n.d., v. 4.4.4, http://gretil.sub.uni-goettingen.de/gret_utf.htm#BrhUp, where the dead person takes on a better body, that of a celestial being (gandharva, pitṛ), just as a goldsmith takes a piece of gold and molds it into a more beautiful shape. Here, like Abhinavagupta, however, we still keep an idea of the body.

19 Ipvv vol. 3: 282: *Tena aham bhāvena ajñatā sarvathaiva tirodhīyate iti punar api nīlam idam iti na prarohet. Tatas tādṛgaparo >ham bhāvo >tra niṣektavyo yas tatra jñatāṃ nirmalatayātiraskartuṃ na śaktaḥ.*

20 Note that Torella points to Utpaladeva's conception of two types of self-awareness (*aham pratyavamarśa*), a pure one related to ascertainment of I as pure consciousness creating the field, and an impure one that relates the I to its manifestation as object, as subtle body (*puryaṣṭaka*) as prāṇa or breath, and as the body (*deha*) in Raffaele Torella's, *Īśvarapratyabhijñākārikā of Utpaladeva with the Author's Vṛtti: Critical Edition and Annotated Translation* (Delhi: Motilal Banarsidass, 2002), 132, v.1.6.4.

21 Ipvv, vol. 3: 310: *śūnyapuryaṣṭakasaṃkucitasaṃvitsvabhāvaḥ, saṃsaraṇaśilaḥ.*

22 Ipvv, vol. 3: 286–287: "*Rudrādes tulanam*" *ity ādau ca* "*so >ham*" *iti tāvat saṃskārapūrṇa eva aham iti parāmarśāt garvakopādyudayā yuktāḥ. Svakṛtasaṃkocasaṃskāravatī yā cit, tanmayatayā pralīnam apasāritaśabdādirūpa viśeṣam ekam iti puryaṣṭakāntarāder bhinnam.*

23 Taken from the Iśa Upaniṣad, verse 16, Olivelle, *Upaniṣads*, 80–81.

24 Ipvv, vol. 3: 335–336: śūnyāhantām ākṣipya vartamānaḥ puryaṣṭakaḥ iti uktaḥ... Yad āhuḥ 'līnaśūnyasamādhāvapyāste liṅgaśarīraḥ |' iti. "Tathā ca" iti yata evaṃ, tata evaṃ yojanā sā śūnye 'hantā prāṇādiprerikā akṣavṛttirūpā puryaṣṭakātmiketi.

25 Ipvv, vol. 3: 334: *Ubhayor api ca ayaṃ yonyantarasañcārī puryaṣṭakaśabdavācyo yato 'tra prāṇādipañcakam indriyavargau dvau niścayātmikā ca tṛtīyā svīkṛtāntaḥkaraṇāntarā dhīrvyajyate.*

26 Ipvv, vol. 3: 306: "*puryaṣṭakātmatātyantasūkṣmadeha eva vā.*" In the text he is quoting Utpaladeva's commentary, and he links the subtle body here, as we saw earlier, to Emptiness.

27 Ipvv, vol. 3: 306: *kālaviśeṣeṇa ca śarīrivat niyatena pārimityabhājā yo 'vacchedas tadrahitaḥ; sāmānyakālayogas tu tasya api asty eva... Puryaṣṭakasya dehatā asty eva mahābhūtaiḥ samanvayād iti tad api iha na vacanīyam iti mohavyapohanāya śaṅkodbhāvanārthaṃ dehagrahaṇam.*

28 Ipvv, vol. 3: 307: *tayor astu prameyatā, tābhyāṃ tu anyat pramīyate ghaṭādi bāhyaśarīreṇa asamparke bhogasaṃpādakatvāyogāt. "Ata eva" iti yato 'nyat na pramīyate tābhyāṃ, tataḥ.*

29 Ipvv, vol. 3: 336: *Yatas tanmātrapañcakamantaḥkaraṇaṃ ceti kecana puryaṣṭakam āhuḥ sparśatanmātreṇa prāṇādisvīkārāt, tata eva atra pakṣavaicitrye vastuno na vaicitryam iti.*

30 It is not exactly clear who these "others" are that Abhinavagupta refers to here, and for Abhinavagupta's perspective, this alternative notion of the subtle body as made of the subtle elements rather than the five breaths, does not substantially alter the involvement of breath as key to the subtle body.

31 Quoting Utpaladeva he tells us, "in the creation of objects the expansion and unfoldment of the objective world belongs to the *prāṇa*, while the dissolution of the world is a process belonging to the subject alone." Ipvv, vol. 3: 344: "*arthānāṃ sarge 'pi asau prāṇasya pravṛttiḥ pramātuḥ pralaya eva.* Lakṣmanjoo also notes this reversal of function for *prāṇa* and *apāna*." This reversal is in keeping with Olivelle's translation of the Upaniṣad, where he also translates *prāṇa* as out-breath, Olivelle, *Upaniṣads*, 100.

32 Ipvv, vol. 3: 337.

33 Ipvv, vol. 3: 335–336.

34 Ipvv, vol. 3: 349.

35 Ipvv, vol. 3: 309.

36 Dominic Wujastyk, "Interpreting the Image of the Human Body in Premodern India," *International Journal of Hindu Studies* 13, no. 2 (2009): 200.

37 Gavin Flood, *Tantric Body: The Secret Tradition of HIndu Religion* (New York: I.B. Tauris, 2006), 13.

38 My translation of the well-known name for this portion of the text called *laghu nyāsa*.

39 Subramania Sarma, ed., *Taittirīya Brāhmaṇa Yajurveda: Krishna Yajurveda Works of the Taittiriya Shaka.*, 2018, vv. 3.10.4-3.10.9, http://www.sanskritweb.net/yajurveda/, 3.10.4-3.10.9: *Agnir me vāci śritaḥ| Vāghṛdaye| Hṛdayaṃ mayi| Ahamamṛte| Amṛtaṃ brahmaṇi||* My translation of this basic formula which substitutes a different deity for each verse.

40 We also see hints of this in Śaṅkara's depiction of the five sensory functions like smell and so on collecting in the subtle body, even as Śaṅkara's adherence to his non-dualism tends toward precluding a sensibility of various deities.

41 Gavin Flood points out that Tantric conceptions of the body rely on a notion of an emanationist cosmology which is implicitly and often explicitly pluralistic in Flood, *Tantric Body*, 29.

42 Abhinavagupta, "Dehasthadevatācakrastrotram," v. 1, accessed September 22, 2018, http://www.abhinavagupta.net/hymns/track-5-dehasta-devata-cakra-strotra/. See also Gavin Flood, *Body and Cosmology in Kashmir Śaivism* (San Francisco, CA: Mellen Research University Press, 1993), 305–308. My translation alters these two only slightly.

43 In Abhinavagupta's case, this would be understood as the in-breath (contrary to what we see in current popular yogic understandings).

44 There is not an exact correspondence. The subtle body, for instance, is comprised of the five breaths, whereas in this hymn, Abhinavagupta only mentions the prāṇa and apāna breaths.
45 Ipvv, vol. 3: 309: *Tata eva brahmahṛdayo viṣṇukaṇṭho rudratālur Īśvarabhrūmadhyāḥ Sadāśivoudhvabrahmarandhro 'nāśritātmakaśaktisopānoparipadaḥ kāraṇaṣaṭkavigrahaḥ parameśvaraḥ iti hṛdayādisvarūpābhidhānena sūcita āgamiko 'rthaḥ.*
46 Merlin Donald, *Mind So Rare: The Evolution of Human Consciousness* (New York: W. W. Norton & Company, 2002).
47 George Lakoff and Marc Johnson, *Philosophy in the Flesh* (New York: Basic Books, 1999).
48 Brian Massumi, "The Autonomy of Affect," *Cultural Critique*, no. 31 (1995): 83–109, https://doi.org/10.2307/1354446.
49 Antonio Damasio, *Self Comes to Mind: Constructing the Conscious Brain* (New York: Pantheon, 2010), 37.
50 Patrick McNamara, *Neuroscience of Religious Experience* (New York: Cambridge University Press, 2014), 37.
51 Timothy Morton, *Hyperobjects: Philosophy and Ecology after the End of the World* (Minneapolis: University of Minnesota Press, 2013), 139.
52 Ipvv, vol. 3: 281: *Nanu adarśanayogyaṃ puryaṣṭakādi prakāśamānatayā nāma saṃbhāvyatāṃ ghaṭādivadeva, tasya tu kim ahaṃ pratītyā adhikayā yena uktaṃ "pratītau" iti. Āha "tasyaiva" iti. "Kevalam" iti iyadadhikamavaśyam aṅgīkāryam. Ahaṃ pratītyabhāve hi sa eva "śuddhājñatvasahita" iti ātmatayāyo na dṛśyate bhāvavargo nīlādiḥ, sa naiva prakāśeta, prakāśate ca asau.*
53 Ipvv, vol. 3: 309: *'pravibhajyātmanātmānaṃ sṛṣṭvā bhāvān pṛthag vidhān |sarveśvaraḥ sarvamayaḥ svapne bhoktā pravartate ||'*. Quote taken from Bhartṛhari, "Vākyapadīya" (Goettingen Register of Electronic Texts in Indian Languages, 1977), v. 1.140, http://gretil.sub.uni-goettingen.de/gretil/1_sanskr/6_sastra/1_gram/vakyp1pu.htm.

Bibliography

Abhinavagupta. "Dehasthadevatācakrastrotram." Accessed September 22, 2018. http://www.abhinavagupta.net/hymns/track-5-dehasta-devata-cakra-strotra/.

———. *Īśvara Pratyabhijñā Vivṛti Vimarśinī*. Vol. 3. 3 vols. Delhi: Akay Reprints, 1985.

———. "Parātriṃśikāvivaraṇa." Goettingen Register of Electronic Texts in Indian Languages. Accessed November 8, 2016. http://gretil.sub.uni-goettingen.de/gretil/1_sanskr/6_sastra/3_phil/saiva/partrvau.htm.

Bhartṛhari. "Vākyapadīya." Goettingen Register of Electronic Texts in Indian Languages, 1977. http://gretil.sub.uni-goettingen.de/gretil/1_sanskr/6_sastra/1_gram/vakyp1pu.htm.

Damasio, Antonio. *Self Comes to Mind: Constructing the Conscious Brain*. New York: Pantheon, 2010.

Dawkins, Richard. *River Out of Eden: A Darwinian View of Life*. Reprint. New York: Basic Books, 1996.

Donald, Merlin. *Mind So Rare: The Evolution of Human Consciousness*. New York: W. W. Norton & Company, 2002.

Flood, Gavin. *Body and Cosmology in Kashmir Śaivism*. San Francisco, CA: Mellen Research University Press, 1993.

———. *Tantric Body: The Secret Tradition of Hindu Religion*. New York: I.B. Tauris, 2006.

Heilijgers-Seelen, Dory. *The System of Five Cakras in Kubjikamatatantra 14–16: A Study and Annotated Translation*. Leiden: Brill, 1994.

Johnston, Jay. "Subtle Subjects and Ethics: The Subtle Bodies of Post-Structuralist and Feminist Philosophy." In *Religion and the Subtle Body in Asia and the West: Between Mind and Body*, edited by Jay Johnston and Geoffrey Samuel, 239–248. New York: Routledge, 2013.

Lakoff, George, and Marc Johnson. *Philosophy in the Flesh*. New York: Basic Books, 1999.

Massumi, Brian. "The Autonomy of Affect." *Cultural Critique*, no. 31 (1995): 83–109. https://doi.org/10.2307/1354446.

McAuliffe, Kathleen. *This Is Your Brain on Parasites*. Boston: Mariner Books, Houghton Miflin Harcourt, 2016.

McNamara, Patrick. *Neuroscience of Religious Experience*. New York: Cambridge University Press, 2014.

Morton, Timothy. *Hyperobjects: Philosophy and Ecology after the End of the World*. Minneapolis: University of Minnesota Press, 2013.

Olivelle, Patrick, trans. *Upaniṣads*. New York: Oxford University Press, 1996.

Prandovsky, Emese, Elizabeth Gaskell, Heather Martin, J.P. Dubey, Joanne P. Webster, and Glenn McConkey. "The Neurotropic Parasite Toxoplasma Gondii Increases Dopamine Metabolism." *PLoS One* 6(9): e23866 (September 21, 2011). https://doi.org/10.1371/journal.pone.0023866.

Samuel, Geoffrey. "Subtle-Body Processes: Towards a Non-Redutionist Understanding." In *Religion and the Subtle Body in Asia and the West: Between Mind and Body*, edited by Geoffrey Samuel and Jay Johnston, 249–266. Johnston. New York: Routledge, 2013.

Sanderson, Alexis. "World's Religions." In *Śaivism and the Tantric Traditions*, edited by Stewart Sutherland, F Hardy, L. Houlden, and P. Clarke, 660–704. London: Routledge, 1988.

Śaṅkara, and Bṛhadaraṇyaka. *Bṛhadaraṇyaka Upaniṣad with Śaṅkara's commentary*. Kanva recension with the commentary ascribed to Śaṅkara. n.d. http://gretil.sub.uni-goettingen.de/gretil/1_sanskr/1_veda/4_upa/brupsb_u.htm

Sapolsky, Robert. "Interview: Toxoplasmosis." *Edge TV*. Accessed August 25, 2018. https://www.youtube.com/watch?v=m3x3TMdkGdQ.

———. Sapolsky on Free Will. August 2018. https://www.youtube.com/watch?v=ihhVe8dKNSA.

———. *Stanford Biology Lectures #25*. 2010. https://www.youtube.com/watch?v=-PpDq1WUtAw&index=25&list=PL150326949691B199.

Sarma, Subramania, ed. *Taittirīya Brāhmaṇa Yajurveda: Krishna Yajurveda Works of the Taittiriya Shaka*. 2018. http://www.sanskritweb.net/yajurveda/.

Smith, Frederick. *Self Possessed: Deity and Spirit Possession in South Asian Literature and Civilization*. New York: Columbia University Press, 2006.

Torella, Raffaele. *Īśvarapratyabhijñākārikā of Utpaladeva with the Author's Vṛtti: Critical Edition and Annotated Translation*. Delhi: Motilal Banarsidass, 2002.

Wujastyk, Dominic. "Interpreting the Image of the Human Body in Premodern India." *International Journal of Hindu Studies* 13, no. 2 (2009): 189–298.

6 Embodied experience in the *Mahārthamañjarī* of Maheśvarānanda

Sthaneshwar Timalsina

Convergence of frameworks

Tantric texts are opaque, and visualizations are bizarre. The esoteric philosophy that supports these practices is perplexing. Initiates are secretive about their practice. In every account, the Tantric world is saturated through and through with misconceptions. My approach in this chapter is to utilize a cognitive theory of body-schema, engage some body-centric visualization practices, and explore the ways to interpret the mechanisms and teleology behind Tantric visualization.[1] In so doing, I am retracing the footsteps of Tantric philosopher Maheśvarānanda because his text *Mahārthamañjarī* (MM), composed around the thirteenth century, is very concise, making it possible to address central tenets of Tantric embodiment in a single chapter by solely relying on this text.

This chapter focuses on the body, mostly the imagined body, which is the body generated through the processes of imagination, and the ways in which the fantasized imagery interacts in transforming somatosensory responses.[2] At this nexus, I find the esoteric world comfortably communicating with cognitive science and phenomenology. My contention here is that remapping the conceptual parameters in framing Tantric philosophy in a new light allows us to bring the body in to discourse. And this body is not the gendered body, not the body confined within the epidermis, but the placeholder of subjectivity, the bodily subject. In this account, I find relevance in establishing communication between Maheśvarānanda and the phenomenologists.

Before entering into the topic, I need to clarify some categories. By body-image, I mean the beliefs regarding one's own body. On the other hand, body-schemas are sensory-motor capacities that regulate somatosensory functions. Body-schemas provide organized models of ourselves, allowing us to use tools to function in our given environment. For the purposes of this discussion, this understanding suffices, that both body-schema and body-image are subject to change but are not biological processes: they are rather the cognitive and sensory negotiations of ourselves with the surroundings. For both mapping our movements in space and localizing stimulation in our body, we are constantly using the schemas, even though alterations to them remain an unconscious process. It is a mental framework, a way of organizing knowledge, a map for us to evaluate the situation and develop a response. Following Piaget, a schema is "a cohesive, repeatable action sequence possessing component actions that are tightly interconnected and governed by a core meaning."[3] Following George Lakoff and Mark Johnson, I introduce "image schema" as a category for the structure of our cognitive process that helps us establish patterns of understanding and reasoning.

Broadly, image schemas are pre-linguistic structures of experience that guide the process of mapping over domains in forming conceptual metaphors. We can have schema for everything, for our own subjective states, for the roles that we play at different times and in different places, for events or functions, for a specific individual or even for collective actions. This framework, following the cognitive scientists, is pre-linguistic and at the basis of human cognitive behavior. Mapping reality inside and out, far and near, tall and short, and extending the metaphors borrowed from up and down, based on our bodily mapping, are all guided by the schema at the background.[4]

Consciousness, for Maheśvarānanda, functions in degree and not in kind. In his paradigm, every entity has the potential to express its embodied nature of consciousness. This thesis contradicts the schema theory, as the premise for the latter is that even the schemas, not just the body, fall under the category that lacks consciousness. For Maheśvarānanda, there is some form of language even in the atomic structure, or in today's language, the genetic structure, as his monistic philosophy rests on the assumption that there is no dichotomy between the corporeal and the mental. Jerry Fodor, in the *Language of Thought Hypothesis*, for instance, maintains that we have a distinctive mental language with which we organize our thoughts and even the basis of thinking. The proponents of this theory have identified propositional attitudes in belief, hope, desire, and so on, and maintain that there is something represented in each and every propositional attitude. This mental representation is a basis for behavioral attitudes that include verbal exchange. Like sentences, token mental representations have syntactic and semantic structure. In other words, these representations are complex symbols that in themselves demand semantic analysis.

Combining this theory with schema theory, we can argue that there is a passive process involved in framing and reframing the schemas which are not unconscious, albeit not actively conscious. This modification allows us to engage graphic visualization processes that aim to interact in human cognitive and behavioral attitudes with the intent to bring about change, not merely altering the subject's beliefs or his subjective assessment, but also his corporeality. Body, in this account, is an extended mind, just as the mind is an extension of the body. This gives a greater fluidity for the interaction between body and mind, and gives subjects greater freedom in formulating each individual's response to stimuli. One of the fundamental premises of Tantric practice is that our bodily experience is elastic and alterable: the way we experience certain things or events is determined in our engagement with the environment or in negotiation with our *saṃskāras*, the habit patterns guided by our past actions. By means of deconstructing and reconstructing these patterns, we can reprogram our habit tendencies as well as our cognitive assessment of the environment. This reprogramming relies heavily on the bodily schema, and the subject's projection of body-image aims toward altering the schema for the desired response.

Tantric strategies of remapping the body first problematize common language while endorsing the semantics for mapping the altered body-image. By language, I mean here the transformed imagery that stands for or substitutes the objectified body and becomes a template for a negotiated interface between the body and the mind. This transformed bodily vision, I argue, allows the subject to reconfigure reality. The enactive approach championed by Francesco Varela, Evan Thompson, and Eleanor Rosch, which maintains that cognition arises through a dynamic interaction between organism and environment, can assist here, as what it maintains is that our organisms are not mere receptors of the world out there, but rather, the environment and organism interact in constructive ways, and what results is not merely an informational but rather transformational interaction.[5]

Body-image and body-schemata can be cognitively engineered, resulting in the breakdown of distinction between the body and what constitutes the mind. Tantric models of what the West has called the body-mind problem, emphasize a mutual and reciprocal creation of body-mind articulation and structure. Yogic practices, particularly visualization focused on altering sensory and motor functions, demonstrate a process wherein the subject can alter his own bodily self. This makes the breach between the body and the flesh, as Merleau-Ponty would have it, possible. Just as the lived body is not identical with the flesh, the visualized body is not the lived body, although it does transform the subject's bodily awareness, paving the path for altering somatosensory experiences. Although Tantric visualization practices are focused on esoteric and liberating experiences, there is no reason this transformation cannot function as a way to generate assertive roles for subjects who feel trapped within their own epidermis.

For Maheśvarānanda, visualization practices are for altering the subject's body-image and body-schemata, thus effecting their transformation. Grounded on his Śākta philosophy nourished by the developments in Trika, Spanda, and other Kashmiri monistic traditions, Maheśvarānanda's project of transforming embodied experience while encapsulating the totality within the lived body is oriented toward cultivating mystical experiences. These mechanisms have the potential to address the plasticity of bodily schema and body-image, allowing subjects to address their own somatic experiences. Maheśvarānanda's project is itself therapeutic, given that he views subjects as trapped within their own subjective horizons, localizing their experiences as confined within the body, giving the subjects a sense of entrapment. For him, visualizations, particularly those focused on altered bodily forms and multiple body-imagery, alter the subject's identification with the body, renegotiate the horizon of consciousness bound within the body, and amplify bodily consciousness to incorporate the totality to eventually transform the subject's assessment about himself and his being in the world. His proposal, if translated into today's language, is that Tantric practice can facilitate a twofold transformation: (1) an overall subversion of the existing body-schemas and body-image, which also includes self-image and self-schemas, and (2) the imposition of a new map to reconfigure bodily response with an intent to redirect somatic interactions and cognitive processes to accommodate a new projected body-image and body-schemata. This process, vividly portrayed in his visualization practices, rests on remapping the reality and altering both the somatic and cognitive self-experiences.

When this thesis is applied to the Tantric philosophy of embodiment, particularly the image body, it becomes clear that Tantras recognize the basic bodily mapping of reality, and practitioners use this premise to advance the argument that we can reprogram our bodily awareness and map our environment with this new body-schemata, thereby enhancing our ability to experience freedom and bliss. In order to extract this thesis from an esoteric text, the MM, we not only need to demystify the language and scope of the text, we also need to shift the parameters in which the text is traditionally read. And one may find this a hermeneutical breach. This, to me, is inevitable, as any attempt to read classical texts involves bridging the temporal gap between the author and the reader, and renegotiating the grounds in which the texts were written and are being read. This, however, does not involve a subversion of the textual thrust which could impose a new sense that we cannot extract by reductively translating the texts the way they are.

Maheśvarānanda does not say his is a project of reconfiguring reality. However, his is a project that stems from the understanding that the given bodily consciousness is extremely narrow and needs to be altered in order to acquire a liberating experience. The deconstruction of the bodily consciousness is not a thesis for him, as this rather is the premise that underlies the transformation of the bodily sense to enclose the totality, to find one's self-presence in the reality extended beyond one's corporeality. Clearly he uses certain concepts as deconstructive in the sense that they interact with the existing schema and nullify their foundation, and as a consequence, he explores the possibility of liberating from the existing framework and replace it with a new structure, with an intent to cultivate a new body-image that envelops all that exists, and a self-image in which there is no inside or outside between the self and the other. I analyze this plasticity of the body and the self, as portrayed by Maheśvarānanda.

Remapping Maheśvarānanda's body schema

Body, for Maheśvarānanda, is suffused with unsurmountable power. The reason why subjects are not capable of accessing this power is because of *saṃskāras*, the habit patterns that control our access to the potential of the body. In other words, if we were to reprogram the schema by means of altering our body-image, we could tap into the forces that constitute the body. Freedom, for Maheśvarānanda, has an inherent embodied character. Maheśvarānanda proclaims:

> If [you] observe, there is so much power in the body of an insect with the size of a sesame seed. How much power would there be of someone with the totality as his body, with him having a self-regulated body. To whatever extent is there the expansion of the Lord in his mode of expressing the world, the same extension is there in the embryonic stage when the world is absorbed within.[6]

Maheśvarānanda has identified three distinctive bodies in this passage. The first is the insect body, the body as a metaphor for triviality. The second is the cosmic body, the totality as the body. And the third is the embryonic body. Insect body is a metaphor that also describes the embryonic body, identical with the body experienced by human subjects. His central argument here is that whether or not the latent energies are expressed, or whether the world is felt outside of the body or encapsulated within, this does not change the fact that bodily experience is elastic and retains even in its most embryonic form the capacity to express itself as the totality. The body-image that Maheśvarānanda advocates is the all-encompassing cosmic body. By establishing identity in a hierarchical order where the individual subject equals the supreme divinity, individual body equals the totality, and the psychosomatic energies equal the totality of the physical forces, Maheśvarānanda explores the possibility of a total awakening, arguing for the surge of awareness wherein bodily sense encapsulates the totality.

By repeatedly identifying that the world is the body-image of the subject, which is the central premise of *bhāvanā* or visualization in his philosophy, Maheśvarānanda aims to alter the subject's self-evaluation, including the body-schemas, in order to transform his convictions regarding his own body. The body, in this altered paradigm, is the divine abode, *deva-gṛha*, with the energies expressed in the body being equated with the cosmic forces. He cites the following passage from the *Parātrīśikā* to further his argument:

> Just as the great tree [is] within the seed of a banyan in the form of latency, this world comprised of both sentient and non-sentient entities is within the heart as if the seed.[7]

The heart, in the aforementioned metaphor, stands both for the corporeal and psychological center: just as the body is an expression of the heart, so also is the world the expression of consciousness. This is the metaphoric embryonic body that the yogin finds himself within as he begins his practice, and the course of visualization evolves with him finding the totality as his own expression or expansion (*prasara*). Further noteworthy is the terminology for discovering oneself identical with the cosmos, as Maheśvarānanda identifies this as *prasara*, derived of *pra* + √*sṛñ* + *ac*, with the prefix confirming progression, giving a positive sense to finding materiality. This, therefore, is not an emancipation from matter, as the way the subjective experience is given is already bereft of matter; it is already expunged from the objective realm. On the contrary, this is the rediscovery of the self in its expressions of both subject and object. This is the autopoiesis or self-generation that explains the concept. The metaphor he uses in the commentary for describing this embryonic phase is *śikhaṇḍyaṇḍa* or a peacock-egg. Just as myriads of colors are latent in the yolk, albeit not expressed or visible in any form, the peacocks could not display colors that did not already exist as potential in the egg.

Maheśvarānanda describes the unsurmountable power underlying the body with an example of an insect body that is endowed with both autonomous cognitive (*parisphuraṇa*) and behavioral powers (*pari-bhramaṇa*). The first, *sphuraṇa*, explains the expansive expression of the self or consciousness, while the second relates to bodily fluidity. Human bodily awareness is yet another corporeality, although with greater freedom of self-expression and corporeal mobility than lower life forms. Grounding his thesis on the *Śiva Sūtra* (III.30), "the entire world is the constellation of his inherent powers" (*svaśaktipracayo'sya viśvam*), Maheśvarānanda argues that all that is manifest in the totality as an expression of the cosmic powers is an inherent potency of the subject expressed as if outside.

By borrowing the concept from the *Spandakārikā* I.1, Mahesvarānanda argues in MM 30 that the "manifestation" or expression (*unmeṣa*) of the self implies withdrawal or closing (*nimeṣa*) of the world, and vice versa. This amounts to maintaining that commonsense experience of the self and the world relies on mutual abnegation. On the other hand, the yogic consciousness presupposes recognizing or rediscovering oneself as the totality, dissolving the difference that underlies the cognitive modalities of subject and object. In this remapping of somatic experience, Maheśvarānanda develops a semantics to reconfigure horizon of embodiment, where the body expands outward from its epidermis and interacts as an open system, encapsulating the totality within the seeker's bodily awareness. With these new somatic schemata, a Tantric subject interacts while dwelling in the world and also experiences the world as his own body. The other in this dialogical transaction is not located "out there" where the bodily horizon reaches its physical limits. On the contrary, the other is mirrored within oneself in this newly mapped bodily image. Further buttressing his argument from the *Triśirobhairava*, "*sarvatattvamayaḥ kāyaḥ*" that "the body is comprised of all the elements," Maheśvarānanda confirms: "there lies identity between the body and the cosmos" (*aṇḍapiṇḍayor aikyam* | Parimala in MM 34).

The expansion of bodily consciousness is one of the recurring themes of MM. According to Maheśvarānanda, our response to the environment during bondage is controlled by our habit patterns shaped in reaction to the world, with the world as "this," an entity outside of the self, bereft of consciousness. His philosophy rests on the assumption that greater empathy is possible by means of reversing this habit pattern, and he proposes the course of visualization toward achieving this goal. His conviction is that subjects can mirror the world and vice versa, and the self-discovery in his paradigm rests on reaffirmation of the totality as the self, and not in expunging self-consciousness further from the body and the world. An insect, according to Maheśvarānanda, surpasses its expression of powers in relation to its body. The body in this depiction is recognized by means of its demonstration of power – bodily force compared with mechanical power and the powers of the sensory faculties compared with the powers of the luminous divinities.

We know today that a single strand of neuron or a single virus is observed to be capable of conducting complex functions, and the amount of information squeezed within the genome is mind-boggling. Following Maheśvarānanda's hypothesis, every cell within our body is capable of the same expression. He considers the body as a hub, a constellation of all the karmic predispositions and personal volitions, and for this, he refers to the body using the Sanskrit term *kāya* that derives from √*ciñ*, to accrete. Even in a biological sense, the body is merely a system, with each cellular structure having a certain degree of individuality. The consciousness I have of my body is subject to change, with bodily awareness shifting in different modes. This fluidity of bodily consciousness provides the platform for addressing Maheśarānanda's thesis that our bodily consciousness is not fixed and can be expanded to incorporate the totality. Visualization practices are directed toward allowing subjects to acknowledge this bodily elasticity. To further support his argument, he cites the *Virūpākṣapañcāśikā*: "All of this [that I see] is my body, with me having the character of consciousness."[8]

Maheśvarānanda gives a mirror-test example to demonstrate the present self-experience encased within the body. Recognizing oneself in the mirror has been considered a hallmark of self-awareness. The application here of the same example is for a different purpose: (1) to demonstrate that one can project one's bodily subjectivity outside, and (2) to make an argument that an awakened yogin, while finding his bodily presence enveloping the totality, can still recognize his corporeality within his body. In the words of Maheśvarānanda:

> While experiencing a dullness of being in the embryonic state corresponding to the expansion that has the form of one's own power with the character of descending [and becoming] the entities of cognition, the subject that has transcended the world [retains] reflexive consciousness (*vimarśa*) [that has] the character of autonomous pulsation. Following

> the precepts such as "just as an elephant [recognizes] oneself as big as a mansion and also oneself [reflected] within a mirror, the absolute subject relishes both the entire expansion of the world and also the body," the recognition [at this state] is similar to a sexually aroused elephant recognizing [himself] in the mirror.[9]

For Maheśvarānanda, the body is merely a composite. What is it composed of? The body, accordingly, is an aggregate of previous modes of consciousness, retained in the form of *saṃskāra*. The body accumulates what we undergo, both physically and psychically. There is not even a categorical difference between these, as what is physical is merely mental. And all that is the body is what our past modes of consciousness have experienced. Our bodily directionality implies our being in the world, with our interactions in various corporeal and mental modes. It is not the self-governing capacity alone that puzzles Maheśvarānanda; it is also the capacity to self-express. And this self-expression is not an expression of bodily being in time and space, but rather this is the self-expression of the cosmic being, being itself, the self that experiences itself in terms of the totality. Bodily schemas are what our *saṃskāras* form, and visualization is what forces us to reorganize these formations. Just as the subject's expression of being short or tall is merely mapped in his bodily presentation, Maheśvarānanda's self as the totality is a remapping of the subject in light of immanence and in terms of cosmic awareness. The bodily image that the practitioner imposes during the course of visualization is that of the cosmos as the body. For Maheśvarānanda, this becomes the yardstick to measure self-realization.

Ritualizing the body-image

Vivid in the earlier description, Maheśvarānanda's project sought to impose a new body-image, and he created a manual to guide the aspirants to repeatedly observe themselves within the framework of the new body-image. The first, the cosmic body-image, follows his philosophy, while the second, the manual, emerges from his Śākta ritual experience, in which the aspirant is guided toward recognizing cosmic forces and bodily energies as integral to Kālī. By all accounts, when Maheśvarānanda uses terms to refer to body, what he really means is the lived body. Moreover, his lived body is constantly interacting with his visualized world, the cosmic planes and psycho-physical centers projected within the body. The body here is both the imagined body and the body-image that is used as a template for the recognition of oneself as both the absolute subject and the one having no boundaries caused by the epidermis. For Maheśvarānanda, there are no limits to the body, and whatever the limitations are, they are merely self-imposed. By actively creating an alternative body-image, Maheśvarānanda seeks to establish an altered body-schema, changing the subject's self-assessment as well as his interaction in the world. His ritualized body-image needs to be read in this light.

What grounds both subject and object is experience (*anubhava*). It is in the immediate mode of experience wherein the subjective meets the objective: what constitutes as subject and object is determined within the very flash of consciousness. The project of visualization, then, is to shift experience from being temporal and finite to being infinite, from being located within the body to locating the body within experience, by liberating experience from all the frameworks.

The liberated experience, accordingly, is a consequence of freeing experience from the chains of habit patterns or *saṃskāras* that condition and constrain the experiences to be the way they are felt. Beyond what the *Language of Thought* and cognitive theories have proposed—that our cognitive and verbal exchange relies on a deeper structure, our experiences per se—there is a deep ecological domain where the body and the environment are in a fluid exchange, mutually reshaping each other. Accordingly, in the basic sensation that reveals the world to us or the moment in which we are exposed to the world, there already is a "mapping," a reconfiguration, or schematization in process. By ritually articulating an alternative body-image, Maheśvarānanda explores the ways to reshape human experience,and with it, both the subject and the way he interacts in his environment.

The flesh or the clinical body can be as if bracketed, as in paralysis, in dream, or in deep sleep states. We are able to repress some basic sensations or to postpone them when encountering other urgent concerns. Embodied experiences are constantly changed in relation with the environment, suggesting that there is a ground for negotiation. While this exchange is mostly an unconscious process, Maheśvarānanda explores the ways to consciously engage by means of visualization. Telos, after all, is not predetermined, as what amounts to a higher telos for one subject may not mean the same for another. Maheśvarānanda explores the ways to reconstitute the higher telos by giving a philosophy of cosmic oneness, with the bodily energies being harmonized with the cosmic forces that govern the physical world. Even clinically speaking, phantom limb experience suggests that bodily sensation can be extended beyond the epidermis, and the habit tendencies preserve the bodily sense beyond the existing corporeal boundaries. This is all the more vivid in the examples of pregnancy or in the case of conjoined twins.

Body, for Maheśvarānanda, is an expression of energies, with these being indistinct from consciousness or the self. He constitutes a hierarchy on which the self ascends from its materiality or descends toward inertia, both being the play of consciousness or the self. For him, this is the *svātantrya-śakti* or the capacity of freedom, that bestows upon the individual the possibility of self-concealment and self-illumination, with the first referring to materiality and the second to self-recognition. In the MM (verse 30), Maheśvarānanda introduces the terminology of the state wherein the world manifests (*viśvonmeṣadaśā*) with its counterpart term, "the retrieval or closing of the world" (*viśvanimeṣa*). Having bodily consciousness that is circumscribed by the epidermis, in Maheśvarānanda's opinion, is an embryonic phase, with the subject possessing the potential of experiencing himself as the totality.

With a holographic imagery of the body, Maheśvarānanda maintains that whatever lies in the cosmos exists in the body, albeit in unmanifest forms. Similar to what the gestalt theories would propose, what we actually experience is something in alignment with our predeterminations, predispositions, and our need to see something in terms of units as wholes. The embodied self has both its natural state with the expansion of the totality and its conditioned state with the body finding its limits within the epidermis. The body-image of Maheśvarānanda is thus not merely a projection of new imagery but a meticulous negation of the existing and limited body-image with a thorough deconstruction of what amounts to the body prior to replacing the bodily vision, and this sequence articulates his philosophy and mediates his ritual paradigm. Maheśvarānanda, while doing so, separates himself from other non-dual philosophers, as the enlightened subject in his depiction is not disembodied but rather super-embodied, wherein bodily consciousness expands to capture the totality.

The metaphor of the peacock egg (*śikhaṇḍyaṇḍa*) explains this phenomenon: even while in bondage and separated from the rest of the world, the embodied subject retains his dormant capacities to eventually have the all-encompassing embodiment expressed. Liberation in his depiction is one such mode of consciousness that confirms total bodily consciousness that gives full access not only to the body at its cellular level but also to the entire cosmos as one's own body. Accordingly, the confinement within the epidermis is a condition and not a natural state for the self, and awakening is not a negation of the embodied self but rather an embrace of its ultimate expression in terms of totality.

The ritual visualization in this regard is a mechanism utilized to transform the gaze that allows the subject to articulate their body-image and identify with the projected image. MM can be broadly identified as a text that guides the aspirant toward implanting this altered vision. *Darśana*, philosophy, in this light, is not some speculation but rather a vision, and having a correct vision requires dismantling false convictions. Above all, one needs to rely on transformed insights in order to correct existing visions. This strategy of Maheśvarānanda is particularly vivid in the verses 34–46 where he provides the theoretical framework to alter bodily consciousness in order to transform it to encapsulate the totality within. Rather than going to the detail of how he aims to achieve this schematic transformation, it is enough to give a quick summary of the salient features of this manual. What underscores this conversation is the statement that:

> The energies characterized by the sensory faculties which are also equated with the cosmic energies [of the limbs corresponding to the absolute subject] (*karaṇadevī*) shine forth in what has been the altar.[10]

One of the recurring themes in this course of visualization is that the body is an altar, that deities are to be worshipped within one's own heart, that one's self-experience is identical to the experience of the absolute subject, that the way the individual subject experiences his body is identical with how the absolute subject experiences his embodiment within the totality. And this is what we encounter in the course of visualization practices. For instance:

> The highest divinity (*parameśvara*) in the form of the individual subject is the deity presiding at the center that is differentiated as external and internal deities within the circles. The placeholders for the deities in the enclosures are the powers of the sensory faculties. It is only within the body which is the major altar that their worship is possible.[11]

Along these lines, an unliberated subject only has a vague idea about himself, with his consciousness drifting in the temporal flux. Awakening in this regard is a full affirmation of the body, wherein the body extends to and embraces the cosmos. The very self immediately given in the experiential modes becomes the divinity or the absolute subject to be recognized by means of visualization. Maheśvarānanda adds further:

> The highest divinity whose essential nature is confirmed by means of the Vedas and Āgamas is to be worshipped upon the sacred altar of the form of the body.[12]

A general understanding of worship as an activity that is directed outward needs a correction here, as in this internalized gaze, worship is nothing distinct from the acknowledgment of the roles that the sensory faculties play in the flow of consciousness outward and their retrieval from the external realm after having encountered the objective world. What visualization implies then is an observation of consciousness in its dynamic mode of being engaged with the world. Maheśvarānanda states:

> The essence is that the very *effulgent modes of consciousness manifest in the form of objects* [lit. nectar] (*vedyāmṛta*) that are the substances for the Kula ritual (*kuladravya*) are the very objects (*tāni*) that are the instruments for worship. These objects (*tāni*) are to be offered, with them being skillfully contained in the [metaphoric] cup of one's own mind. [emphasis mine][13]

In an external ritual, there is a deity and a worshipper, while both become identical when the ritual is internalized. In an external ritual, there are ritual objects and instruments such as cups to hold those objects, while in the internal ritual, the mind becomes the cup and the engagement of consciousness through the sensory modalities becomes the ritual objects. The very will of the subject to enter into the collective consciousness and erase the sense of a separated individuality becomes the mechanism of conducting the ritual. Self-realization is the anticipated outcome of such a ritual. Maheśvarānanda confirms this concept in the following statement:

> First, one should worship the body as the altar. [After that,] one should seek in the center of the heart the supreme divinity of the character of absolute luminosity that is identical to the self. One should [thereafter] visualize the potencies in the form of the sensory faculties encircling the [metaphoric center,] the self. Thereafter, one should fill the mind, which is the collective form of all the inner faculties, with the libation objects which are characterized by the expression of the objects of cognition. One should then purify these objects (*tad*) with the power of *mantra* that is comprised of the reflexive consciousness of the supreme divinity. This deity [or the self] encircled by divinities [or the sensory faculties] is to be worshipped with this very *kula* nectar (*kulāmṛta*) [of experiencing bliss].[14]

Reaffirmation of oneself as the divinity, or the subject with absolute freedom, is at the core of Maheśvarānanda's visualization. The fundamental problem he observes for human suffering is the sense of lacking freedom. This sense of lack extends not only in subjective limitation, but it also results in conditioning the sensory and corporeal functions to be limited. Subjects enter into the inertia of dullness simply by giving up their inherent nature that possesses absolute freedom. Maheśvarānanda initiates the course of visualization by first deconstructing what constitutes subjectivity, that an individual subject is not what the subject considers himself to be, nor is his body what he understands it to be. This shift in the subjective horizon targets a transformation in the objective horizon, opening the possibility of experiencing the other as the very self, extended in space and time. Other bodies and other subjects in this philosophy are different clusters woven like prayer beads or like different cells constituting a single body. With this underlying premise, Maheśvarānanda argues:

> This has been said and will be reiterated that the deity [to be worshipped] is the absolute subject (*parameśvara*) that is of the character of the pulsation of one's own heart. *Bala,* or the force, refers to the reflexive consciousness that has the character of enduring the perturbation in the form of the world that has entered within the self, being identical with it. The very observation of this [force] is what constitutes worship. This [capacity to maintain the inner gaze] is what is described as the force [*bala*].[15]

Tantric vocabulary is replete with terms for force, power, and strength. The rituals are often prescribed to be carried out by a hero (*vīra*), and even the states of realization are invoked with the terminology of *sāhasa,* referring to force. For Maheśvarānanda as well as for other Tantrics, it is a matter of strength to explore the possibility beyond an individual's immediately given subjectivity, and it takes stamina to expand the self-experience beyond the epidermis.

Transforming bodily awareness

The mirror test, for whatever reason Maheśvarānanda cites, suggests his understanding of a projected body. Mirror body is the projected body "out there," and this is not the immediately felt body. With the totality as the body of a yogin, Maheśvarānanda argues that the bodily sense is retained objectively, just as the elephant is able to recognize its reflection. This example as well as the mirror metaphor invokes a much wider discussion in Tantric philosophy of reflection (*pratibimba*). For this paper, it suffices to say that bodily consciousness is elastic and can be extended beyond the epidermis, just as in the case of recognizing the mirror image as one's own body. Yogic awakening for Maheśvarānanda is the immediate experience of oneself as the collective, and this is dependent upon liberation from the fragmented self-image. For him, this fragmented image is not actually fragmented but rather is in its early evolutionary phase or in the embryonic stage. There are certain stages understood in this leap to the absolute:

1. A yogin begins his journey with the epidermis as the extended horizon of the body.
2. He distills the information processed through the sensory faculties by capturing them in the mind and allowing the images to merge into the self, making them dissolve their forms.
3. He breaches the sense of the external and the internal with the sensory capacities, both roaming inside and out, by means of engaging them in the world and at the same time saturating them with pure consciousness. Sensory organs are considered here as breaching the realms of the subject and object, negotiating their boundaries within both horizons. These are the energies that constitute the inside and outside, the self and the other. The total extension of these energies relates to the awakening of the individual subject by means of affirming absolute subjectivity.
4. In the awakened state, the yogin reverses his experience of the body, with the totality being his body and the flesh being a mere mirror image.

In Maheśvarānanda's philosophy, there are two stages of mirroring. In the everyday state of consciousness, there is a mirroring of the world, where the self is merely cognizing mirror images. In the liberated state, both the body and the individual self appear as the mirror image. Here, the outside becomes the inside and the inside morphs into the outside. The totality becomes the source, and the body, the target. How does Maheśvarānanda envision such a possibility? The response rests on his epistemology and cosmology. He understands consciousness in terms of energy. Sensory faculties are further extensions of this very energy, and the self is the core or a unified field of consciousness. In his epistemology, sensory faculties are the energies of the self, and a *maṇḍala* with center and periphery describes his image of the self and the sensory capacities. Even when these energies are scattered in the world, these are the very aspects of the self, the sparks of consciousness often equated with fire (*cidagni, citivahni*). In passively or naturally engaging with the world, the self is fragmented into pieces as sparks of consciousness.

A yogin, according to Maheśvarānanda, allows the flow of energies through the sensory faculties but retains their information in the mind metaphorically described as a cup, and rather than allowing it to constitute *saṃskāras* or retain their individual traits, the yogin absorbs these images within the self. What arises in the form of images, accordingly, is the very self that is manifest as the object-image which therefore has the potential to be reabsorbed into its pristine form. Whatever exhilarates the self, food, drink, and, of course, sex, are the means to worship the self that is divine, and in its contentment lies the possibility of self-realization. With this underlying premise, Maheśvarānanda also displaces the body-negating theology, supplanting it with a world-affirming vision in which the body is the beginning for further expression of the self and not an impediment.

For Maheśvarānanda, body-image and body-schemas are flexible; we can morph our body-image into something new, and meticulous visualization can constitute the new synoptic structures and habit patterns to alter our body-schemas. Is the imagery that he provides absolutely real? In his own metaphysics, both the internal and external acts of worship as well as meticulous visualizations are merely for the alteration of the subject's horizon of consciousness. In this regard, one can argue that the images that he provides are merely for rearticulating the body-schemata. Visualization, in this paradigm, is merely for transforming the way we are accustomed to experience the world. Regulated breathing or *prāṇāyāma*, along with the mental exercises that constitute the corpus of his yogic practice, affirms this very notion of subjective transformation.

Ultimately, the acts of allowing the flow of consciousness through the sensory faculties and restraining it from its external engagement, observing the flow of consciousness through different conduits in grasping the world, and transcending these processes, all result in regulating consciousness, making it possible to experience beyond the body as if it were touched. Reality and encountering the reality both become visceral, as awakening is measured in terms of having a corporeal or tactile sensation in the interaction with the world. Sensory faculties are not deprived in this process. On the contrary, they are engaged and are enlivened, being further empowered to the extent of their potentialities. By means of acknowledging the pristine nature of consciousness that is shared among the sense organs, the yoga here is as if recollecting the pieces of consciousness fragmented into a myriad of forms as the sensory faculties. The limitation of the senses in this depiction can be compared with slumber, where a subject is unable to perform the tasks that he can accomplish while awakened.

Yogic liberation is repeatedly identified as the real awakening, with bondage being compared with slumber. The self is thus literally engaged when actualizing itself by means of the effulgence of the sensory modalities. Knowing the world and knowing the self become one and the same, as the very modes of consciousness can be compared to ripples, with the oceanic consciousness remaining one and the same. The spiritual awakening in the philosophy of Maheśvarānanda is orgasmic, and the language he uses to describe it is visceral. The affirmation of the body in the absolute sense allows the subjects to have their attitude transformed while living their everyday lives and still enjoying the bliss of absolute freedom.

Notes

1 For salient issues relevant to visualization practices, see Sthaneshwar Timalsina, "Visualization in Hindu Practice," *Religion, Oxford Research Encyclopedias*, 2017; Sthaneshwar Timalsina, "A Cognitive Approach to Tantric Language." *Religions* 7, no. 12 (2016): 139; Sthaneshwar Timalsina, *Language of Images* (New York: Peter Lang, 2015); Sthaneswar Timalsina, *Tantric Visual Culture: A Cognitive Approach* (London: Routledge, 2015); Sthaneshwar Timalsina, "Cosmic Awareness and Yogic Absorption in the Nāth Literature," *Studien zur Indologie und Iranistik* 25 (2008): 137–168; and Sthaneshwar Timalsina, "Metaphors, Rasa, and Dhvani: Suggested Meaning in Tantric Esotericism," *Method and Theory in the Study of Religion* 19, no. 1–2 (2007): 134–162.

2 Somatosensory responses are the bodily and sensory effects of the internal visualization practices.

3 Jean Piaget, *The Origins of Intelligence in Children* (New York: International Universities Press, 1952).

4 This chapter does not need to address the controversies surrounding body-image and body-schema theories. Those interested can consult Helena De Preester and Veroniek Knockaert, eds. *Body Image & Body Schema. Interdisciplinary Perspectives on the Body* (Amsterdam: John Benjamins, 2005); Douwe Tiemersma, *Body Schema and Body Image: An Interdisciplinary and Philosophical Study* (Amsterdam: Swets & Zeitlinger, 1989); and Shaun Gallagher, "Body Image and Body Schema: A Conceptual Clarification," *The Journal of Mind and Behavior* 7, no. 4 (1986): 541–554.

5 Some of the concepts I have borrowed in this conversation come from the following sources: for embodied mind, autopoiesis, and enactivism, see Francisco Varela, Evan Thompson, and Eleanor Rosch, *The Embodied Mind: Cognitive Science and Human Experience* (Cambridge: MIT Press, 1991); for ecological perception see J.J. Gibson, *The Senses Considered as Perceptual Systems* (Boston: Houghton-Mifflin, 1966); for early development on the gestalt theory, see Husserl and von Ehrenfels and Wolfgang Köhler; and for a wide range of phenomenological issues, see Maurice Merleau-Ponty, *Phénoménologie De La Perception.* [in French] [Phenomenology of Perception] (London: Routledge, 2012 [1945]).

6 *tilamatte vi sarīre pekkhaha kīḍassa ettiī sattī* | *sā sacchandaasiriṇo vīsasarīrassa kettiī hou* || 29 || *vīsummesadasāe desiaṇāhassa jattiyo pasaro* | *kalalāvatthāe ṭhio vīsaṇimese vi tattio hoi* || 30 ||
7 *yathā nyagrodhabījasthaḥ śaktirūpo mahādrumaḥ* || *tathā hṛdayabījastham jagad etac carācaram* | *Parātrīśikā* 24 cd-25ab.
8 *sarvaṃ mama caitanyātmanaḥ śarīram idam* | *Virūpākṣapañcāśikā* I.1.
9 *vedyāvarohaunmukhyaśālini svasāmarthyarūpe vibhave kalalāvasthayāvasthānātmakaṃ staimityam anubhavaty api viśvottīrṇasya svātmaparispandamayo vimarśaḥ –viśvasyaiva vilāsaṃ me śarīraṃ cāśnute śivaḥ* | *śālām iva viśālāṃ svātmādarśaṃ ca yathā dvipaḥ* || *ityādinītyā darpaṇamaṇḍalāntaḥpraviṣṭagandhagajendrādyanusandhānasthānīyaṃ paryālocanam* | MM, 43.
10 *pīṭhībhūte karaṇadevya indriyalakṣaṇāḥ śaktayaḥ sphuranti*. MM, 34.
11 *svātmarūpaḥ parameśvara evāntaś cakradevatā bāhyāntarabhinnāḥ* | *karaṇaśaktayaś ca tadāvaraṇadevatāsthānīyāḥ* | *tadarcanaṃ ca svaśarīrātmani mahāpīṭha evopapadyate* | MM, 34.
12 *saḥ vedāgamādiprasiddhasvabhāvaḥ parameśvaras tatra piṇḍātmani pīṭhe pūjanīyaḥ* | MM, 35.
13 *yāni tāni vedyāmṛtamayāni kuladravyāṇi tāny eva pūjāsādhanānīty arthaḥ* | *tāni ca svacittātmani caṣake grahaṇayuktyā kayācid arpaṇīyāni* | MM, 35.
14 *pūrvaṃ tāvat pīṭhatayā deham abhyarcya tanmadhye hṛdayavyomarūpe svātmarūpamahāprakāśalakṣaṇaṃ parameśvaram anusandhāya tam abhitaḥ prasarantīrindriyaśaktīś ca vicintya tadanu sarvāntaḥkaraṇasamaṣṭilakṣaṇe svacitte viśvavedyavilāsalakṣaṇam arghyadravyam āpūrya tac ca pārameśvaraparāmarśamayyā mantraśaktyā saṃskṛtya tenaiva kulāmṛtena nijāvaraṇadevatāparimaṇḍalito 'yaṃ parameśvaraḥ pūjanīyaḥ* | MM, 35.
15 *svahṛdayasphurattārūpaḥ parameśvara eva devatety uktaṃ vakṣyate ca* | *tatra yan nijaṃ svātmatādātmyānupraviṣṭaṃ balaṃ viśvavikṣobhasahiṣṇutvalakṣaṇaṃ vimraṣṭṛtvaṃ tatparyālocanam eva varivasyā* | *tac ca balam ity eva vyapadiśyate* | MM, 42.

Bibliography

Abhinavagupta. *Parātrīśikā: With the Laghuvṛtti Commentary by Abhinavagupta*. Srinagar: Mercantile Press, 1947 [circa 10th C].

De Preester, Helena, and Veroniek Knockaert. *Body Image & Body Schema. Interdisciplinary Perspectives on the Body*. Amsterdam: John Benjamins, 2005. doi:10.1075/aicr.62.

Gallagher, Shaun. "Body Image and Body Schema: A Conceptual Clarification." *The Journal of Mind and Behavior* 7, no. 4 (1986): 541–554.

Gibson, J.J. *The Senses Considered as Perceptual Systems*. Boston: Houghton-Mifflin, 1966.

Maheśvarānanda. *Mahārthamañjarī with Parimala*. Edited by Mukunda Rama Shastri. Bombay: Tattva-Vivechaka Press, 1918.

Merleau-Ponty, Maurice. *Phénoménologie De La Perception* [in French] [Phenomenology of Perception]. London: Routledge, 2012 [1945].

Piaget, Jean. *The Origins of Intelligence in Children*. New York: International Universities Press, 1952.

Tiemersma, Douwe. *Body Schema and Body Image: An Interdisciplinary and Philosophical Study*. Amsterdam: Swets & Zeitlinger, 1989.

Timalsina, Sthaneshwar. "A Cognitive Approach to Tantric Language." *Religions* 7, no. 12 (2016): 139. https://doi.org/10.3390/rel7120139.

———. "Cosmic Awareness and Yogic Absorption in the Nāth Literature." *Studien zur Indologie und Iranistik* 25 (2008): 137–168.
———. *Language of Images*. New York: Peter Lang, 2015.
———. "Metaphors, Rasa, and Dhvani: Suggested Meaning in Tantric Esotericism." *Method and Theory in the Study of Religion* 19, no. 1–2 (2007): 134–162.
———. *Tantric Visual Culture: A Cognitive Approach*. London: Routledge, 2015. doi:https://doi.org/10.4324/9781315748528.
———. "Visualization in Hindu Practice." *Religion, Oxford Research Encyclopedias*, 2017. doi:10.1093/acrefore/9780199340378.013.103.
Varela, Francisco, Evan Thompson, and Eleanor Rosch. *The Embodied Mind: Cognitive Science and Human Experience*. Cambridge: MIT Press, 1991.
Virūpākṣa. "Virūpākṣapañcāśikā." Edited by Ganapati Shastri. Tiruvandrum: Travancore Government Press, 1912.

7 Sensing the ascent

Embodied elements of Muhammad's heavenly journey in Nizami Ganjavi's *Treasury of Mysteries*

Matthew R. Hotham

Introduction

One night, early in his prophetic career, Muhammad is awakened by the Angel Gabriel, bid to mount a strange beast and ascend to heaven for a face-to-face encounter with God. On his way there, he subdues Scorpio's poisonous tail with his mint-scented breath and perfumes the heavens with his musk. After perfuming the fixed stars and heavens with his bodily odors, he finally ascends to the highest heaven where he approaches the divine throne and views God with his two physical eyes.[1]

Or so the story is told in the introduction to the poet Nizami Ganjavi's (d. 1209) *Treasury of Mysteries*. In these 67 lines of poetry, Nizami offers a unique vision of the Prophet's ascension (*Mi'raj*)[2] than that found in the works of his predecessors and contemporaries. He also sparks a centuries-long tradition of emulation, in which most major Persian poets include a sustained passage on the ascension in the introduction to their epics. Ascension narratives can be found at the center of theological debates, are used to draw boundaries between religious communities, have been deployed as tools of conversion, and taught to children and converts as a means of learning about their ritual obligations.[3] In the *Treasury of Mysteries*, Nizami's ascension narrative posits Muhammad as a paradigmatic mystic whose journey to God can be emulated by other mystics—but who remains distinct and superior to them through his *embodied* ascension. Such an investigation reveals the importance of the body to Sufi[4] understandings of mysticism.

The *Makhzan al-Asrar* is a unique text in Nizami's opus. The first of five major *masnavis* (long narrative poems written in rhyming couplets), it does not tell a single sustained story like his other works in the genre. Instead, the poem collects a number of short essays followed by exempla. These essays range in topic, from the proper comportment around a king to the value of renouncing worldly wealth. Nizami's *Quintet* provides a comprehensive vision for the structure and regulation of Islamic civilization. His poems advocate models of courtly love, mystical experience, and religious ritual, setting forth the requirements for a properly regulated society and outlining the contours of divine kingship. The size and scope of his project was attempted by a host of later poets, who mimicked the subject matter, meter, and structure of his opus.

Nizami's *Quintet* also perpetuated the practice of beginning these epics with a fixed series of introductory remarks, covering topics such as God's unity, praise of the Prophet, and the Prophet's ascension. Though the nature of Nizami as poet, mystic, ethicist, and scientist has been a topic of debate for several decades, barely discussed in this ongoing conversation is the first poem in his *Quintet*, the *Treasury of Mysteries*. A mystico-ethical text, it serves as a prolegomenon to his *Quintet*, outlining the major contours of his poetic vision, and was emulated in both meter and structure by a vast number of Persian poets after him, most notably Amir Khosrow Dehlavi (d. 1325) and 'Abd al-Rahman Jami (d. 1492). These poems were enormously popular—they circulated in lavishly illuminated manuscripts, were displayed in imperial libraries, passed down along Sufi lineages, and were turned into songs performed at saints' shrines. Ownership of and command over Nizami's *Quintet,* among several other texts, was one way that medieval Muslim kings and saints constructed their religious and political legitimacy.[5]

In spite of their immense popularity and importance, these poems, especially their long introductory sections, are often overlooked in contemporary scholarship. This is in part because they challenge long-held but problematic definitions of Sufism as a private, interiorizing tendency within Islam that is primarily interested in human love as a metaphor for divine proximity. Tied to this understanding of Sufism is the notion that it was a predominantly antinomian tradition always at odds with "orthodox" Sunni legalism and political authority. This has led many contemporary scholars to read Sufi critiques of religious legalism and political authority as being largely defensive, that is, that they represent Sufi attempts to carve out a space for themselves in a public sphere dominated by hostile voices. The confidence with which these texts caricature and confront religious and political authorities, along with their centrality to medieval Islamic political and religious discourse, belies this simple explanation. This chapter challenges such characterizations of medieval Sufism by investigating the importance of the model of the Prophet Muhammad for bodily practice and religious authority in a prominent medieval poem.

The ascension

Virtually every aspect of the ascension (*Mi'raj*)[6] has been up for debate at some point in Islamic history. Questions have ranged from whether the ascension was physical, spiritual, or metaphorical to where Muhammad departed and returned from. Modernist thinkers, such as Sir Seyyed Ahmed Khan, have objected to *mir'aj* narratives based on their fabulosity. Other contemporary Muslims have discounted the ascension for the problematic influence of Isra'iliyyat[7] in fleshing out the larger narrative. Yet others object to the materialistic descriptions of heaven, arguing that heaven cannot be captured in such mundane imagery. Fazlur Rahman attacks bodily ascension as part of his broader critique of hadith.[8] More recent writers have plugged the *mir'aj* story into ancient astronaut theories.[9] Even the date of the occurrence has probably shifted.[10]

What follows is the general outline of the ascension based on Ibn Ishaq's biography of Muhammad. Ibn Ishaq notes that his narrative is pieced together from the accounts of a number of close associates of the Prophet Muhammad. Medieval ascension narratives added to, amended, or rearranged elements of this tale according to genre conventions and rhetorical function, but Ibn Ishaq's account provides a baseline for comparison:

One night, as Muhammad is sleeping beside the Ka'ba,[11] he is awoken by the angel Gabriel. Gabriel escorts the Prophet to the door of the mosque and shows him a white "half mule, half donkey" whose strides spanned "the limit of its sight."[12] He mounted this creature, called Buraq, and swiftly traveled to Jerusalem where he meets a number of prior prophets, whom he leads in prayer. He is then offered a choice of drink—in this account he may choose between milk and wine—and chooses the milk. Gabriel then explains that because of this apt choice, wine is forbidden to Muhammad and his people.[13] At this point, a ladder descended from heaven and Gabriel and Muhammad climb to the gates of heaven together. The angel Ismail greets them and asks Gabriel if Muhammad has been sent for, which Gabriel confirms. At this, Ismail allows them to enter heaven. He then meets the angel Malik who shows him a vision of hell, which is described as a blast of flames that Muhammad fears will consume all creation. He is then shown a number of people being punished for the sins of stealing from orphans, usury, and adultery. From here, Muhammad leaves the first heaven and ascends the remaining six levels of heaven, encountering a different prophet or prophets at each level along the way. In Ibn Ishaq's account, the prophets occur in the following order, though this order varies widely in later retellings of the ascension:[14]

2nd Heaven: Jesus and John the Baptist
3rd Heaven: Joseph
4th Heaven: Idris[15]
5th Heaven: Aaron (Moses' brother)
6th Heaven: Moses
7th Heaven: Abraham

After meeting Abraham, he is taken to "Paradise" where he meets his companion Zayd's heavenly wife, a compensation for his failed marriage to Zaynab, whom the Prophet later married. Finally, Muhammad meets with God who requests that Muhammad and his people pray 50 times per day. When he returns to the 6th Heaven, Moses notes that this is too much to ask of people and advises that he return to request a reduction. Muhammad gets several incremental reductions to the prayer obligations, with Moses continuing to object to the heavy prayer burden. Finally, when the daily prayer is reduced to five, Muhammad is too embarrassed to request a further reduction.

This is where the ascension narrative ends in Ibn Ishaq. Issues of Muhammad's return to Mecca from heaven and Jerusalem are notably handled in relation to the first part of the narrative, the night journey to Jerusalem. Here, the emphasis is on the miraculous nature of Muhammad's swift journey as a testament of faith, as well as the proofs he offered of the physicality of his journey.

Ascension as paradigm for mystical experience

A number of scholars and commentators have noted the important role the ascension (*mir'aj*) has played as a paradigm for mystical experience.[16] Several features of the ascension made it particularly fruitful for Sufi exploration and explication. Muhammad's journey through the seven heavens, for example, was frequently analogized to the stages of the Sufi path. His face-to-face encounter with God comes to represent the goal of the Sufi path: mystical union with God.

We see early evidence of the use of the *mir'aj* by Sufis in the writings of Abu Abd al-Rahman Sulami (d. 412 AH/1021 CE). Sulami was an important early biographer of Sufi saints, whose writings helped to consolidate and mark the boundaries of the Sufi tradition. In *Subtleties of the Ascension*, Sulami collects 56 sayings by earlier Sufis on the topic of the *mir'aj*. In Fredrick Colby's translation and commentary on Sulami's work, he notes four major themes in the collected sayings:[17]

1 The ascension as confirmation of Muhammad's unique position among created beings.[18]
2 The ascension as an initiatory journey in which Muhammad gets clothed in garments of light.[19]
3 Muhammad's vision of God as a model for Sufi mystical encounters.[20]
4 The ineffability of mystical encounters.

Thus, for Sulami, Muhammad is an ontologically unique being who nevertheless provides a model for Sufi practice. He provides a model in four different ways: confirming the necessity of approaching God through stages;[21] affirming the practice of garment bestowal as sign of acquiring spiritual authority; highlighting the dangers of temptation along the path and the importance of rejecting lesser heavenly rewards in favor of a direct encounter with God; and, finally, asserting the difficulty and potential danger in putting into words what one experiences in God's presence. These themes all arise, to lesser or greater degrees, in Nizami's writing as well.

In Sulami's work, the ascension is primarily a metaphor for the Sufi path. One might compare and contrast Sulami's understanding of the ascension with Ibn Sina's approach.[22] For Ibn Sina, the ascension is not an embodied, but a spiritual, occurrence depicted through embodied metaphors. A lengthy discussion of Ibn Sina's psychology and cosmology is beyond the scope of this chapter, but, in short, for Ibn Sina, the Prophet's heavenly journey occurred in the *Ilm al-Mithal*, or realm of similitudes. For Ibn Sina, Buraq is a metaphor for the Active Intellect who descends to take Muhammad for an encounter with the Intelligibles. As a Prophet, describing these non-material forms in language is not a problem—Muhammad's perfected Imaginative Faculty does that work for him. Thus, Ibn Sina is able to draw one-to-one parallels between Muhammad's metaphorical description of his ascent, which is meant for the masses, and his own philosophical understanding of the experience, which can only be understood by the elite. In contrast to Sulami, who argued for the ineffability of Muhammad's encounter with God, Ibn Sina argues that the Prophet Muhammad did not have trouble putting the ascension into words at all. Rather, he put them into the ideal metaphorical terms to convey meaning to the masses.

In other Sufi writings, however, the *mir'aj* functions less as a metaphor and more as a map to guide Sufis as they ascend toward God during their own mystical journeys. Given Ibn Sina's interpretation of the ascension, one can see how it may be difficult to maintain Muhammad's uniqueness while also arguing that his most unique act could be replicated. For many writers, this tension was resolved by insisting on the bodily nature of Muhammad's ascension in contrast with the spiritual or dream ascensions available to others.

Saintly ascensions

The ascension of Bayazid Bistami

One of the earliest and most prominent Islamic mystics was a ninth-century Iranian named Bayazid Bistami. Though he predated the organizational structures, technical vocabularies, and signature rituals that would come to be hallmarks of Sufism, he is nevertheless looked to as a foundational figure for later Sufi groups. He also claimed to have ascended to heaven for a face-to-face encounter with God. His ascension narrative is as among the earliest writings in this genre.

Within the Sufi context, as Michael Sells notes, "What is at stake in these symbolic worlds is the goal of the mystical path" as framed by the author, whether that is "to become more purely intellectual, more angelic, or more deeply human."[23] Bistami's ascent is framed as a competition with the angels, who provide a series of tests to see whether he will settle for a reward of lesser worth than a direct encounter with God.[24] Since his focus is on the angels' tests, his description of the heavens themselves is sparse—he notes landscape features only to highlight how they were used to tempt him to halt his journey before its completion. He repeatedly states that the angels showed him sights that would "wear out the tongue to describe."[25]

This allows him to nod to the vast glories of heaven, without expending ink describing them. For Bistami, the rewards of heaven are not only beside the point, they are temptations to be avoided: it would be unfruitful or even dangerously tempting to recount them.

In contrast to Muhammad's ascension, where his meetings with previous prophets are key to affirming his status as Seal of the Prophets, Bistami's ascension features no prophetic encounters. Instead, Bistami encounters a variety of angels who attempt to awe him with their numbers, size, or brightness. Bistami pointedly rejects their overtures, sometimes boasting or demonstrating his superiority to the angels, such as in the Fifth Heaven, when the angels greet him in a number of languages, and he greets them back in all the same languages.[26] In each heaven, however, he ends his encounter with respect and humility, declining the angels with the phrase, "My goal is other than that which you are showing me."[27] As a metaphor for the Sufi path, Bistami's ascension narrative warns prospective mystics of the dangers of the Sufi path. Much like Farid al-din Attar's *Conference of the Birds*, in which each valley represents a danger on the path to union with God, for Bistami, each level of heaven has the potential to harmfully waylay a Sufi.

Bistami's ascension also differs from the Prophet Muhammad's because it does not include a journey overland or upward through the stars and spheres. At the start of his narrative, he simply finds himself "risen to the heavens."[28] The only mention we get of the stars in Bistami's account is when he encounters the angels in the first heaven, who are "standing with their feet aflame among the stars."[29] Jumping straight into the heavens emphasizes the spiritual and disembodied nature of his ascension. Accounts of Muhammad's ascension often spend as much time describing his journey overland and through the stars as his encounters in the heavens. This is because Muhammad's embodied ascension provides proof of its miraculousness. Questions of how he was able to travel so quickly in one night and overcome normal human limitations abound in discussions of Muhammad's ascension. This aspect of Bistami's journey is precluded with a very simple opening: "I saw myself in a dream."[30] Bistami traveled to heaven in a dream, so his journey through the material realm becomes insignificant. What matters are the spiritual insights he gained while in the heavens. This critical distinction between Bistami's ascension and that of Muhammad's would prove important for other Sufis who wished to write about their personal ascensions. His work provided a model for a number of later Sufis writing on the topic, including Ibn Arabi[31] and Qadi al-Numani.[32] And, as we shall see in the next section, failure to properly frame one's ascension as disembodied could have severe consequences.

The ascension of Muhammad Ghwath

Muhammad Ghwath was a sixteenth-century South Asian Sufi whose claim to have had an embodied ascension (*mir'aj*) both allowed him to garner a large popular following and caused him to run afoul of religious and political authorities. His narrative begins somewhat differently from that of Bistami's, with clear parallels to Muhammad's own *mir'aj*. Muhammad Ghwath states that he spends the night half-sleep and half-awake before hearing a voice calling him to prayer. Instead of being called to ascend by Gabriel, Muhammad Ghwath is called forth by Khidr.[33] Unlike Bistami, Muhammad Ghwath does not state that this encounter happened in a dream, but instead leaves it ambiguous, noting that he remained in the half-waking, half-sleeping state throughout. One key to the potential embodied nature of Muhammad Ghwath's ascent is that he requires a means of transport up to heaven. In his narrative, all of creation and then the elements of water, air, and fire transform into a series of immense human beings upon whose heads he steps to ascend to heaven.[34] Allowing Muhammad Ghwath to place his feet upon their heads is a sign of utmost respect for the saint, who "encompasses, completes, and perfects each element."[35] As Kugle notes, these elements also represent the constituent parts of the human body, so "ascending upward is also delving inward, through bodily materiality."[36] The very contours of Muhammad Ghwath's ascent make little sense if he leaves his body behind on the journey.

Once Muhammad Ghwath reaches the seven heavens, his narrative further diverges from that of Bistami's, since he meets a number of saints and prophets, not just angels. These figures greet him with warmth rather than with temptation and testing. They note that Muhammad Ghwath accompanied Muhammad in spirit on his *mir'aj*, but appear surprised at his current ascent. What most shocks the denizens of heaven is that Muhammad Ghwath is "fully attached to [his] body!" which is "a completely new and different spectacle."[37]

Throughout the narrative, Muhammad Ghwath attempts to unite or resolve binaries. His body joins his soul on the ascent, he sees a vision of heaven and hell as one form with two essences, he resolves esoteric and exoteric religious knowledge, he places male and female piety on equal footing.[38] This appears most starkly in his descent from heaven, where, after attaining union with God, the denizens of heaven appear not as distinct entities, but abstract emanations of God. Thus, the goal of Muhammad Ghwath's *mir'aj* is to attain a loss of self within God, which afterward makes apparent the mystical principle of *wahdat al-wujud*, or unity of being.[39]

Though Muhammad Ghwath's ascension highlights mainstream Sufi principles and is couched in a number of qualifications,[40] it nevertheless caused controversy. As with prior controversial Sufi figures, it seems Muhammad Ghwath's theologically problematic claims would not have garnered attention had he not run afoul of political authorities.[41] Once he did, however, his ascension narrative became a key site of contention. His embodied ascension, for example, threatened the uniqueness of Muhammad's own *mir'aj*. Muhammad Ghwath seems to anticipate this difficulty, for he explicitly preserves the distinction between saint and prophet. He notes:

> *When I heard this command call out to Muhammad to rise and ascend, I was confused. I turned to Jesus who was standing beside me, and*

> *asked, "I thought that this was the night of my ascension, so why should Muhammad be called up now to ascend to the Divine Throne?" Jesus answered, "Each saint is a member of the community that was founded by a specific prophet. The Prophet must ascend first, so that the saint can follow after him up to the appointed place. That way, the structure of prophethood and sainthood can be established in good order."*[42]

Of greater concern to religious authorities than his embodied ascension was the fact that Muhammad Ghwath seems to articulate a form of monism, arguing that heaven and hell will be united on the Day of Judgment. Nevertheless, it was only when he conceded that his vision had been a dream, rather than an embodied experience, that his persecution on theological grounds came to an end.[43]

From this brief survey of two non-prophetic ascension narratives, we can draw a few conclusions about how Sufis deployed the *mir'aj*. First, the structure of the ascent represents a metaphor for the Sufi path to God. Second, the nature of the figures and challenges encountered on the journey tells us how the author perceives the ultimate goal of the mystical path. Third, when discussing Muhammad's ascension as a model for Sufi practice, Sufis had to be careful to preserve the uniqueness of Muhammad's ascent. They often did so by emphasizing his bodily ascent in contrast to their disembodied or dream ascent.

Embodiment in the Makhzan's ascension narrative

The ascension narrative in the *Makhzan al-Asrar* is 68-lines-long and directly preceded by a brief, 25-line section praising Muhammad in more general terms. This section highlights Muhammad's importance to salvation history and to creation itself: the "'A' drawn on the First Tablet" was a doorway to Ahmad[44] (another name for Muhammad) whose name spans from the "A of Adam to the M of messiah."[45] He is the "brightest center of the circle of 'Be'."[46]

Existing alongside these descriptions of Muhammad as integral to existence are verses which incorporate imagery of kingship and the bestowal of kingly authority. Thus, the letters of Muhammad's name become a signet ring—Ha ح, a necklace—Dal د, and a belt—Mim م, marking his authority over the two worlds, which bow before him.[47] Throughout this section, Nizami juxtaposes images of humility with those of royalty, inadequacy with super-efficacy—thus Muhammad is the illiterate who is more loquacious than all eloquent speech.[48]

Body/heart

Muhammad's preeminence in creation and the images of kingship continue in the next section—the *mir'aj* narrative itself. Here, Nizami makes a distinction between body and soul. The words he uses form a sonic as well as conceptual binary: body or outward form—*qāleb* and heart/soul—*qalb*. As early as Hasan al-Basri, Muslim mystics and ascetics began to develop a heart-symbolism out of Qur'anic references to the word *qalb*. In *Revival of the Religious Sciences*, Abu Hamid Al-Ghazali defines *qalb* as the immortal and spiritual essence of a human being, through which one comes to know God.[49]

This focus on the physicality of the ascension begins with the metaphors Nizami uses to describe Muhammad's journey. He notes:

> *With the body's birdcage [qafas-e qāleb] from this world of traps [dām-gah]*
> *His heart-bird [morgh-e del-esh] left for the realm of rest [ārām-gah]*[50]

The metaphor of the soul as a bird and the world as a snare is a familiar Sufi trope, deployed in brief treatises by Ahmad al-Ghazali (d. c. 1123–26) and Shahab al-din Suhrawardi Maqtul (d. 1191), and at length in the *Mantiq al-Tayr* of Farid al-Din 'Attar (d. c. 1221)—a rough contemporary of Nizami. The idea that the world is rife with snares liable to tangle up a soul-bird is also common in these works. He continues to describe the heart's role in lifting Muhammad to heaven:

> *His divine bird [morgh-e alhīsh] carried aloft the cage*
> *His body [qāleb] became lighter than soul [qalb]*[51]

In these lines, it is not simply the world which is a snare for the soul, but the body itself which is a cage for it. Muhammad's soul, however, is particularly buoyant, and can lift the body out of this world of snares. It can't, however, do all the work by itself:

> *As he moved on step-by-step,*
> *he was seized and carried higher toward God's blessing...*[52]

So Muhammad's initial impetus is met with an enthusiastic divine response—a reciprocal interaction which echoes that found in a Hadith Qudsi[53] popular with Sufis: "and if he [a devoted servant] draws near to Me [God] an arm's length, I draw near to him a fathom's length. And if He comes to me walking, I go to him at speed."[54] Thus, Muhammad sets out a path for future mystics to follow: seek proximity with God and God will meet you more than half way.

Perhaps most interesting about this passage is the apparent ambivalence toward the body. The world is a place of snares to be escaped, the body is a cage which traps the heart. Yet even though Muhammad departs from "the seven climes and the four cardinal directions and the six orientations," his ascension is not an escape from the body, it is a journey with it.[55] And it's not just his body that ascends in Nizami's account, but Muhammad's clothing also comes along for the ride.[56]

Clothing and gift bestowal

References to clothing and the exchange of clothing as gifts are a prominent feature of Nizami's ascension narrative. Sometimes Muhammad is metaphorized as an article of clothing himself, such as when "the heavens bore him as a crown."[57] Elsewhere the situation is reversed, such as when he enters the presence of God and "His head poked out from the collar of nature"[58] and he thus wears all creation as a robe of discipleship. Elsewhere, the stars themselves disrobe in his presence, such as when the celestial spheres throw down their patched woolen cloak (*khirqa*), the distinctive garment of Sufis from which the name Sufi is derived, in Muhammad's presence.[59] Some commenters, such as Vahid Dastgirdi, take this line to mean that the fixed stars threw off their cloak to begin a *sama* in Muhammad's honor.[60] This resonates with Nizami's portrayal of Muhammad's encounter with the star constellation Libra. Finding that her scales aren't up to the task of weighing Muhammad's infinite worth, according to one interpretation which toys with the definition of *sanj*, she turns the plates of her scales into castanets to play Muhammad a song.[61]

Other constellations honor Muhammad through the exchange of gifts. Taurus allows Muhammad to ride him as a steed, and Sagittarius slays Aries with his arrow, to lay a feast for the Prophet. More interestingly, however, is a pair of verses in which Cancer and Orion give over their crown and belt to Muhammad as *pesh-kash*, a term that denotes extraordinary gifts given to superiors, especially royal ones. Thus, throughout Muhammad's ascension, the signs of the Zodiac break, transform, or give up their characteristic symbols in order to welcome Muhammad as a guest and in recognition of his superiority to and authority over them.[62]

Once he leaves the realm of the fixed stars and enters into heaven proper, we discover that Muhammad has not only received clothing as gifts upon his journey, but also brought clothing with him from Earth. The furniture of heaven engages with Muhammad physically, just as the fixed stars did. But rather than gifting the Prophet clothing, they instead touch (or even become) his clothes.[63] For example, "The Lote Tree reached his vest [*pīrāhan*] / the Throne touched the hem of his skirt [*dāman*]."[64] The terms here have Sufi valences: the *pīrāhan* is associated with *futuwwa,* Islamic chivalric codes developed and promoted within young men's organizations that had considerable overlap with Sufi orders, and was worn as a "finishing garment" on top of a *khirqa*.[65] As such, it represented the outer form to the *khirqa's* inner meaning. These physical interactions between the Prophet and the very symbols of Divine proximity are slightly ambiguous, however: is Muhammad receiving blessings through these exchanges, or are the Lote Tree and Throne acknowledging his preeminence?

Scent and spit

The Prophet's uniqueness and purity, even before the ascent, is demonstrated, in part, through the scents he emanates. A number of recent historians have pointed to the importance of scent and perfumery in premodern texts. Though our own noses are poorly trained, premodern elites were well-versed in the character of odors, components of perfumes, and the uses to which certain scents were best put.[66] From their perspective, scent had both internal and external component—it could alter one's interaction with others but also reflect or even have an effect on one's own state. This is because scent was seen to involve an element of touch—particles of the thing being smelled were understood to enter the nose as part of the process of smelling them. Thus, it was an intimate sense—and could be more intimate than sight, for example, because of its partially involuntary nature.

Muhammad's scent is key to several verses in Nizami's account. First, he notes that on the night of the ascension, "Midnight was filled with the musk of his lips."[67] Numerous ascension accounts depict Muhammad returning from his ascent with a musky odor, which is understood as the scent of heaven. For Al-Ghazali, heavenly muskiness is a solution to the question of eating and excrement in the afterlife —he has resurrected bodies sweating and belching musk. Nizami inverts this, having Muhammad enter the heavens already emitting a musky scent with which he perfumes the night. Thus, all of heaven is touched by particles of the Prophet on his ascent.

His bodily odors do not simply perfume those they touch, however, they also have alimentary powers. In one evocative line, Nizami has Muhammad exhale his minty breath upon Scorpio's tail, which cures its poison.[68] Though the odor of Muhammad's breath is key to Nizami's depiction, the moisture exhaled with his breath clearly also plays a role in its curative power. Amir-Moezzi notes that the etymology of the word *baraka* (blessing) contains traces of its embodied origins. He argues an affiliation between *taḥnīk*[69] and *baraka/tabarruk*.[70] Originally *baraka* meant abundant rain, or a place to water camels, or mother camels feeding children prechewed food at such a site, but "this latter meaning led to the interpretation of *baraka* as the spiritual energy that the father transmits to his newly born child by placing him upon his knees and putting saliva in his mouth, blessing him, and in this way according him his protection."[71]

Nizami explicitly makes this connection in his second section praising the Prophet. The second praise poem begins by immediately focusing on the Prophet's body: "Your body [*tan*] is purer than pure soul [*jan*]."[72] A few lines later, Nizami picks up the thread of the relationship between *baraka* and bodily fluids, saying: "Open your mouth, so that all may eat of your sweet words[73] / from the fountain of your mouth, feed us moist dates."[74] Here Nizami is engaging with a long tradition of venerating the Prophet's bodily fluids, where Muhammad uses saliva to cure epilepsy, transmit secret knowledge to Ibn Abbas, and convey blessings and virtues upon children and new converts.[75] Exchanges of bodily fluid can transmit not just spiritual blessing, but also knowledge or even religious authority.

> We know that in a number of ancient belief systems, body fluids such as blood, sperm, saliva, milk, sweat, are considered agents for thaumaturgic transmission; they bear and transmit beneficial or harmful elements, faculties, virtues or spiritual influences from the bearer to another, more specifically, by heredity, to their descendants.[76]

Notably, this was a power specifically attributed to the *kahin* in pre-Islamic Arab culture.[77] It is also a mode of transmitting spiritual authority, such that Muhammad's contact with the divine during the ascension can be transmitted to others through bodily fluid transfers.

In concluding his second praise poem to Muhammad, Nizami mourns his physical absence, saying "You of two worlds, why are you beneath the ground? You are not a treasure [to be buried], why are you clothed in dirt?"[78] This absence of the Prophet's physical presence, which denies the world of his light, perfume, and voice,[79] is then turned to political and even apocalyptic ends. Nizami implores the Prophet to return in order to "renew the world" by deposing those who live in ease, and cleansing the *minbar* [pulpit] of the ritually impure.[80] Nizami seems particularly interested in the corruption he witnesses in the Persianate world, calling Muhammad to leave the land of the Arabs and come to Persia to enact this purification. On the apocalyptic side, he calls for Muhammad to "Arise and command *Israfil* to blow out these few candles"[81] and then to intercede for those who call on him on the day of judgment.[82]

In the fourth praise poem to the Prophet, Nizami compares Muhammad to prior prophets, arguing for his preeminence and superiority to them. One running theme throughout the work is the role that wheat played in the corruption of humans. Here Nizami notes that Adam was defiled by that indigestible grain, wheat. All the other Prophets have their own worldly entanglements, most revolving around food and drink.[83] In this section, Muhammad alone amongst the prophets is framed as an ascetic whose worldly renunciation was sufficient to grant him a direct encounter with God. Nizami notes that Muhammad alone "discarded everything,"[84] and calls on him to "annihilate [*fana'*] annihilation"[85] Thus, in these introductory sections, we see Nizami frame Muhammad as the perfect ascetic whose denial of worldly desire has granted him unique, embodied access to God. Blessings from this encounter can be obtained through bodily contact with the Prophet, but he is no longer bodily present. Thus, through emulating his example, practicing proper withdrawal from the world, Nizami argues one can obtain a direct, though disembodied, encounter with God for themselves.

Vision of God

The association of senses with physical contact also plays a role in Nizami's account of Muhammad's vision of God. Nizami insists that Muhammad saw God with "this eye and that eye of his head."[86] Likewise, when encountered with the brilliance of the divine vision "His Narcissus[87] had the collyrium[88] of '*Mazagh*'."[89,90] Nizami's repeated, emphatic insistence on the Prophet's bodily ascension and encounter with God gives us hints about the audience of his poem. The insistence on Muhammad's direct vision of God has some resonance with Sufi deployments of the ascension narrative. From Bayazid Bistami to Ibn Arabi, Sufis utilized the *mir'aj* as a model in a number of ways. First, they analogized the stages of Muhammad's ascent to stages of the Sufi path itself. Second, they pointed to Muhammad's direct face-to-face encounter with God and the momentary loss of consciousness that Muhammad experiences in God's presence as the preferred goal of human existence. For example, Nizami notes that Muhammad was "bewildered [*muttaḥīr*]" as he knocked on the door to the court of heaven.[91] This bewilderment is an angelic quality and is compared to the state of the angels Muhammad has left behind at the Lote Tree. Bewilderment, *hayra,* is also an important, usually late stage on the Sufi path in a number of mystical manuals and allegorical poems. Finally, Sufis used Muhammad's ascension to put an asterisk next to the assertion found in hadith literature that humans will not see God before the Day of Judgment. Muhammad did, and he did because direct encounters with God happen along a different temporal axis than linear eschatological time. Nizami is emphatic on this point, stating: "God can be seen / may he who says otherwise go blind."[92]

Conclusion

In Seyyed Hossein Nasr's apologetic account of the ascension in *Muhammad: Man of God,* he emphasizes the importance of the body to a proper understanding of the ascension (*mir'aj*). He asserts that "it refers to a journey to the higher states of being and not simply through astronomical space," and that "the ascension of the Blessed Prophet physically as well as psychologically and spiritually meant that all the elements of his being were integrated in that final experience which was the full realization of unity (*al-tawhid*)."[93] Nasr directly confronts contemporary Muslims who are keen to reject the bodily ascension, saying:

> certain modernized Muslims who want to reduce Islam to a rationalism and empty it of all its beauty and grandeur have sought to explain this central event away along rationalistic lines…there is nothing worse than reducing the majestic events associated with the great founders of religion to harmless events of 'ordinary life' in order to make them acceptable.[94]

He notes that scientific rationalism can't tell us about higher planes of existence, but that the bodily ascension is necessary to confirm the inherent dignity of creation and the human being, because Muhammad's "corporeal ascent signifies also the nobility and dignity of the human body as created by God."[95] Nasr argues that bodily ascension becomes comprehensible if we avoid the mistake of "tak[ing] to be unreal whatever is not accepted by the modern scientific worldview," which he calls "a kind of totalitarianism which converts, often unconsciously, a science of a particular plane of reality to the science of the whole of reality."[96] Though medieval theologians and philosophers, influenced by Neoplatonic thought, divided material reality into multiple levels, it is not entirely clear that they would agree with Nasr's assertion that these levels were immaterial or beyond the scope of human observation and rational inquiry.

The fact that Nasr gives the *mi'raj* such attention in a contemporary biography of the Prophet Muhammad highlights its importance to Islamic identity and the problem embodied ascension poses for contemporary Muslim thinkers. This problem is not, however, a new one that only arises in the face of Western science. Central Muslim thinkers, such as Ibn Sina, have rejected embodied ascension. From very early in the history of Islam, the majority of both Sunni and Shi'i philosophers and theologians accepted Muhammad's bodily ascension, though some went to great lengths to resolve embodied ascension with the known laws of the universe. In spite of the intellectual challenges posed by embodied ascension, rejecting it outright posed its own challenges. Muhammad's ascension played an important role in distinguishing between Islam and other monotheistic traditions,[97] marking Islamic sainthood as distinct from prophethood and, in *hadith* accounts, drawing the border between Islam and *Jahiliyya*.[98] Those who did and did not believe in Muhammad's embodied ascension are also the central figures in the story of Muhammad's struggle with the Quraysh and polytheism.[99]

The embodied ascension provided a challenging, but not insurmountable, intellectual problem for Islamic philosophers. As scientific knowledge improved, a number of philosophers set out to prove that bodily ascension was possible according to known laws of physics. Fakr al-Din al-Razi (d. 1210 CE), and many after him, focus on the possibility of fast travel as essential to their proofs. For these thinkers, miraculous acts can push the physical laws of the universe to their limits, but cannot break them, so it seems. Another question involved the physical wholenesss of the celestial spheres. Muhammad must "break through" them in order to ascend to a higher sphere, but such rupture would leave a hole. Questions abounded regarding whether or not this hole could be repaired or the implication of the hole for the perfection of the spheres.[100] Of greater concern is whether or not this journey could occur in one night. Fakr al-Din al-Razi turns to both scientific and scriptural sources for such confirmation. Citing the speed at which the sun moves through the sky, he argues that such movement is easily possible. He also relies on a theory of sight involving extra-vision. Noting that eye-rays move at impossibly quick speed in order to facilitate sight, he again argues that such speedy movement is well within God's power within the limits of the material world. In terms of scriptural proofs, al-Razi cites verses related to Solomon and Bilquis[101] that mention movement between Jerusalem and Yemen occurring within "a twinkling of an eye." He also cites the speed at which Satan can move to spread whispers and deceit among believers.[102]

Such a tradition of scientific rationalization of the bodily ascension obviously runs into difficulty as the scientific understanding of the cosmos changes—the distances traveled become daunting, the upward trajectory through spheres untenable, and Buraq's winged propulsion insufficient. On the other hand, the idea of a human ascending into space becomes more plausible once astronauts have landed on the moon.[103] Contemporary Muslims are left with a few possibilities for discussing the *Mir'aj:* (1) reject the physical ascension outright, (2) mark the physical ascension as happening in a different realm of reality (as Nasr does), and (3) apply ancient astronaut theories of alien space visitation and powerful technology to the ascension.[104] None of these solutions are ideal. In the latter approach, Buraq and the *rafraf*[105] become premodern descriptions of alien space vehicles.[106] In Nasr's approach, the line between metaphorical ascension and physical ascension becomes a bit wobbly. And in the former approach, Muslims run into the problem of the miraculous ascension as litmus test of faith. Buckley notes several modernist objections to the physical ascension. Some, such as Sir Seyyed Ahmed Khan, posit the physical ascension as a by-product of the wild medieval imagination.[107] Others note the problematic influence of Israeliyyat in the development of ascension narratives.

In short, though contemporary Muslims may wish to get away from medieval depictions of the Prophet's bodily ascension, the *Mir'aj* remains an important issue with which they must grapple. It remains significant because of its early role in defining the boundaries of community. Contemporary scholarly approaches to the ascension further enrich our understanding of just how significant *Mir'aj* accounts were to the development of Muslim identity in the medieval period. The *mir'aj* becomes an important narrative in the development of the image of Muhammad as intercessor, which marks his community as special and distinct from those of other monotheist prophets. This intercessory power can be characterized in a number of ways;but, as Shahzad Bashir notes, sometimes intercession can be triggered by partaking in physical contact with God through touching one who has touched God—and in one hadith, this physical connection can be carried through up to seven degrees of remove.[108] As Nizami's ascension narrative demonstrates, for medieval Sufis, Muhammad's physical ascent is critical for both differentiating him from mystics who might later experience a disembodied encounter with God and as a way of physically transmitting to the rest of the world the blessings obtained during his ascent.

Notes

1 Nizami Ganjavi, *Makhzan al-asrar*, ed. Bihruz Sarvatiyan (Tehran: Tus, 1984).

2 In Arabic, *mi'raj* literally means "instrument of ascension," usually glossed as "ladder" or "staircase." As a technical term in Islamic Studies, it refers to the heavenly ascension of the Prophet Muhammad. Mohammad Ali Amir-Moezzi, "Meʿrāj," *Encyclopedia Iranica*, June 25, 2010, http://www.iranicaonline.org/articles/meraj-i.

3 Christiane Gruber and Frederick S. Colby, eds., *The Prophet's Ascension: Cross-Cultural Encounters with the Islamic Mi'raj Tales* (Bloomington: Indiana University Press, 2010).

4 Sufism is often unhelpfully glossed as "Islamic Mysticism." Following Carl Ernst's "family resemblance" model, I use the word to point toward a complex of texts, institutions, objects, communities, and individuals who have been marked as Sufi or connected with and to Sufis. Carl Ernst, *Sufism* (Boston: Shambhala, 2011), xvii.

5 Lisa Balabanlilar, *Imperial Identity in the Mughal India: Memory and Dynastic Politics in Early Modern South and Central Asia* (New York: I.B. Tauris, 2012), 149.

6 It is worth noting that though I will discuss the ascension here in the singular, it is not a given that Muhammad ascended to meet God only once. In many Shi'i traditions, Muhammad had as many as 120 heavenly ascensions. (Mohammad Ali Amir-Moezzi, *The Spirituality of Shi'i Islam: Belief and Practices* (London: I. B. Tauris in Association with the Institute of Ismaili Studies, 2011), 142). In early traditions, the Isra (night journey from Mecca to Jerusalem) and Miʿraj (ascension into heaven) are discussed as separate occurrences. In Sunni sources, consensus forms around one bodily ascension and multiple spiritual ascensions thereafter (R.P. Buckley, *The Night Journey and Ascension in Islam: The Reception of Religious Narrative in Sunnī, Shī'ī and Western Culture* (New York: I.B. Tauris, 2013).

7 A term describing information derived from biblical and extra-biblical Jewish and Christian sources used by Qur'anic interpreters to flesh out narratives in the Qur'an or provide additional information about figures mentioned in the Qur'an. For a variety of reasons, these narratives have been viewed with suspicion by modernist thinkers. G. Vajda, "Isrāʾīliyyāt," *Encyclopaedia of Islam, Second Edition*. October 5, 2018.

8 Buckley, *Night Journey*, 97–99.

9 See, for example, Edward E. Curtis, "Science and Technology in Elijah Muhammad's Nation of Islam" *Nova Religio* 20, no. 1 (August 1, 2016) on Minister Farrakhan's ascension to the Mother Plane, or Abdul Aziz Khan, *UFOs in the Quran* (N.p.: Strategic Book Publishing, 2008) who reads the Qur'an and hadith as a record of alien encounters, citing Erik Von Daniken's best-selling pseudo-history book, *Chariot of the Gods* as liberally as *Sahih al-Bukhari*.

10 Traditionally it is placed on Monday, 12 Rabi' al-awwal, but this date seems to be largely symbolic, since it is also the date of Muhammad's birth, death, first revelation, and the hijra. It also marks the coming of spring, which is a key aspect of Nizami's depiction of Muhammad's ascent through the Zodiac. Uri Rubin, *The Eye of the Beholder: The Life of Muhammad as Viewed by the Early Muslims—A Textual Analysis* (Princeton, NJ: The Darwin Press, 1995), 190.

11 A cube-shaped building in Mecca purportedly initially constructed by Abraham and toward which Muslims turn in prayer.

12 Ibn Ishaq, *The Life of Muhammad*, trans. A. Guillaume (New York: Oxford University Press, 2002), 182.

13 This appears to serve as an etiological myth explaining the prohibition on wine and clarifying the three differing Qur'anic verses on the topic. Qur'an 4:43 advocates bodily purity in prayer, which includes sobriety; 2:219 argues that wine (رخَمْلا), along with gambling, has some benefits, but is a greater source of sin (مثْإ). In 5:90, wine, gambling, idol worship, and divination are lumped together as abominations (سجْر). Ibn Ishaq's biography was penned before the legal tradition had formulated its theories of abrogation to account for seemingly contradictory Qur'anic verses, so this part of the ascension story might have served a similar purpose for earlier communities.

14 Subtelny argues that the order of the prophets can be used as a tool of polemic or conversion, depending upon the religious community to which the ascension narrative is targeted. She documents, for example, that ascension narratives circulating amongst Jewish communities with a Christian population will remove Jesus from the first heaven, but place Adam in the seventh, with Adam symbolizing both himself and Jesus, who was understood to be the 'second' or 'last' Adam by many Christian communities for his role in restoring humanity to its pre-Fall condition—an attempt to assuage Jewish audiences, while appeasing Christian ones. Maria E. Subtelny, "The Jews at the Edge of the World in a Timurid-Era Mi'rajnama: The Islamic Ascension Narrative as Missionary Text," in *The Prophet's Ascension: Cross-Cultural Encounters with the Islamic Mi'raj Tales*, ed. Christiane Gruber and Frederick S. Colby (Bloomington: Indiana University Press, 2010).

15 Idris is often associated with Enoch, father of Methuselah, in the Book of Genesis.

16 See, for example, Annemarie Schimmel, *And Muhammad Is His Messenger: The Veneration of the Prophet in Islamic Piety* (Chapel Hill: The University of North Carolina Press, 1985), 168–170.

17 Frederick S. Colby, *The Subtleties of the Ascension: Lata'if Al-Mi'raj: Early Mystical Sayings on Muhammad's Heavenly Journey* (Louisville, KY: Fons Vitae, 2006), 16–20.

18 We've seen this theme before, especially in relation to Muhammad's status as intercessor on the Day of Judgment. Many Sufi writers link Muhammad's departure from Gabriel at the Lote Tree as a paradigmatic instance of *fana* or annihilation in God.

19 As we will see later in this chapter, garment bestowal is a typical Sufi symbol of investiture that becomes a critical feature of Nizami's own ascension narratives.

20 For Sulami, Muhammad's ability to see God provides a way around the Qur'anic interdiction of such a vision. See Colby, *Subtleties of the Ascension,* xx. The wording here is especially important, for as noted in Cyrus Ali Zargar, *Sufi Aesthetics: Beauty, Love, and the Human Form in the Writings of Ibn 'Arabi and 'Iraqi* (Columbia: University of South Carolina Press, 2011), 13-15, ru'yah is the highest mode of Divine vision and requires a divine unveiling to occur.

21 For example, in one saying, an anonymous commentator asserts that Muhammad's journey through the seven heavens was "so that he would learn propriety" before encountering God directly. Colby, *The Subtleties of the Ascension,* 41. The implication here is that Sufis too must learn proper manners before a direct encounter with God, and that the stages along the Sufi path provide an analogous experience to Muhammad's encounter with angles and prophets on his ascent.

22 Peter Heath, *Allegory and Philosophy in Avicenna (Ibn Sina): With a Translation of the Book of the Prophet Muhammad's Ascent to Heaven* (Philadelphia: University of Pennsylvania Press, 1992).

23 Michael Sells, ed., *Early Islamic Mysticism : Sufi, Qur'an, Mi'raj, Poetic and Theological Writings*, (New York: Paulist Press, 1996), 243.
24 As Sells notes, this is related to Qur'an 2:30, in which the angels object to God's creation of Adam.
25 Sells, *Early Islamic Mysticism*, 245–248.
26 Presumably this is a testament to his spiritual excellence, not that he is a studious polyglot. Sells, *Early Islamic Mysticism*, 247.
27 Ibid., 245–248.
28 Ibid., 245.
29 Ibid.
30 Ibid.
31 James Winston Morris, "The Spiritual Ascension: Ibn 'Arabī and the Mi'rāj Part I," *Journal of the American Oriental Society* 107, no. 4 (October 1, 1987): 629–652; James Winston Morris, "The Spiritual Ascension: Ibn 'Arabī and the Mi'rāj Part Ii," *Journal of the American Oriental Society* 108, no. 1 (January 1, 1988): 63–77.
32 Elizabeth Alexandrine, "The Prophetic Ascent and the Initiatory Ascent in Qadi Al-Nu'mani's Asas Al-Ta'wil," in *The Prophet's Ascension: Cross-Cultural Encounters with the Islamic Mi'raj Tales*, ed. Christiane Gruber and Frederick S. Colby (Bloomington: Indiana University Press, 2010).
33 Khidr is a complex figure who is associated with an unnamed spiritual guide to Moses in the Qur'an 18:65-82 and plays an important role in Sufi devotional practice. He is viewed as a still-living saint who one may occasionally encounter, especially in remote mosques and saints tombs. He can also initiate people into the Sufi path. For more on Khidr, see Ethel Sara Wolper, "Khidr and the Changing Frontiers of the Medieval World," *Medieval Encounters* 17, no. 1/2 (March 2011): 120–146.
34 Scott A. Kugle, "Heaven's Witness: The Uses and Abuses of Muhammad Ghawth's Mystical Ascension," *Journal of Islamic Studies* 14, no. 1 (January 1, 2003): 1–36.
35 Ibid., 17.
36 Ibid.
37 Ibid.
38 Ghwath visits Hell and meets with Eve, whom he is surprised to see in Hell. In some of accounts of Muhammad's ascension, he notes that Hell is mostly full of women. This was taken by a number of male authorities as an indication of women's inferior religiosity. In his own ascension, Ghwath provides a new explanation for it, showing that Eve and her attendants are there to minister to the damned.
39 Kugle, "Heaven's Witness," 23.
40 He notes, for example, the ultimate ineffability of his experience, stating "this description is really only a tissue of allusions and metaphors for the ungraspable reality of the experience." Ibid., 24.
41 See, for example, Carl W. Ernst, *Words of Ecstasy in Sufism* (Albany, NY: SUNY Press, 1985).
42 Kugle, "Heaven's Witness," 21.
43 Ibid., 34.
44 Another name for Muhammad, drawn from the same trilateral rootح-م-د meaning "to praise."
45 Nizami Ganjavi, *Makhzan al-asrar*, 12.
46 Ibid., 13.
47 "Lord of the Two Worlds," is a common honorific for God in the Qur'an. The two worlds are generally glossed as heaven and earth. Ibid., 12.
48 Ibid., 13.

49 Hellmut Ritter, *The Ocean of the Soul: Man, the World, and God in the Stories of Farid Al-Din 'Attar* (Leiden: Brill, 2003).
50 Nizami Ganjavi, *Makhzan al-asrar*, 14.
51 Ibid.
52 Ibid. Sarvatiyan glosses this by explaining that as he ascends, Muhammad encounters layers of veils between reality and God. As he encounters the first veil, which appears to be the limit of how far he can ascend, a hand appears and pulls him through to the next, higher veil, at which point, a new hand appears and pulls him through, and so on. Since this must happen repeatedly and in rather swift succession, Nizami's verb choice, which could be translated as "abducted," captures the involuntary and disorienting nature of this experience.
53 Literally "Sacred Hadith." Hadith are the collected sayings and deeds of the Prophet Muhammad passed down through long chains of oral transmission. The final line of this chain is usually "and so-and-so heard the Prophet Muhammad say...." Hadith Qudsi take this formula and add an extra link to the chain: "and so-and-so heard the Prophet Muhammad say that God says..." Hadith Qudsi thus have Muhammad delivering extra-Qur'anic speech from God. Hadith Qudsi play a prominent role in Islamic mystical traditions, since many contain esoteric sayings calling for supererogatory acts in exchange for greater closeness with God.
54 Javad Nurbakhsh, *Traditions of the Prophet, Volume 1* (N.p.: Khaniqahi Nimatullahi Publications, 1981).
55 Nizami Ganjavi, *Makhzan al-asrar*, 14.
56 For more on anxiety over Muhammad's nakedness in the hadith, see Rubin, *Eye of the Beholder*.
57 Nizami Ganjavi, *Makhzan al-asrar*, 15.
58 Ibid., 18.
59 Ibid., 14.
60 Ibid., 14, footnote 7. *Sama* means "listening" and is a Sufi musical performance used to induce remembrance of and reflection on God. In some Sufi orders, it is accompanied by ritualized body movements to induce meditation or trance, such as the distinctive whirling of the Mevlevi Order.
61 Ibid., 15.
62 Ibid., 15–16.
63 In a later portion of the introduction in praise of the Prophet, Nizami notes that "The Lote Tree [sidrat] is a brooch on your chest [sudrat]; the heavenly throne is an lowly chair in your palace." Ibid, 24.
64 Ibid., 17. The Lote Tree of Farthest Limit, mentioned in the Qur'an 53:14-16, is seen as a marker between the level of heaven in which created beings can exist within and the portion of heaven beyond which no created being, save Muhammad, may enter without being utterly destroyed by close proximity to divine might and majesty.
65 Lloyd Ridgeon, *Jawanmardi: A Sufi Code of Honour: A Sufi Code of Honour* (Edinburgh: Edinburgh University Press, 2011), 82; Lloyd Ridgeon, *Morals and Mysticism in Persian Sufism: A History of Sufi-Futuwwat in Iran* (London: Routledge, 2010), 79.
66 See, for example, Alain Corbin, *The Foul and the Fragrant: Odor and the French Social Imagination* (Cambridge: Harvard University Press, 1986), Emma J. Flatt, "Spices, Smells and Spells: The Use of Olfactory Substances in the Conjuring of Spirits," *South Asian Studies* 32, no. 1 (January 2016): 3–21, or James McHugh, *Sandalwood and Carrion: Smell in Premodern Indian Religion and Culture* (New York: Oxford University Press, 2013).
67 Nizami Ganjavi, *Makhzan al-asrar*, 16.

68 Ibid.

69 A custom of acknowledging paternity by chewing food and spitting it in an infant's mouth.

70 A complex term often translated, not unproblematically, as "blessing" or "grace."

71 Amir-Moezzi, *The Spirituality of Shi'i Islam*, 37. Contemporary positivists have attempted to give this practice a scientific gloss by arguing that it passes antibodies on to the child, therefore "blessing" them with improved health.

72 Nizami Ganjavi, *Makhzan al-asrar,* 22.

73 Here the word-play is quite ingenious, as *shakkar* can mean sweet words, the most literal usage here, but also sugar – a possible meaning which Nizami plays with in the second hemstitch. Likewise, *shakkar* is a homograph of *shuker,* which means "blessing" and is thus a synonym for *baraka.*

74 The implication here is that the dates have been moistened because the Prophet has pre-chewed them for us. Nizami Ganjavi, *Makhzan al-asrar*, 22.

75 Amir-Moezzi, *The Spirituality of Shi'i Islam*, 36–37. See also: Michael Muhammad Knight, ""Muhammad's Body: Prophetic Assemblages and the Baraka Network," ProQuest Dissertations Publishing, 2016.

76 Amir-Moezzi, *The Spirituality of Shi'i Islam*, 31.

77 Ibid., 31. Kahins were pre-Islamic prophetic figures who Muslim tradition portrays as receiving their "revelations" through becoming possessed by *jinn*—immaterial beings with free will whose motives and interactions with humans are not dissimilar to how faeries are portrayed in Irish folklore. These revelations were delivered in rhyming, rhythmic verses, and though they were not necessarily false, Muslims tradition viewed them as unreliable at best. In pre-Islamic Arabic, however, they were powerful and revered authorities who advised or even became tribal leaders and were consulted before major military or economic undertakings.

78 Nizami Ganjavi, *Makhzan al-asrar,* 24.

79 Ibid., 25.

80 Ibid., 25.

81 Ibid., 26. Israfil is the angel who Islamic tradition says will blow the trumpet to announce the End Times.

82 Ibid., 27.

83 For example, in Jalal al-Din Rumi's *Masnavi al-Manavi*, he tells the story of how Jesus was barred from the highest heaven because he remained attached to the world. Though he gave up all his worldly possessions—cup, comb, etc—according to Rumi, he held on to a needle to repair his clothing which relegated him to the Fourth Heaven instead of the highest heaven.

84 Ibid., 29.

85 Ibid.

86 Ibid., 19.

87 This is a common Persian poetic metaphor for the iris of eye.

88 *Surmah*, an eye-treatment made with antimony. Based on hadith accounts, it plays a role in prophetic medicine.

89 Or "not turning away"—a reference to Qur'an 53:17.

90 Ibid., 17.

91 Ibid.

92 Ibid., 19.

93 Seyyed Hossein Nasr, *Muhammad: Man of God* (Chicago: Kazi Publications, 2007), 36.

94 Ibid., 35–36.

95 Ibid., 36.

96 Ibid., 31 and 36.

97 Tabari highlights the importance of the irrational, unproven bodily ascension as proof of Muhammad's prophecy. For Tabari, the *Mir'aj* must be a miracle, and it is only miraculous if it occurs bodily. He notes that were Muhammad's ascension spiritual or metaphorical, it would not be a miracle. Yet it must be a miracle to confirm Muhammad's special role as Prophet. Through this tautology, he confirms that belief in Muhammad's bodily ascension as a prerequisite for membership in the Muslim community *per se* (Buckley, *The Night Journey*, 67).

98 A term meaning "Age of Ignorance," before Muhammad's revelation when polytheistic Arabs were ignorant of the existence of and their duties to the one God.

99 Several versions of the ascension narrative foreshadow the disbelief with which Muhammad's tale will be met, with various characters warning Muhammad not to share his experience with the Meccans. When he does declare it, he is met with disbelief. Some traditions resolve this disbelief by having the Prophet produce proof of his *'isra*, such as detailed descriptions of Jerusalem or information about caravans traveling between Mecca and Jerusalem that he passed during the night journey. Early traditions seemed to keep separate the *'isra* and *mir'aj,* only later combining them into a single outing in the same night. This combination allows the proofs of the *'isra* to also serve as confirmation of the *mir'aj*. In other discussions of the ascension, however, there is no suitable confirmation of Muhammad's travels—it is an article of faith which divides those who believe, such as Abu Bakr (from whence, by some accounts, he attains his nickname Siddiq, "Trustworthy") and Abu Jahl (Buckley, *The Night Journey,* 61–62 and Nerina Rustomji, *The Garden and the Fire: Heaven and Hell in Islamic Culture* (New York: Columbia University Press, 2008), 30.

100 Buckley, *The Night Journey*, 79.

101 The proper name of the Queen of Sheba, according to Qur'anic exegetes.

102 Buckley, *The Night Journey,* 78.

103 Buckley, *The Night Journey*, 119.

104 See, for example, Curtis, "Science and Technology in Elijah Muhammad's Nation of Islam" or Khan, *UFOs in the Qur'an.*

105 The *Rafraf* is not mentioned in Ibn Ishaq's ascension account, but appears in other *hadith* narratives and is described as a green conveyance, often a cushion or bed, that transports Muhammad from Gabriel into God's presence. This interpretation brings together descriptions of heaven found in Qur'an 55:76, with the, at times, confusing temporal and spatial movements described in Qur'an 53:7-18, verses generally associated with the ascension. Colby, *Narrating Muhammad's Night Journey,* 47 & 185.

106 One author argues of Buraq: "Keeping in mind the aerodynamic description, the mention of wings, the shiny glittering surface, and lightning (which is most likely the jet wash from the afterburner), it seems more likely that this beast that took the Prophet in the skies was mechanical rather than biological. Since animals were the only mode of transportation that people of that time were familiar with, it would be quite normal for them to interpret a small space vessel as a flying beast," Khan, 140.

107 Khan writes that arguments for the embodied ascension were "brought forward by only those persons who, blinded as they were by religious zeal and fanaticism, maintained that everything pertaining to religion, however absurd, ridiculous, or impossible that thing might be, must be believed as true." Khan, "Essays on Shakki-Sadr and Meraj," 8–9, as cited in Buckley, *The Night Journey*, 95.

108 Shahzad Bashir, *Sufi Bodies: Religion and Society in Medieval Islam* (New York: Columbia University Press, 2011), 5.

Bibliography

Alexandrine, Elizabeth. "The Prophetic Ascent and the Initiatory Ascent in Qadi Al-Nu'mani's Asas Al-Ta'wil." In *The Prophet's Ascension: Cross-Cultural Encounters with the Islamic Mi'raj Tales*, edited by Christiane Gruber and Frederick S. Colby. Bloomington: Indiana University Press, 2010.

Amir-Moezzi, Mohammad Ali. "Meʿrāj." *Encyclopedia Iranica*, June 25, 2010. http://www.iranicaonline.org/articles/meraj-i.

———. *The Spirituality of Shi'i Islam: Belief and Practices*. London: I. B. Tauris in Association with the Institute of Ismaili Studies, 2011.

Balabanlilar, Lisa. *Imperial Identity in the Mughal India: Memory and Dynastic Politics in Early Modern South and Central Asia*. New York: I.B. Tauris, 2012.

Bashir, Shahzad. *Sufi Bodies: Religion and Society in Medieval Islam*. New York: Columbia University Press, 2011.

Buckley, R. *The Night Journey and Ascension in Islam: The Reception of Religious Narrative in Sunnī, Shī'ī and Western Culture*. New York: I.B. Tauris, 2013.

Colby, Frederick S. *The Subtleties of the Ascension: Lata'if Al-Miraj: Early Mystical Sayings on Muhammad's Heavenly Journey*. Louisville, KY: Fons Vitae, 2006.

Corbin, Alain. *The Foul and the Fragrant: Odor and the French Social Imagination*. Boston, MA: Harvard University Press, 1986.

Curtis, Edward E. "Science and Technology in Elijah Muhammad's Nation of Islam: Astrophysical Disaster, Genetic Engineering, UFOs, White Apocalypse, and Black Resurrection." *Nova Religio: The Journal of Alternative and Emergent Religions* 20, no. 1 (August 1, 2016): 5–31. https://doi.org/10.1525/novo.2016.20.1.5.

Daniken, Erich Von. *Chariots of the Gods: 50th Anniversary Edition*. New York: Penguin, 1999.

Early Islamic Mysticism: Sufi, Qur'an, Miraj, Poetic and Theological Writings. New York: Paulist Press, 1996. http://search.lib.unc.edu?R=UNCb2932363.

Ernst, Carl. *Sufism*. Boston, MA: Shambhala, 2011.

Ernst, Carl W. *Words of Ecstasy in Sufism*. Albany, NY: SUNY Press, 1985.

Flatt, Emma J. "Spices, Smells and Spells: The Use of Olfactory Substances in the Conjuring of Spirits." *South Asian Studies* 32, no. 1 (January 2016): 3–21. https://doi.org/10.1080/02666030.2016.1174400.

Gruber, Christiane, and Frederick S. Colby, eds. *The Prophet's Ascension: Cross-Cultural Encounters with the Islamic Mi'raj Tales*. Bloomington: Indiana University Press, 2010.

Heath, Peter. *Allegory and Philosophy in Avicenna (Ibn Sina): With a Translation of the Book of the Prophet Muhammad's Ascent to Heaven*. Philadelphia: University of Pennsylvania Press, 1992.

Ibn Ishaq. *The Life of Muhammad*. Translated by A. Guillaume. New York: Oxford University Press, 2002.

Khan, Abdul Aziz. *UFOs in the Quran*. N.p.: Strategic Book Publishing, 2008.

Kugle, Scott A. "Heaven's Witness: The Uses and Abuses of Muhammad Ghawth's Mystical Ascension." *Journal of Islamic Studies* 14, no. 1 (January 1, 2003): 1–36. https://doi.org/10.1093/jis/14.1.1.

McHugh, James. *Sandalwood and Carrion: Smell in Premodern Indian Religion and Culture*. New York: Oxford University Press, 2013.

Morris, James Winston. "The Spiritual Ascension: Ibn ʿArabī and the Miʿrāj Part I." *Journal of the American Oriental Society* 107, no. 4 (October 1, 1987): 629–652.

———. "The Spiritual Ascension: Ibn ʿArabī and the Miʿrāj Part Ii." *Journal of the American Oriental Society* 108, no. 1 (January 1, 1988): 63–77.

Nasr, Seyyed Hossein. *Muhammad: Man of God.* Chicago: Kazi Publications, 2007.

Nizami Ganjavi. *Makhzan al-asrar.* Edited by Bihruz Sarvatiyan. Tehran: Tus, 1984.

———. *Makhzan al-asrar.* Edited by Hasan Vahid Dastgirdi and Saʿid Hamidiyan. Tehran: Nashr-i Qatrah, 1997.

Nurbakhsh, Javad. *Traditions of the Prophet, Volume 1.* N.p.: Khaniqahi Nimatullahi Publications, 1981.

———. *Traditions of the Prophet, Volume 2.* N.p.: Khaniqahi Nimatullahi Publications, 1983.

Ridgeon, Lloyd. *Jawanmardi: A Sufi Code of Honour: A Sufi Code of Honour.* Edinburgh: Edinburgh University Press, 2011.

———. *Morals and Mysticism in Persian Sufism: A History of Sufi-Futuwwat in Iran.* London: Routledge, 2010.

Ritter, Hellmut. *The Ocean of the Soul: Man, the World, and God in the Stories of Farid Al-Din 'Attar.* Leiden: Brill, 2003.

Rubin, Uri. *The Eye of the Beholder: The Life of Muhammad as Viewed by the Early Muslims--A Textual Analysis.* Princeton, NJ: The Darwin Press, 1995.

Rustomji, Nerina. *The Garden and the Fire: Heaven and Hell in Islamic Culture.* New York: Columbia University Press, 2008.

Sarvatiyan, Bihruz. *Sharh-i Makhzan al-asrar-i Nizami Ganjavi.* Tehran: Barg, 1991.

Schimmel, Annemarie. *And Muhammad Is His Messenger: The Veneration of the Prophet in Islamic Piety.* Chapel Hill: The University of North Carolina Press, 1985.

Subtelny, Maria E. "The Jews at the Edge of the World in a Timurid-Era Mi'rajnama: The Islamic Ascension Narrative as Missionary Text." In *The Prophet's Ascension: Cross-Cultural Encounters with the Islamic Mi'raj Tales*, edited by Christiane Gruber and Frederick S. Colby. Bloomington: Indiana University Press, 2010.

Vajda, G. "Isrāʾīliyyāt." In *Encyclopaedia of Islam,* 2nd ed., n.d. Accessed October 5, 2018.

Wolper, Ethel Sara. "Khidr and the Changing Frontiers of the Medieval World." *Medieval Encounters* 17, no. 1/2 (March 2011): 120–146. https://doi.org/10.1163/157006711X561730.

Zargar, Cyrus Ali. *Sufi Aesthetics: Beauty, Love, and the Human Form in the Writings of Ibn 'Arabi and 'Iraqi.* Columbia: University of South Carolina Press, 2011.

8 Bodies in translation

Esoteric conceptions of the Muslim body in early-modern South Asia[1]

Patrick J. D'Silva

Introduction

> First, that the entire human body is held together with veins.
> It is necessary that one of these veins has information (*khabar*).
> Second, namely that the veins of the body are the source of the human breath, which appears from those veins.
> Third, one should know that each breath (*nafas*) individually goes by three paths.
> The first is from the right side, they say it is of the sun.
> The second is from the left side, they say it is of the moon.
> The third is in the middle of two nostrils, they say it is heavenly (*asmani*).
> Every breath (*dam*) has a special quality.[2]
>
> Sayyid al-Din Bukhari, *Miz al-nafas*

When does a body *become* Hindu or Muslim? Indian or Persian? Esoteric or exoteric? Mystical or mundane? In pre- and early-modern South Asia there were numerous translations and interpretations of a set of divination techniques known in Sanskrit as *svarodaya* ("the attainment of the toned breath"). As early as the fourteenth century CE, these techniques were translated into Persian as *`ilm-i dam* ("the science of the breath"). Classified at different times as astrology, medicine, and mysticism, the science of the breath has attracted sustained interest through the twenty-first century in both India and Iran.

Given that interest in these practices crosses the boundaries between modern nation-states, what then is the relationship between the science of the breath and other ways of knowing such as yoga and Ayurveda? Are there places where one could say that a body is deemed "yogic" or "ayurvedic"? These are all manifestations of the ways in which examining corporeal boundaries yields a study in how those limits are perpetually shifting and refusing to be fixed in material realms. As Judith Butler notes in *Bodies that Matter*, it is no small feat to hem in and bind the body:

> ...but I found I could not *fix* bodies as simple objects of thought. Not only did bodies tend to indicate a world beyond themselves, but this

> movement beyond their own boundaries, a movement of boundary itself, appeared to be quite central to what bodies 'are.'[3]

This chapter situates the science of the breath within systems of bodily knowledge that are typically seen as distinct from one another. Ayurveda and yoga are usually associated with "traditional" Indian religions such as Hinduism, Buddhism, and Jainism. However, the science of the breath offers a window into an example where Persianate Muslim communities in the pre- and early-modern periods actively engaged with practices that demonstrate a conception of the body that is closely linked to that of Ayurveda and yoga (implicit in the former, and explicit in the latter). While there is substantial literature on the ways that people of many different religious communities collectively patronize Sufi shrines and festivals, there is less work on how this type of permeable membrane manifests in conceptions of the body.[4] This chapter asks questions as to what can be learned by foregrounding esoteric or "subtle" conceptions of the body, and using that to support an understanding of the exoteric or "gross" bodies bound up in these boundary-defying conceptions. Citing examples from Persian manuscripts written in India and Iran dating to the sixteenth to nineteenth CE, and with particular references to the *Bahr al-hayat* ("Ocean of Life") of famed Shattari Sufi master Muhammad Ghawth (d. 1563 CE) and Sufi yoga texts from Bengal, this chapter argues for a broader conception of "the Islamic body." Ghawth discusses differences between teachings of the Prophet Muhammad and the yogis regarding the body's need for the spirit, but he does not dismiss the yogis, instead asking his readers to take advice from both sides in order to realize the shared link between them that is only available through esoteric contemplation.[5] As I discuss in more detail below, contemporaneous texts from Bengal map the yogic *cakra*s ("subtle centers") onto the *maqam*s ("stations") and *manzil*s ("abodes") that known from Sufi discourses on the spiritual path.[6] How does one make sense of these searches for equivalence? Recognizing that there are different visions of the physical body leads to the notion that there are more visions that usually acknowledged in terms of bodies of knowledge. Studying the science of the breath facilitates connections with approaches to reconciling cosmological differences in Islam and yoga that confound the modern-day imposition of boundaries between these ways of knowing.

These primary sources include instructions on using knowledge of the breath for divination purposes, as well as manipulating other people, specifically other people's bodies. Practitioners of this science must learn to discern the quality of the breath. At any given moment, is the breath connected to the sun or the moon? The left side or the right side of the body? Which of the five elements (earth, air, fire, water, and ether) is strongest at the moment of contemplation? An added layer of complication involves combining knowledge of the breath with time of day, day of the week, and position of celestial bodies such as planets and the stars. Properly harnessing the power of all these bodies and their myriad forms holds the promise of incredible power, all made possible by a conceptualization of the breath is the simultaneously concrete and ephemeral. Concrete, because one can use knowledge of it to destroy others as well as navigate the struggles of daily life, including success with one's rulers, purchasing livestock, getting dressed, and discerning the health and gender of unborn children. Ephemeral, because the breath is constantly in motion, forcing a practitioner of this science to learn to chart its transitions in order to best take care of oneself and others. The science of the breath demonstrates how esoteric knowledge holds highly practical information, aiding practitioners in dealing with daily struggles.

By drawing on work by Judith Butler and Gilles Deleuze for theoretical resources on materializing the body and rhizomatic models for exchange, respectively, and scholarship by Joseph Alter, Shahzad Bashir, Carl Ernst, and Shaman Hatley on South Asia and the study of Islam, this chapter articulates a model of the body that is equally Islamicate and Indic, raising the question of how precisely scholars working on Islam in South Asia can develop theoretical frameworks for belief and practice in the pre- and early-modern period that are grounded in solid textual evidence.[7] These frameworks invite scholars to further develop an Islamic imaging of the body in a pluralistic religious environment. This is an equally relevant inquiry whether situated in South Asia or other regions around the world.

Ayurveda

Moving to non-Islamic perspectives, one important system to take into consideration is Ayurveda, an ancient set of knowledge and techniques for maintaining bodily health that has enjoyed a great deal of popularity in recent times, spreading beyond India to Europe and North America. Of key importance for this project are the two visions of the body found in ayurvedic treatises. First, there is the "material body," corresponding to the notion of the body as static or fixed in nature, as it might appear in illustrated form on the pages of a medical textbook. Second, there is the "embodied self," which is of an entirely different conception. Where the first may be treated as an object that stands apart from any context, the second "presents a modal case of being-in-the-world; it presents a portrait of an active patient whose experience of health or illness cannot be fully knowable apart from her or his relationships with other people and the natural world."[8] This distinction in the ayurvedic traditions could be one example of developing a new approach to theorizing the vision of the body in the science of the breath texts. There is no discussion of homologous categories such as "embodied self" or "material body." Even in the *svarodaya* texts, one does not find these categories; thus, it is unsurprising that they do not appear in the *`ilm-i dam* texts. Yet, the body in this context is certainly potent, and one is able to generate great powers through attuning an awareness of the breath. But who precisely is permitted to practice this science, and dispense the wisdom gained through its mastery? There are no stipulations listed as to bodily purity (anatomical, physiological, or ritually construed).

The clearest indication regarding the practice for learning these skills comes in generalities:

> This should be paid attention to with experience (*tajriba*), so that one is able to understand: one should make known from which side one inhales.[9]
>
> When its knowledge (*ma`rifat*) is apprehended, after every practice, I will say which breath was good in correspondence to these actions, and which was not good.[10]

The context for the first excerpt here is that the practitioner must learn to discern on which side the breath is flowing. However, in the second excerpt, the author speaks in the first person—a rare occurrence even within the corpus as a whole, where most of the references are oblique third-person plurals such as "they say"—telling the reader what to expect in the passages that follow, where the author lays out a series of situations, identifying which type of breath is preferable.

Yoga

Another system identified very closely with India is that of yoga, which has seen exponentially more growth in India as well as its export to Europe, North America, and all over the world in the past century. Yoga is a term that has come to encompass a great many sets of philosophies and practices. At present, the goals of those practicing yoga include everything from increased bodily flexibility to the attainment of union with the divine, with a great many stages in between. Just as the ends diverge, so too do the means. Control of one's breathing, mastery of the body, increased physical (and spiritual?) strength; all of these become considerations. One of the other names of *svarodaya* is *svara-yoga*, as shown in the twentieth-century English translation from Sanskrit by Swami Muktibodhananda entitled *Swara Yoga: The Tantric Science of Brain Breathing.*[11] One challenge with invoking a term like yoga is that its definition is decidedly heterogeneous in nature. As David Gordon White outlines in the introduction to *Yoga in Practice*, yoga can refer to things ranging from the literal yoking of one's animals, to an astral conjunction, to a type of recipe, incantation, combination, application, contact, "...and the Work of alchemists. But this is by no means an exhaustive list."[12] In so far as it is possible to determine a fixed list of priorities or aims from such a vast discursive tradition, White stipulates that yoga encompasses four main principles: first, "an analysis of perception and cognition"; second, "the raising and expansion of consciousness"; third, "a path to omniscience"; and fourth, "a technique for entering into other bodies, generating multiple bodies, and the attainment of other supernatural accomplishments."[13] *Svarodaya* and *`ilm-i dam* could fit quite easily within the first three of these, while the fourth would be a bit of a stretch. For my purposes, the fact that the arts and sciences of understanding one's *svara* has already been construed as a type of yoga makes the connection worth exploring in greater detail.

Even in cases that would typically not be classified as philosophical or religious, there are still connections to the notion of the body as an organism whose most effective functioning is rooted in knowledge of the breath. As Alter writes about wrestling in north India, *pranayama* (controlled breathing) is recognized as an important technique that wrestlers must master in order to improve their bodily powers. Breathing just to breathe is insufficient, because it "only satisfies the needs of the gross body. To breathe properly harmonizes the body with the mind: the spiritual with the physical."[14] That the practice is understood to streamline the mind-body connection is clear, but the details are key: a wrestler must breathe through his nose while expanding his diaphragm. A great deal of emphasis is placed on this point. If one gasps for air with an open mouth and heaving chest, it is likened to the agency of an inanimate bellows. Breathing in this fashion performs the function of putting air into the body and taking it out, but as such it is purely mechanical.[15] Here, the body is seen as being animated by the breath in very powerful ways. Beyond simple inhalation and exhalation, all breathers—that is to say, all human beings—are advised to pay attention to their breath in such a way as to transcend the "purely mechanical" experience of the world, and move into a more empowered state. In the case of wrestling, this has very clear applications to physical combat with one's opponent. In the *`ilm-i dam* texts, there is little to no explicit references to this type of one-on-one fighting. Instead, the contexts in which combat takes place at larger-scale military ventures (i.e., one army fighting another), or more political or courtly intrigue (i.e., using knowledge of the breath to defeat one's adversary while enjoying an audience before one's ruler).

> By comparison, for example, to the role of *brahmacarya* (celibate) that Joseph Alter describes playing a prominent role in northern Indian notions of masculinity and bodily control, in which practices such as semen retention could have important consequences, in the *`ilm-i dam* texts, one does not get the impression that practitioners would have understood the consequences of the breath in quite the same manner. The breath is vital, a potentially powerful aspect through which the universal power is literally taken into the body, but the body conceived here is a more passive entity than the wrestlers that Alter mentions.[16] In the cases of Ayurveda and yoga, there are very rich philosophical contexts explicitly linked to these practices. As Cerulli describes, the conceptualization of the "embodied self" is rooted in specific notions of *atman*, "a nonmaterial self," which in turn is tied to the idea that caring for the body "is the foundational *dharma* to which all people must attend

> before everything else in their lives to ensure optimal performance of the complex array of all the other *dharmas* in the social and religious arenas."[17] In the case of yoga, one finds so many references and descriptions of the term that it is almost impossible to speak of the term in the singular. Instead, there are many different yogas, with each varying depending on specific context. I agree with Alter's statement: It is problematic to think of knowledge, ideas, and forms of embodied practice in terms of the same categories that define either trade and travel or the bounded geopolitical units between which these things are conducted. Although one can construct a history of ideas that outlines the ultimate development of a tradition as encompassing as Yoga, and locate the development of those ideas in a particular place, there is no need to think of this tradition *as it developed through time as an essentially bounded entity.*[18]

Part of the challenge in triangulating *`ilm-i dam*'s historical context is dealing with the porous nature of its boundaries. Deciding which analytic(s) to use in differentiating between the various potential classifications is no simple matter. Like so many others with yoga, I am attempting here to "construct a history of ideas" encompassing *`ilm-i dam*, but I find that each of the qualifiers (Islamic, Hindu, Indic, Persian(-ate), mystical, magical, religious, scientific, medical, etc.) leaves out important material.

It is helpful here to situate *`ilm-i dam* within the broader framework of *svarodaya*. The Sanskrit and Hindi texts include significant astrological material, with specific information on the role played by the position of the planets and other celestial bodies alongside assessing the nature of one's breath in determining the auspicious or inauspicious nature of particular actions.[19] Known in India as *jyotisha*, practitioners of this knowledge have at times enjoyed prominent roles in courtly settings. Even today, there has been a resurgence in the active promulgation of this knowledge in Indian universities.[20] By linking *`ilm-i dam* explicitly to South Asian astrological traditions, I aim to contextualize these breathing practices in a cosmopolitan milieu where knowledge passed fluidly back and forth across religious, ethnic, and linguistic boundaries.

I want to exercise caution here in drawing a direct equivalence between those practicing *`ilm-i dam* and those who see themselves as astrologers. This is because while the Sanskrit *svarodaya* texts contain astrological content, in most cases the Persian and Arabic *`ilm-i dam* texts do not. Still, because the *`ilm-i dam* material consistently contains not only directives for understanding one's own fortunes, but also the fortunes of others, it stands to reason that there is much to be gained from taking scholarly insights on astrologers and apply them to those practicing *`ilm-i dam*. This is an extension of the methodology employed for this chapter, that there are important connections between systems of knowledge that we as scholars might ordinarily divide up due to differences in terminology, religion, language, or geography. While respecting differences is important, so too is cultivating an understanding of when we can break down some of these barriers. At the end of the day, my concern is analyzing how these bodies function in the world—both physically and figuratively.

Islamicate views of the body

In exploring these various contexts, I have made recourse to different knowledge systems that circulated in India alongside *svarodaya* and *`ilm-i dam*. Examining each system—even briefly—helps to triangulate the boundaries of the science of the breath. Given that I am primarily concerned with *`ilm-i dam* as an expression of Muslim interest in Indian esotericism, and that many of the Muslim interlocutors in this process are explicitly affiliated with Sufi organizations, I will begin with a brief sketch of Islamic conceptions of the body with an emphasis on Sufi expressions thereof. In *Sufis and Saints' Bodies*, Scott Kugle argues that Sufis' affirming of God's immanent nature leads them "to value the body in ways fuller and deeper than other Muslim authorities."[21] This casts the interest in the body as part of a broader articulation and experience of God's love for creation, and puts Sufis in the position of seeing the body differently than non-Sufis due to a type of theological position that is more than doctrine. Kugle makes recourse to a text by Chishti Sufi Diya' al-Din Nakhshabi (d. 1350) entitled *Juz'-yat o Kulliyat* ("The Parts and the Wholes") as a guiding frame for his broader inquiry into Sufi conceptions of the body. "Sufis came to see the body not as the enemy to be opposed by strenuous ascetic effort...but, more subtly, as a sign of the creator, or rather as a whole constellation of signs."[22] As one might understand the universe through studying the stars, so too can one understand divine purpose and plan through studying the signs in the body. Most pertinent for connecting to *`ilm-i dam* is the Qur'anic account of Adam's creation, which reads "I molded him and breathed into him of My spirit."[23] Kugle's interpretation of this scripture is key because it establishes an anchor point for one of the many understandings of the body in this essay:

> This magisterial image of the material body being enlivened with the breath of the spirit that blows into it and through it from beyond is the central paradox of the human body from an Islamic point of view. It is material, therefore ephemeral, limited in space, fragile, even brittle; however, it is material infused with spirit and is therefore eternal, unbounded in space, opening into the infinite beyond waking consciousness and participating in durable cosmic being beyond personal weakness.[24]

The vision that Kugle conveys here maps nicely onto the conception of the body found in Ayurveda and yoga. The particular cosmology cited may differ, but there is a shared sense of the body as inspired (literally) with a type of breath that is cosmic and divine in nature.

Shahzad Bashir's work reevaluating the historiography of Persianate Central Asia is focused more on the fourteenth and fifteenth centuries, specifically on the way that Sufi texts from this period carry with them a sense of the body inscribed "not out of explicit intention but as a reflection of a socioreligious habitus that was integral to [the authors] way of seeing the world."[25] I would not argue that there is an explicit theory of the body in the *`ilm-i dam* corpus. Instead, the normative standards, expectations, and potentialities incumbent on the practitioners is implicit. While Bashir examines textual and visual depictions of dream narratives involving the body, the *`ilm-i dam* corpus does not offer the same type of data. Still, Bashir's insights are helpful for giving a fuller form to a sense of the body rooted in Islamicate contexts that are roughly contemporaneous to some of the *`ilm-i dam* texts. Both Kugle and Bashir work to integrate the study of Islam and Muslims within the broader—and rapidly growing—framework of modern-day scholarship on religion and embodiment. In the work that follows on *`ilm-i dam*, I seek to emphasize systems of understanding the body that are more contemporaneous with the pre- and early-modern periods in South Asia. Accordingly, Shaman Hatley's work on yoga and Sufism in Bengal provides perspective that is more grounded in the cultural milieu that I associate with many of the *`ilm-i dam* texts.

In examining the process through which Bengali Muslims translated yogic categories of the body into Islamic ones, Hatley identifies the Nātha yogis as a starting point, specifically the sixteenth century, with links to Śaiva Tantra dating to the eleventh and twelfth centuries.[26] Hatley points out that since Tantric yoga was integrated with Śaivism, Buddhism, Vaiṣṇavism, and Jainism, it should not be surprising that it made its way into Islam, most notably Sufism.[27] This translation process was not patronized by a singular authority, but instead is polycentric in nature, with authors emphasizing or dealing with aspects of the translation process in a different way. For example, sometimes the references to Nātha practice would be retained, while other times they were left out. Islamic categories would usually be translated into Bengali or Sanskrit equivalents, and both Persian and Arabic would be used as a type of technical vocabulary.[28] This delineation between using one language as for technical terms, while another is used for the vernacular, or applied register, is also found in the *`ilm-i dam* corpus. For the key terms of sun and moon, authors frequently use the Arabic terms *shams* and *qamar* when referring to the esoteric solar and lunar breaths, while the Persian terms *aftab* and *mehtab* are used when discussing the physical celestial objects. While Hatley finds differences between "classical Sufism" and the Sufi yoga texts over issues such as the immortality of the body, or the latter genre's lack of discussion of divine love, he nonetheless identifies a sustained interest concerning the organization of the subtle body, namely the homology between Tantric *cakras* (centers) and Sufi *maqams* ("stations"). Additionally, the body is mapped onto the system of *manzils* ("abodes"), all of which undergirds the Sufi spiritual life:

> *Shari`ah*, Islamic orthopraxis, *tariqah*, the path of Sufi discipline; *haqiqah*, the experience of truth or reality; and *ma`rifah*, ultimate gnosis. This homology of the *cakras* with Sufi *maqams* and the stages of the religious path seamlessly integrates Islamic orthopraxy within the framework of Islamic yoga and relegates it, as in many forms of Sufism, to a low but foundational station.[29]

I would urge caution in evaluating these homologies. There is no unitive moment of exchange between Sufis and yogis. As the review of texts demonstrate, this is a dynamic series of exchanges, with individual actors expressing creative agency along the way. Adapting Judith Butler's invocation from above, to study the esoteric body is to see the myriad ways that the definitions of that body move with each attempt to capture an essence.

Nadis: channels mediating the connection between macro- and microcosms

With Hatley's work on Bengali Sufi translations of yogic works in mind, I want to introduce another way of following the breath's path across religious and linguistic boundaries, all the while staying within the same vision of the body. The concept of the *nadi* is central for understanding the visioning of how and where astral power flows through the body. These *nadis* are channels that map onto both the micro- and macrocosmic realms. Some renditions count millions of such channels labeled as such in Yogic and Tantric renderings of human physiology, in which they serve as conduits for the energy that drives the human body. Within the Sanskrit *svarodaya* corpus, there are references to three principle channels, flowing through the left side (*ida*), right side (*pingala*), and central axis (*susumna*) of the body. For example, one *svarodaya* text informs readers that

> [t]here are numerous *nadis* of different sizes in the body and they should be known by the erudites for the knowledge about their own bodies. Originating like sprouts from the root situated a little above the navel, there are 72,000 *nadis* in the body.[30]

In his work on *nadi* divination and astrology, Martin Gangsten outlines a history of the different practices typically subsumed under this heading.[31] In the course of his investigation, Gangsten comments that there are several different derivations for the term. He notes that the Sanskrit term means "tube, hollow stalk," and dates back to the time of the Upanishads, and

> is thought to pulsate through the body; hence, a derived meaning of *nadi* is 'pulse.' Some writers would connect the word in this sense with the divinatory art, while others again focus on *nadi* as a particular measure of time (synonymous with *ghati*), related to the rising of minute divisions of the zodiac over the horizon.[32]

For a comparison from the *`ilm-i dam* corpus, in Abu'l Fazl ibn Mubarak's text from the *A'in-i akbari*, he specifically references the three principle *nadis*, connecting *Ida* (vital spirit), or *Chandra-nadi*, with the left nostril, while *Pingala* (sun or fire), otherwise known as *Surya-nadi*, connects with the right nostril. The third type of breath is called *Sushumna* or *Sambhu-nadi*, and is "attributed to the influence of *Mahadeva*" (*nam-zad-i maha-dev namand*).[33]

The discussion of the correspondence between the macro- and microcosmic worlds is by no means limited to the *`ilm-i dam* corpus, or even the broader genre of astrology. The *nadis* are key, but equally important is the role played by the person who understands themselves as the nexus point at which the micro- and macrocosms meet. Lyssenko argues that "one common point characteristic of the micro-mascrocosmic speculations in India" is that

> ...it is not the universe that is its starting point and basis, but the individual, the human being and more precisely his/hers sense capacities to grasp some properties (stimuli) of the surrounding world and to communicate with it in different manners proper to the human psychosomatic structure.[34]

This emphasis on the individual, thus the individual's body, is important because it highlights individual agency. However, at the same time, none of these individual bodies exist without some type of collective society that shapes and molds them. The next sections introduce a series of examples of different types of individuals and views on the role that the body plays mediating the relationship between the individual and their social context.

Risalah-i dam az [hawz?] al-hayat

Second, the *Risalah-i dam az [hawz?] al-hayat*[35] ("Treatise on the Breath from the [Sea] of Life") is from the library of an important Indian Muslim court: Tipu Sultan, who died in battle against the British in 1799 at Seringapatam. The preface contains no information about the provenance of the knowledge contained in the text, but does include explicit references to correspondences between macro- and microcosms: *aftab va mahtab har che ta'sir-i dam dar `alam-i kabir darand va dar `alam-i saghir hami aftab va mahtab ast* ("the sun and moon each have an influence on the breath on the macrocosm, and they are also present in the microcosm").[36] This is the same conceptual language found in Sanskrit texts expounding upon the existence of the *nadis*, the channels running throughout the microcosm of the human body that then directly correspond to channels in the macrocosmic universe. Similar to other texts described in this section, the author of this particular text invokes Arabic terminology for technical terms such as *`alam-i kabir* and *`alam-i saghir*, literally meaning "large world" and "small world," respectively. Different from other texts, this author retains the Persian terms *aftab* and *mahtab* for sun and moon throughout the text, rather than the Arabic terms *shams* and *qamar*.

While this author eschews Arabic in some contexts, he invokes in others. The text includes instructions on using some Arabic phrases to enable success, such as *bi-tawfiq allah ta`ala* in a section on obtaining victory in warfare, or *qul huwa Allah ahad* ("say: he is Allah, the One").[37] At one point during the text, the author appears to switch from the Persian *dam* to the Arabic *nafas*, a combination that raises questions about how we might differentiate the valence of each term when (unlike as raised above) the Arabic is not being introduced as a technical term. At the conclusion, the author stitches together an assortment of amazing references. He writes that "most scholars of India" (*aksar `ulama'-i hind*) undertake these practices, and that "some of the people of Islam" (*ba`zi ahl-i islam*) undertake "the above-mentioned action" (*`amal-i mastur*) as they "draw near knowledge" (*nazd-i ma`rifat*).[38] The final passage contains several lines that help draw out the distinctions between this manuscript and the other members of the corpus:

> This practice should be done repeatedly in other work. Most of the scholars of India (*'ulama'-yi hind*) carry out this work (*'amal*) have reached their essence, [and] some of the people of Islam (*ahl-i islam*) carried out the above-mentioned work [for] knowledge (*ma`arifat*), as it should be in order to obtain in practice (*shughl*) is not negligence (*ihmal nist*), whether it happens or not. After that the forty-day retreat will be recorded, according to which the master (*pir*) and disciple (*murshid*) have ordered that work be done.[39]

What emerges from this passage is the explicit links to other aspects of Sufi practices, specifically the reference to the forty-day retreat, the "scholars of India" as an identified class of individuals, as well as the aforementioned master/disciple relationship, and, last but not least, the "people of Islam." This is not so much a normative statement about what particular groups of Muslims believe, but invoking these terms makes the "Islamic" nature of the text much harder to debate.

Sufi treatise on macro- and microcosms

As a third example, there is an untitled and anonymous Sufi treatise from the Delhi Persian collection at the British Library that speaks of the connections between the macrocosm (*`alam-i kabir*) and the microcosm (*`alam-i saghir*), but in this case the connection is one in which the latter is a reflection of the former, and there is no mention of channels such as the *nadi*s serving as channels mediating the flow of power or correspondence from one realm to the other.[40] While the manuscript is untitled and anonymous, the final page contains a Kubrawi, followed by a Naqshbandi *silsila*, thus establishing affiliations with two important Sufi *tariqa*s in India. The text contains repeated mentions of the prophets Jesus, Moses, Noah, and Muhammad. It also tells the reader that the world is made up of ten things: five of which are the five elements of earth, water, air, fire, and "breath" (*nafas*).[41] These brief examples demonstrates that discussion of the correspondences between the gross and subtle realms was by no means the exclusive domain of authors writing in Sanskrit, Hindi, or other Indian languages.

My goal in this brief overview of the *nadis* and other approaches to micro- and macrocosmic correspondences has been to demonstrate that within pre- and early-modern India there were indeed different models for approaching and discussing this issue. The *nadis* may literally operate as channels through which the *svara* or *dam* flows to great effect; however, I see further theoretical implications for them. Through understanding the vocabulary that authors use for discussing the interaction of the subtle and gross realms, I argue that we can analyze those authors' vision of the body as an entity inter-woven with the world around it.

Miz al-nafas and bodily control of self and others

In this section, I move the discussion from comparing across *`ilm-i dam* texts to focusing on a single example. In this brief case study, I demonstrate how one *`ilm-i dam* text from early-modern India provides scholars with important insight into the powers available to those who are able to use the breath. The quote opening this chapter provides the clearest vision of the relationship between the body, the breath, and the information (*khabar*) conveyed from the latter to the former. This vision of the body and the breath comes from *Miz al-nafas*, which details the circumstances surrounding the translation of an *`ilm-i dam* text from Hindavi into Persian at a shrine known as Piranpatan in Gujarat. This text would come to be collected with ten others, all on different topics, but including medicine, physiognomy, interpretation of pulses, meaning of sneezes, and sexology, which were edited together in the sixteenth century in a volume that was included in the royal Mughal library held at the Red Fort in Delhi. There are no other known copies of this text, so there is no way to determine with any accuracy how much earlier the reported translation took place, or if this manuscript itself is the original product of the exchange between the patron, Shaykh Jalal al-Din al-Bengali, and the translator, Sayyid Burhan al-Din Bukhari. The excerpt from the epigraph above, taken from the very beginning of the text, points to a very specific understanding of the relationship between the body and the breath. The fact that this breath comes *from* the veins (*rig-ha*), and not from some other source, indicates that in these practices, the body produces this breath all on its own. This would appear to be the very definition of mutually constitutive. Additionally, one of these veins "has information" (*khabar darad*). While the precise scope of this *khabar* is left unspecified in this passage, reading through the rest of the text helps a great deal in narrowing it down. The *khabar* referenced here is the information that comes with the awareness of the breath, which of the five elements is dominant, and the link to the sun or moon. This stands in important distinction to other terms of "ways of knowing" that are included in the text, such as *`ilm* or *ma`rifat*. The term for vein, *rig*, could be one translation of the Sanskrit term *nadi*, referring to the channels through which the breath flows, and in turn through which the macro- and microcosms are connected. Another possibility is that the term *tariq*, here rendered as "path," would be the Persian gloss of *nadi*. Given that the three principle *nadis* (*ida*, *pingala*, and *sushumna*) are often listed in *svarodaya* and *`ilm-i dam* texts, if not by name than according to their associations with the moon and the sun, then I am persuaded by the latter over the former. As explained earlier in this chapter, the concept of *nadi* is rather expansive, so both *rig* and *tariq* would be operable translations into Persian.

The complete and empty breaths

Consider this brief example of one application of this knowledge of the breath:

> If somebody wants to go on a short journey, let him go with the solar breath, but on the condition that the breath should be complete. Every breath that should be empty, let him ignore it. In the breath of fullness, let him expel it. If there is fullness in the lunar breath, go out with the left foot. If there is fullness in the solar breath, go out with the right foot.[42]

This is another layer beyond ascertaining the lunar or solar affiliation, for here the practitioner has to understand when the breath is either complete (*kamuliyyat*) or empty (*khali*). Later on, the text introduces another element, which is determining when the breath is full (*purri*). These technical terms carry with them a distinct sense of the breath that is in turn linked to the body. A body holding a "complete" breath is capable of different things than one holding an "empty" breath, which in actuality is no longer holding a breath at all, or perhaps the very potential for creating the breath constitutes a type of breath unto itself. As the excerpt above demonstrates, when the solar breath courses through the body, this has consequences for how one controls that body (i.e., starting travel with the right foot), compared to the lunar breath and the left food. This begs the question, what would happen to someone who did the opposite of the prescribed order of operations, and knowingly started their travels with the left foot even with the solar breath was present? Such a person would be flying in the face of the very cosmic order of things, and as such would most likely bring doom and destruction upon themselves and possibly those around them.

Three-dimensional breathing and envisioning of the body

> Know that of the six aspects [*jihat*], three aspects are related to the sun breath. Three aspects are related to the moon breath, whereby if it is before, above, and to the right, it is related to the sun breath. In front of, to the left, and under is related to the moon breath.[43]

In this passage, the author presents even more layers for understanding and visioning the way that the breath relates to the human body. In 360 degrees, three dimensions, the practitioner can develop a sense of the breath where it envelops them, flowing in and out not just of their body but also the space immediately around them. In so doing, the body extends outside of its physical limits, powers generated solely through attuning one's knowledge of the breath to the cosmic rhythms that—like the ocean's tide—operate whether one notices them or not. In the same section, the author provides a detailed exposition in which the practitioner is faced with a question from someone "asking which army was victorious":

> If asking with the sun breath about an army distant from the person, there will be victory. If asking with the moon breath about an army that is nearby him, he will be victorious. If asking with the full breath, the friend will be victorious. If asking with the empty breath, the enemy will be victorious.[44]

Note the different elements that the practitioner must determine in order to ascertain the result of the battle: sun and moon, far and near, full and empty, friend and foe. There are associations drawn between the full breath and the friend's victory, and then the empty breath and the enemy's victory, but these associations are not consistently applied throughout the text.

> If someone is asking with the moon breath: If the letters of the name of lord of the army are even, he will be victorious because even letters are related to the moon breath. If someone is asking with the sun breath: If the letters of the name of the lord of the army are odd, he will be victorious because odd letters are related to the sun breath.[45]

Here in this passage, immediately following the one cited above, the author introduces numerology in a manner consistent with other *`ilm-i dam* texts.

A numerical value is determined by using the *abjad* system, in which each letter of the army leader's name has a specific value, and then the total is either an odd or even number. But note here the added wrinkle: the outcome is dependent on both the sum total determined by the *abjad* system, and whether the solar or lunar breath is dominant in the body *of the person asking the question.* The implication here is that the practitioner is able to assess not only the status of their own breath, but also the status of another person's breath. This sets up a scenario in which practitioners of *`ilm-i dam* are able to see (or sense?) inside other human beings, understanding how they relate to the cosmic order of things. This (literal) insight is a powerful ability with great ethical responsibilities.

Conclusion

Future research is necessary to firm up the theoretical framework for understanding how to isolate the "ayurvedic" body from the "yogic" body and the "*`ilm-i dam*" body. In particular, I would like to closely examine this notion that each of these bodies is commensurable with one another. It is worth pointing out that in arguing for the ease with which notions of the body travel across permeable boundaries, scholars should keep in mind that the differences are just as important as the similarities. Treating *svarodaya* and *`ilm-i dam* as simultaneously distinct *and* unified creates exciting analytical possibilities, while also raising some problems. The boundaries I speak of in this context are not just the texts themselves (i.e., the languages, time periods, and places in which they were composed), but also the ways that modern-day scholarly approaches to these texts are defined so much by arbitrary constructions of disciplines and departments, particularly in the Euro-American academy. While this type of isolation is inimical to the general approach I endorse, I can also acknowledge the utility of pulling back for a broader view when attempts at the granular level microscopic view yield an image with too much overlap and permeability to make for useful description and analysis.

Importantly, while this chapter is rooted in the early-modern period, it sets the stage for work pursuing these lines of inquiry into the modern period. In the late twentieth century, Hindu teachers in India have translated texts on the science of the breath into English, while as recently as April 2013, Ayatollah Hassan Zadeh Amali of Iran posted a related text in Persian on his personal website.[46] Taken together, these anecdotes suggest that studying the science of the breath enables scholars to study esoteric knowledge in order to understand the porous nature of boundaries between religious traditions.

In his work on dance and performance, Benjamin Spatz asks:

> How can we understand the depths at which technique changes us through practice, over time and sometimes radically? What is the

relationship between knowledge and power, in the practice of embodied technique? Do we sing the song, or does the song sing us?[47]

If I substitute the word "breath" for "song," then I am left with a number of startling implications. In examining the different perspectives on the power of the breath in the above materials, there is little question for me that practitioners of *`ilm-i dam* saw the breath as a powerful force, and that learning to control that force could yield equally powerful results. What is less clear is whether or not these authors saw this detailed observance of the breath as a way of bringing their bodies, and thus the actions that they undertook with those bodies, into concert with any type of balance, or perhaps I would say, "in-tune" with the rhythm of the universe. This would be one area for future research related to these practices, especially if brought into conversation with other breath-centered divination practices in different cultural and historical settings. If the breath is fully commensurable between bodies—no matter how human communities mark those bodies—then questions arise as to how scholars might ascertain and evaluate the degree of overlap and difference between the conceptions of the breath itself.

Notes

1 An abridged form of this chapter was presented at the "Material Islam Seminar" at the 2018 American Academy of Religion conference in Denver, CO. I would like to thank the Material Islam's conveners, Anna Bigelow and Kambiz Ghanea Bassiri, for their invitation to present this work as part of their seminar, as well as Katherine Zubko for the subsequent invitation to contribute to the present edited volume.

2 *Miz al-Nafas*, British Library Delhi Persian 796d (London), folio 57b-58a.

3 Judith Butler, *Bodies that Matter: On the Discursive Limits of "Sex"* (New York: Routledge, 1993), *ix*.

4 There is substantial literature on this subject, but two examples would be Joyce Flueckiger, *In Amma's Healing Room: Gender and Vernacular Islam in South India* (Bloomington: Indiana University Press, 2006), and Anna Bigelow, *Sharing the Sacred: Practicing Pluralism in Muslim North India* (Oxford: Oxford University Press, 2010).

5 Muhammad Ghawth, *Bahr al-hayat*, trans, Carl W. Ernst, cited in "Sufism and Yoga According to Muhammad Ghawth," in *Refractions of Islam in India* (Delhi: Sage Publications, 2016), 157.

6 Shaman Hatley, "Mapping the Esoteric Body in the Islamic Yoga of Bengal," *History of Religions* 46, no. 4 (2007): 362–363.

7 I would like to thank Danielle Wideman Abraham for pointing out to me that in India, at least, there is no real questioning of the degree to which these different bodies (Hindu and Muslim, for example) are *commensurable*. That is to say, our bodies as fundamentally the same, regardless of how we mark them in terms of religious identity or communal membership. An area for further thought and research would be to analyze the limits of this commensurability. In what ways do powers leveraged by state (and other) actors work to place firm boundaries on the body that conflict with the type of commensurability seen in corporeal visions witnessed across yoga, Ayurveda, and *`ilm-i dam*?

8 Anthony Cerulli, "Body, Self, and Embodiment in the Sanskrit Classics of Ayurveda," in *Refiguring the Body: Embodiment in South Asian Religions*, ed. Barbara Holdredge and Karen Pechilis (Albany: State University of New York Press, 2016), 61.
9 *Kamaru Panchashika abridgment* (Browne recension), folio 59b.
10 *Kamaru Panchashika abridgment* (Browne recension), folio 60a.
11 Swami Muktibodhananda, *Swara Yoga: The Tantric Science of Brain Breathing* (Yoga Publications Trust: Munger, Bihar, India, 1984), 72.
12 David Gordon White, "Introduction," in *Yoga in Practice* (Princeton: Princeton University Press, 2012), 2.
13 White, *Yoga in Practice*, 6–10.
14 Joseph Alter, *The Wrestler's Body: Identity and Ideology in North India* (Berkeley: University of California Press, 1992), 95–96.
15 Joseph Alter, *The Wrestler's Body*, 96.
16 Joseph Alter, "Celibacy, Sexuality, and Nationalism in North India" in *Bodies in Contact: Rethinking Colonial Encounters in World History*, eds. Tony Ballantyne and Antoinette Burton (Durham, NC: Duke University Press, 2005), 310–322.
17 Cerulli, "Body, Self and Embodiment," 61.
18 Joseph Alter, "Yoga in Asia—Mimetic History: Problems in the Location of Secret Knowledge," *Comparative Studies South Asia, Africa, and the Middle East* 29, no. 2 (2009): 217, emphasis added. I differ from Alter in rendering yoga in lower-case letters, which in my view helps emphasize its unbounded nature. By contrast, my readings of Ayurveda lead me the opposite direction, and so I follow Cerulli in capitalizing Ayurveda.
19 For representative examples of this material, see Ram Kumar Rai's translation and commentary, *Śivasvarodaya*. Tantra Granthamala No. 1 (Varanasi: Prachya Prakashan, 1980), as well as Yogi Ramacharaka, *The Hindu-Yogi Science of Breath: A Complete Manual of the Oriental Breathing Philosophy of Physical, Mental, Psychic and Spiritual Development* (Chicago: Yogi Publication Society, c. 1905).
20 Caterina Guenzi, "Faculté de prévoir. L'astrologie dans les universités indiennes," *Extrême-Orient, Extrême-Occident* 35 (2013): 141–170.
21 Scott Kugle, *Sufis and Saints' Bodies: Mysticism, Corporeality, and Sacred Power in Islam* (Chapel Hill: University of North Carolina Press, 1997), 4.
22 Kugle, *Sufis and Saints' Bodies*, 29.
23 Qur'an 13:29, my translation.
24 Kugle, *Sufis and Saints' Bodies*, 30.
25 Shahzad Bashir, *Sufi Bodies: Religion and Society in Medieval Islam* (New York: Columbia University Press, 2011), 13.
26 Hatley, "Mapping the Esoteric Body," 362–363.
27 Ibid., 352.
28 Ibid., 354.
29 Ibid., 355.
30 Rai, *Śivasvarodaya*, 6.
31 Martin Gangsten, *Patterns of Destiny: Hindu Nāḍī Astrology* (Stockholm: Almqvist & Wiksell International, 2003).
32 Ibid., 9–10.
33 Abu'l Fazl ibn Mubarak ibn 'Allami, *A'īn-i Akbari*, ed. H. Blochmann (Calcutta: Baptist Mission Press, 1869), 125.
34 Viktoria Lyssenko, "The Human Body Composition in Statics and Dynamics: Āyurveda and the Philosophical Schools of Vaśesika and Sāmkhya," *Journal of Indian Philosophy* 32 (2004): 31–32.

35 *Risalah-i dam az khavass al-hayat*. London, British Library IO Islamic 464, ff. 1b-5b. The copyist is likely referring to the *Hawd al-hayat*, which is why I have labeled this text as *Risalah-i dam az [hawd?] al-hayat*.
36 *Risalah-i dam az khavass al-hayat*, folio 1b.
37 *Risalah-i dam az khavass al-hayat*, ff. 3a and 5a (Qur'an 112:1), respectively.
38 *Risalah-i dam az khavass al-hayat*, folio 5b.
39 Ibid.
40 Delhi Persian 1030b, London, British Library, ff. 97b-102a. While little information is available to aid in dating the manuscript, the text's presence within the Delhi Persian collection would put it at mid-nineteenth century at the absolute latest, since the collection is taken from the royal Mughal library in 1857.
41 Delhi Persian 1030b, 97b. *Nafas* could possibly be translated here as "ether," but the author's use of one of the possible Persian terms for "breath," in a place where the five-fold typologies of the breath to follow in this discussion all mention these same four elements *plus* the additional "ether" or "heavenly" element (*dam-i asmani*), stands out as another example of ways in which these cosmological references do not quite fit with another.
42 *Miz al-Nafas*, folio 58a.
43 *Miz al-Nafas*, folio 59a. The anonymous author of the *Kamaru Panchashika abridgment* (Browne recension) employs a similar typology, but using only four aspects instead of six, leaving out the aspects of above and under.
44 *Miz al-Nafas*, folio 59a.
45 Ibid.
46 Amuli, Hassan Zadeh Hassan. *Ma`arifat-i `ilm-i dam-i hazarat-i `allamat ayatollah al-`azima Hassan Zadeh Amuli (raz va ramz-i `ulūm-i ghariba `ilm-i anfas)*, accessed January 9, 2017, http://ansarolmahdiirdemousa.mihanblog.com/post/432.
47 Ben Spatz, *What a Body Can Do: Technique as Knowledge, Practice as Research* (New York: Routledge, 2015), 8.

Bibliography

Unpublished manuscript sources

Kamaru Panchashika abridgment (Browne recension). Cambridge University Library V. 21,

Cambridge. Ff. 59a-66b.

Miz al-nafas. British Library Delhi Persian 796d, London. Ff. 57b-63a.

Risalah-i dam az khavass al-hayat. London, British Library IO Islamic 464, ff. 1b-5b.

Delhi Persian 1030b, London, British Library, ff. 97b-102a.

Secondary sources

ibn 'Allami, Abu'l Fazl ibn Mubarak. *A'īn-i Akbari*, edited by H. Blochmann. Calcutta: Baptist Mission Press, 1869.

Alter, Joseph. "Celibacy, Sexuality, and Nationalism in North India." In *Bodies in Contact: Rethinking Colonial Encounters in World History*, edited by Tony Ballantyne and Antoinette Burton, 310–322. Durham, NC: Duke University Press, 2005.

———. *The Wrestler's Body: Identity and Ideology in North India*. Berkeley: University of California Press, 1992.

———. "Yoga in Asia—Mimetic History: Problems in the Location of Secret Knowledge." *Comparative Studies of South Asia, Africa and the Middle East* 29, no. 2 (2009): 213–229.

———. *Yoga in Modern India: The Body between Science and Philosophy*. Princeton: Princeton University Press, 2004.

Ballantyne, Tony and Antoinette Burton. *Bodies in Contact: Rethinking Colonial Encounters in World History*. Durham, NC: Duke University Press, 2005.

Bashir, Shahzad. *Sufi Bodies: Religion and Society in Medieval Islam*. New York: Columbia University Press, 2011.

Bigelow, Anna. *Sharing the Sacred: Practicing Pluralism in Muslim North India*. Oxford: Oxford University Press, 2010.

Butler, Judith. *Bodies that Matter: On the Discursive Limits of "Sex."* New York: Routledge, 1993.

Cerulli, Anthony. "Body, Self, and Embodiment in the Sanskrit Classics of Ayurveda." In *Refiguring the Body: Embodiment in South Asian Religions*, edited by Barbara Holdredge and Karen Pechilis, 59–88. Albany: State University of New York Press, 2016.

Ernst, Carl W. *Refractions of Islam in India*. Delhi: Sage Publications, 2016.

Flueckiger, Joyce. *In Amma's Healing Room: Gender and Vernacular Islam in South India*. Bloomington: Indiana University Press, 2006.

Gangsten, Martin. *Patterns of Destiny: Hindu Nāḍī Astrology*. Stockholm: Almqvist & Wiksell International, 2003.

Guenzi, Caterina. "Faculté de prévoir. L'astrologie dans les universités indiennes." *Extrême-Orient, Extrême-Occident* 35 (2013): 141–170.

Hatley, Shaman. "Mapping the Esoteric Body in the Islamic Yoga of Bengal." *History of Religions* 46, no. 4 (2007): 351–368.

Kugle, Scott A. *Sufis and Saints' Bodies: Mysticism, Corporeality, and Sacred Power in Islam*. Chapel Hill: University of North Carolina Press, 1997.

Lyssenko, Viktoria. "The Human Body Composition in Statics and Dynamics: Āyurveda and the Philosophical Schools of Vaśesika and Sāmkhya." *Journal of Indian Philosophy* 32 (2004): 31–32.

Muktibodhananda, Swami. *Swara Yoga: The Tantric Science of Brain Breathing*. Bihar: Yoga Publications Trust, 1984.

Rai, Ram Kumar, ed. and trans., *Śivasvarodaya*. Tantra Granthamala No. 1. Varanasi: Prachya Prakashan, 1980.

Ramacharaka, Yogi. *The Hindu-yogi Science of Breath: A Complete Manual of the Oriental Breathing Philosophy of Physical, Mental, Psychic and Spiritual Development*. Chicago: Yogi Publication Society, c. 1905.

Spatz, Ben. *What a Body Can Do: Technique as Knowledge, Practice as Research*. New York: Routledge, 2015.

White, David Gordon. *Yoga in Practice*. Princeton: Princeton University Press, 2012.

9 The prostituted body of war

U.S. military prostitution in South Korea as a site of spiritual activism

Keun-Joo Christine Pae

Introduction

As Australian feminist scholar Sheila Jeffreys points out, "military prostitution was a most important vector in the globalization and industrialization of prostitution in the late 20th century."[1] Although many women have long been recruited in various ways to offer sexualized labor for male soldiers in the global war theater, this reality has been generally ignored. How would war look if it were seen through the eyes of military prostitutes? What kind of knowledge of war, and even peace activism against militarism, would these prostitutes embody? My chapter contemplates these questions, arguing that military prostitutes are important characters in sovereignty's war project and that their boides are the active space of producting knowledge about war—militarized international politics, military policy, gender-based violence, racialized gender, sexualized human relations, and even religion that resists or supports war. As the site of knowledge, the body of war in which this chapter engages is the collective body of Korean prostitutes, who are pejoratively called by the name "Western Princess." The U.S. military's presence in South Korea and the militarized tension in East Asia cannot be properly analyzed without considering Western Princesses, who have catered to American soldiers in South Korea for more than seven decades.

Defining military prostitution as a form of necropolitical labor, this chapter first analyzes the racialized and sexualized U.S.–Korea relations through the bodies of Western Princesses. The knowledge accumulated in their bodies concerns how the state's war project has relied on two different groups of people (military prostitutes and soldiers) who perform necropolitical labor for the sake of security for others. The second half of this chapter will examine the roles which Christian "faith" has played in Western Princesses' healing journey and political activism against state-sanctioned violence. More specifically, I delineate how Western princesses claim and reclaim their bodies as the space of healing and resistance. I finally propose the idea of "spiritual activism" as an alternative to war. This chapter searches for the knowledge of peace activism as spiritual activism through the embodied knowledge of Western Princesses.

Necropolitics: U.S. military prostitution in South Korea

In his influential essay "Necropolitics," African postcolonial theorist Achille Mbembe argues that "the ultimate expression of sovereignty resides, to a large degree, in the power and the capacity to dictate who may live and who must die."[2] If sovereignty manifests its power by controlling mortality and defining life, then war becomes "as much a means of achieving sovereignty as a way of exercising the right to kill."[3] Imagining politics as a form of war, Mbembe interrogates "what place is given to life, death, and the human body" and "how they are inscribed in the order of power."[4] Death takes many forms: slavery (with a loss of a "home," loss of rights over one's body, and loss of political status), concentration camps, historical colonies, colonial occupation (i.e. occupied Palestine), and war including war making, war machines, soldiering, terrorism, and resource extraction.[5] U.S. military prostitution in South Korea is a good example of Mbembe's necropolitics or sovereignty's exercise to kill; more specifically, that a group of socially and economically vulnerable women has been subjugated to death, conducting sexualized labor within America's quasi-colonial camptowns across South Korea. Just as the realities of occupied people's daily lives are invisible to outsiders, so that those of Western Princesses have been unknown. Their invisibility has enabled sovereignty to condemn them to death more easily.

U.S. military prostitution in South Korea began in 1945, only a few months after the arrival of the U.S. Twenty-Fourth Army Corps, consisting of some 72,000 soldiers through the port of Incheon. Their mission was to transfer power from the crumbled Japanese empire to Korea, which was supposedly emancipated from Imperial Japan's thirty-five-year ruling (1910–1945).[6] By the end of 1945, Bupyeong, a small town nearby Incheon, was turned into an entertaining camptown with simple bars where the soldiers sought out alcohol and women for recreation.[7] Since then, camptown prostitution has evolved in different stages: the early stage (1945–1949), the foundation of the Relaxation and Recreation business (1950s), the golden days (1960s), the systematic corporation (1970s to mid-1980s), and the declining period (mid-1980s to present). These stages correspond to the number of American GIs stationed in South Korea, changes in American military policy, and the economic development of South Korea.

Military prostitution is built upon the heterosexual masculinist ideology that soldiers' sex drives are uncontrollable. Hence, to ensure their willingness to kill and to be killed in war, a means of easy, cheap, and safe sex must be provided.[8] During the Korean War, from 1950 through 1953, U.S. military prostitution spread throughout Korea as American soldiers were stationed across the Korean peninsula. Although the public prostitution system (e.g. public brothels occupied by licensed prostitutes), which had been installed by Imperial Japan in Korea, became outlawed in 1947, the Korean government adopted the Japanese institution of "comfort stations" to serve U.N. Allied Forces and Korean soldiers. The Korean version of the "comfort women" system was justified in the name of "protecting respectable women and rewarding soldiers for their sacrifice."[9] There was not much difference between the Japanese military "comfort women" system and U.S./U.N. military prostitution. Western Princesses, in fact, had been called America's comfort women for a long time.

Since their arrival on Korean soil, the U.S. military had fought two wars: one against communism and the other against venereal disease. While venereal disease threatened the soldiers' readiness to fight in the war, the U.S. military could not properly control the soldiers' sexual behaviors. To control venereal disease (VD) among the soldiers, both the U.S. military and the Korean government regulated prostitution rather than abolished it. Under the government's supervision, Western Princesses were allowed to sell sex only in designated areas after having proven to be clean of VD. However, the effort to control VD failed because the soldiers could take sexual advantage of poverty-stricken Korean women, mostly war widows and orphans who had multiple dependents. Although the U.S. Armed Forces in Korea (USFK) restricted the soldiers' contact with local Korean women, the soldiers' attitudes toward the women resembled those of white European colonialists toward colonized women of color, who were seen as sexually exploitable.

Since the Korean War ended in a truce in 1953, the U.S. military has remained stationed in South Korea for an indefinite period. The Korean War, followed by the U.S.–Republic of Korea Mutual Defense Treaty (known as SOFA), provided recourses for U.S. military prostitution. The War produced a large supply of girls and women without homes and livelihood who flocked to the areas where UN/U.S. forces were bivouacked, searching for food, shelter, and work. The majority of strategic areas, close to the border with North Korea, developed into Rest and Relaxation (R&R) boomtowns beginning in the mid-1950s.[10] Entertaining camptowns built upon the R&R business sprang up all around U.S. bases, becoming the borderlands between the United States and South Korea and the quasi-colonies of the United States. Korean American international relations scholar Katharine Moon describes the turning of sparsely populated rural villages into hustle and bustle camptowns:

> ...Tongduch'on sprouted from agricultural fields into one of the most notorious camptowns, having housed four different U.S. infantry divisions since the end of the Korean War. During its "golden age" in the mid-1960s, Tongducho'on boasted approximately 7,000 prostitutes... Songt'an, which had been a small unknown farming village until the Korean War, grew to be the "darling" of U.S. Air Force camptowns since the early 1950s. On July, 1951, the 417th Squadron came to Songt'an with bulldozers to construct an airfield, causing 1,000 families, or 5,000 people, to lose their homes and land.[11]

Camptown economies were exclusively dependent on U.S. bases where Western Princesses' sexual labor was used to connect American soldiers to local Korean men. For example, in Songtan, by the late 1970s, 80% of its 60,000 residents, including approximately 2,500 prostitutes, lived on income earned from U.S. military personnel.[12] The system of U.S. military prostitution has been considered a necessary evil to satiate American soldiers' sexual desires and to protect respectable Korean women from wild foreign soldiers. However, the system generated lucrative profits, especially for military dictator Jung Hee Park's regime in the 1960s through 1970s. Western Princesses were the crucial dollar earners whose labor was extracted into the construction of modern Korea. The U.S. military's presence in Korea has been justified through anti-North Korean rhetoric and arguments for international peace and security, but has always been framed in economic terms.

As Korean American sociologist Grace Cho insightfully points out, the body of the Western Princess has been "materially and discursively constructed by competing ideologies of Korean nationalism" as well as "the object of violence and a site of contestation."[13] The Western Princess embodies the hypermilitarization of East Asia, Korea's collective history of trauma (particularly from Japanese colonialism to the ongoing Korean War), American military imperialism, and Korea's ambivalent relationship with the United States. Depending on Korea's (international) political situation, the body of the Western Princess became a self-sacrificial site for national development, an occupied territory by the United States, a source of national shame and secrecy, or a symbol of anti-Americanism. This was especially true after 1992 when the murder case of a Western Princess Gum-yi Yoon was publicized. The slain body of Yoon by Private Kenneth Markle emerged as a significant space of anti-American military imperialism. Masculinized Korean nationalists equated her death with South Korea's sub-colonial status, and Yoon became the symbol of innocent Korean women prostituted and raped by American imperialists due to poverty and the lack of Korea's sovereign power.[14] Juxtaposed to the victims of the Japanese military "comfort women" system during World War II, Western Princesses, who had been previously condemned as sexually immoral women, suddenly became the representatives of South Korea's subordination to the United States.[15] Although Yoon's death was brutal enough to bring public attention to the necropolitical realities of camptown prostitution marred with violence, death, and exclusion, political activism revolving around Yoon's death did not comprehend the normalized military violence based on race and gender in camptowns. Neither did male-dominated nationalists see the case as a violation of human rights. Rather, the body of Yoon and many other Western Princesses, who were neither innocent nor evil, proves that their prostituted body, and even death, did not belong to themselves but to the nation.

Necropolitical labor: military prostitution and soldiering

Expanding Mbembe's necropolitics, Korean American cultural theorist Jin-kyung Lee elaborates on the idea of "necropolitical labor," which means "the extraction of labor from those 'condemned' to death…is limited to serving the labor demands of the state or empire."[16] Necropolitical labor, as the most disposable form of labor, highlights an intermediate stage where "the extraction of labor is related to and premised on the possibility of death, rather than the ultimate event of death itself."[17] Both soldiering and prostitution are considered forms of necropolitical labor because both constantly expose the laborers to deadly violence, the possibility of death, and the ultimate disposability. Moreover, their labor is controlled for the sake of the lives of others.

Defining military prostitution as a form of necropolitical labor, Lee first argues that an essential dimension of South Korean modernization consists of "commodifying the transformation of sexuality and race into labor power."[18] More specifically, the mobilization of female sex has two related stages: the militarization of prostitution and the industrialization of prostitution.[19] Like many other third-world countries, South Korea's economy in the 1960s through the early 1980s relied on women's sexualized labor—poor women were recruited into various forms of prostitution to bring foreign currencies for their developing country, including U.S. camptown prostitution and *kiseang* (courtesan in English) tourism for rich Japanese tourists. For prostitutes, whether they are selling sex to soldiers or domestic men, the psychological, physical, and sexual violence incurred by the commercialization of sex are daily realities. The brutal murder of Gum-yi Yoon was not a unique case in camptown prostitution for its seventy-year history.

The possibility of death and the ultimate disposability, as Lee accentuates, is "an integral element of prostitution as an occupation."[20] In the case of U.S. camptown prostitution, the South Korean government and the USFK indeed occupied Western Princesses' bodies by monitoring and controlling their sexual acts, interactions with American soldiers, and, most importantly, venereal disease. The Korean-government–led Camptown Clean-Up Campaign would best show camptown prostitution as necropolitical labor.

In the early 1970s, in response to the Nixon Doctrine that announced the reduction of the number of G.I.s in Korea, the South Korean military government launched the Camptown Clean-Up Campaign, "which was intended to improve channels of communication and cooperation in camptown politics."[21] The Campaign modernized camptowns with new lights, roads, and buildings so that American soldiers could relax and recreate in cleaner environments. In order to reduce the racial tension among G.I.s, USFK asked the Korean government to educate Western Princesses not to discriminate against black soldiers. The club owners were asked to play blues and jazz more frequently. Western Princesses were divided into "white-only" and "black-only" prostitutes because white soldiers, the majority of the USFK, did not want to buy the women who sexually catered to the soldiers of color. Associating with blacks further stigmatized the prostitutes, not only to white soldiers but also to Korean residents. Therefore, for most prostitutes, racial discrimination against black men was a means to exercise their limited freedom of choice of customers and retain their compromised sense of self-dignity.[22] Although the Clean-Up Campaign might have alleviated the racial tension among G.I.s, the camptown environment became more oppressive toward Western Princesses, for they were surveilled by multiple groups such as club owners, the U.S. military police, local Korean leadership, and both black and white soldiers. Western Princesses' subjectivity was erased by a government that exercised the right to kill over them.

In response to the USFK's concern about the increasing rate of VD among G.I.s, the Clean-Up Campaign regulated and disciplined Western Princesses' bodies through rigorous VD education and mandatory VD check-ups. All the prostitutes who passed VD checks were required to register their names and work places with local authorities and to wear nametags while working in the bars and clubs. VD cards sanctioned the prostitute's body as clean flesh to be safely used. Nametags were used by the G.I.s to identify possibly diseased women when the soldiers were found infected with VD. In many cases, G.I.s failed to identify the women with whom they had slept but pointed out random women. Whether they were infected with VD or not, the women pointed out by the G.I.s with VD were quarantined in a special facility, called "the monkey house," until they were declared clean and, thus, reusable.[23] While G.I.s should share the responsibility for the VD problem, the VD control fell only on the shoulders of Western Princesses and the Korean government. The prostitutes found VD check-ups humiliating and financially burdensome, and the aggressive VD control often caused deaths and disabilities for Western Princesses.[24] Since the value of the prostitutes relied on clean and safe bodies as commodities, they were to be discarded when they became useless due to disease and if they could not be restored to a usable condition. The VD control shows one aspect of prostitution as necropolitical labor.

Although necropolitical labor was disposable, the Korean government relied on it for its economic development, national security, and relationship with the USFK in particular. For this reason, the Clean-Up Campaign subcommittee regularly gathered Western Princesses only to indoctrinate them to the belief that they contributed to the modernization and security of their country through prostitution.[25] In order to survive in camptowns, Western Princesses internalized the patriotic dimension of their work but had no illusions about prostitution being viewed as dirty work condemned by society. Ironically, the dispossessed population is condemned to death for the prosperity of others, but, in fact, the livelihood of sovereignty relies on the condemned population.

The South Korean-government–designed U.S. camptowns were segregated from the rest of Korean society, disciplining Western princesses' bodies through VD clinics and sex education. Camptowns were neo-colonies of the United States until recently, so most South Koreans and Americans do not know what has happened inside said neo-colonies. At the turn of the twenty-first century, as South Korea emerged as a sub-imperialist state, it has smuggled Filipina, Central Asian, and Russian women into camptowns and exported Korean women to prostitution in the United States, Australia, and Japan.

Soldiering is another kind of necropolitical labor, as the job is carried out only by necessarily risking one's life.[26] Yet soldiers' necropolitical labor is embellished with noble values, such as honor, pride, discipline, sacrifice, and patriotism, cherished by society. Killing the enemy, the lowest form of "survival" during war, is the crucial aspect of soldiering as necropolitical labor which is constructed upon not only patriarchal gender ideologies but also the separation between body and spirit. Military labor, according to Lee, is a particular kind of sexual proletarian labor, "where certain aspects of masculine sexuality are (re)constructed, (re)appropriated, and deployed as a range of tasks."[27] Similarly, feminist theologian Susan Thistlethwaite's analysis shows that militarism constructs the sex industry through the forced separation of the sexes in military life. Usually men are recruited into the military, taken out of their familial patterns of human relationship, and no longer governed by civilian norms for sexual and moral conduct.[28] Military training (i.e. reflexive shooting) relies on the ideology that requires a soldier's body to be suppressed and disciplined to intentionally kill the enemy and to overcome fear. The construction of the warrior's body is interwoven with masculinized ideologies such as dominance over femininity and direct denial of human vulnerability. Sex, then, is used as a vehicle to appease soldiers' fear and vulnerability or to show their superiority to women and the enemy. Hence, Thistlethwaite further argues that militarism is both a product of and a support for "the gnosticizing tendency in Christianity to denigrate the body and sexuality and to exclude them from the realm of the spirit."[29] In this case, necropolitical labor should be understood as the extraction of labor from both the body and the spirit of those who are condemned to death.

The consequences of the necropolitical labor of soldiering are detrimental. Even long before the idea of "necropolitical labor" or "necropolitics" had been pronounced, American military hero Major General Smedley Butler accentuated how ordinary soldiers paid the true cost of America's wars: death, disgifurement, dismemberment, and psychological injury. The American soldiers were not equipped with proper tools to fight the war due to a small number of self-interested capitalists who made a huge profit from it. If the soldiers had not been killed in the battlefield, they could have suffered from post-traumatic stress disorder,[30] bankruptcy, and various forms of disabilities.[31] Today various psychologists and theologians produce critical research that shows how the labor of soldiering is truly necropolitical by harming soldiers' body, mind, spirit, and morality.[32] These studies reveal the negative psychological, spiritual, and moral impact on soldiers after they have been involved in killing the enemy or witnessing the tragic deaths of their comrades. The state's lack of proper medical support and respect for veterans illustrates the disposability of military labor after war.

Ironically, Western Princesses could comprehend the necropolitical nature of soldiering. They knew that American soldiers came to Korea to make money, not to protect the country, and that these soldiers were recruited among the poor in the United States. These women had no illusions about America but criticized the U.S. mismanagement of its economy, high unemployment rates, low educational standards in public schools, racial discrimination, and imperialistic actions toward developing countries.[33] In terms of class backgrounds and as the state's neglected population, Western Princesses saw similarities between G.I.s and themselves.

Christian faith and activism in camptowns

Camptowns are gendered, racialized, and culturally hybridized spaces where Western Princesses' values are solely measured by their sexualized bodies. Through intimate interactions with American soldiers, wage-based relationships with Korean club owners, and contested relations with local authorities, Western Princesses have accumulated knowledge of American military imperialism, including a sense of sexual exceptionalism and entitlement to buy Korean women's sex, the Korean government's sexual exploitation of poor women, and the club owners' often dishonest ways of making profits. This intimate knowledge has often motivated the prostitutes to organize themselves by directly confronting their employers, G.I. customers, or local authorities for their rights to earn fair wages and to work in a safe environment. Their actions are mostly issue-based and episodic, although it is crucial to recognize how they use their limited power of agency to rectify injustice. The unilateral U.S.–Korea relations, the physical isolation of camptowns, and public apathy toward Western Princesses make it challenging to organize social movements in camptowns. Nonetheless, outside activists and Western Princesses collaboratively organized various forms of activism for human rights. In many cases, Christianity as people's faith (i.e. popular religion), rather than as an institutionalized religion, has played an important role in camptown activism.

Christian women's anti-prostitution activism in Korea has a long history. In the 1920s, when Imperial Japan systematized public brothels, Korean women's Christian organizations first led the anti-prostitution movement.[34] After Korea's independence over Imperial Japan in 1945, Christian women's organizations demanded that the U.S. Military Government in South Korea abolish public prostitution, the system left behind after the Japanese ruling. In 1948, the U.S. Military Government outlawed public prostitution, although prostitution had been privatized with the exception of U.S. camptown prostitution.[35] In the 1970s and the 1980s, various Christian groups based on *Minjung* theology, a Korean version of liberation theology, protested against military dictatorship. The Korean Church Women United was one of the core organizations who first challenged *kisaeng* tourism.[36] Christian women's groups might be the most persistent actors in the anti-prostitution movements in Korea. These women's organizations saw prostitution as the byproduct of systemic poverty and gender-based violence, although many Korean Christians equated prostitution with privatized moral issues caused by sexually corrupt men and women. Most recently, the Korean Council for the Women Drafted for the Military Sexual Slavery by Japan helps the public see military prostitution and wartime rape from anti-war feminist perspectives.

In 1986, Durebang (known as My Sister's Place in the English-speaking world), the first women's center for Western Princesses in camptowns, was founded by two Christian women leaders, Fay Moon and Bok-nim Yoo. Moon, an American woman married to a well-known Korean *Minjung* theologian, learned about the realities of camptown prostitution while counseling and teaching English for Korean military brides in the United States Eighth Army. Bok-nim Yoo of the Presbyterian Church in the Republic of Korea is a feminist activist whose faith and social activism are rooted in *Minjung* theology. Opening Durebang next to Camp Stanley in Uijeongbu, the two leaders articulated the mission statement of Durebang: "To help camptown women and interracially married military wives liberate themselves and live life originally created by God."[37] Durebang's mission was not to abolish prostitution but rather to help Western Princesses to overcome alienation from Korean society and to find a means of survival in their unequal relationships with American soldiers. It is important to note that Durebang understood camptown prostitution in terms of the unilateral U.S.–Korea relations that reflect American soldiers' imperialistic attitudes toward Korean culture and Western Princesses.[38] Teaching survival skills for Western Princesses and their bi-racial children, Durebang serves as a shelter, advocacy group, educational center, and healing space. In the 1990s, especially after the death of Gum-yi Yoon, Durebang was a center for outside activists to meet Western Princesses and to organize various activisms in the camptown so that the camptown could enter larger social movements. However, male-dominated nationalist movements in the 1990s (and today) did not overcome the patriarchal prejudice toward Western Princesses due to the view that these women volunteered to prostitute for economic gains. As Korean feminist Na-young Lee critically analyzes, male-dominated Korean activists are only interested in stopping Americans from using Korean women's bodies. Hence, a Western Princess' body represents national shame, as if it should be hidden from the official national history, while her body becomes visible "only when there is a need to mobilize feelings of unity as one nation."[39]

If, as outsiders of military prostitution, Christian women's organizations participated in social activism in camptowns, the story of Yonja Kim would show the transformation of a former Western Princess into a camptown activist through her Christian faith. She was the first woman who publicly spoke about her life in camptown prostitution, including its horrible realities, the construction of corporate Americatown solely for U.S. military prostitution in Gunsan, Western Princesses' church community, and protests against G.I. violence. Kim, a survival of incest rape and other forms of sexual violence, entered U.S. military prostitution for meager earnings. Working in clubs and bars, Kim had played various leadership roles in representing Western Princesses to local law enforcement and club owners. Mbembe might agree that the environment, people's lives, and politics inside Americatown, which were described in Yon-ja Kim's autobiography, resemble the occupied territory of Palestine, a modern example of an occupied colony of necropower.[40] Like the West Bank and Gaza Strip, Americatown was surrounded by walls that separated the town from the rest of Korea. Security guards checked out visitors at the gate to the town. Western Princesses in Americatown occupied the bottom of the social hierarchy—club owners, bathhouse owners, the head of the Americatown Corporation, landlords, pimps, and the local residents living around the town all surveilled Western Princesses' everyday lives, extracting their sexualized labor from their bodies.[41]

Long before the death of Gum-yi Yoon and the following public outrage, in 1977 Yon-ja Kim and about two hundred Americatown prostitutes protested in front of the U.S. Air Base, demanding that Steven Warren Towerman, an American soldier who brutally murdered two Western Princesses, be judged at the Korean court.[42] Bok-hi Yi was found strangled and scorched in her room in Americatown after having been seen with Towerman. A month after Yi's death, Towerman killed another Americatown prostitute, Young-soon Yi, and mutilated her body. Both the local Korean police and the U.S. military police had been indifferent to the two murder cases until Western Princesses protested in front of Warren's base. Finally, Warren was persecuted at the Korean court and sentenced to life in prison. He could avoid capital punishment because the Korean court respected his service for Korea.[43] Although no one outside Americatown paid attention to the mutilated bodies of the Yis, Western Princesses used their agency to protest against their unjust deaths and the sexual violation against them. In the 1970s, however, Western Princesses' collective actions were suppressed by Korean authorities and the U.S. military, and they were even stigmatized as communists if they did not silently perform their sexualized labor. The series of deaths of Western Princesses, whose bodies were mutilated, beaten, strangled, burnt, hung on trees, and drowned in reservoirs, ironically made Yon-ja Kim desire to live. Praying to God, she searched for the meaning of her life in Christian faith.[44]

She would later study Christian theology and become a Christian minister and activist for Western Princesses and their bi-racial children. With other Western Princesses who had found renewed purpose to their lives through Christian faith, Yon-ja Kim opened mission centers in Gunsan and Songtan camptowns.[45] Christian faith embodied by Kim and the Western Princesses in the mission centers radically reclaim their human dignity in God. Differently from institutionalized Christianity of which understanding of Divinity is expressed through doctrines and rituals, Kim's faith enables her to see God's presence among Western Princesses, whose bodies are condemned to death and sin by the mainstream Christian doctrine of sin and redemption. Their survival strategies, thus, translate to God's power of life, and violation of their bodies is what God denounces. The mission center, as the space to proclaim God's presence among Western Princesses, must be present in the camptown.[46] Kim's understanding of God renounces necropolitics because her value is not defined by her sexualized labor but affirmed by God, who has led her to survive through hardships in camptowns.

According to Kim, both scholars and public audiences only want to hear about the tragic stories of Western princesses, victimizing these women by poverty, sexual violence, and the unilateral U.S.–Korea relations. However, what she wants to share with the world is how Christian faith helped her heal her wounds and trauma from the various forms of violence, reclaim her dignity, and resist structural injustice.[47] She also wanted to emphasize the human dignity of Western Princesses as a whole and these women's power for survival. Refusing to victimize Western Princesses, Yonja Kim says that they are not innocent from what they did to G.I. customers, who were barely out of their teens and often confused about their mission in Korea. Western Princesses took advantage of these soldiers—according to Kim, they played the games with the lone soldiers' hearts.[48] Furthermore, engaging in pity toward Western Princesses, for Kim, fails to resolve the structural problems around camptown prostitution and to recognize the realities of camptown life. Pity and sympathy for Western Princesses would disrespect their agency and power to claim their dignity.[49]

Kim's testimony shows the complex politics inside camptowns, which resonates with Gloria Anzaldua's analysis of the Southwestern borderlands between the United States and Mexico. In the borderlands, the third world clashes with the first world and bleeds, and death and violence are normalized.[50] Like the prostitutes in camptowns in South Korea, women of color in the borderlands are alienated from both their culture and white-dominated society, but their identity is rooted in the spirit of women's resistance (i.e. Chicana women's resistance of European colonialism and Korean women's resistance of militarism, nationalism, and imperialism).[51] Similarly, Kim's critical reflection on the role of Christian faith among camptown prostitutes shares some common traits with Anzaldua's spiritual activism or spirituality for social change, the radically inclusionary politics that refuses the dichotomy between the victims and the victimizers. Kim alludes to the possibility of creating empathy between the two necropolitical laborers—low-ranking soldiers and Western Princesses. Furthermore, Kim's experience of Christianity also speaks with Dorothee Soelle's emphasis on mysticism as resistance against the status quo.

From here, let us turn to the idea of spiritual activism by engaging with feminist scholars such as Gloria Anzaldua, M. Jacqui Alexander, and Dorothee Soelle, and by looking at the activism of the Sunlit Center, a unique organization which advocates for the elderly who used to work in camptown prostitution.

Spiritual activism: resistance of necropolitics, an alternative to transnational militarism

Gloria Anzaldua's spiritual activism intertwines inner works with public acts and private concerns with social issues. Spiritual activism begins at the level of the personal; "it combines self-reflection and self-growth with outward-directed, compassionate acts designed to bring about material change."[52] Anzaldua's spiritual activism is rooted in both a feminist belief in interconnectedness between the personal and the political and a religiously and spiritually holistic view on interrelationality among all living beings. The recognition of the radical interrelationality does not allow for the dichotomy between body and spirit as well as between the oppressors and the oppressed.

Talking about spirit and spirituality in the context of political activism is often confusing and even dangerous. As transnational feminist scholar M. Jacqui Alexander argues, Christianity's historical participation in colonization, the patriarchal and masculine dominance over the theological understanding of spirituality, and the rise of the Religious Right collapse an imagination of spirituality into hierarchical religion that is separated from the secular, the body, politics, etc.[53] Namely, the vast traditions of mysticism as social engagement in Christianity have been lost, just as the mainstream political activism has been developed upon oppositional consciousness. It is insightful when Alexander says that:

> What we have devised as an oppositional politic has been necessary... but it can never ultimately feed that deep place within us: that space of the erotic, that space of the Soul, that space of the Divine.[54]

Spirituality as the work of the spirit is critical self-reflection on the foundation of human life, grounded in the Divine, the Sacred, or God. Conversing with Anzaldua, Alexander accentuates that spirituality leads us to the ultimate truth that "we are connected to the Divine through our connections with each other."[55] Therefore, spiritual work cannot glorify the self as an atomized being but must lead to the realization that the self is always unfolded in community and with community. Spirituality is necessary in political activism because it grounds the activists in the Sacred, encourages them to imagine revolutionary visions, and brings patience and courage. It is crucial to note that spirituality is not separated from the human body or the material world. Rather, spirituality enables one to freely cross the boundaries of the body and the spirit, the sacred and the secular, and sensuality and sexuality, because all of these are what sustain, mold, and make human life. The body is ultimately a means of encountering spirituality and the Sacred.

German feminist theologian Dorothee Soelle's study of mysticism helps expand my understanding of spiritual activism. Soelle explains mysticism and mystic spirituality with three key terms: Being Amazed (*via positive*), Letting Go (*via negative*), and Healing/Resisting (*via transformative*). Amazement is the soul's pure wonder and realization of the beauty in all living beings and in ordinary life. Soelle states:

> The soul needs amazement, the repeated liberation from customs, viewpoints, and convictions, which, like layers of fat that make us untouchable and insensitive, accumulate around us. What appears obvious is that we need to be touched by the spirit of life and that without amazement and enthusiasm nothing new can begin.[56]

Letting go means letting go of false desires, needs, possession, violence, and ego. The more one lets go of these, the more s/he makes room for amazement.[57] Letting go would take one to what ancient mysticism called "being apart," or living out concretely her/his farewell to the customs and norms of her/his culture such as capitalism, patriarchal heterosexism, and militarism.[58] In this second stage of mysticism, one experiences the missing of God in the "dark night" or suffering from God due to the destruction of God's creation.

Letting go leads one to a life in God. To live in God means to take an active part in God's ongoing creation.[59] Thus, the third stage of mysticism is healing and, simultaneously, resistance. In terms of salvation, Soelle articulates that in the third stage, just as Jesus' disciples understood themselves to be "healed healers," humans live in compassion (healing) and justice (resistance) cocreatively; in being healed (saved), we, humans, experience also that we can heal (save).[60] In compassion and justice we can move beyond and change death-oriented reality or necropolitics.

Yon-ja Kim's life story resonates with Soelle's mysticism. Kim found long-lost amazement in her life through faith, or being touched by God: while crying out to God for help she mysteriously realized that it was God who enabled her to survive through life's hardships.[61] Letting go of the life of camptown prostitution and the identity of a prostitute, she still struggled to find her dignity in God and experienced isolation from a society that stubbornly saw her as a prostitute rather than a human. Through social activism in camptowns, Kim continued to heal herself and heal others with compassion, resisting the oppression and exploitation of sexualized and commodified women. Kim's life reflects Anzaldua's spiritual activism that combines "self-reflection and self-growth with outward-directed, compassionate acts designed to bring about material change."[62]

Crucial aspects of spiritual activism are seen also through the Sunlit Center's activism. The Sunlit Center, located in the Anjeongri camptown, adjacent to the United States Army Garrison Humphreys (known as Camp Humphreys or Camp K-6), first began as a gathering place for single senior women who were involved in camptown prostitution and continued to live in the camptown even after their bodies were unwanted in prostitution. Due to the ghettoization of camptowns and the negative social stigma of Western Princesses, they cannot easily leave the towns once they entered prostitution there. When Soon-deok Woo, a Christian lay leader and social worker, offered a space for senior Western Princesses, they were initially reluctant to visit the center because of their long experience of exclusion from mainstream society. However, they would soon regularly come to the center for meals and social events. When local church people visit the center, the senior women ask them to sing Christian hymns and pray for them. The women have memories of visiting the church with their G.I. lovers. With Christian volunteers at the center, these women began creating new memories of the church and being amazed by their lost memories of intimate love that they had felt for others. Based on their experience with camptown prostitution and a Christian God, the women also interpret biblical narratives in their words. Although the center is not a faith-based organization, it has come to embody Christian faith of its own. This faith has played a role in strengthening their gathering and collaborating with activists from the outside.

In 2014, the Sunlit Center presented two plays to the public, based on their life stories: *The Story of Sookja*, performed by the center women, and *The Village of Seven Houses*, performed by professional actors and actresses. *The Story of Sookja* was born out of the center women's healing journey through acting out their previous lives in camptown prostitution. Performing their own lives as if they were actresses, the women started seeing their bodies differently, not as something only useful for prostitution, but as flesh with souls that can feel and express joy and tears. Since they intentionally separated their body from their mind (spirit) in order to survive prostitution, the healing play gave them the opportunity to reflect on their bodily experience rather than forgetting or hiding it. After one-year-long sessions of the healing play, the center women decided to perform the play at a local theater in order to meet the public audience and to raise awareness of the historical presence of camptown prostitution. In the summer of 2017, the Sunlit Center women also performed a musical, *Jukebox*. In this musical, the women revealed themselves as human beings of memories by singing the songs that they used to sing with their G.I. lovers. Although Western Princesses do not know the whereabouts of their ex-lovers now, their bodies remember the love that once brightened their lives.

The Village of Seven Houses was a collaborative work of the Sunlit Center women and outside activists. Yanggu Lee, the director and writer of the play, is a longtime volunteer at the Sunlit Center and social activist in camptowns. After he had encountered the lone death of an old Western princess, he began writing the play. During my informal conversation with Lee in summer 2013, he shared the image of God that emerged from the faces of elderly Western Princesses:

> A Western princess's lonely death tells me certain truth about life. In my play, a dying elderly Western princess asks Hana from the United

> States who researches camptown prostitution to pray for her. As Hana hesitates, the dying woman says, "When you pray for me, my tears flow into your eyes, and yours into God's eyes. God is the one whose eyes are full of tears." I wish everyone in audience shares the tears with Western princesses and will see the teary eyes of God.

Lee's body image of a God with eyes full of tears perhaps represents the physical expression of Her/His empathy toward victims of necropolitics. Namely, God (the Sacred) resides in the concrete body of empathy rather than merely remaining in the metaphysical realm. In addition, religious rituals such as prayers may create a space of empathy among the participants of the rituals.

Sunlit Center women are currently filing a lawsuit against the Korean government for the violation of their human rights through the government's aggressive regulation of VD. For this lawsuit, in 2013 the Sunlit Center women initiated the Solidarity Network for Human Rights in the Camptown (*Kijichon Inkwon Yeondae*) that includes various advocacy organizations for military prostitutes.

The Sunlit Center women's social activism shows at least two aspects of spiritual activism that were previously mentioned. First, their activism redefines who they are through their inner work (spiritual work) intertwined with their bodily performance, as seen in their play, *The Story of Sookja*. If the prostituted body previously defined who they were, now the women reclaim the spirit of their bodies through intentionally performing their memories of camptown prostitution. Their bodies interpret military prostitution. Furthermore, as healed healers, the Sunlit Center women continue to heal themselves with compassion through performing their memories of military prostitution and resist injustice through conscious engagement with the public audience.

Second, their inner transformation grounded in Christian faith that articulates the sanctity of human life leads them to courageously embrace structural suffering and to engage in social changes without demonizing the perpetrators. This empathetic embracing of suffering embodies the idea of radical interconnectivity among living beings and generates the new body image of the Divine, the Sacred, or God who empathizes with the victims of the unjust system. Hence, the sacred, or God, cannot represent sovereignty that "exercises the right to kill," but Her/His eyes are full of tears for the sufferers.

Conclusion

Concluding this chapter, I propose that spiritual activism, particularly exercised by Western Princesses, can be an alternative to war and militarism built upon necropolitics. If war were defined as sovereignty's exercise of its right to kill, namely, a politics of death at the expense of certain groups' necropolitical labor, then an alternative to war should be a politics of life and empathy that refuses to reduce any human body to necropolitical labor. The theories of necropolitics primarily question which body is subscribed to death in colonial and post-colonial contexts. In response, many faith and spiritual traditions may strive to generate different discourses, including how to analyze the spiritual and psychological impact of death on human bodies in war and violence, how to resist a politics of death, and how to claim and reclaim a politics of life which can be tangible only through human body.

Notes

1 Shiela Jeffreys, *The Industrial Vagina: The Political Economy of the Global Sex Trade* (London: Routledge, 2008), 107.
2 Achille Mbembe, "Necropolitics," trans. Libby Meintjes, *Public Culture* 15, no. 1 (Winter, 2003): 11. Project MUSE.
3 Ibid., 12.
4 Ibid.
5 Ibid., 20; 25–27; 33.
6 Seung Sook Moon, "Regulating Desire, Managing the Empire: U.S. Military Prostitution in South Korea, 1945–1970" in *Over There: Living with the U.S. Military Empire from World War Two to the Present*, ed. Maria Höhn and Seungsook Moon (Durham, NC: Duke University Press, 2010), 40.
7 Ji-Yeon Yuh, *Beyond the Shadow of Camptown: Korean Military Brides in America* (New York and London: New York University Press, 2003), 20.
8 Cynthia Enloe, *Maneuvers: The International Politics of Militarizing Women's Lives* (Berkeley: University of California Press, 2000), 51.
9 Moon, "Regulating Desires, Managing the Empire," 41.
10 Katharine Moon, *Sex among Allies: Military Prostitution in U.S.–Korea Relations* (New York: Columbia University Press, 1997), 28.
11 Ibid.
12 Ibid., 28.
13 Grace Cho, *Haunting the Korean Diaspora: Shame, Secrecy, and the Forgotten War* (Minneapolis: University of Minnesota Press, 2008), 90.
14 Ibid., 116–117.
15 Many political changes in South Korea in the early 1990s enabled the Yoon Gum-yi case to appeal to the public. South Korea elected the first non-military president in 1992 which gave the Korean citizens hope for the democratization of the country. At this time, the survivors of the Japanese military "comfort women" system finally broke the silence about their experiences with the militarized sexual slavery. In addition, in the late 1980s, the Korean public learned about the U.S. Eighth Army's alleged involvement in brutally quelling the Gwang Ju Democratization Movement in May 1980. Anti-American sentiments escalated.
16 Jin-kyung Lee, *Service Economies: Militarism, Sex Work and Migrant Labor in South Korea* (Minneapolis: University of Minnesota Press, 2010), Introduction, Kindle.
17 Ibid.
18 Ibid.
19 Ibid.
20 Ibid.
21 Moon, *Sex among Allies*, 128.
22 Ibid., 129.

23 Ibid., 132–133.
24 Ibid., 131.
25 Ibid., 135.
26 Lee, *Service Economies*, Introduction. Kindle.
27 Ibid.
28 Susan Thistlethwaite, "Militarism in North American Perspective" in *Women Resisting Violence: Spirituality for Life*, eds. Mary John Mananzan et al. (Maryknoll, NY: Orbis Books, 1996; reprint, Eugene, OR: Wipf and Stock Publishers, 2004), 120.
29 Ibid., 121.
30 Although in Butler's time PTSD was relatively unknown, his description of the psychological status of the veterans locked in the psychic institutions was similar to the soldiers suffering from PTSD.
31 Major General Smedley Butler, *War Is a Racket* (The Bulter Family, 1935; reprint, Port Townsend, WA: Feral House, 2003), 23–26; 56–57.
32 The particular literatures in my mind are: Judith Herman, *Trauma and Recovery: The Aftermath of Violence—From Domestic Abuse to Political Terror* (New York: Basic Books, 2015); Lt. Col. David Grossman, *On Killing: The Psychological Cost of Learning to Kill in War and Society*, revised ed. (New York: Back Bay Books, 2009); and Rita Nakashima Brock and Gabriella Lettini, *Soul Repair: Recovering Moral Injury after War* (Boston, MA: Beacon Press, 2013).
33 Moon, *Sex among Allies*, 30.
34 Na-Young Lee, "Negotiating the Boundaries of Nation, Christianity, and Gender: The Korean Women's Movement against Military Prostitution," *Asian Journal of Women's Studies* 17, no. 1 (2011): 34–66.
35 Yi-Soo Gang, "Prohibition of Public Prostitution and Women's Movements during the American Military Occupation," in *Social Changes and History of Korea during American Military Occupation*, Vol. II (Chooncheon, South Korea: Hanrim University Institute of Asian Cultural Studies, 1999), 275 (Korean).
36 Lee, "Negotiating the Boundaries of Nation, Christianity, and Gender."
37 K. Christine Pae, "A Politics of Empathy: Christianity and Women's Peace Activism in U.S. Military Prostitution in South Korea" in *Women and Asian Religions*, ed. Zayn Kassam (Santa Barbara, CA: Praeger, 2017), 228–229.
38 Lee, "Negotiating the Boundaries of Nation, Christianity, and Gender."
39 Ibid.
40 Mbembe, "Necropolitics," 27.
41 Yon-ja Kim, *A Big Sister in Americatown Screams until Five Minutes before Her Death* (Seoul: Samin, 2005), 168–169.
42 Ibid., 184–185.
43 Ibid., 187; also Hyun-sook Kim, "Yanggongju as an Allegory of Nation: Images of Working-class Women in Popular and Radical Texts," in *Dangerous Women: Gender and Korean Nationalism*, eds. Elaine Kim and Choongmoo Choi (New York: Routledge, 1998), 194–195.
44 Kim, *A Big Sister in Americatown Screams until Five Minutes before Her Death*, 192.
45 Ibid., 259–260.
46 Ibid., 222–224.
47 Ibid., 260; 275.
48 Ibid., 139–140; 157.
49 Kim, "Yanggongju as an Allegory of Nation," 195.
50 Gloria Anzaldúa, *Borderlands: La Frontera*, 3rd ed. (San Francisco, CA: Auntie Lute Press, 2007), 3–4.

51 Ibid., 20–21.
52 AnaLouise Keating, "'I'm a Citizen of the Universe': Gloria Anzaldúa's Spiritual Activism as Catalyst for Social Change," *Feminist Studies*, 34, no. 1/2, *The Chicana Studies Issue* (Spring-Summer, 2008): 58.
53 M. Jacqui Alexander, *Pedagogies of Crossing: Meditations on Feminism, Sexual Politics, Memory, and the Sacred* (London and Durham, NC: Duke University Press, 2005), 281–282.
54 Ibid., 282.
55 Ibid., 283.
56 Dorothee Soelle, *The Silent Cry: Mysticism and Resistance*, trans. Barbara Rumscheidt and Martin Rumscheidt (Minneapolis: Fortress Press, 2001), 90.
57 Ibid., 92.
58 Ibid.
59 Ibid., 93.
60 Ibid.
61 Kim, *A Big Sister in Americatown Screams until Five Minutes before Her Death*, 220.
62 AnaLouise Keating, "'I'm a Citizen of the Universe,'" 54.

Bibliography

Alexander, M. Jacqui. *Pedagogies of Crossing: Meditations on Feminism, Sexual Politics, Memory, and the Sacred*. London and Durham, NC: Duke University Press, 2005.

Anzaldúa, Gloria. *Borderlands: La Frontera*, 3rd ed. San Francisco, CA: Auntie Lute Press, 2007.

Butler, Smedley. *War Is a Racket*. The Bulter Family, 1935; reprint, Port Townsend, WA: Feral House, 2003.

Cho, Grace. *Haunting the Korean Diaspora: Shame, Secrecy, and the Forgotten War*. Minneapolis: University of Minnesota Press, 2008.

Enloe, Cynthia. *Maneuvers: The International Politics of Militarizing Women's Lives*. Berkeley: University of California Press, 2000.

Jeffreys, Shiela, *The Industrial Vagina: The Political Economy of the Global Sex Trade*. New York and London: Routledge, 2008.

Keating, AnaLouise. "'I Am a Citizen of Universe': Gloria Anzaldua's Spiritual Activism as Catalyst for Social Change." *Feminist Studies* 34 no. 1/2 (2008): 53–69.

Kim, Hyun-sook. "Yanggongju as an Allegory of Nation: Images of Working-Class Women in Popular and Radical Texts." In *Dangerous Women: Gender and Korean Nationalism*, edited by Elaine Kim and Choongmoo Choi, 175–202. New York and London: Routledge, 1998.

Kim, Yonja. *A Big Sister in Americatown*. Seoul: Samin, 2005 (Korean).

Lee, Jin-Kyung. *Service Economies: Militarism, Sex Work, and Migrant Labor in South Korea*. Minneapolis: University of Minnesota Press, 2010. Kindle.

Lee, Na-Young. "Negotiating the Boundaries of Nation, Christianity, and Gender: The Korean Women's Movement against Military Prostitution," *Asian Journal of Women's Studies* 17, no. 1 (2011): 34–66.

Mbembe, Achille. "Necropolitics." Translated by Libby Meintijes. *Popular Culture* 15, no. 1 (Winter 2003): 11–40.

Moon, Katharine. *Sex among Allies: Military Prostitution in U.S.–Korea Relations*. New York: Columbia University Press, 1997.

Moon, Seung-Sook. "Regulating Desire, Managing the Empire: U.S. Military Prostitution in South Korea, 1945–1970." In *Over There: Living with the U.S. Military Empire from World War II to the Present*, edited by Maria Höhn and Seung-sook Moon, 39–76. Durham, NC: Duke University Press, 2010.

Pae, Keun-Joo Christine. "A Politics of Empathy: Christianity and Women's Peace Activism in U.S. Military Prostitution in South Korea." In *Women and Asian Religions*, edited by Zayn Kassam, 223–239. Santa Barbara, CA: Praeger, 2017.

Soelle, Dorothee. *The Silent Cry: Mysticism and Resistance*. Translated by Barbara Rumscheidt and Martin Rumscheidt. Minneapolis, MN: Fortress Press, 2001.

Thistlethwaite, Susan. "Militarism in North American Perspective." In *Women Resisting Violence: Spirituality for Life*, edited by Mary John Mananzan, et al., 119–128. Maryknoll, NY: Orbis Books, 1996; reprint, Eugene, OR: Wipf and Stock Publishers, 2004.

Yuh, Ji-yeon. *Beyond the Shadow of Camptown: Korean Military Brides in America*. New York and London: New York University Press, 2004.

10 Frisky methods: subtle bodies, epistemological pluralism and creative scholarship

Jay Johnston

Introduction

Over many years the ethical and aesthetic ramifications of subtle body forms of subjectivity have been a specific focus of my research: in particular considering the subtle body a radical form of intersubjectivity.[1] In summation, I have considered subtle bodies in several registers—(1) philosophically: as a concept of radical intersubjectivity, with parallels to other post-structural forms of subjectivity; (2) culturally: examining the way that the concept of subtle bodies is used in various spiritual practices, including investigating a type of aesthetics engendered by this model of the body—Esoteric Aesthetics—and the related ethics of "cultivation of perception"; and (3) methodologically: considering how scholars of religion can study phenomena that are understood to be perceived by non-normative forms of the senses.

Central to this work of analysis and proposition has been a concern with the cultivation of perception—including "alternate" perception—and the attendant epistemologies that emerge as a result of such an "expanded" perceptual field. This analysis has included consideration of relation with other-than-human subjects.[2]

In the last paragraph two terms were presented within "scare" quotation marks: *alternate* and *expanded.* The distinction and qualification of both terms relies on pervasive but extremely general conceptualizations in dominant western discourse regarding the boundaries of perception and knowledge. The scare quotation marks are used to signal that what counts as alternative perception and knowledge is socio-culturally specific. Their use is intended to stress the slippery foundation of normative epistemological categories and the associated designation (often negative or feminized) of skills and knowledge deemed to fall outside that ambit.

The conceptualization of alternate knowledge(s) is of relevance to this chapter because concepts of the subtle body can be understood to destabilize the normative-deviant binary that is commonly employed to frame such epistemological difference. Further, I contend (and have argued elsewhere) that subtle body schemas—and the implicit cultivation of perception that accompanies them—are a useful case study from which to advocate for the identification and valorization of epistemological pluralism within academic practice.[3] That is, that the form of subjectivity necessarily requires different modes of knowing and that such an experience sits uncomfortably within mainstream academic work. Therefore, *frisky* methods are required. Rather than simply position these knowledges as "less-than-reason" or to denigrate them as dodgy—or even "spiritual," if that term is deployed to minimize their viability—I would argue that the task at hand is one in which debates about "truth" claims are set aside and the scholar is required to work at sitting uncomfortably with epistemological plurality and difference. That is, there should be a refusal to smooth the jagged—or invisible—edges of subtle body models of experience and subjectivity that threaten to deflate the balloon of empiricism.

These are bodies that simply cannot be seen with "everyday" sight, and that at the same time require and elicit epistemologies that disrupt easy categorization. Therefore, this chapter knowingly asks unanswerable—or perhaps partially answerable—questions. How does one study invisible bodies? How can one incorporate—with due critical rigour—more intuitive, creative forms of epistemology (implicit in the perception of spiritual anatomy) into contemporary scholarship? Although eluding concrete answers, it is hoped this consideration is not merely futile. Rather, it seeks to open out and sit with the confusion, difficulties and possibilities. Before treading that unstable ground, a swift overview of issues of subtle body composition and its ramifications for the conceptualization of subjectivity is warranted.

Frisky matter: subtle, invisible and infuriating

As exemplified by the scholarship in this volume, concepts of the subtle body are found in numerous religions and self-directed spiritual practices, including Asian, western and Indigenous traditions.[4] The presentation in western discourses of subtle anatomy—whether, for example, networks of *chi* (foundational to the practice of Traditional Chinese Medicine, inclusive of acupuncture) or interpenetrating sheaths of spirit–matter (Theosophical subtle bodies)—commonly links their recognition and utilization to specific forms of body–mind cultivation. This may be, for example, learning to read a variety of pulses via touch (acupuncture) or to perceive the dynamics of invisible bodies utilizing extrasensory skills (seeing auras for example). Such skills can be known by many names—the sixth sense, clairvoyance, intuition, clairsentience, "mystic" vision, etc.—and are in general positioned in an unequal binary with reason (on this reductive view of reason see Ruth Barcan).[5]

My own previous research has primarily utilized concepts of the subtle body developed by the Theosophical Society (and their adaptation of schemas from Hindu and Esoteric traditions). This is a seven-body schema, in which the individual subject is considered to be comprised of seven sheaths of subtle matter (often termed "energy" in contemporary subtle body discourse): only three of which are understood to manifest in this physical plane and of those, only one—the physical body—is perceived by empirical senses. There is no need to recount the complexities of the system here (which includes detailed cosmological and evolutionary schemas); it is suffice to note that this engenders a profoundly extensive subject: one that expands far beyond the physical skin border. Each sheath of these subtle bodies interpenetrates and exceeds the preceding bodies: therefore, the self that they form is extensive and largely invisible to the normative capacities attributed to the five senses. Further, due to the ontological "material" of which they are composed—subtle matter (the degree of density and vibration understood to differentiate the subtle bodies from one another)—also being considered to constitute the broader world, this is a self that is radically open.

Therefore, subtle body forms of subjectivity present a radically extensive version of the body: the individual is simultaneously plural, open to the universe and in constant energetic exchange with it. This type of subjectivity (subtle subjectivity) can be thought of as a radical form of intersubjectivity—a corollary to concepts proposed in phenomenological and post-structuralist thought—although this ramification is rarely considered in popular culture discourses.[6] However, what is prioritized in many accounts of energetic anatomy in alternative therapies and well-being culture is the way in which subtle bodies challenge the definitions of body given by biomedicine. By proposing the self as comprised of invisible relations of energy or subtle matter, a core understanding of health is generated in which both disease and cure are simultaneously physical, emotional and metaphysical.

Such fundamental considerations of the boundaries of individual subjectivity and its intersubjective relation with others and the broader environment give rise to a number of ethical questions (to say the least), including the vexing: how is one to be responsible for bodies that they may not even perceive? How is one to apprehend the subtle dynamics of others?

These tricky issues regarding the perception of subtle matter draw considerable relation with issues of other-than-human agency espoused as part of the so-called "ontological turn" in recent theoretical debates.[7] This "turn" encompasses the approaches of New Materialism (e.g. "vibrant" matter) and "New" Animism: albeit these umbrella terms encompass a vast range of diverse theories.[8] Broadly, both approaches recognize, and seek to carve out in academic discourse, space for other-than-human agencies. These are agencies not generated (even indirectly) by the human and whose affects and knowledge are apprehended in a variety of ways, utilizing a range of perceptive skills.

Subtle bodies and the subtle matter of which they comprise sit in an ambiguous relationship with concepts of other-than-human agency. On the one hand, subtle matter must necessarily be considered of the human; yet, it is also attributed as a shared ontological foundation for other beings, the environment, the cosmos and various metaphysical beings (angels for example). As such, radical difference can be conceptualized as constitutive of the self. That is, a shared ontology of "subtle substance" does not necessarily need to result in a collapse of ontological difference—including the dangerously reductive (neoliberal) "we are all one" perspectives associated with (New Age belief) that elide socio-cultural difference and ethical responsibility.[9] Subtle subjectivity can maintain individual personhood while at the same time acknowledge via embodied practice radical difference and interconnection.[10] However, rather than trace these ontological ramifications that rupture neat binaries of self and other,[11] this chapter is focused upon its epistemological ramifications.

Frisky experience: ways of knowing subtle bodies

The next few sections open out the epistemological pluralism enacted by subtle body forms of subjectivity. Uncharacteristically this will not be done in detailed philosophical dialogue with a particular theorist (my usual mode!); rather, it will more generally converse with a range of approaches and examples. The term "frisky" is employed to denote the gentle deviance these bodies engender. This deviance refers to the critical acknowledgement of alternative forms of knowledge. Although they may be denigrated in particular fields (particularly those with an unwavering commitment to reductive forms of empiricism), alternative forms of knowledge, for example the many forms of intuition, extra-sensory perception and dream knowledge that are fundamental fixtures of embodied existence and as such have produced long histories of experience and investigation. Indeed, it is well accounted that mind–body training regimes may elicit an increased facility in "expanded" or "alternate" modes of perception and an accompanying capacity to apprehend subtle body dynamics (mediation, or Reiki training for example).

Yet, these sensory capacities and knowledges are not fixed and self-evident. They are part of dominant discourse—dominant discourse that both constructs and restricts their understanding—and they can be recognized and represented in many different ways. Although more recent western philosophical and literary movements have associated these epistemologies with Romanticism, the legacy of which remains in popular discursive construction of an emotion–intuition corollary *contra* reason, what counts as intuition, mystic experience or alternative perception (even in western contexts) is socio-culturally constructed and subject to change. Indeed, depending on cultural context what is considered deviant or "alternative" may be rendered normative or everyday. However, the discussion in this chapter is built upon their representation in dominant western discourse.

Indigenous and esoteric worldviews have long traditions taking into account the invisible agency of the other-than-human; whether that is conceived of as spirits of place, the agency of a stone, an animal "spirit" or individuated spirit-beings. Specific humans are also attributed the capacity to be able to direct or manipulate the subtle energies attributed to such other-than-humans: variously termed within western discourses (and some indigenous traditions), shamans or magicians. This invisible agency is understood to effect invisible cause at a distance, is attributed an ontological agency distinct from others and is also considered the essence of individuated subjectivity. The popular engagement with such type of agencies in contemporary forms of self-directed spirituality is well attested and the subject of numerous academic studies.[12]

These forces, forms of subtle matter, other-than-human ontological agencies—whether in ancient or contemporary discourse practice—are all conceptualized within dominant discourse. So too is the capacity for an individual to apprehend them and to direct them (for example, in magical practice). Therefore, as I have previously noted:

> It is not just that these modes of knowing are often presented as antithetical to dominant discourse, but also that the positing of their very existence and efficacy—embodied or manifest in symbolic or literary systems—is profoundly intertwined with normative conventions. As von Stuckrad argues: "the power of discursive structures clearly limits the ways in which scholars can construct meaningful narratives."[13]

Recognizing these limits and the dominant tropes of any specific discourse is crucial to its analysis. This impacts directly on the terminology that scholars use to describe and identify aesthetic practice and relations.[14]

Therefore, delineating intuition, alternative perception, etc. becomes an exercise in Foucauldian-inspired discourse analysis. Although generally understood as a collective "other" to dominant forms of rationalism, what "counts" as each form of knowledge individually is quite complex and can differ markedly depending upon the socio-cultural group. For example Ruth Barcan's analysis of intuition demonstrates that it can be considered both an embodied and an entirely disembodied form of knowledge, that it can be linked to deeply practical, habituated skills and practice (nursing) or rendered implicit in psychic forms of knowing understood as an essential aspect of the self or as "given" by an external agent.[15] Significantly, what such studies elicit is a picture of alternate forms of knowing as being quite routine epistemological practices for many people—a part of the "everyday" ways in which an individual relates to and understands their world—rather than a rarefied form of epistemological deviance. Further Barcan notes that the simple binary intuition–reason also masks the plurality of "reason(s)" and the necessary lived interrelationship of intuition(s) and reason(s):

> We spend years learning how to reason, including being trained in specific forms, styles, and vocabularies of reasoning. Even so, no one,

> when they reason, can be absolutely certain that their conclusions have been derived free of the workings of habit, assumption, prejudice, cultural limitations, or, for that matter, 'intuition.'[16]

Therefore, as Barcan goes on to claim, there is no "pure" intuition *or* reason. Just as subtle body models of subjectivity disrupt mind–body dualisms via their plural form and ontological substance, so too the knowledges accorded with their apprehension disrupt dominant epistemological boundaries that would position them in an oppositional binary relation. Of course, the reclamation of legitimacy and strategic use of knowledges historically marginalized and denigrated within western contexts has been (and continues) to be an important strategy for the representation and *presencing* of difference and the practice of inclusivity in a variety of contexts including academic. These are important social, political and cultural interventions. Without minimizing this strategy and its effects, another approach (following Barcan) is to emphasize the under-acknowledged presence of "alternate" knowledges within the realms of dominant, reasoned discourse and to develop research methods that presence and acknowledge these modes of knowing more directly.[17] It is towards this topic that the next section turns.

Frisky methods: ways of working with subtle bodies

As is in keeping with the multiple, porous and nebulous bodies with which this volume is concerned, there are numerous ways in which the forms of alternate knowledge, which are deemed requisite to apprehend them, can be incorporated into academic research practice. This is inclusive of respecting and working with—via material engagement and taking up different modalities of "vision"—the specific worldviews of the practice and its material affects being studied.[18] Indeed, I contend that one salient way is for the researcher to cultivate a particular aesthetic–ethic approach: Esoteric Aesthetics.[19] This use of the term "aesthetics" is not bounded by traditional Kantian disinterested agendas but is akin to more recent approaches, for example those of the Aesthetics of Religion.[20] Esoteric Aesthetics requires an acknowledgement of the dynamics of invisible, other-than-human agency and the conscious cultivation of specific types of extra-sensory perception while remaining cognizant of the discursive construction of such. As previously summarized,[21] the core features that the practice of an Esoteric Aesthetics is founded upon are:

1 the relationship between viewer and object is considered radically intersubjective and co-constitutional;
2 this relationship is constitutive of extended human and other-than-human agencies that may not be perceptible to the five senses, but may be perceived by forms of extrasensory perception;

3 an Esoteric Aesthetics requires the utilization of a range of scopic regimes, some of which may require conscious cultivation;
4 the practice of an Esoteric Aesthetics requires an embodied and self-reflective relationship that often requires elongated periods of time to cultivate;
5 the practice requires a conscious and reasoned continual questioning of socio-culturally defined concepts of "materiality," "subjectivity" and their interrelation; and
6 it embraces epistemological plurality in the understanding of subject-object relations and seeks to acknowledge, respect and communicate this plurality.

In particular regard to subtle subjectivity (a subjectivity comprised of subtle bodies) especial attention would be directed to the space "in between" subject and object. A space more usually constructed as empty or as filled with atmosphere. An Esoteric Aesthetics would stress this as a field of dynamic, agential interrelation: the site of emergent ontologies as well as a "space" in which the subject and object are radically intertwined.

A central aspect of the Esoteric Aesthetic approach, the cultivation of perception has also become a feature of the methodological furniture in contemporary environmental humanities. These discourses are often premised upon a close attention to intersubjective relations and to redirection of attention to the specific, from the macro to the micro; or from one sense (vision for example) to another (sound). In the field of studies in religion, Donovan O. Schaefer has adapted these approaches and affect theory (Deleuzian) in order to make a case for "animal religion."[22]

While Schaefer is focused on the other-than-human ethics of these approaches, the issue of the change in orientation of perception and an accompanying issue of religious experience or perception accompany other more human-centric analysis, and are often presenced in the discourse via the terminology of "enchantment." Enchantment and the call to be "re-enchanted" are terms that often accompany animist or new materialist approaches to relation with the other-than-human world. Such a perspective can be found in David Abram's extended phenomenology that focuses upon an earth-based relation with invisible "spirits."[23] He argues:

> The reciprocity between our body and the earth is enabled by a host of unseen yet subtly palpable presences, fluid often fleeting powers whose close-by presence we may feel or whose influence we can intuit yet whose precise contours remain unknown to us. Felt presences whose lives sometimes mesh or move through us so seamlessly that they cannot be rendered in thought, but only acknowledged or honoured with simple gestures of greeting, and sometimes of gratitude.[24]

According to Abrams, developing a close relationship with place, with particular environments, will necessarily place an individual in relation with other-than-human invisible agencies, which he terms "spirits." The acknowledgement of such is also key to the development of alternate epistemologies according to Abrams:

> By speaking of the invisibles not as random ephemera, nor as determinate forces, but as mysterious and efficacious powers that we sometimes felt in our vicinity, we loosen our capacity for intuition and empathic discernment, unearthing a subtlety of sensation that has long been buried in the modern era.[25]

Subtle knowledge, subtle senses are linked here with embodied concentration on and in particular places. This is exactly the type of relation encompassed by an Esoteric Aesthetics. Abrams contends: "to live is to dance with an unknown partner."[26] This statement clearly renders the irreducible difference of other-than-human agencies. However, from the perspective of subtle subjectivity, the individual self is also comprised at an ontological level of expansive bodies unknowable in their entirely; therefore, the self is also already an unknown partner. Distinguishing the different invisible agencies/ontologies from one another—and appropriately respecting radical difference—remains a fraught issue and one of the most enduring ethical conundrums of such perspectives.

The reconsideration of animism to which Abrams contributed his phenomenological, sensory, earth-based insights also garnered M. J. Barrett's overview of her research methodology that explicitly sought to "*research and write through* (rather than just about) animist ways of knowing and being."[27] Identifying as an "academic, animist and trained practitioner in a variety of energy-healing modalities," she advocates "porosity" (related to porousness) as "the episto-ontological position from which I write. It refers to an openness to and engagement with animate Earth, particularly in the process of knowledge acquisition and meaning-making."[28] Indebted to Val Plumwood's "dialogic" method, and working from a base that "thought and matter are, to a great extent, manifestations of energy" (the Theosophical concept of "thought-forms" is a direct corollary to this belief[29]), Barrett's worldview and academic practice is thoroughly embedded in subtle material: "The word 'porosity' underscores the porousness, or lack of boundaries, between human-beings and that which exists well beyond the physicality of human thought and body."[30]

To render this perspective and practice not only palpable but as a core aspect of her research practice for her doctoral dissertation, she incorporated "a variety of intuitive knowledge-making practices, energy work, and a multi-media hypertextual form."[31]

The first two steps of her method are forms of the cultivation of perception: "Quieting the mind" and "Being open and attuned to porosity." The third step is to discover and develop particular body–mind practices: "various forms of meditation, dowsing, dreaming, and non-local communication. They also include artistic practice and simple, quite attention."[32]

I am not sure about the discursive conventions that often lead to the description of paying attention as "simple"; it would seem that such practices of focused attention can be quite hard work and require substantive training and practice (for example the proliferation in a secular, commodified context of mindfulness guides, workshops and retreats). However, other methods Barrett advocates are already embedded as research strategies in the Humanities, in particular artistic practice as Critical Practice or Practice-Led Research. This approach in the visual arts involves an active exploration of critical concepts via art production. However, its products are not considered as necessarily finished artwork, but rather coalesced moments of dialogue or intervention with dominant discourse. It is thought that the experimental processes integral to such exploration will enable new emergent knowledges to develop. Barrett's particular dissertation actively sought to open spaces for the non-discursive—"poetry, collage, music, prose, recorded human voice and photographic images together with multi-media hypertext"—the latter enabling the reader to choose (actively or randomly: or a little bit of both!) in what order to read and how deeply to engage with the knowledge and arguments that she presented.[33]

These processes enable the presentation of plural epistemologies; however, I would contend that the apprehension of such—as with subtle bodies themselves—will always only ever be partial. Ethically that is to be valorized, not only for the relinquishing of discourses of mastery it affords, but also because of the "space" (albeit a very active one) for radical difference (also only ever partially apprehended) it engenders.

To Barrett's approach I would append Barcan's insight in regard to the plurality of reason and its (unknown) admixture with intuition. Academic argument, conceptual intellectual knowledge not only bears its own often under-recognized plurality, but need not be considered or positioned as antithetical to other modes of knowing. Although it must be acknowledged that in its name violent, reprehensible atrocities and discrimination have been and continue to be committed; these considerations about epistemology are profoundly intertwined with human rights and respect for cultural difference. Academic reasoning(s) is not pure, and can itself be the expounded result of other modes of knowing: the following of a hunch, the accidental discovery of a text/theorist/object that was not sought for but directly leads to new academic knowledge. Respectable academic methods of research/writing genres *already* incorporate, dialogue and represent the intuitive, emotive, invisible, affective knowledges and dialogue with other-than-human agencies. It is generative of the context from which the work emerges. It is the acknowledgement and respect for this creatively messy ground of thought-being that frisky methods advocate. Ranging from the majority creative practice to the tightest of empirical frameworks alternate knowledges are already operational.

Conclusion: subtle epistemology

Subtle bodies are nothing if not wonderful to "think with." They enable reconceptualization of a vast range of binaries, including the vexed issues of body–mind and matter–consciousness relations. As this chapter has sought to explore, they also enable a more conscious representation of intersubjectivity and other-than-human agencies within academic research and practice. As I have noted previously, alternate knowledges are no less embedded in cultural paradigms and dominant discourse than any other aspect of lived experience. As such, their acknowledgement requires the same critical, ethical imperative to investigate the discourses that construct them and limit their representation. There is the same imperative to trouble our own assumptions about what "intuition" or "alternative perception" is and/or can be. This should be part of the work of developing frisky methods in the study of subtle bodies.

As an active researcher in this area I have also been a participant in a vast swathe of subtle-body–related practices. My well-developed (and well-reasoned) cynicism has at times baulked at the discourse through which these experiences are presented to me. In its very worst forms it has been racist, sexist and spiritually elitist. Simultaneously I cannot deny the affectivity and agency of the practices. To do so would be churlish and similarly elitist and disrespectful. It is not, or at least not only, a *matter* of belief.

To be frisky I need neither to denigrate the experience (mine and others) with my well-developed capacity to critically strip anything to shreds; nor to imbibe a position of gullible naiveté or support discourses I find ethically reprehensible. I have to agree to be baffled and to not let that get in the way of continued observation, analysis and questioning. I have and continue to struggle with subtle body experiences and their ramifications personally-professionally. I have no viable framework in which I can place the experiences that would make them acceptable to a conservative academic context. Techniques of multi-vocality, creative critical practice and explorations of mixed methods can assist with this task.

Being frisky requires allowing multiple knowledge worlds to exist concurrently and to sit and work in the uncomfortable intersections with as many modalities of enquiry as available. What is available will be dependent upon the scholar's epistemological skill and cultivation of perception. This is no easy task. More often than not I falter: it is more comfortable to pick apart discursive tropes, trace conceptual lineages and search for signs of fraudulence in practice. I catch myself doing this and reflect upon the impulse (especially for the latter) and what is at stake. If we wish to glimpse subtle bodies and other-than-human agencies—and the epistemological pluralism with which they are intertwined—then we have to allow ourselves to be undermined by the unknown and uncontrollable (within and without) and continue to think–play anyway.

Notes

1 For example, *Angels of Desire: Esoteric Bodies, Aesthetics and Ethics* (London: Equinox, 2008) and Geoffrey Samuel and J. Johnston, *Religion and the Subtle Body in Asia and the West: Between Mind and Body* (London: Routledge, 2013).
2 Jay Johnston, "Rewilding Religion: Affect and Animal Dance," *Bulletin for the Study of Religion* 46, nos. 3–4 (2017): 11–16.
3 Jay Johnston, "Slippery and Saucy Discourse: Grappling with the Intersection of 'Alternate Epistemologies' and Discourse Analysis," in *Making Religion: Theory and Practice in the Discursive Study of Religion*, eds. F. Wijsen and K. von Stuckrad (Berlin: Walter de Gruyter, 2016), 74–96.
4 Maureen Lockhardt, *The Subtle Energy Body: The Complete Guide* (Rochester: Inner Traditions, 2010) and Samuel and Johnston, *Religion and the Subtle Body*, 2013.
5 Ruth Barcan, "Intuition and Reason in the New Age: A Cultural Study of Medical Clairvoyance," in *The Sixth Sense Reader*, ed. David Howes (Oxford and New York: Berg, 2009), 209–232.
6 Johnston, *Angels of Desire*, Op. Cit.
7 Johnston, "Slippery and Saucy Discourse," Op. Cit.
8 For example, Jane Bennett, *Vibrant Matter* (Durham, NC and London: Duke University Press 2010); Donovan O. Schaeffer, *Religious Affects: Animality, Evolution, and Power* (Durham, NC and London: Duke University Press 2015); Graham Harvey, ed. *The Handbook of Contemporary Animism* (London: Routledge 2014 [2013]).
9 Ruth Barcan and Jay Johnston, "Fixing the Self: Alternative Therapies and Spiritual Logics," in *Mediating Faiths: Religion and Socio-Cultural Change in the Twenty-First Century*, eds. Michael Bailey and Guy Redden (Surrey: Ashgate, 2011), 75–87.
10 Johnston, *Angels of Desire* (section III Ethics), Op. Cit.
11 I have done this elsewhere, see Johnston, *Angels of Desire*, Op. Cit.
12 For example, Ruth Barcan, *Complimentary and Alternative Medicine: Bodies, Therapies, Senses* (London and New York: Berg, 2011); Paul Heelas, *Spiritualities of Life: New Age Romanticism and Consumptive Capitalism* (Malden and Oxford: Blackwell, 2008); Christopher Partridge, *The Re-Enchantment of the West*, Volume 1 (London: T & T Clark, 2004) and *The Re-Enchantment of the West*, Volume 2 (London: T & T Clark, 2005); Steven Sutcliffe and Ingvild Saelid Gilhus, eds. *New Age Spirituality: Rethinking Religion* (London: Routledge, 2014).
13 Kocku von Stuckrad, *The Scientification of Religion: An Historical Study of Discursive Change 1800–2000* (Berlin: Walter de Gruyter 2014), 182.
14 Johnston "Saucy and Slippery Discourse," Op. Cit., 77.
15 Johnston "Saucy and Slippery Discourse," Op. Cit.
16 Ruth Barcan, "Intuition and Reason," and *Complimentary and Alternative Medicine*, Op. Cit.
17 Johnston "Saucy and Slippery Discourse," Op. Cit.
18 Jay Johnston and Iain Gardner, "Relations of Image, Text and Design Elements in Selected Amulets and Spells of the Heidelberg Papyri Collection," in *Bild und Schrift auf 'magischen' Artefakten*, eds. Sarah Kiyanrad, Christopher Theiss and Laura Willer (Berlin: de Gruyter, 2018), 139–148; Johnston "Saucy and Slippery Discourse," Op. Cit.
19 On Esoteric Aesthetics see Johnston, *Angels of Desire*, Op. Cit.; Jay Johnston, "Esoteric Aesthetics: The Spiritual Matter of Intersubjective Encounter," in *Aesthetics of Religion: A Connective Concept*, eds. A. K. Grieser and J. Johnston (Berlin: Walter de Gruyter, 2017), 349–365.

20 Alexandra Grieser and Jay Johnston, eds. *Aesthetics of Religion: A Connective Concept* (Berlin: Walter de Gruyter, 2017).
21 Jay Johnston "Enchanted Sight/Site: An Esoteric Aesthetics of Image and Experience," in *The Relational Dynamics of Enchantment and Sacralization: Changing the Terms of the Religion Versus Secularity Debate*, eds. P. Ingman, T. Utriainen, T. Hovi and M. Broo (Sheffield: Equinox, 2016), 97–114.
22 Schaefer, *Religious Affects*, Op. Cit.
23 David Abrams, "The Invisibles: Towards a Phenomenology of the Spirits," in *The Handbook of Contemporary Animism*, ed. G. Harvey (London and New York: Routledge, 2014), 124–132.
24 Ibid., 131.
25 Ibid., 132.
26 Ibid., 124.
27 M. J. Barrett, "Researching Through Porosity: An Animist Research Methodology," in *The Handbook of Contemporary Animism*, ed. Graham Harvey (London and New York: Routledge, 2014), 416–422.
28 Ibid., 416–417.
29 On Thought–forms see Annie Besant and Charles W. Leadbeater, *Thought-Forms* (Wheaton; Madras; London: Theosophical Publishing House, 1969 [1901]).
30 Barrett, "Researching Through Porosity," 417.
31 Ibid.
32 Ibid., 418.
33 Suze Adams, "Practice as Research: A Fine Art Contextual Study," *Arts & Humanities in Higher Education* 13, no. 3 (2014): 218–226.

References

Abrams, David. "The Invisibles: Toward a Phenomenology of the Spirits." In *The Handbook of Contemporary Animism*, edited by Graham Harvey, 124–132. London and New York: Routledge. 2014 [2013].

Adams, Suze. "Practice as Research: A Fine Art Contextual Study." *Arts & Humanities in Higher Education*. 13, no. 3 (2014): 218–226.

Barcan, Ruth. *Complimentary and Alternative Medicine: Bodies, Therapies, Senses*. London and New York: Berg, 2011.

———. "Intuition and Reason in the New Age: A Cultural Study of Medical Clairvoyance." In *The Sixth Sense Reader*, edited by David Howes, 209–232. Oxford and New York: Berg, 2009.

Barcan, Ruth and Jay Johnston. "Fixing the Self: Alternative Therapies and Spiritual Logics." In *Mediating Faiths: Religion and Socio-Cultural Change in the Twenty-First Century*, edited by Michael Bailey and Guy Redden, 75–87. Surrey: Ashgate, 2011.

Barrett, M. J. "Researching Through Porosity: An Animist Research Methodology." In *The Handbook of Contemporary Animism*, edited by Graham Harvey, 416–422. London and New York: Routledge, 2014 [2013].

Bennett, Jane. *Vibrant Matter: A Political Ecology of Things*. Durham, NC and London: Duke University Press, 2010.

Besant, Annie and Charles W. Leadbeater. *Thought-Forms*. Wheaton; Madras; London: Theosophical Publishing House, 1969 [1901].

Grieser, Alexandra K. and Jay Johnston, eds. *Aesthetics of Religion: A Connective Concept*. Berlin: Walter de Gruyter, 2017.

Harvey, Graham, ed. *The Handbook of Contemporary Animism.* London and New York: Routledge, (2014 [2013]).

Heelas, Paul. *Spiritualities of Life: New Age Romanticism and Consumptive Capitalism.* Malden and Oxford: Blackwell, 2008.

Johnston, Jay. *Angels of Desire: Esoteric Bodies, Aesthetics and Ethics.* London: Equinox Publishing, 2008.

———. "Enchanted Sight/Site: An Esoteric Aesthetics of Image and Experience." In *The Relational Dynamics of Enchantment and Sacralization: Changing the Terms of the Religion Versus Secularity Debate*, edited by P. Ingman, T. Utriainen, T. Hovi and M. Broo, 97–114. Sheffield: Equinox, 2016.

———. "Esoteric Aesthetics: The Spiritual Matter of Intersubjective Encounter." In *Aesthetics of Religion: A Connective Concept*, edited by A. K. Grieser and J. Johnston, 349–365. Berlin: Walter de Gruyter, 2017.

———. "Rewilding Religion: Affect and Animal Dance." *Bulletin for the Study of Religion* 46 nos. 3–4 (2017): 11–16.

———. "Slippery and Saucy Discourse: Grappling with the Intersection of 'Alternate Epistemologies' and Discourse Analysis." In *Making Religion: Theory and Practice in the Discursive Study of Religion*, edited by F. Wijsen and K. von Stuckrad, 74–96. Berlin: Walter de Gruyter, 2016.

Johnston, Jay and Iain Gardner. "Relations of Image, Text and Design Elements in Selected Amulets and Spells of the Heidelberg Papyri Collection." In *Bild und Schrift auf 'Magischen' Artefakten,* edited by Sarah Kiyanrad, Christopher Thiess and Laura Willer, 139–148. Berlin: de Gruyter, 2018.

Lockhardt, Maureen. *The Subtle Energy Body: The Complete Guide*, Rochester: Inner Traditions, 2010.

Partridge, Christopher. *The Re-Enchantment of the West.* Volume 1. London: T & T Clark, 2004.

———. *The Re-Enchantment of the West.* Volume 2. London: T & T Clark, 2005.

Samuel, Geoffrey and Jay Johnston, eds. *Religion and the Subtle Body in Asia and the West: Between Mind and Body.* London and New York: Routledge, 2013.

Schaefer, Donovan O. *Religious Affects: Animality, Evolution, and Power.* Durham, NC and London: Duke University Press, 2015.

Sutcliffe, Steven and Ingvild Saelid Gilhus, eds. *New Age Spirituality: Rethinking Religion.* London: Routledge, 2014.

Von Stuckrad, Kocku. *The Scientification of Religion: An Historical Study of Discursive Change 1800–2000.* Berlin: Walter de Gruyter, 2014.

11 Bliss and bodily disorientation

The autophagous mysticism of Georges Bataille and the *Taittirīya Upaniṣad*

Matthew I. Robertson

Introduction

Discussions of the body's role in mystical experience exhibit a tendency to think in terms of a threshold. The subject turns inward or outward from it, imploding toward an unseen center or exploding into the outer and/or the all. The dichotomous typologies that have been forwarded over the last seventy years—Eliade's enstatic/ecstatic,[1] Stace's introvertive/extrovertive,[2] Forman's trophotropic/ergotropic,[3] and Sarbacker's numinous/cessative[4]—have all essentially retained this bodily oriented inner-or-outer basis. And even though none of these typologies are in widespread use today (owing especially to the decline of comparative and phenomenological approaches to the study of religion), a basic distinction they forward thrives unspoken: the body is the locus of orientation according to which we ascribe an inner or outer character to the mystical experience. In other words, the presumption of the body as a stable, orienting point of reference, as the threshold from which the inner or outer turn of mysticism occurs, remains the uncritically accepted point of orientation for our manner of thinking and speaking about mystical experiences.

This has a way of occluding an essential feature of the body's role in such experiences. For is it not true that, insofar as the turn occurs, the body-as-threshold can lose its orienting significance, no longer able to make the otherwise crucial distinction between inner and outer? This is quite clearly illustrated in certain Indic traditions. For instance, a twelfth–thirteenth CE Nāth Siddha work, "The Manual on the Final Aim of the Perfected One" (*Siddhasiddhāntapaddhati*), outlines how the practitioner should realize that the outer cosmos he is "in" is equally within his own embodied self, while his true embodied self is nothing less than the entire cosmos. In the conflation of the within of the body and the without of the world he becomes spatially ambiguous; he lacks any true inner or outer side.[5] A similar spatial ambiguity is suggested in the early Upaniṣads, according to which the hidden truth of reality is grasped when the Self (*ātman*) is understood in its identity relation to *brahman*, the "power of growth and expansion" that is the unseen and omnipresent basis of all that exists. In spite of the fact that this identity relation clearly locates the Self as both within and beyond bodies—and thus the Self is not a personal, individual self, but rather a trans- or inter-personal Self—the process by which the Self is discovered is almost exclusively read as involving an inward turn. Hence, the term *antarātman* is universally translated as "inner Self" despite the fact that the prefix *antar-* could just as easily be translated as "inter-" or "in the midst." It seems rather quite likely that the authors of the early Upaniṣads consciously played upon this ambiguity, in the hopes that others might see that what is typically thought to be merely "within" is, in truth, "in the midst."

With such thoughts in mind, the present chapter aims to more deeply examine the role of the body in two strikingly parallel descriptions of mystical experience. The first is Georges Bataille's "The Practice of Joy before Death," a densely poetic encapsulation of his "base materialist" philosophy (summarized below), which is framed in terms of an atheistic mysticism that categorically rejects the existence of any transcendent reality.[6] The second is found in the second and third chapters of the *Taittirīya Upaniṣad*, an early Upanishadic text that radically reconceives one of the most celebrated of Vedic rituals—the Agnicayana, or "the piling of the fire altar"—outlining thereby a novel technique for inducing a mystical experience of the "bliss" of the supreme state of being, *brahman*. There is no direct historical connection between these sources. Moreover, their contents reflect worldviews that many would see as fundamentally incompatible: the one modern, Western, and staunchly irreligious; the other ancient, South Asian, and part of a long-standing religious tradition. Yet there are strong parallels between them that make such a comparison irresistible: both works were written in times of rising political uncertainty and violence, and both respond to their times by the use of shockingly parallel thematic imagery. It is the latter of these parallels that most relevantly draws my attention to these sources as emblematic of a certain kind of bodily disorienting mysticism. Nevertheless, I hope the reader will indulge a brief consideration of the historical contexts attending these sources; for it not only deepens our sense of the kinship between them, but invites us to think in a different fashion about the deep contexts that inspire mystical experiences, and thus about the place of bodily disorientation in our thinking about not only the category of mystical experience, but also the broader categories of religion and the sacred.

Let us consider first the historical context of "The Practice of Joy before Death." It was published in the summer of 1939, on the eve of the Second World War, mere months before Germany would invade Poland. At this point, Bataille had already long fantasized in his writing about the possibility of his own violent demise—eventually discerning therein the promise of an "impossible" category of experience that remains a hallmark of his thought—and with the increasing likelihood of war on a global scale his fantasies seemed on the verge of becoming reality.[7] But whereas his previous works had elements of a direct social and political engagement, "The Practice of Joy before Death" records a stark shift in his thought toward the liberating apoliticism of mysticism.[8] As noted by Jules Monnerot (who co-founded the Collège de Sociologie with Bataille and Roger Caillois), it was in this moment, when the political state of the world was becoming a dominant concern in public discourse, that Bataille "almost ceased to use the words of politics and sociology which previously he used frequently."[9]

Monnerot believed that Bataille's turn to the language of mysticism marked a retreat from politics or the rising violence of the world. But in fact he was beginning to develop an intuition that the practice of mysticism shares key features—a curious blending of violence, exhilaration, and terror—with war and ritual sacrifices; and that therefore a broader social engagement with mysticism, detached from notions of transcendence or supreme beings, could perhaps circumvent or curb the human impulse to engage in catastrophically violent conflict.[10] In "The Practice of Joy before Death," Bataille puts to page this irreligious and joyfully war-like mysticism. It is a testament to Bataille's evolving views on politics and violence and their relation to experiences typically deemed mystical in the religious sense only. It represents an attempt to confront the realities of violence in a way that he believed to be more honest, and a hope that such an honest confrontation could transform humanity's engagement—social, political, etc.—with the world. The result is an essay that seeks, through the cultivation of mystical experience, to transmute violence into an enviable gift that affords the necessary conditions for all of life's possibilities for joy and bliss.

A parallel set of circumstances attends the *Taittirīya Upaniṣad*. It too was composed during a time of significant political uncertainty—between the fifth and sixth centuries BCE, in the twilight of the great tribal polities of northern India and on the eve of an age of "Great" men with imperial ambitions. Urban city centers began to spring into existence as a sedentary, agrarian pattern of life took hold. Meanwhile, vast highways, facilitating both trade and shifts of power, brought about the existence of an increasingly interconnected world. As a result, the established orders underwent a remarkable decline.[11] As a text that developed in the midst of such changes, the *Taittirīya Upaniṣad*, like "The Practice of Joy before Death," appears to seek refuge in an apolitical turn: whereas the preceding tradition of the Vedic Brahmins was explicitly steeped in politics,[12] the *Taittirīya* reflects the general outlook of the early Upaniṣads, which gives voice to a rising class of ascetics who turned away from a direct participation in society and politics in order to seek a more individualistic, mystically informed engagement with the world.

Here too, however, the apparent turn away from social and political participation more accurately marks a search for a new approach. The ascetics of the early Upaniṣads cut a middling path between the old ways of Vedic sacrifice and the upstarts of the "heterodox" traditions of Jainism and Buddhism. The Jains and Buddhists most strongly embraced the doctrine of non-violence (*ahiṃsā*), and rejected outright the sociopolitical organization proffered by the Vedic orthodoxy, faulting especially its practice of ritual sacrifice as a wholly violent affair that merely perpetuated a woeful existence borne out through cyclical patterns of life, death, and rebirth. By contrast, and in a manner reminiscent of Bataille's essay, the *Taittirīya*

Upaniṣad forwards a new paradigm of political sovereignty and engagement with the world based upon a more honest confrontation with the violent nature of an existence rooted in cycles of birth and death. The final goal, as in the rest of the early Upaniṣads, was to inculcate a knowledge, a mystical realization that one's true self is *brahman*, the abstract Absolute characterized in one respect by a sovereign power over life and death, and in another by a bliss that is fundamentally without measure. Thus, rather than seek outright escape from the violent nature of cyclic existence, the ascetics of the early Upaniṣads discovered therein a new kind of political power and a pathway to embrace the fullness of life in all its expressions with ecstatic gratitude.

Both Bataille's "The Practice of Joy before Death" and the *Taittirīya Upaniṣad* were thus composed in times of significant social and political strife, when the issue of violence as a tool for organizing and administrating the world was under a certain intense scrutiny. Both likewise respond to the issue of violence in a parallel fashion by positing a reconfiguration of engagement with the world through techniques of mystical realization. There are even more impressive and deeper parallels evident at the level of their thematic imagery. The remainder of this chapter will focus on these other parallels, in particular their use of a textual imagery of autophagy—of self-consumption—to describe the true nature of existence that is realized in the midst of the mystical experience. Furthermore both arrive at this imagery by following parallel courses, involving a meditative confrontation with death and an affective transformation in which an initial dread or fear turns into an overwhelming bliss. It is in these parallels especially that we glimpse the *pathosformel* working across these texts;[13] or, to put the same in an Indic idiom, the stirring of echoes across the cycles of time.[14] They have duly emboldened the comparison I will draw below by tracing the unique paths they take from death to the bliss of autophagy. I trust that the true value of reading these sources together will become self-evident as a result. But more importantly, I trust that it will raise important questions about the role of the body in mystical experiences of the sort described herein. For both texts compellingly accentuate the ambiguities of embodiment in the mystical experience by arguing that bodies, which we typically view as having a spatially orienting effect on our existence, in fact exert a fundamentally *disorienting* influence, which mystical experience alone can rectify. And this urges us to think anew about how bodies engaged in mystical experiences are framed in academic discourses.[15]

Georges Bataille

Death

"The Practice of Joy before Death" is a densely poetic, somewhat erratic set of meditations that cannot be well understood apart from several broader trends in Bataille's body of work. Most important in this regard is his on-going attempt to think in terms of a "base materialism."[16] As this thinking is expressed in "The Practice of Joy before Death," base materialism rests upon the assertion that there is no transcendent force that governs our existence. There is instead only the perpetually unstable, ceaseless, and useless flow of energy throughout the cosmos. Thus the base materialist rejects all discourses involving notions of God or some existence "beyond" the immediately present reality, and instead embraces the "base" reality of an existence comprised of flesh that presses upon, penetrates, violates, and consumes other flesh. Understanding the ramifications of this outlook is crucial, not only to grasping the general thrust of Bataille's thought, but more importantly to grasping how it is that Bataille is able to still speak to the possibilities of a mystical experience. For it is our inability to reckon with the instability of our nothing-more-than-material manner of existing that has led, according to Bataille, to the perpetuation of a fundamental misunderstanding about the nature of ourselves and our relationship to the world. And this fundamental misunderstanding has profoundly negative social, political, and economic consequences—war being chief among them—that could be avoided if our thinking, our values, and our behaviors were reformed. The mystical experience outlined in "The Practice of Joy before Death" provides one possible avenue for such a reformation, aimed ultimately and more broadly at the development of new paradigms of social, political, and economic systems of power.

The misunderstanding of which Bataille speaks is rooted in two wrong assumptions. The first is that there is a certain degree of stability to our existence and that the world is not in a constant state of change. Speaking to this error and its effect, he writes:

> We can ignore or forget the fact that the ground we live on is little other than a field of multiple destructions. Our ignorance only has this incontestable effect: It causes us to *undergo* what we could *bring about* in our own way, if we understood. It deprives us of the choice of an exudation [of destructive energies] that might suit us.[17]

The second wrong assumption is that our harnessing of the energies that flow throughout the cosmos, which we most often use toward our own, specifically human ends, is essentially without consequence. In other words, we wrongly assume that the resources of the Earth and the cosmos-at-large are there as a free reserve for us, for our immediate and unlimited use, and that these resources are not inextricably part of the larger movement of energies in the cosmos. In Bataille's words, "Humanity exploits given material resources, but by restricting them as it does to a resolution of the immediate difficulties it encounters... it assigns to the forces it employs an end which they cannot have."[18] The modern reliance on fossil fuels is a case in point: not only has the struggle for the control of this resource been a major source of conflict among nations, its broader unforeseen consequences include the deforestation of the planet, the acidification of the oceans, and the alteration of climatic patterns. This is just one example of the way in which our behavior neglects the reality that there is "a circuit of cosmic energy on which [human activity] depends, which it cannot limit, and whose laws it cannot ignore without consequences." Instead, our behavior is that of "those who, to the very end, insist on regulating the movement that exceeds them with the narrow mind of the mechanic who changes a tire."[19]

The corrective to these wrong assumptions is likewise twofold. First, an awareness of the instability of our nothing-more-than-material existence must be raised. Second, and as a corollary to the first, our use of energies must be brought more in line with the greater flow of energies in the cosmos (a flow which our own uses only temporarily succeed in redirecting at best). Bataille's brand of mysticism aims toward both of these goals by means of a direct, experiential confrontation with death, "the wonder-struck cry of life,"[20] which Bataille frames in a manner perfectly in line with the outlook of base materialism.

In the "The Practice of Joy before Death," Bataille defines death as a "happy *loss of self*," a "dark unknown," and an "unintelligible and bottomless space."[21] Death thus lay beyond the rational and experiential horizons of embodied life, and in this regard it is situated beyond the limited sphere of human activity and the modes of life that are rooted in the wrong assumptions identified above. In short, death refers us to the greater movement and characteristic instability of cosmic energies. Other forms of mysticism, according to Bataille, gravely error when they approach death in spiritual terms rather than these base material terms. Joy before death—though perhaps it is more accurate to say joy at the recollection of death—"belongs only to the person for whom there is no *beyond*," and is therefore a means by which "life can be glorified from root to summit."[22] In other words, death directly refers us to the nothing-more-than-material grounding of our embodied existence. Consequently, a profound mortality, widespread and absolute, is the *sine qua non* of our embodied existence, the immediate reality of the world and our life therein.

Bataille sees this reality expressed concisely by our Sun, an orb that burns ceaselessly, without sense of reserve, and essentially catastrophically by pouring forth light in the manner of a profusely bleeding wound.[23] The Sun's profound mortality is the source of all life on our earth, and by its ever-excessive nature the Sun proclaims the base nature of that life: as given above all by death, without which the excessiveness of our life—its conscious individuality, its consumptive enjoyment, and its self-proliferation through sex—would not arise nor could persist. The mystical experience that Bataille seeks in practicing joy before death, which reveals and makes plain the excessiveness of life, resides in this mortality. As he writes,

> death appears to be of the same nature as the [Sun's] illuminating light… [and thus] it appears that no less a loss than death is needed for

> the brilliance of life to traverse and transfigure dull existence... [Consequently, through the mystical experience,] I cease to be anything other than the mirror of death, just as the universe is only the mirror of light.[24]

Bliss

Our everyday concealment of the reality of death marks a retreat into the illusions of stability and separate human activity. Bataille refers to these illusions as the basis for what we normally recognize as the "real order,"[25] a chief effect of which is the concealment of the excessiveness of life. But through this retreat from death, from the excessiveness of life, the *intimacy* of life is lost—its immediate nature of being "caught up" in the vast movement of cosmic, living energies, in which the strict limits of embodiment and individuality are overwhelmed by a consciousness of continuity. Indeed, the whole existence of the "real order" requires that it "annul – neutralize – that intimate life and replace it with the thing that the individual is in the society of labor."[26] The sacred, which is rooted in intimate life, and religion, whose aim it is to bring the intimacy of the sacred to bear upon our existence,[27] are thus opposed to the "real order" insofar as they aim to reveal these things that the "real order" conceals.

The excessive nature of life that underlies death reveals itself more fully in the act of sexual reproduction, and more immediately in the bliss of the sexual orgasm. That is, in the act of sex, the excessive qualities of the reproductive orgasm and death are exposed simultaneously. In his most provocative works, Bataille paints literary scenes that superimpose sex and death in a manner that recalls the revulsionary force of social taboos. He concludes his *Story of the Eye* with the rape and murder of a priest, and *My Mother* with the protagonist masturbating over the corpse of his mother. The shocking nature of such scenes reflects not only Bataille's willingness to break past the social barriers of perversion, but also his understanding that mystical experience is driven by a "profound love [that] burns [and leads us to a] point which, being both the life and death of the loved one, has the blast of a cataract"—a violent blow that "strikes down" and brings about "the nullification of all possible illusion."[28]

The orgasm is indeed a *little death*, and "between death and the reeling, heady motion of the little death, the distance is hardly noticeable."[29] Orgasms exhibit above all "the desire to live while ceasing to live, or to die without ceasing to live."[30] And it is precisely because the orgasm affords no final consummation of death that it touches on the very heart of the mystical experience of dying without ceasing to live. That is, it provides a moment of intimacy in and through which the limitations of human embodiment and individuality can be transgressed and, at least temporarily, overcome. As such, the orgasm is an object lesson that nevertheless fails to achieve what it intends. Through it, one learns that "the impossibility of satisfaction in love is a *guide* toward the *fulfilling leap* at the same time that it is the nullification of all possible illusion."[31] The illusion, in this case, is the existence of discrete bodies, while the dispelling of that illusion is like a moment of violent rupture, in which the spatial delimitation of bodies is erased, as is the distinction between life and death.

These insights coalesce in a line from the "Heraclitean Meditation"[32] that concludes "The Practice of Joy before Death." With characteristic flourish, Bataille writes, "I imagine the gift of an infinite suffering, of blood and open bodies, in the image of an ejaculation cutting down the one it jolts and abandoning him to an exhaustion charged with nausea."[33] The orgasm is an imperfectly killing blow, and precisely in this manner it provides a glimpse of that which, so long as we are in fact alive, touches something otherwise impossible: a union of two discontinuous beings that betrays the consequence of death's destruction of the individual; the revelation of the world as the intimacy of a "continuity of being."[34] Here, then, lies the core of Bataille's characterization of the mystical experience: an obliteration of the inner and the outer, and an orthogonal turn away from the illusory isolation of embodiment.

Self-consumption

Clearly, the turn away from embodiment is marked by a certain violence toward the body. Without it, Bataille sees no access to the continuity of the mystical experience. He was famously fascinated by images of torture and bodily suffering, especially a set of photographs of a person[35] being subjected to the truly horrific corporal punishment, the "death by a thousand cuts," in which the body is flayed, carved, and disarticulated, bit by bit, until the victim dies. Purportedly given to him by his personal psychotherapist,[36] Bataille's ruminations on these images span the rest of his career as a writer and seem to have stood as a monument to the transgressive, inverted view of mysticism that he championed. In one instance he writes:

> [The victim] communicated his pain to me or perhaps the excessive nature of his pain, and it was precisely that which I was seeking, not so as to take [sadistic] pleasure in it, but in order to ruin in me that which is opposed to ruin.[37]

In seeking to express the exuberant bliss capable of being found in the greatest of all horrors, a bliss that smiles at the prospect of a headlong fall into the "impossible" continuity of being in death, Bataille returned again and again to the transfixed look of agony on the photographed victim's face. It was, for Bataille, precisely the expression of the highest religious sentiment.

In his *Theory of Religion*, Bataille sees this same sentiment evident in the dynamics of the eater and the eaten. The animal that is killed and eaten by another emits a primal scream in the throes of death, a "supreme affirmation of life."[38] He sees such consumption, and the moment of primal affirmation it affords, as the very nature of the universal economy, the act that makes clear how truly excessive life is in the universe—always more of it, at every level of existence, irrupting into the world to eat and be eaten. It is for this reason that the mystical experience, which above all exposes and makes intimate the excessiveness of life, manifests in a manner that encapsulates the dynamics of animal consumption, one animal subsumed by another, like waves overtaking each other in a vast ocean. In other words, the particular violence of the mystical experience is one of autophagy. Bataille makes this abundantly clear in the series of visualizations that conclude his essay on attaining the "Joy before Death," the most immediately relevant of which read as follows:

> I imagine... everything that exists destroying itself, consuming itself and dying, each instant producing itself only in the annihilation of the preceding one, and itself existing only as mortally wounded. Ceaselessly destroying and consuming myself in myself in a great festival of blood.
>
> ...
>
> This death is only the *exploding* consumption of all that was, [and] the joy of existence of all that comes into the world... I imagine myself covered with blood, broken but transfigured and in agreement with the world, both as prey and as a jaw of TIME, which ceaselessly kills and is ceaselessly killed.[39]

Taittirīya Upaniṣad[40]

Death

The *Taittirīya Upaniṣad* too proposes that death and bliss reveal the fundamentally self-consumptive nature of reality. Though we must bear in mind that in giving expression to these themes, it relies upon the uniquely Indic idioms of sacrifice and asceticism. In the analysis that follows below, these idioms will be privileged without modification in order to develop a more robust basis for comparison. For it is precisely the distance between these two sources, in terms of their idioms of expression, that renders the parallels between them all the more impressive.

The *Taittirīya Upaniṣad* is structured around a reinterpretation of the Vedic-era rite known as the Agnicayana, the "piling of Agni."[41] Agni, it must be noted, is the Vedic god of fire who is present in each and every fire in existence—those burning on the Earth's ground, those burning in the heavens in the guise of the Sun and the stars, and even those burning within our bodies, exuding warmth and digesting food. The ritual in which Agni is "piled" corresponds to a cosmogonic myth that privileges the connection between these fires, but that in certain ways emphasizes the Sun's fire as the greatest and most expansive fire in existence. According to it, Prajāpati, the creator god whose name avers that he is the "Lord of the Creatures," creates the cosmos by a toilsome practice of austerities (*tapas*) that eventually brings him to a death-like state of total exhaustion. It is precisely this act of self-sacrificing exhaustion, in which the *prāṇa*, or "breath of life," leaves Prajāpati, which gives rise to the multiplicity of beings that populate the cosmos. In other words, all mortal beings owe their existence to this sacrifice of the creator god's original integrity, his unitary immortality. Afterward, his body thus dispersed throughout (and as) the cosmos, Prajāpati pleads for rescue from Agni, his first-born son. Agni dutifully puts his father back together, but does so *in his own image*. Hence, Prajāpati is reborn as the son of his son, a second Agni, and a Sun-like fire. In this way the god whose body became the cosmos found restoration and unity by becoming the fire whose light reaches every corner of the world.

In the Agnicayana's ritual context, a human sacrificer symbolically repeats this creative act through a protracted process that involves significant toil and exhaustion as the sacrificer goes about "re-piling" himself in the image of Agni. This he does (aided by a retinue of brahmin priest specialists) by the construction of a five-layered, eastward-oriented altar in the shape of a bird, which simultaneously represents himself and the Sun. The altar, along with the clay bricks of which it consists, is built to the specifications of the sacrificer's own height, and it is in this regard that the sacrificer is said to be the "same measure" as the sacrifice and the cosmos it models for the sake of his ritualized identity transformation.[42] By the conclusion of the rite, the sacrificer, like Prajāpati, is exhausted to a death-like state and subsequently reborn[43] as the reconstituted creator of the cosmos, and therefore he knows himself to be united with the whole world by virtue of his own identification with the Sun and its world-filling light. The elevated status of the sacrificer and the lofty identity secured by the Agnicayana's performance are indicative of the fact that, historically speaking, the rite's primary performers were members of the royal class, and a key function of its performance was to consolidate the sovereignty of the sacrificer through the series of complex identifications it affords. That is, the rite legitimized political authority by symbolically transferring the title of "Lord of the Creatures," thereby granting the new "Lord" an expansively luminous identification with the full scope of the kingdom/cosmos over which he ruled.

The *Taittirīya Upaniṣad* reflects a historically later development, by which time concerns about the sovereignty of the individual had expanded to include those not engaged in actual political office. Instead, it offers a comparatively apoliticized manual for developing this same cosmic identification and a similarly sovereign status in a non-ritual setting. Excised from the complicated ritual setting of the Agnicayana, the *Taittirīya* relies upon an imaginative journey through an ascetic-practitioner's five "selves" (*ātmans*—consisting of food, breath, mind, perception, and bliss; and collectively mirroring the five brick layers of the traditional Agnicayana rite[44]) culminating in the discovery of one's most essential and immortal nature. It is also an imaginative journey through death, via the passage beyond all those selves that have temporary existence only (specifically, those selves made of food, breath, mind, and perception). This has a twofold benefit: on one hand, it guides the ascetic toward a mystical death-without-dying, and thus a living transcendence of mortal life; on the other, it prepares the ascetic for an eventual journey toward immortality that will come at the moment of his[45] actual physical death. The goal in either case is to reach the fifth and final Self, which consists of *ānanda*, or bliss. The ascetic's goal thus involves the experiential realization of his most fundamental *blissful* nature that is exposed in and through death. Doing so introduces the ascetic to the capital-S Self that is non-different from *brahman*, the essence of all that lives, grows, dies, and is reborn again.

The centrality of death in all of this cannot be overstated. Death is here not the cutting off or the absence of life; it is its very source. It is that unarticulated state or space out of and through which all living forms are articulated. Indeed, it could be said that the capital-S Self that is non-different from *brahman* is quite close to death, if not, in a sense importantly different than our usual thinking about what death is, wholly identifiable with it. And so too is death linked to bliss, which qualifies the fifth and final self-discovered in and through death.

Bliss

The reframing of the Agnicayana in terms of bliss, and its linking of bliss thereby to *brahman*, is arguably the signature innovation of the *Taittirīya Upaniṣad*. It is also a highly significant development for the history of Indic philosophy, as centuries later the school of Advaita Vedānta will rely upon it to argue that one of *brahman*'s most essential characteristics (along with "being" and "consciousness") is bliss.[46] Yet even before the *Taittirīya* forwarded its innovative argument, the centrality of bliss to the early Upaniṣadic worldview could have been anticipated on two interrelated counts. On the first, bliss was already conceived as the root cause behind all births, and therefore as the driving force that perpetuates the cycle of rebirth. On the second, bliss was already beginning to be conceived as the very nature of liberation (*mokṣa*) from that same cycle.

As that which perpetuates the cycle of rebirth, the authors of the early Upaniṣads explicitly understand bliss in terms of sexual pleasure. Sex organs are treated essentially like the organs of sense, their unique "power" being the sensation of bliss.[47] The true nature of bliss is thus best glimpsed in the moment of orgasm, which not only unleashes an engulfing wave of bliss, but also releases the very stuff of life (which is in this context especially identified with male semen[48]). In effect, bliss is treated as identical to semen and no real distinction is admitted between the physical and the experiential dimensions of the reproductive process.[49] The *Taittirīya* attests to this understanding when, speaking to the origins of existence, it draws a link between bliss (*ānanda*) and the "essential fluid," *rasa*: "That [origin of all life] is *rasa*. Indeed one obtains *rasa* only when one obtains bliss."[50] Paraphrased in plainer terms, this would read: "The origin of all life is semen. Indeed, semen comes only when one has an orgasm." Clearly, there could be neither birth nor rebirth were it not for bliss, thus understood. Whence then this bliss-*qua*-semen perpetuates the "miserable round" of cyclic existence?

The origin of bliss—insofar as one can be found in a cyclic cosmos—is food. Specifically, semen is the end result of the process of digestion, whereby food is transmuted in the fires of the belly until only its most refined essence, its *rasa*, remains. This much is avowed in the "five fire doctrine" (*pañcāgni-vidyā*), the earliest systematization of the process of cyclic existence found in the Upaniṣads (that is, prior to the *Kaṭha Upaniṣad*'s introduction of the originally non-Brahmanical concept, *saṃsāra*). The five fire doctrine builds upon an explicitly Vedic, sacrificial worldview, according to which the cosmos is ultimately reducible to the two chief substances of a sacrifice, which are also lauded as deities in their own right—fire (*agni*) and liquid (*soma*). A cosmogonic myth in the *Bṛhadāraṇyaka Upaniṣad*, in which a personified and ravenously hungry Death stands as the originary creative impulse, claims, "The extent of this whole world is food and the eater of food. *Soma* is verily the food; *agni* is the eater of food."[51] The five fire doctrine expands upon this vision of the cosmos to explain where a living being goes at death and how it is that he tends to return to life on Earth once more. In brief, when the body of a dead man is offered into a cremation fire, its refined essence (the transmigrating "soul") exits the body and begins a journey throughout the vast digestive apparatus that is the sacrificial cosmos. The steps along this journey are conceived as a series of offerings made into a series of fires until, eventually, the essence of the dead returns once again to the earth as food, which is eaten by men, transformed into semen, and then deposited into female wombs in a moment of blissful orgasm, after which the dead are reborn. Of course, once alive again, these reborn beings will resume the whole process, eating food and seeking their own moments of bliss throughout.

In short, bliss—as the phenomenal *rasa* of semen—is crucial to the continuation of cyclic existence. In this regard, it is perfectly intelligible that certain ascetics of the early Upaniṣadic era would seek to avoid rebirth by abstaining from sex or food. And yet (and this is nowhere more than case than in the *Taittirīya Upaniṣad*) bliss is also conceived as the very nature of liberation. The apparent paradox this implies vanishes when the experience of bliss is analyzed. For the characteristic feature of the bliss of the sexual orgasm is that it momentarily overcomes the separation between two otherwise distinct beings. Hence, "a man completely enveloped by a woman lover knows nothing at all about 'outside' or 'inside.'"[52] His spatial orientation, the boundary between his body and all else, disappears in a moment. And it is out of this moment, in which self and other merge, that new life comes forth, effectively heralding the unseen creative power that is *brahman*. The experience of bliss in the orgasm is thus an object lesson, and one that should be understood in such a way that one permanently overcomes disorientation of embodiment that separates self and other by knowing oneself as *brahman*, the blissful basis of all existence.

Prior to the liberating awareness of being *brahman*, existence in a cyclical manner is filled with sorrow and fear.[53] The sole hope for escape rests upon a person's ability to comprehend this bliss that is the source of mortal life—this bliss that wipes away the inner and the outer, that is un-spatializable, and according to the *Taittirīya*, "supportless and incorporeal." And yet, as the above should make clear, the escape offered is not one of absolute transcendence. It is one of total acceptance and a merging into the blissful, underlying power of cosmic transformation. So whereas there is a definitely non-spatial quality to bliss, and likewise to *brahman*, the identification with that power of cosmic transformation carries with it an identification with the entire expanse of the cosmos. That is, there is a poetic sense of bliss as a cause of magnification or expansion that accompanies the sense of bliss as doing away with spatial boundaries between self and other. So it is, for instance, that semen, as a physical manifestation of this power, is said to be found in the vacuity of space,[54] or founded upon the heart,[55] within which lies a space "as big as this space outside us."[56]

The *Taittirīya Upaniṣad* echoes this trend in a section on the "analysis of bliss," the primary aim of which is to distinguish the bliss of *brahman* as being orders of magnitude greater in scope from the greatest possible human bliss. "Take a young man," the text states, "an accomplished youth who is learned, possessed of a great appetite,[57] highly resolute, and exceedingly strong. And assume that this whole earth filled with wealth should be his. That is a single [measure] of human bliss."[58] From this point of an already rarified bliss the text then describes the bliss experienced by every class of being within the divine hierarchy, each a hundred times greater than the last. It concludes its blissful survey of the upper echelons of the great chain of being with the declaration that the bliss of *brahman* is the greatest of all possible blisses, fully one quintillion times greater in measure than the greatest possible human bliss.

Throughout the whole of this analysis, the referent of that bliss has clearly shifted away from the sexual, non-spatial idiom to one of increasingly cosmic spatiality. But the core meaning of bliss, as an experience in which self and other merge, is nonetheless retained. This is evident in the opening lines, when the measure of human bliss is given in terms that are most appropriate to a sovereign ruler, whose qualities of youth, erudition, strength, and ownership of the world have been emphasized variously since Vedic times. Indeed, in those Vedic times, the qualities of the human sovereign were patterned after those ascribed to Indra, the king of the gods. Indra's quintessential feat in the Vedic mythology was to overcome his rival, Vṛtra ("The Constrictor"), by transacting with *agni* and *soma*—those same substance deities whose digestive interactions underlie all cosmic transformations—and thereby expanding in both might and size to a cosmic scope, breaking past his constrictive foe. In the process, the world is created, the extent of which is no less than the extent of Indra's expansive size. Consequently, a sovereign is fundamentally a strong one who, in owning the wealth of the whole world, is considered non-different from it. In other words, the sovereign is the one whose self is the kingdom over which he rules. He has merged his embodied self with all the others in its expanse. In this regard, the spatial expansive characterization of the bliss of an orgasm bears a fundamental resemblance to even the spatially expansive characterization of the Vedic sovereign.

And yet the prototypical sovereign of the *Taittirīya* is not Indra, but Prajāpati, specifically as he appears in the Agnicayana mythology. Consequently, the sovereign and either non-spatial or expansive character of bliss in the *Taittirīya* is ever-linked to the encounter with death. A verse from an Upaniṣadic analysis of dreamless sleep is helpful in sorting out the relation of all of these themes. A man in a dreamless slumber, he states, "can rest like a young man, a great king, or a great brahmin who has reached the total oblivion (*atighnī*) of sexual bliss."[59] As any recollection (or rather, the impossibility of any recollection) of the dreamless state affirms, a non-dreaming person rests in a state of profound indifference, in which there is no hint at all of spatial distinctiveness or orientation. In the phrasing of the analysis this marks a "total oblivion," the equal of one who has been "utterly struck down" (*atighnī*), i.e. "killed."[60] The expansive spatial footprint of the sovereign is in this way essentially considered the same as the non-spatial non-difference of the one killed by bliss. This fits well with structure of the *Taittirīya Upaniṣad*, wherein the passage to the bliss of *brahman* proves to be a passage (imagined and then later realized) through death.

Self-consumption

In sum, one must be obliterated by bliss in order to reside in bliss—in *brahman*—permanently. But what survives the obliteration of bliss is both of the highest and lowest order. As both root and summit, the knower of *brahman* encapsulates all of life and death, a feat which requires a joyous abandonment of self to the digestive transformations of fires and liquids in the sacrificial cosmos, and thus a gleeful sense of self as that which consumes and that which is consumed. Put differently, the knower of *brahman* enters a state of immortality predicated on a persistent and profound mortality that survives and surpasses by dwelling in the bliss that is without self or other. Hence, to truly know bliss is finally to know oneself as the same as the processes by which bliss arises and through which it is infinitely expressed. To attain immortality is to embrace a profound mortality, and thus rather than know oneself as merely a body, one should know oneself as both eater and eaten.

The revelation of the *Taittirīya Upaniṣad* is in this manner a revelation of the autophagy of one's truest self. It is for this reason that the text closes by identifying the blissful knower of *brahman* with the Sun, the greatest of all fiery eaters and the light that daily rises and swells to fill the whole world. It is the Sun's fire, in the minds of the Upaniṣadic sages, that stands as the originary basis of all fires, and that therefore dwells both outside and within all bodies, consuming them as its food. Upon knowing this, experiencing it as the truth of oneself, "one travels across the worlds, eating whatever he likes and assuming whatever appearance he likes, and sings this chant:

> I am food! I am food! I am food!
> I eat food! I eat food! I eat food!
> ...
> I eat him who eats the food!
> As the Sun, the light, I have conquered this whole world!"

Concluding remarks

Both "The Practice of Joy before Death" and the *Taittiriya Upaniṣad*'s reimagining of the Agnicayana aim at cultivating a mystical experience through an engagement with death. Both assert that the engagement results in an overwhelming experience that transforms what is normally full of dread into a source of joy or bliss. Both hold that this bliss matches the sexual orgasm's momentary obliteration of self and other and inner and outer. And thus both give expression to the intimate relationship between death and the bliss by which life originates. As a result, both envision human, embodied life to be suspended between bliss and death, which are conceived as two facets of the same phenomenon that recurs throughout the cosmos at every moment. Thus both see the fullness of life and its true character reflected in the action of consumption on a cosmic scale, directly knowing which one is transfigured into that greater reality—the autophagous cosmos that nullifies the illusions of separate natures and embodied selves in an endless gnashing of teeth and Time.

In considering the value of these parallels, I offer the following observations. First, both Bataille and the *Taittirīya Upaniṣad* propose a kind of mystical destabilization of bodies that does not presuppose a concomitant spiritualization of the subject. In other words, there is nothing precisely *beyond* flesh in these texts. Nevertheless, this flesh—especially when considered as that which belongs to merely mortal, temporary beings—is characteristically unstable. It transforms continuously, takes birth and dies, eats and is eaten. In viewing flesh and bodies in this light, Bataille considers our existence according to its base materiality. Later post-structuralists have sought to operationalize this view through the conception of an "unstable third term" that disrupts distinctions between self and other.[61] The Upaniṣadic material discussed here understands *brahman* in essentially the same manner. *Brahman* is by name the "power of growth and expansion," and as the Upaniṣad argues, this power manifests as a transformative force that disrupts stability through acts of consumption and digestion. In this regard, both Bataille and the Upaniṣad stand against those mysticisms that merely reject flesh and seek an escape therefrom through an inactive, inward turn. They instead seek flesh in the mode of its naturally active exuberance.[62]

Second, this disruptive movement, regardless of the terms involved, disrupts above all the spatial or spatializable dimensions of experience, which are often understood from the locus of bodies. In normal, everyday states, bodies afford a stable point of orientation in and to space. In the extra-normal states of the mystical experiences described in these sources, these same bodies *disorient*, and so must be torn by teeth and consumed in order to reveal a state not beyond flesh, but rather radically *enfleshed*. Not quite embodied, insofar as embodiment presupposes delimitation and stability, but flesh extended past all formal limits and yet kept mortal, and thereby a flesh made sovereign by virtue of its irrepressibility rather than its transcendence: the Sun that rises daily to conquer the world with its light; "TIME that ceaselessly kills and is ceaselessly killed."

With such thoughts in mind, we can return to the consideration I outlined at the start of this chapter. Our usual way of thinking about mystical experiences begins with a presumption of the body as a fixed threshold, a site where boundaries and differences are constituted. Hence, the body becomes the site from which the mystical experience inwardly or outwardly proceeds. This same way of thinking tends to inflect our approach to the categories of religion and the sacred, as evidenced by recent work among spatial theorists.[63] These theorists too think of the body in terms of its capacity for orientation, its capacity to effect the differencing of "internal and external relations, [of] situatedness and movement in space to produce spatial metaphors that can be used to articulate differences and relationships between persons, things, places, and values."[64] And because religion and the sacred are fundamentally determined by their difference from the secular and the profane, the body is envisioned as the "bio-spatial starting point" from which the formation of the categories of religion and the sacred occurs.[65] Yet if mystical experience can reveal bodies that are fundamentally disorienting and unstable in themselves, as constantly eating and being eaten, to what extent could they ever rightly serve as a threshold? How could they effect the differencing of interiorities and exteriorities or of the sacred and the profane? If bodies in the midst of the kinds of mystical experience described here fail to orient—to be sources of space and differencing—then are we in the presence of something other than religion or the sacred?

Fixed or static notions of bodies fail to afford an appropriate point of orientation for our thinking about such questions precisely because the bodies uncovered in these mystical experiences are not discrete. Instead, they are extended throughout vast spatial and temporal contexts, enfleshed in the illimitable flows of cosmic energies. When everything is "profoundly cracked," as Bataille wrote in "The Practice of Joy before Death," and bodies begin to fail in their usual role as boundary markers and makers of space, consequently distinctions between the religious and the secular, the physical and the spiritual, or the sacred and the profane become thoroughly confused. It is precisely for this reason that the irreligious mysticism of Bataille can so neatly fit alongside the religious mysticism of the *Taittirīya Upaniṣad*. This is not to say, however, that we cannot effectively speak in terms of the religious or the sacred in considering such expressions of mystical experience. For it seems readily apparent that it is out of such experiences, with their disoriented spaces and threshold-less bodies, that the presence of the sacred or the religious becomes most evident. That is, it is possible to imagine that categories like religion and the sacred, which do indeed rely upon the presence of a boundary setting them apart from the secular and the profane, are in certain cases first formed and made recognizable by their reference to an originary moment—a recurrence of the order of a *pathosformel*, an echo reverberating across cyclical time—in which bodily disorientation (perhaps of a blissful character) overrides all possible loci of orientation or conceptual differencing. More work is necessary to further examine this possibility. Nevertheless, one thing is now certain: the uncritical acceptance of fixed bodies as a locus of orientation for our thinking about such events occludes our capacity to even begin to think in this direction. In other words, so long as notions of bodies as a locus of orientation continue to orient our thinking about mystical experience and the related categories of religion and the sacred, our conclusions may themselves prove to be decisively disorienting.

Notes

1 See Mircea Eliade, *Yoga: Immortality and Freedom* (Princeton: Princeton University Press, 1958) and Mircea Eliade, *Shamanism: Archaic Techniques of Ecstasy* (Princeton: Princeton University Press, 1964).

2 See Walter Stace, *Mysticism and Philosophy* (London: MacMillan, 1960).

3 See Robert K. C. Forman, *The Problem of Pure Consciousness* (New York: Oxford University Press, 1990).

4 See Stuart Sarbacker, "'Enstasis and Ecstasis'" *Journal for the Study of Religion* 15, no. 1 (2002): 21–37, and Stuart Sarbacker, *Samādhi: The Numinous and Cessative in Indo-Tibetan Yoga* (New York: SUNY Press, 2005). Sarbacker's typology breaks somewhat with the others in this list. While he correlates his numinous-cessative typology with Eliade's, he adds important nuance in arguing that "the *enstatic* and *ecstatic* modalities can be better seen as being dynamically related rather than mutually exclusive" (Sarbacker, "'Enstasis and Ecstasis,'" 22).

5 David G. White, "Le monde dans le corps du Siddha: Microcosmologie dans le traditions médiévales indiennes," in *Images du Corps dans le Monde Hindou*, eds. Gilles Tarabout and Véronique Bouillier (Paris: CNRS Editions, 2003), 189–212.

6 Georges Bataille (b. 1897, d. 1962) was a librarian and archivist by trade and an intellectual and prolific writer by calling. His works made their profoundest impact after his lifetime, capturing the imaginations of French post-structuralist intellectuals such as Michel Foucault, Jacques Derrida, Jean Luc Nancy, Jacques Lacan, Julia Kristeva, and Henri Lefebvre, to name a few. His writings were characteristically transgressive and sometimes surrealist, and they treated a wide range of subjects to include economics, sociology, literature, erotism, and religion.

7 Stoekl, *Visions of Excess*, 263–264.

8 According to Stoekl's introduction to the collection of essays in *Visions of Excess*, the beginnings of this turn are linked to the foundation of the Acéphale secret society, which Stoekl characterizes as "a group of adepts, operating in the margins of (and acting against) official society" with the hopes of elevating the "lower" and more essential human drives that were so ill-served by the failures of art, science, and politics (Stoekl, *Visions of Excess*, xix). Giorgio Agamben faults Bataille for this apolitical turn, noting that whereas Bataille had discovered (perhaps unwittingly) the connection between sovereignty and "bare life," he otherwise failed to recognize "bare life's eminently political (or rather biopolitical) nature"; and as a result "in his thought [this bare] life still remains entirely bewitched in the ambiguous circle of the sacred" (Agamben, *Homo Sacer*, 112–113). Agamben essentially agrees with Walter Benjamin's critique of the Acéphale group in this regard: "You are working for fascism" (ibid., 113). A response to these criticisms would exceed the scope of the present chapter, but it is worth pointing out Agamben's uncritical insistence upon the physical body as a central point of orientation for thinking about issues of sovereignty and modern biopolitics. In this regard, he seems to ignore the manner in which Bataille's thought resists the physicality and limitedness of bodies, and bases his thought instead upon the observation that "everything is profoundly cracked" (Bataille, "Practice of Joy," 238). This raises the question of whether Bataille's turn away from a direct engagement with politics and toward mysticism was perhaps more profoundly political in nature than critics like Agamben and Benjamin have allowed, as I will suggest below.

9 Michel Surya, *Georges Bataille*, 288.

10 Bataille's views in this regard were inspired in part by the warrior mysticism of Ernst Jünger and in part by his developing interest with yoga and tantra (in which he saw an embrace of contradictory themes like violence and sexuality). Whatever little can be said about the kinds of yoga or tantra to which Bataille was exposed and/or sought to practice, it seems clear that the attraction was twofold: on one hand, involving the embrace of sexuality as a technique for attaining liberated states ("In the first days when I meditated … I suddenly felt as if I were an erect penis"); on the other, involving an Orientalizing fascination with non-theological (in a strictly Western sense), non-rational representations of the experience of the sacred (when "the limit of knowledge as the end is transgressed"). See Roland Champagne, *Georges Bataille* (New York: Twayne Publishers, 1998), 8–9, and 66–67 on these points. For Bataille's most fully developed thoughts on the capacity of mysticism (and "festivals") to circumvent war and political violence, see his *Theory of Religion* and *The Accursed Share* (especially volume 1).

11 For a more complete summary of the social and political situation during the period in which the *Taittirīya Upaniṣad* is thought to have been composed, see

Matthew Robertson, "The Autophagous Absolute: Revelations of Cosmic and Sovereign Violence in the *Bhagavad Gītā* and the *Taittirīya Upaniṣad*," *Journal of Religion and Violence* 6, no. 1 (2018): 73–105.

12 See especially Theodore Proferes, *Vedic Ideals of Sovereignty and the Poetics of Power* (New Haven, CT: American Oriental Society, 2007), and Jarrod Whitaker, *Strong Arms and Drinking Strength: Masculinity, Violence, and the Body in Ancient India* (New York: Oxford University Press, 2011).

13 The German art historian, Aby Warburg, developed the *pathosformel* concept to describe a certain type of iconographic recurrence evident in works of art that draw from the culture of Western antiquity, most especially its mythological and astrological systems of knowledge. Conceived apart from this specifically Western context, a *pathosformel* is an "emotionally charged visual trope" (Becker, "Aby Warburg's *Pathosformel*," 1) that appears in a number of otherwise disconnected instances, and that functions to recall "primary experiences of mankind, present continuities and transformations on the historical longue durée" (Vidal, "Rethinking the Warburgian Tradition," 2). Similar concepts appear in the Giorgio Agamben's work on the significance of the paradigm (*The Signature of All Things: On Method* (New York: Zone Books, 2009)) and Henri Lefebvre's theorization of "moments" (*Critique of Everyday Life* (New York: Verson, 2002)). Each of these concepts—*pathosformel*, paradigm, and moment—refers to a recurrent event that is (and here I paraphrase Agamben) always archaic and originary; its historicity rests in the crossing of diachrony and synchrony (Agamben, *Signature*, 31).

14 That is, if it could be said that something of the same order as a *pathosformel* (or Agamben's paradigm or Lefebvre's moment) exists in Indic thought, it is expressed especially through a thinking about the cycles of time (day, year, and *yuga*). Indic thinking about time allows for historical events to be both novel and repetitions of long past events. This is indeed the basic premise of the epic *Mahābhārata*—that the long ago struggle between the *deva*s and *asura*s is playing out once more in the world of men. Such originary repetitiveness is likewise the case for the textual imagery of autophagy—applied especially to the Absolute or God—that is found across Indic traditions. In addition to the instance in the *Taittirīya Upaniṣad* that I will address here, we find repeated instances in the *Mahābhārata* (most famously in the *Bhagavad Gītā*'s description of Krishna's *viśvarūpa*, or "all-form"), in Tamil narratives belonging to the Śaiva tradition (see Shulman, *The Hungry God*, 38-40), and in the well-known Buddhist image of the *bhavacakra*, the "wheel of existence." In this regard, we could easily say that the imagery of autophagy already marks a distinctive *pathosformel* in Indic thought. Yet there is an important difference between the autophagy of the *Taittirīya* and these other instances that draws the *Taittirīya*'s imagery in a more direct alignment with Bataille's in "The Practice of Joy before Death." Namely, only in the *Taittirīya* and in the "Practice of Joy before Death" do we see that distress explicitly transmuted into bliss.

15 Especially as they relate to the formation of the categories of "religion" and "the sacred" as framed by spatial theorists. See the concluding remarks below.

16 The concept of base materialism first appears in the 1930 essay, "Base Materialism and Gnosticism," but it is widely recognized as a cornerstone of Bataille's entire oeuvre.

17 Georges Bataille, *Tears of Eros*, 23-24; emphasis in the original.

18 Ibid., 21.

19 Ibid., 26.

20 Georges Bataille, *Theory of Religion*, 46.

21 Bataille, "Practice of Joy," 237.

22 Ibid., 236–237. Bataille connects this rejection of transcendence to sovereignty in strong terms in his essay "The Sacred": "God represented the only obstacle to the human will… [By contrast, the human without God] suddenly has at his disposal all possible human convulsions, and he cannot flee from this heritage of divine power—which belongs to him" (Stoekl, *Visions*, 245).
23 E.g., Georges Bataille, *Erotism: Death and Sensuality*, 28–33.
24 Bataille, "Practice of Joy," 239.
25 Bataille, *Theory*, 46.
26 Ibid., 47.
27 See, e.g., Bataille, *Theory*, 57.
28 Ibid., 238.
29 Bataille, *Erotism*, 239.
30 Ibid.
31 Bataille, "Practice of Joy," 238.
32 Heraclitus (sixth–fifth BCE) is distinguished by his doctrines of ceaseless change (immortalized in the aphorism, πάντα ῥεῖ, "everything flows") and the unity of opposites, both of which Bataille assiduously avers throughout his writings.
33 Bataille, "Practice of Joy," 239.
34 Bataille, *Erotism*, 20–21.
35 Bataille mistakenly identified the victim captured in his photographs (in his *Tears of Eros*) as Fu Chou Li, a man sentenced to death by torture for the murder of the Mongolian prince Ao Han Ouan. The subject in Bataille's photographs remains unidentified. See Timothy Brook, et al., *Death by a Thousand Cuts* for a compelling critique of the history of Bataille's engagement with these photos and of his reading thereof.
36 Bataille's therapist, Adrien Borel, shared these photos with him in 1925, fourteen years prior to the publication of the "Practice of Joy before Death" (Champagne, *Georges Bataille*, 8–9). The biographer Michel Surya names Borel as the photographer behind the images and thus as a first-hand witness to the torture.
37 Georges Bataille, *Inner Experience*, 120.
38 Bataille, *Theory*, 40.
39 Bataille, "Practice of Joy," 238–239.
40 I have recently written elsewhere on the broader complexities of this Upaniṣad as part of an investigation into the ways that Brahmanical authorities dealt with the problematic nature of violence and its associations with political office in ancient Indic society. My treatment of the Upaniṣad in the present chapter will be comparatively cursory. Those readers wishing to gain a more thorough understanding of this highly significant text, as well as a summary of the recent scholarship on it, may consult Robertson, "Autophagous Absolute."
41 Henk W. Bodewitz, *Jaiminīya Brāhmaṇa I, 1-65* (Leiden: Brill, 1973), 282; Yitzhak Freedman, "Altar of Words," *Numen* 59 (2012): 322–343.
42 E.g., *Śatapatha Brāhmaṇa* 3.1.4.23—*puruṣasammito yajña.*
43 On the prevalence in death and rebirth motifs in Brahmanical literature from this period, see Walter O. Kaelber, "The 'Dramatic' Element in Brāhmaṇic Initiation: Symbols of Death, Danger, and Difficult Passage," *History of Religion* 18, no.1 (1978): 54–76.
44 The interpretation of these *ātman*s as "sheaths" (*kośa*s) that is much repeated today is not native to the *Taittirīya Upaniṣad*. It was first popularized by Śaṅkara, the highly influential eighth-to-ninth century CE promulgator of the Advaita Vedānta philosophy, roughly a millennium after the Upaniṣad's accepted date of composition.
45 The Upaniṣad presumes a male subject.

46 Śaṅkara's *Brahma Sūtra Bhāsya*, for instance, relies heavily upon the *Taittirīya Upaniṣad* in developing its argument for the essential link between *brahman* and bliss. For a "semantic history" of bliss in early Indic sources, see Patrick J. Olivelle, "Orgasmic Rapture and Divine Ecstasy: The Semantic History of *Ānanda*," *Journal of Indian Philosophy*, 25, no. 2 (1997): 153–180.

47 In Upaniṣadic thought, the sense organs are more properly speaking sense "powers" (*indriyas*)—the power of seeing converges on the eyes, the power of hearing converges on the ears, and so on. The sex organs are likewise bodily sites where the power of sensing bliss converges. See Olivelle, "Orgasmic Rapture," 162–165.

48 The androcentrism of early Indic thinking about reproduction is best attested by a well-known passage from the *Manusmṛti* (the "Laws of Manu") that reduces the female womb to the status of a field in which a man plants his seed. Semen, in this framing, contains all the necessary constituents of a new life, whereas the womb merely provides the medium for its growth. It is worth noting that this view is not shared by the authors of Āyurveda's foundational medical texts. The *Caraka Saṃhitā*, for instance, more evenly divides the labor of reproduction in holding that certain parts of a fetus come from the sexual fluids of the mother, while others come from those of the father.

49 Olivelle, "Orgasmic Rapture," 166ff.

50 *Taittirīya Upaniṣad* 2.7—*...raso vai saḥ | rasaṃ hy evāyaṃ labdhvānandī bhavati* |.

51 *Bṛhadāraṇyaka Upaniṣad* 1.4.6—*etāvad vā idaṃ sarvam annaṃ caivānnādaś ca | soma evānnam agnir annādaḥ.*

52 *Bṛhadāraṇyaka Upaniṣad* 4.3.21—*priyayā striyā saṃpariṣvakto na bāhyaṃ kiṃcana veda nāntaram.*

53 Insofar as the early Upaniṣads do not appear to be aware of the doctrine of *saṃsāra* (see Johannes Bronkhorst, *Greater Magadha* (Leiden: Brill, 2007) for the most compelling arguments on this debate), the understanding of liberation presented in these texts has little to do with a total escape from *saṃsāra*. Instead, and as Jonathan Geen has convincingly argued, the early Upaniṣads portray the attainment of the state of *brahman* as the attainment of a state beyond *fear* (see Jonathan Geen, "Knowledge of Brahman as a Solution to Fear in the Śatapatha Brāhmaṇa/Bṛhadāraṇyaka Upaniṣad," *Journal of Indian Philosophy* 35, no. 1 (2007): 33–102). This is undeniably the case for the second chapter of the *Taittirīya Upaniṣad*, which concludes in part by citing a verse (from an unknown original source) that claims "One who knows that bliss of *brahman*, he is never afraid" (*Taittirīya Upaniṣad* 2.9; trans. Olivelle, *Upaniṣads*, 307).

54 See *Taittirīya Upaniṣad* 2.7.

55 See *Bṛhadāraṇyaka Upaniṣad* 3.9.17, 22; 6.4.9

56 *Chandogya Upaniṣad* 8.1.3.

57 Here I read *aśiṣṭha* (lit. "eating the most") in place of *āśiṣṭha* ("exceedingly quick"). There is a high likelihood of some minor corruptions in this portion of the text (e.g. *dṛdhiṣṭha* should normally read *dradhiṣṭha*), and the meaning of *aśiṣṭha* is far more appropriate to the broader context of the Upaniṣad than the vulgate's *āśiṣṭha*.

58 *Taittirīya Upaniṣad* 2.8—*yuvā syāt sādhuyuvādhyāyakaḥ | aśiṣṭho dṛdhiṣṭho baliṣṭhaḥ | tasyeyaṃ pṛthivī sarvā vittasya pūrṇā syāt | sa eko mānuṣa ānandaḥ* |.

59 *Bṛhadāraṇyaka Upaniṣad* 2.1.19—*sa yathā kumāro vā mahārajo vā mahābrāhmaṇo vātignīm ānandasya gatvā śayīta* |.

60 In other words, the Upaniṣadic sages considered, in accordance with the French idiom, that the bliss of orgasm is a "little death."

61 Benjamin Noys, "Georges Bataille's Base Materialism," *Journal for Cultural Research* 2, no. 4 (1998): 499.

62 Such is broadly characteristic of both Bataille and the early Upaniṣads. For instance, Bataille was repulsed by his syphilitic father's paralysis, which rendered him an "involuntary ascetic," a "repugnant ascetic" (Surya, *Georges Bataille*, 7). Likewise, the Upaniṣads' emphasis on the active nature of *brahman* stands in a most notable contrast to the world negating asceticism of Jainism. Early Jains harbored such a deep suspicion of action that its most revered figures are iconographized in statues of naked men standing in fixed postures, enacting an entirely voluntary paralysis against the instability of flesh on a cosmic scale—a total rejection of the disruptive ebullience of *brahman*.

63 Here I refer especially to the writings of Kim Knott (*The Location of Religion: A Spatial Analysis* (London: Equinox, 2005); "Spatial Theory and Method for the Study of Religion," *Tenemos* 41, no. 2 (2005): 153–184; and "Religion, Space, and Place: The Spatial Turn in Research on Religion," *Religion and Society: Advances in Research* 1 (2010): 29–43) and Veikko Anttonen ("Space, Body, and the Notion of Boundary: A Category-Theoretical Approach to Religion," *Tenemos* 41 no. 2 (2005): 185–201), as well as the foundational theoretical work of Henri Lefebvre (*The Production of Space, Critique of Everyday Life*).

64 Knott, "Spatial Theory," 157.

65 Knott, "Spatial Theory," 158. Similarly, Veikko Anttonen writes that the sacred is present "when boundaries between the categories of male and female, life and death, pure and impure, left and right, inside and outside of sacralized space, inside and outside of the human body are in transition" (Anttonen, "Space," 191).

Bibliography

Agamben, Giorgio. *Homo Sacer: Sovereign Power and Bare Life*. Stanford: Stanford University Press, 1998.

———. *The Signature of All Things: On Method*. New York: Zone Books, 2009.

Anttonen, Veikko. "Space, Body, and the Notion of Boundary: A Category-Theoretical Approach to Religion." *Tenemos* 41, no. 2 (2005): 185–201.

Bataille, Georges. *The Accursed Share*. 2 vols. Translated by Robert Hurley. New York: Zone Books, 1991–3.

———. *Erotism: Death and Sensuality*. Translated by Mary Dalwood. San Francisco, CA: City Lights Books, 1986.

———. *Inner Experience*. Translated by Leslie Anne Boldt. Albany: SUNY Press, 1988.

———. "The Practice of Joy before Death." In *Visions of Excess: Selected Writings 1927–1939*, edited and translated by Allan Stoekl, 235–239. Minneapolis: University of Minnesota Press, 1985.

———. *Tears of Eros*. Translated by Peter Connor. San Francisco, CA: City Lights Books, 1989.

———. *Theory of Religion*. Translated by Robert Hurley. New York: Zone Books, 1992.

Becker, Colleen. "Aby Warburg's *Pathosformel* as Methodological Paradigm." *Journal of Art Historiography* 9 (2013): 1–25.

Bodewitz, Henk W. *Jaiminīya Brāhmaṇa I, 1–65. Translation and Commentary with a Study of the Agnihotra and Prāṇāgnihotra*. Leiden: Brill, 1973.

Böhler, Arno. "Open Bodies." In *Images of the Body in India*, edited by Axel Michaels and Christopher Wulf, 109–122. New York: Routledge, 2009.
Bronkhorst, Johannes. *Greater Magadha: Studies in the Culture of Early India*. Leiden: Brill, 2007.
Brook, Timothy, Jérome Bourgon, and Gregory Blue. *Death by a Thousand Cuts*. Cambridge: Harvard University Press, 2008.
Champagne, Roland. A. *Georges Bataille*. New York: Twayne Publishers, 1998.
Eliade, Mircea. *Shamanism: Archaic Techniques of Ecstasy*. Translated by Willard R. Trask. 1964. Reprint, Princeton: Princeton University Press, 2004.
———. *Yoga: Immortality and Freedom*. Translated by Willard R. Trask. 1958. Reprint, Princeton: Princeton University Press. 2009.
Forman, Robert K. C., ed. *The Problem of Pure Consciousness*. New York: Oxford University Press, 1990.
Freedman, Yitzhak. "Altar of Words: Text and Ritual in Taittirīya Upaniṣad 2." *Numen* 59 (2012): 322–343.
Geen, Jonathan. "Knowledge of Brahman as a Solution to Fear in the Śatapatha Brāhmaṇa/Bṛhadāraṇyaka Upaniṣad. *Journal of Indian Philosophy* 35, no. 1(2007): 33–102.
Kaelber, Walter O. "The 'Dramatic' Element in Brāhmaṇic Initiation: Symbols of Death, Danger, and Difficult Passage." *History of Religions* 18, no. 1 (1976): 54–76.
Knott, Kim. *The Location of Religion: A Spatial Analysis*. London: Equinox, 2005.
———. "Religion, Space, and Place: The Spatial Turn in Research on Religion." *Religion and Society: Advances in Research* 1 (2010): 29–43.
———. "Spatial Theory and Method for the Study of Religion." *Tenemos* 41, no. 2 (2005): 153–184.
Lefebvre, Henri. *Critique of Everyday Life: Foundations for a Sociology of the Everyday*, vol. II, translated by John Moore. New York: Verso, 2002.
———. *The Production of Space*. Translated by Donald Nicholson-Smith. Oxford: Basil Blackwell Ltd, 1991.
Noys, Benjamin, "Georges Bataille's Base Materialism." *Journal for Cultural Research* 2, no. 4 (1998): 499–517.
Olivelle, Patrick. *The Early Upaniṣads: Annotated Text and Translation*. Oxford: Oxford University Press, 1998.
———. "Orgasmic Rapture and Divine Ecstasy: The Semantic History of *Ānanda*." *Journal of Indian Philosophy* 25, no. 2(1997): 153–180.
Proferes, Theodore. *Vedic Ideals of Sovereignty and the Poetics of Power*. New Haven, CT: American Oriental Society, 2007.
Robertson, Matthew. "The Autophagous Absolute: Revelations of Cosmic and Sovereign Violence in the *Bhagavad Gītā* and the *Taittirīya Upaniṣad*." *Journal of Religion and Violence* 6, no. 1 (2018): 73–105.
Sarbacker, Stuart Ray. "'Enstasis and Ecstasis': A Critical Appraisal of Eliade on Yoga and Shamanism." *Journal for the Study of Religion* 15, no. 1 (2002): 21–37.
———. *Samādhi: The Numinous and Cessative in Indo-Tibetan Yoga*. New York: SUNY Press, 2005.
Shulman, David. *The Hungry God: Hindu Tales of Filicide and Devotion*. Chicago: University of Chicago Press, 1993.
Stace, Walter T. *Mysticism and Philosophy*. London: MacMillan, 1960.

Stoekl, Alan, ed. *Visions of Excess: Selected Writings 1927–1939*. Minneapolis: University of Minnesota Press, 1985.

Surya, Michel. *Georges Bataille: An Intellectual Biography*. Translated by Krzysztof Fijalkowski and Michael Richardson. New York: Verso, 2002.

Vidal, Silvina P. "Rethinking the Warburgian Tradition in the 21st Century." *Journal of Art Historiography* 1 (2009): 1–12.

Whitaker, Jarrod L. *Strong Arms and Drinking Strength: Masculinity, Violence, and the Body in Ancient India*. New York: Oxford University Press, 2011.

White, David G. "Le monde dans le corps du Siddha: Microcosmologie dans le traditions médiévales indiennes." In *Images du Corps dans le Monde Hindou*, edited by Gilles Tarabout and Véronique Bouillier, 189–212. Paris: CNRS Editions, 2003.

Index

Note: *Italic* page numbers refer to figures and page numbers followed by "n" denote endnotes.

Abhinavagupta: *apāna* breath 116; body upward movement 19; *Brahmā* 119; breathing exercise 23; breaths portrayed by 22; conception of subtle body 113–17; consciousness, reality of 23; contemplative practices 16–19; contemplative visualization 17–18, 28; *Dehasthadevatācakrastotram* 118, 120; *dhyāna,* rich history of 17, 114; ecology of beings 111; *Essence of the Tantra* 19; *Īśvara* 119; medieval model 110; new idea for 119–20; non-egoic, autonomous, spontaneous process 19; panentheism 111; panentheist conception 110; *prāṇa* breath 116; *puryaṣṭaka* 110; *Rudra* 119; *samāna* breath 116; subconscious impulses, evocative of 114; subtle body practices of 17, 26, 111; subtle body visualization 18; *Tantrāloka,* descriptions in 17, 21; Tantric articulation of body 118; theological inscription 111; Trika Śaiva tradition of 15, 18; *uccāra* practice 19–21; *udāna* breath 116–17; unitary state 18–19; *Viṣṇu* 119; *vyāna* breath 117; wind energies and awareness 22

abjad system 182

Abram, David 212–13

Abu'l Fazl ibn Mubarak 177

academic knowledge 214

Active Intellect 149

Advaita Vedānta 229

aesthetic–ethic approach 211

Aesthetics of Religion 211

Agnicayana 227, 229

A'in-i akbari (Abu'l Fazl) 177

"alchemical body" 41, 55

alchemical techniques 55

Alexander, M. Jacqui 197, 198

"Alien" 108

Almaas, A.H. 16, 25, 26

Alter, Joseph 170, 172

alternate knowledge 206, 211

"alternate" perception 206

Amir-Moezzi, Mohammad Ali 155

analysis of bliss 231

analytic reflection 66

anātma 112

Angels of Desire (Johnston) 4, 82n3

animal emblems 46

"animal religion" 212

"annihilate annihilation" 156

antarātman 220

Anttonen, Viekko 88; "Rethinking the Sacred: The Notions of 'Human Body' and 'Territory' in Conceptualizing Religion" 90

Anzaldua, Gloria 197–9; *see also* spiritual activism

apāna breath 116

apophatic meditation 37, 38

Arabi, Ibn 150

ascension *(Mi'raj)* 146–8; of Bayazid Bistami 149–50; of Muhammad Ghwath 150–2; mystical experience, paradigm for 148–9; saintly ascensions 149–57

aṣṭatīrthas, Ekaliga temple and 96–8

Attar, Farid al-din 150, 153

autonomic nervous system 70

autonomous cognitive *(parisphuraṇa)* 133

"The Autonomy of Affect" (Massumi) 121
awakening 137, 138, 140–2
"ayurvedic" body 169–71, 182

Bahr al-hayat ("Ocean of Life") 169
Bappaka 86, 104n2
Barcan, Ruth 210
Barrett, M. J. 213, 214
"base materialism" 220, 223
Bashir, Shahzad 170, 175
Bataille, Georges 9, 220, 221, 236n6; bliss 225–6; death 222–5; "The Practice of Joy before Death" 221, 222, 224, 233; *Taittirīya Upaniṣad* 227–33; *Theory of Religion* 226
behavioral powers *(pari-bhramaṇa)* 133
Bell, Catherine 6
"belonging-to" 76
"belonging-with" 76
"betweenness" 77
Bhabha, Homi K. 5
Bhagavad Gītā 113
Bhairava flying-in-the-sky 20, 28
Bhandarkar, D.R. 104n1
bhāvanā 132
Bhils 98, 99, 102, 103
bio-spiritual parasites 48
Bistami, Bayazid 149, 150, 157
Blavatsky, Helena 4
bliss, origin of 230
Bodies that Matter (Butler) 168–9
bodily awareness 133; transforming 140–2
bodily consciousness 131, 134, 136–7, 140
The Body and Society (Brown) 7
body as condition of experience 66–8
body as mountain *51*, 52
body-beyond-the-body 53
body-image 128, 130, 132, 141; cosmic 135; of Maheśvarānanda 137
body-mind problem 130
body-schemas 128–31; Maheśvarānanda's notion of 132–5, 141; ritualizing 135–40
body-self and environment 23
body's information system, circuits of *see* four-circuit body schema
body, temple, landscape 90–4, 100
Bourdieu, Pierre 7
brahman 219–22, 229–34
Brahmins, Vedic 221
breathing exercise 23
"breath of life" 228
Bṛhadāraṇyaka Upaniṣad 230
Brown, Peter 7
Buddhist philosophical conceptions 112
Buddhist soteriology 41
Buddhist *vipassana* (Skt.:*vipaśyana*) practice 37
"building one's own telescope" 80–1
Butler, Judith 168, 170, 176
Butler, Smedley 193
Bynum, Carolyn Walker 7

cakra system 119
camptowns 192; Camptown Clean-Up Campaign 191–2; Christian faith and activism in 194–8; economies 189–90; U.S. military prostitution 188–91
capacity of freedom *(svātantryaśakti)* 136
Casey, Edward 92, 100
Certeau, Michel de 5
chakra-nādī-prāna system 41
Chang, Garma C.C. 26
Chidester, David 103
Chinese medical theory 41
Chinese Pure Land Buddhist visualization 42
Cho, Grace 190
Chretien, Jean-Louis 21, 31n33
circuit of coenesthesis 65, 70
circuit of *ki* 73
circuit of kinesthesis 70
circuit of somesthesis 70
City of Eight 113–15
Clarke, J.J. 75–6
classical Daoism 37
Colby, Fredrick 148
College de Sociologie 221
color-coded cakras pointing 110
"comfort women" system 189, 190, 202n15
"complete" breath *(kamuliyyat)* 180–1
Conference of the Birds (Attar) 150
Confucian moral philosophy 41
consciousness 129, 141; cycle of 18; death of 66; definition of 22; Hunt's explication of 26; reality of 23; yogic 133
"container model of being" 67
contemplative practices 28; academic study of 55; and contemplative experience 36; of *dhyāna* 20; examples of 16–19; experiential methodology 58; expressions of 41; extra-textual guide to 17; Longchenpa's masterly synthesis

22; of subtle body 15, 22; yoga of food 22
contemplative visualization *(dhyāna)* 17, 18
contemporary neuroscientific brain-regions *50*
"contextual grids" 75
"continuity of being" 226
cosmic body 132
cosmogenesis, as topogenesis 93–6
critical adherent discourse (CAD) 55, 58
Critical Practice/Practice-Led Research 214
Crossing and Dwelling: A Theory of Religion (Lefebrve) 6

Damasio, Antonio 121
Dancing with the Virgin: Body and Faith in the Fiesta of Tortugas, New Mexico (Sklar) 7
Daode jing 39
Daoist alchemical body 36
Daoist anthropology 44
Daoist Body Cultivation (Kohn) 3
Daoist body-maps 36, 41–55; contemplative autobiographical account 55–8; Daoist meditation, types of 37–8; "entering the mountains" 52; fragments for daoist body 38–41; macrocosmic/microcosmic views 39
Daoist mystical body 36
dark knowledge 78
Darśana 137
Darwin, Charles 108
Dawkins, Richard 123n2
Day of Judgment 152
decontextualization 22, 31n35
Dehasthadevatācakrastotram (Abhinavagupta) 118, 120
Deleuze, Gilles 170
depth, Merleau-Ponty's concept of 67
depth psychology 71, 74
Despeux, Catherine 44
deva-gṛha 132
dhyāna 17, 18, 114; contemplative practice of 20
Diagram of Ascent and Descent 50, 52
Diagram of Internal Pathways 53, 56
divine bodies 91
divine sound 21
Donald, Merlin 120
D'Silva, Patrick 9
Duden, Barbara 82

Eagleman, David 30n20
East Asian Daoist contexts 3
Eastern mind-body theories 81
Eastern pattern of thinking 80
"eating ambrosia", Longchenpa's description of 28
Eck, Diana 6, 97
"effulgences" 40
egocentric cognition 21
Einstein, Albert 78
Ekaliga temple 86–7, 95; and *aṣṭatīrthas* 96–8
Ekaliṅgamāhātmya (ELM) 86; *aṣṭatīrthas* in 96–8; body, temple, landscape 90–4; chaos and danger 98–103; cosmogenesis as topogenesis 93–6; in historical context 86–7; Madhu and Kaitabha (two evil demons) 94, 98, 101, 102; narrative of wish-granting cow 99–102; space and place in 88–90
"elemental essences" 24
Eliade, Mircea 5, 219
elide socio-cultural difference 209
elitist epistemology 66
"elixir field" 43
ELM see Ekaliṅgamāhātmya (ELM)
embodied mappings 8–9
embodied self 137, 170
embryonic body 132, 133
emotional agitations 71, 72
emotional-instinct circuit 65, 70–5
"empty" breath *(khali)* 180–1
"enchantment," terminology of 212
"energetic experiencing" 56
"energetic perception" 56
"enlightenment" 28
epistemological pluralism 207
epistemologies of enlightenment 41
Ernst, Carl 170
Esalen (Kripal) 4
"esoteric" 84n45
Esoteric Aesthetics approach 211–13
esoteric knowledge 170
esoteric philosophy 128
Essence of the Tantra (Tantrasāra) 17, 19
ethical responsibility 209
"expanded" perceptual field 206
experience *(anubhava)* 136
The Expressiveness of the Body and the Divergence of Greek and Chinese Medicine (Kuriyama) 84n50
extensive version of body 208

Feher, Michel 38
Feldhaus, Anne 95
"five *krośas*" *(pañcakrośa)* 97
"flavor channel" 23
Flegr, Jaroslav 108
Flood, Gavin 117
"flying" *(plavana)* 20
Fodor, Jerry 129
Forman, Robert K. C. 219
For Space (Massey) 5
Foucauldian-inspired discourse analysis 210
Foucault, Michel 5
four-circuit body schema 65, 69–72; circuit of coenesthesis 70; emotional-instinct circuit 70–5; sensory-motor circuit 69, 70; unconscious quasi-body 69, 72–5
Fragments for a History of the Human Body (Feher) 38
frisky methods: experience 209–11; subtle bodies, ways of 209–11; subtle epistemology 215; subtle, invisible and infuriating 207–9; ways of working, subtle bodies 211–14

Gangsten, Martin 176
Gendlin, Eugene 26
Germano, David 15, 16, 22, 23, 25, 29n2
gestalt paradigm 69; benefits of 78–80; Kasulis' assertion of 75
Ghawth, Muhammad 169
Al-Ghazali, Abu Hamid 153
al-Ghazali, Ahmad 153
Godfrey, Edward 8
gods in body 117–19
Governing and Conception Channels 52, 56
graphic visualization processes 129
Great Perfection, synthesis of 22
Guenther, Herbert 22
Gyatso, Geshe Kelsang 26

habit-body, Merleau-Ponty's concept of 67–9, 71
habit patterns *(saṃskāras)* 130, 132, 136, 141
Harris, Sam 80–1
Hatley, Shaman 170, 175
Highest Clarity Daoism 40
Highest Clarity movement 44
highest divinity *(parameśvara)* 138
Hinduism 90
Hindu religious narratives 91
"history of Daoist body" 39, 41
Holdrege, Barbara 3
Holy Feast and Holy Fast (Bynum) 7
Huang, Susan Shih-shan 44
human behavior 111
Hunt, Harry T. 16, 22, 24–6, 32n45, 32n46

"I" *(aham)* 109–11, 113, 122
Ibn Abbas 156
Ibn Sina's approach 149
'ilm-i dam texts 172–5, 177, 179, 182
image schemas 129
imagined body 128
"immortal embryo" 53
"immortality" in Daoist 41, 43
India: A Sacred Geography (Eck) 6
Indian model 111
Indian Tantric vision 109
"I-ness" *(ahantā)* 114, 122
information circuits of body *see* four-circuit body schema
"*in medias res*" 77, 79
"inner elixir" 43
inner landscape map *47, 52*
Inner Landscape Map 46
"inner winds" 16
insect body 132, 133
integrity, characteristics of 75–6
internal alchemy systems 43
internal information apparatus 70
intimacy: characteristics of 77–8; and verification of subtle-body 80–1
Intimacy or Integrity: Philosophy and Cultural Difference (Kasulis) 75
Irigaray, Luce 4
Ishaq, Ibn 147, 148
"Islamicate views of the body" 174–6
Islamic civilization 145
Isra'iliyyat, influence of 146–7
Īśvara Pratyabhijñā Vivṛti Vimarśinī 119, 120

Jainism, "heterodox" traditions of 221
James, William 22
Jami, Abd al-Rahman 146
Japanese military "comfort women" system 189, 190, 202n15
Jeffreys, Sheila 187
Johnson, Marc 120
Johnson, Mark 129
Johnston, Jay 1, 2, 4, 9, 10n1, 83n5, 83n9; *Angels of Desire* 82n3
Juz'-yat o Kulliyat ("The Parts and the Wholes") 174
jyotisha 173

Kaiṭabha (evil demon), in *ELM* 94, 98, 101, 102
Kant's philosophy 66
karmendriya 115
Kāśī 97
Kasulis, T.P. 65–6, 82, 84n35; *Intimacy or Integrity: Philosophy and Cultural Difference* 75
kāya 134
khabar (information) 180
Khidr 151
Khosrow Dehlavi, Amir 146
Kim, Yon-ja 195–7, 199
King, Richard 41
"Kirāta" 102
Knott, Kim 6
knowledge 76–8; dark 78
Kohn, Livia 3, 44
Kong, Lily 5
Korean Church Women United 194–5
Kramrisch, Stella 93
Kripal, Jeffrey 4, 15, 27
krośa 97, 106n29
Kugle, Scott 175; *Sufis and Saints' Bodies* 174
Kulke, Hermann 97
kuṇḍalinī 20
*kuṇḍa*s 105n24

Lakoff, George 120, 129
Lamb, Sarah 7
Language of Thought Hypothesis (Fodor) 129
Laski, Margaret 20
Lee, Jin-kyung 190–1
Lee, Na-young 195
Lee, Yanggu 200–1
Lefebvre, Henri 5, 6, 88, 90
Leland, Kurt 4
"light-of-the-void" experience 25–6
*liṅga*s 100, 105n22
The Location of Culture (Bhabha) 5
The Location of Religion (Knott) 6
Longchenpa: breathing exercise 23; "eating ambrosia" 28; eating of wind-energies 22–4; humanistic dialogue 22; Hunt's explication 26; subtle body contemplative practices 22; yoga of food 22–3, 26
"lucid dreaming" 26
Lyssenko, Viktoria 177

McNamara, Patrick 122
macrocosm *(`alam-i kabir)* 179
Madhu (evil demon), in *ELM* 94, 98, 101, 102
Mahābhārata 104n1
Mahārāṇā Kumbhā (1433–68) 87, 98
Mahārthamañjarī (MM) 128–42
Maheśvarānanda 128–31; body schemas 132–5, 141; ritualized body-image 135–40; transforming bodily awareness 140–2; visualization practices 130
Makhzan al-Asrar (Nizami) 145, 152
Mantramārga 111
*mantra*s/seed-syllables 20
Map is Not a Territory (Smith) 5, 103
Margulis, Lynn 122
masnavis 145
Massey, Doreen 5
Massumi, Brian 121
"material body" 170
Mbembe, Achille 188, 196
medieval methods 44
meditation 71, 72
mental and emotional functions 117
Merleau-Ponty, Maurice 20, 65, 81, 130; body schema 66–8, 73; depth 67; habit-body 67–9; *Phenomenology of Perception* 83n8
"Mewar" 86–7, 90, 94–103, 105n21
microcosm *(`alam-i saghir)* 179
Microcosmic Orbit 44, 53, 56
military prostitution 187, 188, 191–3; *see also* U.S. military prostitution, in South Korea
mind-body 65, 66; correlativity 69; theories 81
mind–body dualism 69, 74
mind–body training regimes 209
mind-controlling parasites 108
mirroring 140
Miz al-nafas 179–82
Monier-Williams, Monier 106n29
Monnerot, Jules 220
Monotheistic and Western Philosophical Contexts 4
Moon, Fay 195
Moon, Katharine 189
Morton, Tim 122
Muhammad Ghwath 150–2
Muhammad: Man of God (Nasr) 157
multiplicity and non-dualities 8
"mystical body" 55
mystical cranial locations 49
mysticism 198, 199

nadis 176–80
Nāgahrada 97, 98

Nanzong movement 38
Nasr, Seyyed Hossein 157, 158
Nāth Siddha work 219
necropolitical labor 187, 190–4
necropolitics 188–90; resistance of 198–201; theories of 202
Needham, Joseph 44
New Age West 117
New Materialism, approaches of 208
Nine Palaces 48, 55, 56
Nishida Kitarō 65
Nizami Ganjavi 145, 154
non-dualist cosmology 112
non-dual philosophy 110
None Higher *(anuttara)* 19
non-violence *(ahiṃsā)* 221
al-Numani, Qadi 150

Olcott, Henry 4
On the Nature of Consciousness (Hunt) 24
"ontological turn" 208
"organ of Being" 21
"orthodox" Sunni legalism 146
other-than-human agency concepts 208, 210
Otto, Rudolph 27
The Outline of Theory of Practice (Bourdieu) 7

Padoux, Andre 29n1
panentheist conception 110
panoramic view 15
parasympathetic nervous system 71
Parātrīśikā 132
"The Parts and the Wholes" *(Juz'-yat o Kulliyat)* 174
pathosformel working across 222, 235
Pati, George 6
peacock egg *(śikhaṇḍyaṇḍa)* 133, 137
Pechilis, Karen 3
perception, cultivation of 206
Phenomenology of Perception (Merleau-Ponty) 83n8
Piaget, Jean 129
Pierce, Steven 7
"piling of Agni" 227
political (in)visibilities 9
"politics of exclusion" 99, 103, 106n34
practice as body 8
The Practice of Everyday Life (de Certeau) 5
"The Practice of Joy before Death" (Bataille) 221, 222, 224, 233
prāṇa breath 116
pranayama (controlled breathing) 172
prasara 133
praxis 81
pre-Islamic Arab culture 156
The Production of Space (Lefebvre) 5
propositional attitudes 129
"psychologies of realization" 41
pure consciousness 122
Puruṣa Sūkta 91, 92
puryaṣṭaka 110, 113–14

"quasi-physical sensations" 20
Quintet (Nizami) 145–6
Qur'anic references 153, 160n7

radical intersubjectivity, concept of 206
Rahman, Fazlur 147
Rainbow Body (Leland) 4
Rāṇā Mokala (1420–9) 87
Rao, Anupama 7
"redoubled yang" 43
Refiguring the Body: Embodiment in South Asian Religions (Holdrege and Pechilis) 3
regulated breathing *(prāṇāyāma)* 141
Reich, William 26
Religion and the Subtle Body in Asia and the West: Between mind and body (Samuel and Johnston) 1
religions, Tweed's understanding of 89–90
"Rethinking the Sacred: The Notions of 'Human Body' and 'Territory' in Conceptualizing Religion" (Anttonen) 90
Ricoeur, Paul 15
Risalah-i dam az [hawz?] al-hayat 177–8
ritual(s) 88; external 138; internal 138; visualization 137
ritualized body-image 135–40
Ritual Theory (Bell) 6
Robertson, Matthew 9
Rosch, Eleanor 130

sacrality of place 103
The Sacred and the Profane: The Nature of Religion (Eliade) 5
sacred spaces 88–9
sacrificial altar 93
saintly ascensions: Bayazid Bistami 149–50; body/heart 152–4; clothing and gift bestowal 154; Makhzan's

ascension narrative 152; Muhammad Ghwath 150–2; scent and spit 155–6; vision of god 157
Śākta philosophy 130
*śākta pīṭha*s 92
Samuel, Geoffrey 1, 2, 4, 10n1, 81, 83n5
Sapolsky, Robert 109, 119
Sarbacker, Stuart 219
Sarukkai, Sundar 81, 83n13
"*sarvatattvamayaḥ kāyaḥ*" 133
"scare" quotation marks 206
Schaefer, Donovan O. 212
schema theory 129
Schilder, Paul 26
Scripture on the Yellow Court 40, 46
Seeking Social Justice (Kitching) 5
"Seizer-Demons" *(graha)* 25
self-cultivation *(shugyō)* 69, 81
self-expression 135
self-realization 139
Sells, Michael 149
sensory faculties 141
sensory-motor circuit 65, 69, 70
sexual reproduction, act of 225
Seyyed Ahmed Khan 146
Shamanistic contexts 3
Shangqing movement 38, 40
Silburn, Lilian 15, 16, 18
Śiva 20
Śiva tattva 112
Sklar, Deidre 7
Skora, Kerry 8
Smith, Jonathan Z. 5, 92; *Map is Not Territory* 103
socio-historical system 25
Soelle, Dorothee 197, 199
Soja, Edward 5
soldiering, necropolitical nature of 193–4
somatosensory responses 142n2
Song-dynasty monastic system 38, 41
"Soul" 16, 21
South Asian yogic and Tantric contexts 2
South Korea: modernization 191; political changes in 202n15; public prostitution system 188; U.S. military prostitution in 188–90; *see also* U.S. military prostitution, in South Korea
Spatz, Benjamin 182
spiritual activism 187, 198–201
spiritual awakening 142
"spiritual breath" 16
spiritualist and New Age contexts 4
spirituality 198; mystic 199
splanchnic nerves 70
splanchnic sensation 70
Stace, Walter 219
"standardized Daoist body" 41, 42
standpoint of intimacy 77
Steinbock, Anthony J. 67
Steiner, Rudolph 4
The Story of Sookja 200
substance-based soul 112
subtle bodies, concepts and practices 1–2
subtle-body as project 81–2
subtle body of vital presence 16
subtle body theory: Abhinavagupta 16–21, 113–17; Buddhist conception of 112; conceptualization of 110, 206–7; contemplative practices of 15, 16; cross-cultural comparison of 15; Daoist name for 43; ethical and aesthetic ramifications of 206; Frisky experience 209–11; gods in body 117–21; inner winds 16; intimacy and verification of 80–1; investigation of 65; Longchenpa's eating of wind-energies 22–4; *sine qua non* of 25; "Soul" 21; spiritual breath 16; "substance" of 74; subtle-body as project 81–2; Tibetan Buddhist practices 26; unconscious functions of 69; Yuasa's understanding of 65, 73
subtle epistemology 215
"subtle substance," ontology of 209
Sufi: conceptions of the body 174–5; treatise on macro- and microcosms 178–9
Sufis and Saints' Bodies (Kugle) 174
Sufism, definitions of 146, 160n4
Sūkṣma śarīra 2
Sulami, Abu Abd al-Rahman 148
Sunlit Center's activism 197–201
śūnya, Buddhist term of 114
śūnyatā (emptiness) 4
svarodaya texts 170, 172, 176, 180, 182
Swami Muktibodhananda 171
Swara Yoga: The Tantric Science of Brain Breathing (Swami Muktibodhananda) 171

"Taima Mandala" 42
Taittirīya Brāhmaṇa 117
Taittirīya Upaniṣad 220, 221; bliss 229–32; death 227–9

Tang-dynasty monastic system 40–1
Tantra in Practice (White) 3
Tantrāloka 16, 20
Tantric philosophy 128; of embodiment 131
Tantric texts 128
Tantric visualization practices 130
"*theōria*" 76, 77, 79, 81
Theory of Religion (Bataille) 226
Theosophical Society 4, 207
Thistlethwaite, Susan 193
Thompson, Evan 130
Three Death-bringers 46
three-dimensional breathing 181–2
Tibetan Buddhist Great Perfection 15
Tibetan Buddhist traditions 25–6
*tīrtha*s 96; Ekaliṅga temple and 96–8
Toxoplasma gondii 109, 119
Traditional Chinese Medicine 207
transmigrating subtle body 115
Treasury of Mysteries (Nizami) 145
Treatise on the Breath from the [Sea] of Life *(Risalah-i dam az [hawz?] al-hayat)* 177–8
Trika Śaiva tradition 15, 18
Turner, Victor 99
Tweed, Thomas 88–90, 99

uccāra practice 19, 21
udāna breath 116–17
ultimate reality 17
unconscious quasi-body 65, 69, 72–5, 82
upward movement in body 19
U.S. Armed Forces in Korea (USFK) 189, 191, 192
U.S. military prostitution, in South Korea 187–90; Camptown Clean-Up Campaign 191–2; in camptowns 188, 189, 191; Christian faith and anti-prostitution activism 194–8; defining necropolitical labor 190–4; Durebang's mission 195; emergence of 188–9; heterosexual masculinist ideology 188; Kim's testimony 195–7; racial discrimination 191; spiritual activism 187, 198–201; Sunlit Center's activism 197–201; VD control 189, 192; "Western Princess" 187, 190, 194; Yi, Bok-hi and Yi, Young-soon deaths 196; Yoon's, brutal murder of 190, 191
U.S.–Republic of Korea Mutual Defense Treaty (SOFA) 189
U.S. Twenty-Fourth Army Corps 188
"utterly struck down" *(atighnī)* 232

Varela, Francesco 130
vāstupuruṣamaṇḍala 93
Vedic "easy invocation" 120
venereal disease (VD) control 189, 192
The Village of Seven Houses 200–1
violent rupture, moment of 226
Virūpākṣapañcāśikā 134
vision of god 157
visualization practices 128, 130, 131, 134, 141
"vital presence" 16, 25, 26
vyāna breath 117

Wallis, Christopher 17, 19
Watsuji Tetsurō 77
Weber, Andreas 28
Webster, Joanne 108–9
"Western" lineages 16, 121
Western mind-body theories 81
Western pattern of thinking 80
White, David 3
White, David Gordon 171, 236n5
White Saris and Sweet Mangoes: Aging, Gender and Body in North India (Lamb) 7
wish-granting cow *(kāmadhenu)* 99–102
de Wit, Han 41
Woo, Soon-deok 200
Wujastyk, Dominik 117

"yang-spirit" 53, *54*
Yi, Bok-hi 196
Yi, Young-soon 196
Yoga in Practice (White) 171
yoga of food 22
yogic and tantric developments 3
"yogic" body 169, 171–4, 182
yogic liberation 142
yogic practices 130
yogin 140, 141
Yoo, Bok-nim 195
Yoon, Gum-yi 190, 191, 196, 202n15
Yuasa Yasuo, contextualization of subtle-body 65–82, 84n35

Zen Buddhism 65